Guide to Programming with Python

Michael Dawson

THOMSON

COURSE TECHNOLOGY

An Introduction to Programming with Python
By Michael Dawson

Vice President, Technology and Trades ABU:
Dave Garza

Director of Learning Solutions:
Sandy Clark

Acquisitions Editor:
Amy Jollymore

Managing Editor:
Tricia Coia

Content Project Manager:
Matt Hutchinson

Editorial Assistant:
Erin Kennedy

Cover Designer:
Steve Deschene

Art Director:
Beth Paquin

Compositor:
Digital Publishing Solutions

Manufacturing Coordinator:
Julio Esperas

Proofreader:
Kathy Orrino

THOMSON

COURSE TECHNOLOGY

Thomson Course Technology
www.course.com

CONTENTS

CHAPTER 3   BRANCHING, while LOOPS, AND PROGRAM
PLANNING: THE GUESS MY NUMBER GAME................. 53

CHAPTER 4   for **Loops, Strings, and Tuples: The Word Jumble Game**.. **93**

CHAPTER 6   FUNCTIONS: THE TIC-TAC-TOE GAME 167

CHAPTER 7 FILES AND EXCEPTIONS: THE TRIVIA CHALLENGE GAME... 203

CHAPTER 10   **GUI DEVELOPMENT: THE MAD LIB PROGRAM............ 307**

CHAPTER 11　GRAPHICS: THE PIZZA PANIC GAME 345

PREFACE

*G*uide to Programming with Python introduces students with little or no experience to the world of programming through the powerful yet easy to learn Python language. It demonstrates how to write console, GUI, and even multimedia applications. The book's unique approach captures a student's attention by using game-related examples—a student sees how to write everything from a text-based version of hangman to an asteroid-blasting classic with graphics, animation, music, and sound effects, all while learning fundamental programming concepts and practicing good style. And since writing code is only one part of successful programming, students also learn how to plan, test, and debug their creations.

Python is a dynamic, object-oriented programming language that's perfect for beginners but also meets the demands of industry. The language's concise nature, intuitive syntax, and interactive interpreter make it eminently approachable. At the same time, Python's expressiveness, deep libraries, and cross-platform capabilities make it perfect for mission-critical applications.

Although this text uses game programs as examples, it teaches fundamental programming and computer science concepts, including types, variables, branching, loops, object-oriented programming, data structures, file handling, exceptions, program planning, GUI programming, and multimedia programming. Because of Python's short learning curve, instructors will likely cover more of these topics in the same period of time as compared to using other popular programming languages.

COVERAGE AND ORGANIZATION

Guide to Programming with Python covers programming concepts and terminology using a professional yet conversational writing style. To facilitate learning, every new concept is introduced with a short but complete working program while each chapter ends with a more complex program that brings these concepts together. All of the programs presented in the text are provided on the CD-ROM that accompanies the book so that students can easily run and modify them.

In Chapters 1 and 2, students are introduced to programming as they learn about types, variables, and output. Chapter 2 also provides a first look at objects. Students continue with essential topics in Chapter 3 with a look at control structures. They finish the chapter by examining how to program the classic number-guessing game.

In Chapters 4 and 5, students tackle data structures by learning to use several of Python's powerful, built-in collection types. At the conclusion of Chapter 5, students see how to apply these data structures in the creation of a complete hangman game. In Chapter 6, students learn all about functions and get a glimpse into the world of artificial intelligence when they see how to create a computer opponent in a game of tic-tac-toe.

In Chapter 7, students study how to read from and write to files. In addition, they examine how to trap for and handle exceptions. In Chapters 8 and 9, students learn how to write object-oriented programs. At the conclusion of Chapter 9, students study a large object-oriented program that spans multiple source files with the blackjack game program.

In Chapter 10, students discover event-driven programming and see how to write GUI programs. Chapters 11 and 12 continue with event-driven programming, but add multimedia to the mix. In these final two chapters, students learn how to write object-oriented, event-driven programs by creating games with graphics and sound.

The text provides not only a breadth of topics, but allows for some flexibility in presentation. For example, instructors may omit Chapter 7 without loss of continuity. In addition, Chapter 10 may be omitted.

By the end of the book, students will have a solid foundation in both procedural and object-oriented programming. In addition, they'll have experience with GUI and multimedia programming. All of this knowledge will serve them in more advanced courses as well as in the study of other languages such as C++, Java, C#, and Visual Basic .NET.

FEATURES

Guide to Programming with Python also includes the following features:

- **Objectives:** Each chapter begins with a list of objectives that cover the chapter topics. In addition to providing a quick overview, this feature acts as a useful study aid.
- **Hints:** Throughout the book are hints—special bits of advice on how to best apply a newly presented concept.
- **Traps:** Throughout the book are traps, which point out where it's easy for a new programmer to make a mistake.
- **Tricks:** Throughout the book are tricks—techniques and shortcuts that can make programming easier.

- **"In the Real World" Features:** Throughout the book are "In the Real World" Features, which describe how a newly presented concept might be applied in a professional setting.
- **Figures:** Each chapter contains many figures. Every program has an accompanying screen shot that shows the program's output. In addition, other figures provide a visual way to understand new ideas.
- **Tables:** Throughout the book are tables that organize and highlight important facts.
- **Summaries:** Each chapter includes a summary that recaps the programming concepts and techniques covered. The summaries also provide a means for students to check their understanding of the main chapter points.
- **Review Questions:** Each chapter also includes twenty questions that ask students to think more deeply about key concepts.
- **Projects:** Each chapter concludes with projects that provide students the opportunity to design and write programs of their own while using new skills and concepts from the chapter.
- **CD-ROM:** The CD-ROM that comes with this book includes the following:
  - Python 2.3.5
  - Pygame 1.6
  - LiveWires 2.0
  - Source code for all programs in the book
  - Project media files

TEACHING TOOLS

The following supplemental materials are available when this book is used in a classroom setting. All of the teaching tools available with this book are provided to the instructor on a single CD-ROM.

Electronic Instructor's Manual. The Instructor's Manual that accompanies this textbook includes additional instructional material to assist in class preparation, including items such as Sample Syllabi, Lecture Notes, Teaching Tips, Quick Quizzes, Discussion Topics, Key Terms and Additional Resources.

ExamView®. This textbook is accompanied by ExamView, a powerful testing software package that allows instructors to create and administer printed, computer (LAN-based), and Internet exams. ExamView includes hundreds of questions that correspond to the topics covered in this text, enabling students to generate detailed study guides that include page references for further review. The computer-based and Internet testing components allow students to take exams at their computers, and they save the instructor time by grading each exam automatically.

PowerPoint Presentations. This book comes with Microsoft PowerPoint slides for each chapter. These are included as a teaching aid for classroom presentation, to make available to students for chapter review, or to be printed for classroom distribution. Instructors can add their own slides for additional topics they introduce to the class.

Solution Files. Solutions to all end-of-chapter questions and projects are provided on the Teaching Tools CD, and can also be found on the Course Technology Web site at *www.course.com*. The solutions are password protected.

Distance Learning. Course Technology is proud to present online test banks in WebCT and Blackboard to provide the most complete and dynamic learning experience possible. Instructors are encouraged to make the most of the course, both online and offline. For more information on how to access the online test bank, contact your local Course Technology sales representative.

Acknowledgements

Writing a book is like giving birth—and I have the stretch marks of the brain to prove it. So, I want to thank all the people who helped me bring my little bundle of joy into this world.

Thanks to Tricia Coia, Managing Editor, for coordinating all of the moving parts—and for keeping me on track. Thanks to Matt Hutchinson, Content Project Manager, for his dedication in overseeing the composition process—his work makes the book look good, literally. Thanks also to Amy Jollymore, Acquisitions Editor, who jumped in mid-project, but worked like she was there from the start.

I am grateful to the reviewers who provided feedback, including Tom Capaul, Eastern Washington University; Mike Michaelson, Palomar College; and Paula Velluto, Bunker Hill Community College. I appreciated all of their suggestions and encouragement. I also want to thank Quality Assurance member John Bosco for his eagle eye and unrelenting attention to detail.

Thanks to Pete Shinners, author of Pygame, and everyone who contributed to the LiveWires package. Because of all of you, writing multimedia programs is now within reach of a new Python programmer.

Thanks to Matt for his audio expertise, Chris for his musical talents, and Dave for wearing a chef's hat.

This book is dedicated to my wife Keren—still my sweet, tough cookie.

Michael Dawson

SOFTWARE INSTALLATION

The following lists the software installations and updates necessary to run all of the programs presented in the book. Please be aware that, although Python is a cross-platform language, some of the software on the CD-ROM that comes with this book will only work under the Microsoft Windows operating system—specifically Microsoft Windows 98 or more recent.

- **Python 2.3.5.** Python is the programming language that this book uses. The version of Python that comes on the CD-ROM that accompanies this book is 2.3.5. Python must be installed before any of the programs in this book can be run. The instructions for installing Python are described in Chapter 1.

- **Pygame 1.6.** Pygame is a multimedia package for Python that is designed for writing games. The version of Pygame on the CD-ROM that comes with this book is 1.6. Pygame must be installed before any of the multimedia programs presented in Chapters 11 and 12 can be run. Python must be installed before Pygame. The instructions for installation are included in the readme.txt file that accompanies the Pygame installer.

- **LiveWires 2.0.** LiveWires is a Python package designed to make writing games easier. The version of LiveWires on the CD-ROM that accompanies this book is 2.0. LiveWires must be installed before any of the multimedia programs presented in Chapters 11 and 12 can be run. Pygame must be installed before LiveWires. The instructions for installation are included in the readme.txt file that accompanies the LiveWires installer.

- **Microsoft DirectX.** Microsoft DirectX is a suite of multimedia application programming interfaces (APIs) built into the Microsoft Windows operating system. To ensure the best possible experience with the multimedia programs presented in Chapters 11 and 12, DirectX should be updated. For more information, visit http://www.microsoft.com/windows/directx.

- **Audio and Video Drivers.** To ensure the best possible experience with the multimedia programs presented in Chapters 11 and 12, a computer's audio and video drivers should be updated. Please visit the appropriate hardware vendors' sites.

GETTING STARTED: THE GAME OVER PROGRAM

Programming basically is getting your computer to do stuff. This is not the most technical definition, but it's a pretty accurate one. By learning Python, you'll be able to create a program, whether it's a simple game, a small utility, or a business product with a full-featured graphical user interface (GUI). It'll be all yours, something you made, and it will do just what you told it to. Programming is part science, part art, and one great adventure. This chapter starts you on your Python programming journey. In it, you'll learn

- What Python is and what's so great about it
- How to install Python on your computer
- How to print text to the screen
- What comments are and how to use them
- How to use Python's integrated development environment to write, edit, run, and save your programs

EXAMINING THE GAME OVER PROGRAM

The chapter project, Game Over, displays the two most infamous words in computer gaming: "Game Over." Figure 1.1 shows the program in action.

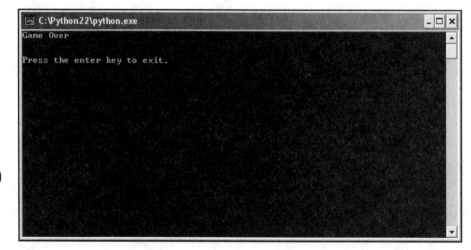

FIGURE 1.1

The all-too-familiar words from a computer game.

Figure 1.1 shows what's called a *console window*, a window that can display only text. Though not as nice as windows with a Graphical User Interface (GUI), console applications are easier to write and a good place for the beginning programmer to start.

The Game Over program is pretty simple; in fact, it's about the simplest Python program you can write. That is the reason it is presented in this chapter. By completing such a modest program, you cover all the setup work required to start programming in Python, such as installing the language on your system. You also work through the entire process of writing, saving, and running a program. Once you finish all of this groundwork, you'll be ready to tackle larger programs with some real meat to them.

IN THE REAL WORLD

The Game Over program is really just a variation of the traditional Hello World program, which displays the words "Hello World" on the screen. The Hello World program is often the first program a beginner writes in order to dip his or her toe in a new language. It's such a common first program that Hello World is an understood term in the programming world.

INTRODUCING PYTHON

Python is a powerful yet easy to use programming language developed by Guido van Rossum and first released in 1991. With Python, you can quickly write a small project. But Python also scales up nicely and can be used for mission-critical, commercial applications.

 If you check out any Python documentation, you may notice an alarming number of references to spam, eggs, and the number 42. These references all pay homage to Monty Python, the English comedy troupe that inspired Python's name. Even though Guido van Rossum named Python after the group, the official mascot of the language has become a cute little green snake. (Which is really for the best, since it would be pretty hard to fit six British comedians' faces on a program icon anyway.)

There are a lot of programming languages out there. What's so great about Python? Let me tell you.

Python Is Easy to Use

The major goal of any programming language is to bridge the gap between the programmer's brain and the computer. Most of the popular languages you've probably heard of, such as C, C++, C#, and Java, are considered *high-level languages*, which means that they're closer to human language than machine language. And they are. But Python, with its clear and simple rules, is even closer to English. Creating Python programs is so straightforward that it's been called "programming at the speed of thought."

Python's ease of use translates into productivity for professional programmers. Python programs are shorter and take less time to create than programs in many other popular languages. According to the official Python site, Python programs are typically three to five times shorter than equivalent Java programs, and often five to 10 times shorter than equivalent C++ programs.

Python Is Powerful

Python has all the power you'd expect from a modern programming language. By the end of this book, you'll be able to write programs that employ a GUI, process files, and incorporate multimedia elements such as graphics, sound, and animation.

Python is powerful enough to attract hundreds of thousands of programmers from around the world as well as companies such as Google, Hewlett-Packard, IBM, Industrial Light + Magic, Microsoft, NASA, Red Hat, Verizon, Xerox, and Yahoo!. Python is also used as a tool by professional game programmers. Activision, Electronic Arts, and Infogrames all publish games that incorporate Python.

Python Is Object Oriented

Object-oriented programming (OOP) is a modern way of thinking about solving problems with computers. It embodies an intuitive method of representing information and actions in a program. It's certainly not the only way to write programs, but, for large projects, it's usually the best way to go.

Languages such as C#, Java, and Python are all object-oriented. But Python does them one better. In C# and Java, OOP is not optional. This makes short programs unnecessarily complex, and it requires a bunch of explanation before a new programmer can do anything significant. Python takes a different approach. In Python, using OOP techniques is optional. You have all of OOP's power at your disposal, but you can use it when you need it. Got a short program that doesn't really require OOP? No problem. Got a large project with a team of programmers that demands OOP? That'll work too. Python gives you power and flexibility.

Python Is a "Glue" Language

Python can be integrated with other languages, such as C, C++, and Java. This means that a programmer can take advantage of work already done in another language while using Python. It also means that he or she can leverage the strengths of other languages, such as the extra speed that C or C++ might offer, while still enjoying the ease of development that's a hallmark of Python programming.

Python Runs Everywhere

Python runs on everything from a Palm to a Cray. And if you don't happen to have a super-computer in the den, you can still run Python on Windows, DOS, Macintosh, or Linux machines. And that's just the top of the list. Python can run on practically every operating system in existence.

Python programs are *platform independent*, which means that regardless of the operating system you use to create your program, it'll run on any other computer with Python. So if you write a program on your PC, you can e-mail a copy to your friend who runs Linux or to your aunt who has a Mac, and the program will work (as long as your friend and aunt have Python on their computers).

Python Has a Strong Community

Most programming languages have a dedicated newsgroup, but Python also has something called the Python Tutor mailing list, a more informal way for beginning programmers to ask those first questions. The list is at http://mail.python.org/mailman/listinfo/tutor. Although the list is called Tutor, anyone, whether novice or expert, can answer questions.

There are other Python communities focused on different areas, but the common element they share is that they tend to be friendly and open. That only makes sense since the language itself is so approachable for beginners.

Python Is Free and Open Source

Python is free. You can install it on your computer and never pay a penny. But Python's license lets you do much more than that. You can copy or modify Python. You can even resell Python if you want (but don't quit your day job just yet). Embracing open-source ideals like this is part of what makes Python so popular and successful.

SETTING UP PYTHON ON WINDOWS

Before you can jump in and write your first Python program, you need to get the language on your computer. But don't worry, because everything required to install Python on Windows 95/98/Me/XP/2000 is on the CD-ROM that is included with this book.

Installing Python on Windows

Okay, go grab the CD-ROM and follow these steps.

1. Insert the CD-ROM into your computer. The CD-ROM comes with a bunch of goodies, but first and foremost, it has Python on it.
2. Run the Python Windows Installer. You can find the Python Windows installer, Python-2.3.5.exe, on the CD-ROM, under the Software section. Click on the Install Python 2.3.5 from this CD-ROM link and run the installer. Figure 1.2 shows it in action.
3. Click Next at each step of the installation wizard to accept the default configuration. Once you're done, you have Python on your computer. Specifically, you have version 2.3.5 in the C:\Python23 folder.

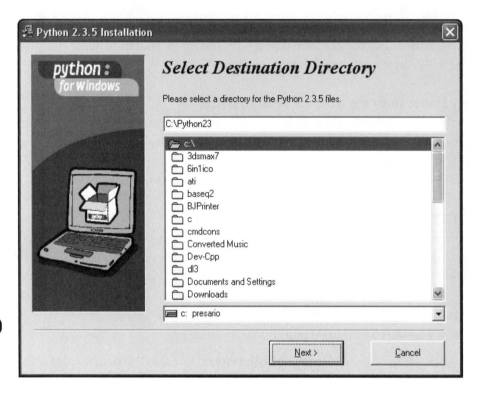

FIGURE 1.2

Your computer is
soon to be home
to Python.

SETTING UP PYTHON ON OTHER OPERATING SYSTEMS

Python runs on literally dozens of other operating systems. If you're running something other than Windows, you'll need to visit the official Python Web site at http://www.python.org, shown in Figure 1.3.

> If Linux is your operating system, you may already have Python on your computer. To check, try running `python` from the command prompt. If that doesn't work, then you'll have to install Python like everybody else.

Under Python versions, click the link of the latest Python release. Follow the links for your particular operating system.

> If you own a Mac, then—even after visiting Python's official home—you owe it to yourself to check out the MacPython page at http://homepages.cwi.nl/~jack/. MacPython integrates Python into the Macintosh environment.

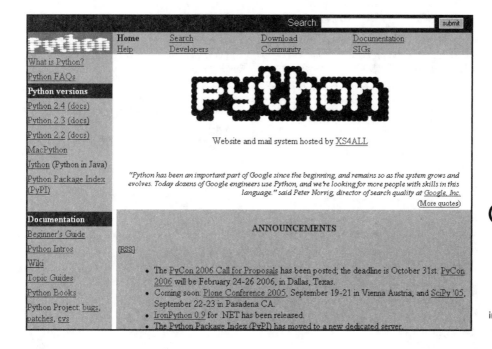

FIGURE 1.3

Visit Python's home page to download the latest version of Python and read loads of information about the language.

INTRODUCING THE PYTHON IDLE

Python comes with a GUI-integrated development environment called IDLE. A *development environment* is a set of tools that makes writing programs easier. You can think of it as a word processor for your programs. But it's even more than a place to write, save, and edit your work. IDLE provides two modes in which to work: an interactive mode and a script mode.

 MacPython has its own integrated development environment called IDE. It works a little differently than IDLE, but allows you to do the same basic things.

Programming in Interactive Mode

Finally, it's time to get your hands dirty with some actual Python programming. The quickest way is to start Python in interactive mode. In this mode, you can tell Python what to do and it'll do it immediately.

Writing Your First Program

To begin your interactive session, from the Start menu, choose All Programs, Python 2.3, IDLE (Python GUI). You should see something very similar to Figure 1.4 on your screen.

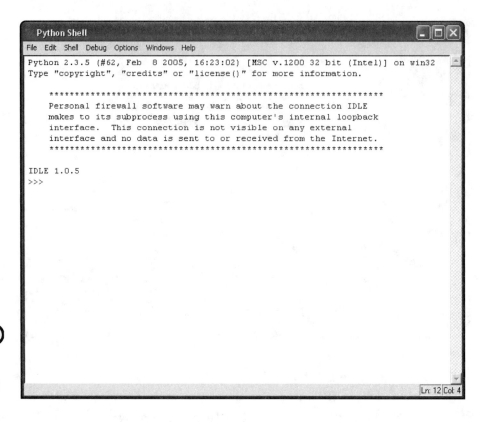

FIGURE 1.4

Python in an
interactive
session, awaiting
your command.

If you have any trouble running IDLE, you may need to modify your Windows System Path—a list of the directories where your computer looks to find program files. You'll want to add the following to the end of your current Path: `;c:\Python23;c:\Program Files\Tcl;c:\Program Files\Tcl\bin`. The process of modifying your Path is different for each version of Windows, so check your Windows Help documentation for Environment Variable (since the Path is one of your Environment Variables).

This window, also called the Python Shell, may look a little different from Figure 1.4. At the command prompt (>>>), type: `print "Game Over"` and press Enter. The interpreter responds by displaying:

`Game Over`

on the screen. Ta da! You've written your first Python program! You're a real programmer (with a little more to learn, but that goes for all of us).

Using the `print` Statement

Take a look again at the line you entered, `print "Game Over"`. Notice how straightforward it is. Without knowing anything about programming, you could have probably guessed what it does. That's Python in a nutshell. It's concise and clear. You'll appreciate this even more as you learn how to do more complex things.

The `print` statement displays whatever text you type between the pair of quotes. You can also use it by itself to print a blank line.

Learning the Jargon

Okay, time to learn some jargon. Now that you're a programmer, you have to throw around those fancy terms that only programmers understand. The line you entered in the interpreter is considered a *statement*. In English, a statement is a complete thought. In Python, a statement is a complete instruction. *It does something.* So, `print "Game Over"` is a statement.

The statement you entered is made up of two parts. The first part, `print`, is a *command*. It's like a verb. It tells the computer to take an action. In this case, it tells the computer to display text on the screen. Python is case sensitive and commands are in lowercase. So, `print "Game Over"` will work, but `Print "Game Over"` and `PRINT "Game Over"` won't.

The second part of the statement, `"Game Over"`, is an *expression*. It doesn't do something. *It is something.* A good way to think about it is that an expression has a value, like the letters in the phrase "Game Over," or even the number 17. An expression can also evaluate to some value. For example, 2 + 5 is an expression that evaluates to 7.

In this particular case, you can be even more specific by saying that `"Game Over"` is a *string* expression. This just means that it's a series of characters, like the ones on your keyboard. "String" may seem like an odd name—"text" or "words" might be more clear—but the name comes from the idea that text is a string or a series of characters. (Not only do you know jargon, but you have some trivia under your belt now too.)

Now that you're a programmer, you can tell someone that you wrote some Python *code*. Code means programming statements. You can use it as a verb, too; you can say that you were up all night eating Doritos, drinking Jolt Cola, and *coding* like crazy.

Generating an Error

Computers take everything literally. If you misspell a command by even just one letter, the computer will have absolutely no idea what you mean. For example, at the interactive prompt I typed `primt "Game Over"`. The interpret responded with:

```
SyntaxError: invalid syntax
```

Translated to English, the interpreter is saying "Huh?!" It doesn't understand `primt`. As a human being, you can ignore my typo and know what I meant. Computers are not so forgiving. This error in my statement, called a *bug* in a program, gets me an error message and nothing else printed on the screen. Specifically, this is a *syntax error*, meaning the computer doesn't recognize something. Syntax errors are usually just caused by a typo and are easily fixed.

Understanding Color Coding

You probably noticed that words on the screen are printed in different colors. This color coding helps you quickly understand what you've typed by visually categorizing it. And there is a method to this coloring madness. Special words, such as `print`, are displayed in orange. Strings, such as `"Game Over"`, are in green. And the output of your statements—what the interpreter prints as a result of what you type—is in blue. As your write larger programs, this color scheme will come in really handy. It will help you take in your code in one glance.

Programming in Script Mode

Using the interactive mode gives you immediate feedback. This is great because you can see the results of a statement right away. But it's not designed to create programs you can save and run later. Luckily, Python's IDLE also offers a script mode, in which you can write, edit, load, and save your programs. It's like a word processor for your code. In fact, you can perform such familiar tasks as find and replace, and cut and paste.

Writing Your First Program (Again)

You can open a script mode window from the interactive window you've been using. Select the File menu, then New Window. A new window will appear that looks just like the one in Figure 1.5.

Now type `print "Game Over"` and press Enter. Nothing happens! That's because you're in script mode. What you're doing is writing a list of statements for the computer to execute later. Once you save your program, you can run it.

Saving and Running Your Program

To save your program, select File, Save As. I gave my copy the name game_over.py. To make it easy to get to later, I saved it on my desktop.

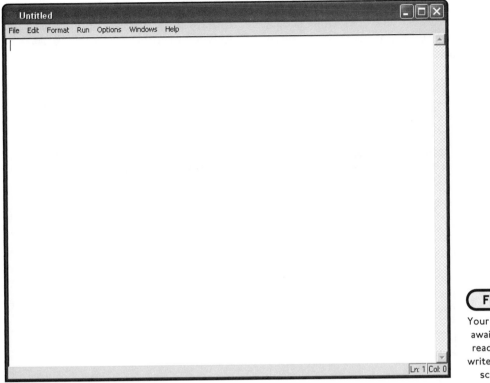

FIGURE 1.5

Your blank canvas awaits. Python is ready for you to write a program in script mode.

To run my Game Over program, I simply select Run, Run Module. Then, the interactive window becomes the active window and displays the results of my program. Take a look at my desktop in Figure 1.6.

You'll notice that the interactive window contains the old text from before. It still has the statement I entered while in interactive mode, print "Game Over", and the results, the message Game Over. Below all of that, you'll see the results of running the program from script mode: the message Game Over.

To run your program from IDLE like I just did, you need to first save your program.

Interactive mode is great for trying out a small idea quickly. Script mode is perfect for writing programs you can run later. Using both modes together is a great way to code.

Even though I need only script mode to write a program, I always keep an interactive window open while I code. As I write my programs in script mode, I jump over to the interactive window to try out an idea or to be sure I have the usage of a command just right.

The script window is where I craft my final product. The interactive window is like a scratch pad where I can think and experiment. Using them together helps me to write better programs more quickly.

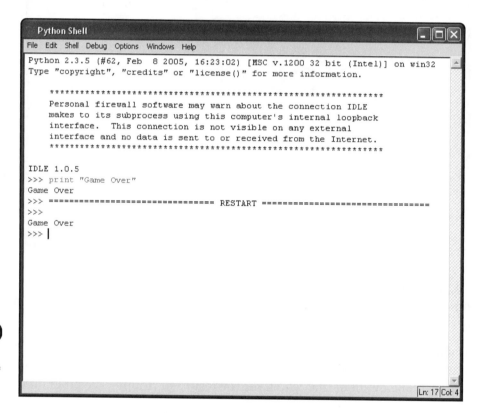

BACK TO THE GAME OVER PROGRAM

So far, you've run a version of the Game Over program through IDLE. While you're in the process of writing a program, running it through IDLE is a fine way to go. But I'm sure you want your finished products to work like any other program on your computer. You want a user to simply double-click your program's icon to launch your program.

If you were to try to run the version of the Game Over program I've shown so far in this way, you'd see a window appear and, just as quickly, disappear. You'd probably think that nothing happened. But something would have happened. It just would have happened too fast for you to notice. The program would run, Game Over would be displayed, and the program would end, all in a split second. What the program needs is a way to keep its console window open.

This updated version of Game Over, the final chapter project, keeps the program window open so the user can see the message. After displaying Game Over, the program also displays the message Press the enter key to exit. Once a user presses the Enter key, the program exits, and the console window disappears.

I'll walk you through the code one section at a time. But I recommend that you load the program from the CD-ROM and take a look at it. Better yet, type in the program yourself and run it.

Using Comments

The following are the first two lines of the program.

```
# Game Over
# Demonstrates the print command
```

These lines aren't statements for the computer to execute. In fact, the computer totally ignores them. These notes, called *comments*, are for the humans. Comments explain programming code in English (or any other language for that matter). Comments are invaluable to other programmers and help them to understand your code. But comments are also helpful to you. They remind you of how you accomplished something that may not be clear at first glance.

You create a comment with the number sign symbol, #. Anything after this symbol (except in a string) on the rest of the line is a comment. Comments are ignored by the computer. Notice that comments are colored red in IDLE to make them stand out.

It's a good idea to start all of your programs with a few comments, like I did here. It's helpful to list the title of the program and its purpose. Although I didn't do so here, you should also list the name of the programmer and the date the program was written.

You may be thinking, "Why have comments at all? I wrote the program, so I know what it does." That may be true a month after you write your code, but experienced programmers know that after a few months away from a program, your original intentions may not be as clear. If you want to modify an old program, a few well-placed comments may make your life much easier.

> ## IN THE REAL WORLD
>
> Comments are even more helpful to another programmer who needs to modify a program you wrote. This kind of situation comes up a lot in the world of professional programming. In fact, it's estimated that the majority of a programmer's time and effort go toward maintaining code that already exists. It's not uncommon for a programmer to be charged with the task of modifying a program written by someone else—and there's a chance that the original programmer won't be around to answer any questions. So, good comments are critical.

Using Blank Lines

Technically, the next line in the program is blank. The computer generally ignores blank lines; these, too, are just for the humans reading the code. Blank lines can make programs easier to read. Usually, I keep lines of related code together and separate sections with a blank line. In this program, I separated the comments from the `print` statement with a blank line.

Printing the String

The next line in the program should seem familiar to you.

```
print "Game Over"
```

It's your old friend, the `print` statement. This line, just as it does in interactive mode, prints Game Over.

Waiting for the User

The last line of the program:

```
raw_input("\n\nPress the enter key to exit.")
```

displays the prompt, Press the enter key to exit. and waits for the user to press the Enter key. Once the user presses the key, the program ends. This is a nice trick to keep a console window open until the user is done with an application.

Normally, this is about the time I'd explain just what is going on in this line. But I'm going to keep you in suspense. Sorry. You'll have to wait until the next chapter to fully appreciate this one line.

SUMMARY

- Python is a high-level, object-oriented programming language that's powerful yet easy to use.
- Python can interface with other programming languages.
- An Integrated Development Environment (IDE) is a set of tools that help a programmer write, run, and save programs.
- IDLE is Python's default IDE.
- IDLE has an interactive mode that offers immediate response to Python code.
- IDLE has a script mode that allows programmers to write, edit, load, save and run their programs.
- Syntax highlighting is displaying programming code in different colors or fonts, according to the category of each item.
- A string is a sequence of characters.
- A statement is a single unit of programming that performs some action.
- An expression is something that has a value or that can be evaluated to a single value.
- The `print` statement displays values on the screen.
- Source code (or programming code) is the instructions in a computer language that a programmer writes.
- A syntax error is a violation of the grammar of a programming language, often caused by a typo.
- A bug is an error in programming code.
- A comment is a note in a program meant only for humans and is ignored by the computer.
- Comments start with the # symbol.
- A program should contain an opening block of comments that list the program's title, purpose, programmer, and creation date.

REVIEW QUESTIONS

1. What is programming?
2. What is a "Hello World" program?
3. What's a console window?
4. Who developed Python?
5. Who or what is Python named after?
6. What is a high-level language?

7. What are three companies that use Python?
8. What is object-oriented programming?
9. How can Python increase programmer productivity?
10. Why might a programmer want to use Python in combination with other programming languages?
11. What does Python's platform-independence mean for programmers?
12. What does the fact that Python is open-source mean for programmers?
13. How does Python's interactive mode help programmers?
14. How does syntax highlighting help programmers?
15. Why include comments in a program if the computer just ignores them?

PROJECTS

1. Create a syntax error of your very own by entering your favorite ice cream flavor in IDLE's interactive mode. Then, make up for your misdeed and enter a statement that prints the name of your favorite ice cream.
2. Using IDLE's script mode, write and save a program that prints out your name. (Hint: Always include an opening block of comments in your program.)
3. Using IDLE's script mode, write and save a program that prints your favorite quote. On the next line, your program should print the name of the person who is credited with the quote. (Hint: Use two different `print` statements.)

Types, Variables, and Simple I/O: The Useless Trivia Program

Now that you've been introduced to the basics of saving and executing a program, it's time to dig in and create some more. In this chapter, you'll learn about different ways computers can categorize and store data and, more importantly, how to use this data in your programs. You'll even see how to get information from the user so that your programs become interactive. Specifically, you'll learn how to do the following:

- Use triple-quoted strings and escape sequences to gain more control over text
- Make your programs do math
- Store data in the computer's memory
- Use variables to access and manipulate that data
- Get input from users to create interactive programs

INTRODUCING THE USELESS TRIVIA PROGRAM

Combining the skills presented in this chapter, you'll create the Useless Trivia program shown in Figure 2.1.

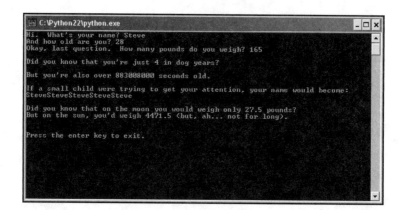

The program takes three pieces of personal information from the user: name, age, and weight. From these mundane items, the program is able to produce some amusing but trivial facts about the person, such as how old the person is in dog years and how much the person would weigh on the moon.

Though this may seem like a simple program (and it is), you'll find that the program is more interesting when you run it because you've had input. You'll care more about the results because they're personally tailored to you. This holds true for all programs, from games to business applications.

USING QUOTES WITH STRINGS

You saw an example of a string, `"Game Over"`, in the previous chapter. But strings can become much longer and more complex. You may want to give a user several paragraphs of instructions. Or you might want to format your text in a very specific manner. Using quotes can help you to create strings to accomplish all of this.

Introducing the Game Over 2.0 Program

Game Over 2.0 improves upon its predecessor program, Game Over, by displaying a more impressive version of the same message, which tells a player that his or her computer game has come to an end. Using single and double quotes, the result is more visually appealing. Check out Figure 2.2 to see a sample run.

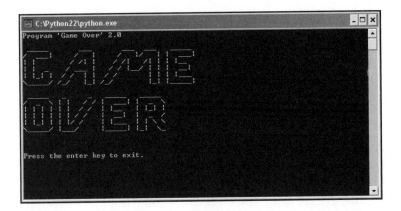

FIGURE 2.2

Now I get it, the
game is over.

The code for the program shows that it's pretty simple to present text using quotes in different ways:

```
# Game Over - Version 2
# Demonstrates the use of quotes in strings

print "Program 'Game Over' 2.0"

print \
"""

  _____        _____            _____   _____
 / ___|      /    |     /    |/    | |  __|
| |         / /| |     / /| |  /| | | | |__
| |  _     / ___ |    / / |__/ | | |  __|
| |_| |   / /   | |  / /        | | | |__
\____/ /_/    |_| /_/          |_| |____|


  _____    _   _   ____   _____   _____
 /  _  \ | | | | / / |  ___| |  _  \
| | | | | | | | / /  | |__   | |_| |
| | | | | | | |/ /   |  __|  |  _  /
| |_| | | | | |/ /   | |___  | | \ \
\____/  |___/       |____|  |_|  \_\

"""

raw_input("\n\nPress the enter key to exit.")
```

Using Quotes inside Strings

You've seen how to create simple strings by surrounding text with quotes. You can use either a pair of single (' ') or double quotes (" ") to create string values. The computer doesn't care. So, `'Game Over'` is exactly the same string as `"Game Over"`. But take a look at the first appearance of a string in the program:

```
print "Program 'Game Over' 2.0"
```

This statement uses both kinds of quotes. Check out the sample run in Figure 2.2 again. Only the single quotes show up, because they are part of the string, just like, for example, the letter *G*. But the double quotes are not part of the string. The double quotes are like bookends, telling the computer where the string begins and ends. So, if you use a pair of double quotes to "bookend" your string, you can use as many single quotes inside the string as you want. And, if you surround your string with a pair of single quotes, you can use as many double quotes inside the string as you like.

Once you've used one kind of quote as bookends for your string, you can't use that type of quote inside your string. This make sense, because once the computer sees the second appearance of the quote that began the string, it thinks the string is over. For example, `"With the words, 'Houston, we have a problem.', Jim Lovell became one of our most famous astronauts."` is a valid string. But, `"With the words, "Houston, we have a problem.", Jim Lovell became one of our most famous astronauts."` isn't valid, because once the computer sees the second double quote, it thinks the string is over. So, the computer sees the string `"With the words, "` followed by the word, *Houston*. And since the computer has no idea what *Houston* is, you get a nasty syntax error.

Continuing a Statement on the Next Line

The next line of code, `print \`, looks awfully lonely. And it should. It's not a complete statement. Generally, you write one statement per line. But you don't have to. You can stretch a single statement across multiple lines. All you have to do is use the line-continuation character, \ (which is just a backslash). Put it anywhere you'd normally use a space (but not inside a string) to continue your statement on the next line. The computer will act as if it sees one long line of code.

The computer doesn't care how long a programming line is, but people do. If a line of your code feels too long or would be more clear as several lines, use the line-continuation character to split it up.

Creating Triple-Quoted Strings

Certainly the coolest part of the program is where it prints out "Game Over" in a big block of text. The following string is responsible:

This is what's called a *triple-quoted string*. It's a string enclosed by a pair of three quotes in a row. Like before, it doesn't matter which kind of quotes you use, as long as you bookend with the same type.

As you can see, triple-quoted strings can span multiple lines. They print on the screen exactly the way you type them.

USING ESCAPE SEQUENCES WITH STRINGS

Escape sequences allow you to put special characters into your strings. These give you greater control and flexibility over the text you display. The escape sequences you'll work with are made up of two characters: a backslash followed by another character. This may all sound a little mysterious, but once you see a few sequences in action, you'll realize just how easy they are to use.

Introducing the Fancy Credits Program

Besides telling a player that the game is over, a program often displays credits, a list of all the people who worked so hard to make it a reality. Fancy Credits uses escape sequences to achieve some effects it just couldn't without them. Figure 2.3 shows the results.

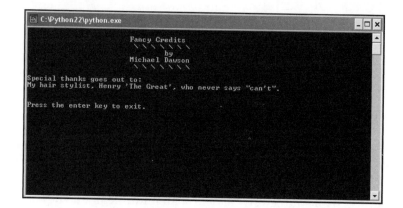

FIGURE 2.3

Please, contain your applause.

The code looks a bit cryptic at first glance:

```python
# Fancy Credits
# Demonstrates escape sequences

# sound the system bell
print "\a"

print "\t\t\tFancy Credits"

print "\t\t\t \\ \\ \\ \\ \\ \\ \\"
print "\t\t\t\tby"
print "\t\t\tMichael Dawson"
print "\t\t\t \\ \\ \\ \\ \\ \\ \\"
```

```
print "\nSpecial thanks goes out to:"
print "My hair stylist, Henry \'The Great\', who never says \"can\'t\"."
```

```
raw_input("\n\nPress the enter key to exit.")
```

But you'll soon understand it all.

Sounding the System Bell

Upon running this program, you'll notice something different right away. It makes noise! The very first statement in the program,

```
print "\a"
```

sounds the system bell of your computer. It does this through the escape sequence, \a, which represents the system bell character. Every time you print it, the bell rings. You can print a string with just this sequence, as I have, or you can put it inside a longer string. You can even use the sequence several times to ring the bell more than once.

TRAP A few escape sequences only work as advertised if you run your program directly from the operating system and not through IDLE. The escape sequences \a and \b are good examples. Let's say I have a program that simply prints the escape sequence \a. If I run it through IDLE, I get a little square box printed on my screen—not what I wanted. But if I run that same program directly from Windows, by double-clicking the program file icon, my computer's system bell rings just as I intended.

Moving Forward a Tab Stop

Sometimes you'll want to set some text off from the left margin where it normally prints. In a word processor, you could use the Tab key. With strings, you can use the escape sequence for a tab, \t. That's exactly what I did in the following line:

```
print "\t\t\tFancy Credits"
```

I used the tab escape sequence, \t, three times in a row. So, when the program prints the string, it prints three tabs and then Fancy Credits. This makes Fancy Credits look nearly centered in the console window. Tab sequences are good for setting off text, as in this program, but they're also perfect for arranging text into columns.

Printing a Backslash

If you've thought ahead, you may be wondering how you can print a backslash if the computer always interprets a backslash as the beginning of an escape sequence. Well, the solution is pretty simple: Just use two backslashes in a row. Each of the following two lines prints three tabs, as a result of the three \t sequences:

```
print "\t\t\t \\ \\ \\ \\ \\ \\ \\"
print "\t\t\t \\ \\ \\ \\ \\ \\ \\"
```

Then, each prints exactly seven backslashes, separated by spaces. Go ahead and count. You'll find exactly seven pairs of backslashes, separated by spaces.

Inserting a Newline

The most useful sequence at your disposal is the newline sequence. It's represented by \n. By using this sequence, you can insert a newline character into your strings for a blank line where you need it. Newlines are often used right at the beginning of a string to separate it from the text last printed. That's what I did in the line:

```
print "\nSpecial thanks goes out to:"
```

The computer sees the \n sequence, prints a blank line, then prints Special thanks goes out to:.

Inserting a Quote

Inserting a quote into a string, even the type of quote you use to bookend it, is simple. Just use the sequence \' for a single quote and \" for a double quote. They mean "put a quote here" and won't be mistaken by the computer as a marker for the end of your string. This is what I used to get both kinds of quotes in one line of text:

```
print "My hair stylist, Henry \'The Great\', who never says \"can\'t\"."
```

The pair of double quotes at both ends are the bookends, defining the string. To make the string easier to understand, look at it in parts:

- \'The Great\' prints as 'The Great'.
- Each \' sequence is printed as a single quote.
- \"can\'t\" prints as "can't".
- Both \" sequences print as double quotes.
- The lone \' sequence prints as a single quote.

As you can see, escape sequences aren't so bad once you've seen them in action. And they can come in quite handy. Table 2.1 summarizes some useful ones.

TABLE 2.1	SELECTED ESCAPE SEQUENCES
Sequence	**Description**
\\	Backslash. Prints one backslash.
\'	Single quote. Prints a single quote.
\"	Double quote. Prints a double quote.
\a	Bell. Sounds the system bell.
\b	Backspace. Moves cursor back one space.
\n	Newline. Moves cursor to beginning of next line.
\t	Horizontal tab. Moves cursor forward one tab stop.

CONCATENATING AND REPEATING STRINGS

You've seen how you can insert special characters into a string, but there are things you can do with entire strings themselves. You can combine two separate strings into a larger one. And you can even repeat a single string as many times as you want.

Introducing the Silly Strings Program

The Silly Strings program prints several strings to the screen. The results are shown in Figure 2.4.

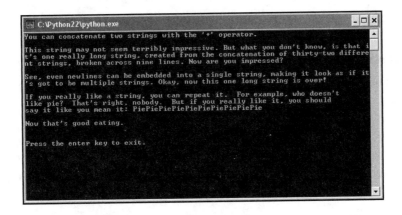

FIGURE 2.4

The strings on the screen appear differently than in the program code.

Though you've already seen strings printed, the way these strings were created is brand new to you. Take a look at the code:

```
# Silly Strings
# Demonstrates string concatenation and repetition
```

```
print "You can concatenate two " + "strings with the '+' operator."

print "\nThis string " + "may not " + "seem terr" + "ibly impressive. " \
    + "But what " + "you don't know," + " is that " + "it's one real" \
    + "l" + "y" + " long string, created from the concatenation " \
    + "of " + "thirty-two " + "different strings, broken across " \
    + "nine lines." + " Now are you" + " impressed?\n\n" + "See, " \
    + "even newlines can be embedded into a single string, making" \
    + " it look " + "as " + "if " + "it" + "'s " + "got " + "to " \
    + "be" + " multiple strings." + " Okay, now this " + "one " \
    + "long" + " string " + "is over!"

print \
"""
If you really like a string, you can repeat it. For example, who doesn't
like pie? That's right, nobody. But if you really like it, you should
say it like you mean it:""",

print "Pie" * 10

print "\nNow that's good eating."

raw_input("\n\nPress the enter key to exit.")
```

Concatenating Strings

Concatenating strings means joining them together, to create a whole new string. A simple example is in the first print statement:

```
print "You can concatenate two " + "strings with the '+' operator."
```

The + operator joins the two strings, "You can concatenate two " and "strings with the '+' operator.", together to form a new, larger string. It's pretty intuitive. It's like adding the strings together using the same symbol you've always used for adding numbers.

 When you join two strings, their exact values are fused together, with no space or separator character inserted between them. So, if you were to join the two strings "cup" and "cake", you'd end up with "cupcake" and not "cup cake". In most cases, you'll want to insert a space between strings you join, so don't forget to put one in.

The next `print` statement shows that you can concatenate 'til your heart's content:

```
print "\nThis string " + "may not " + "seem terr" + "ibly impressive. " \
      + "But what " + "you don't know," + " is that " + "it's one real" \
      + "l" + "y" + " long string, created from the concatenation " \
      + "of " + "thirty-two " + "different strings, broken across " \
      + "nine lines." + " Now are you" + " impressed?\n\n" + "See, " \
      + "even newlines can be embedded into a single string, making" \
      + " it look " + "as " + "if " + "it" + "'s " + "got " + "to " \
      + "be" + " multiple strings." + " Okay, now this " + "one " \
      + "long" + " string is over!"
```

The computer prints one long string that was created by the concatenation of 32 individual strings. One thing you may notice is that the string doesn't correctly wrap in the console window. So be careful when you create super-long strings.

Suppressing a Newline

You've seen how you can add extra newlines with the `\n` escape sequence. But you can also suppress a newline so that the text of two consecutive `print` statements appears on the same line. Python will automatically insert a space between the two printed items. All you have to do is add a comma to the end of a `print` statement, like so:

```
print \
"""
If you really like a string, you can repeat it. For example, who doesn't
like pie? That's right, nobody. But if you really like it, you should
say it like you mean it:""",
```

By adding the comma at the end of this triple-quoted string, the next text printed will appear on the same line as `say it like you mean it:`.

Repeating Strings

The next new idea presented in the program is illustrated in the following line:

```
print "Pie" * 10
```

This line creates a new string, `"PiePiePiePiePiePiePiePiePiePie"`, and prints it out. That's the string `"Pie"` repeated 10 times, by the way.

Like the concatenation operator, the repetition operator, `*`, is pretty intuitive. It's the same symbol used for multiplying numbers on a computer, so repeating a string with it makes sense. It's like you're multiplying the string. You can repeat a string as many times as you want. To repeat a string, just put the string and number of repetitions together with the repetition operator, *.

WORKING WITH NUMBERS

So far, you've been using strings to represent text. That's just one type of value. Computers let you represent information in other ways, too. One of the most basic but most important ways is as numbers. Numbers are used in almost every program. Whether you're writing a space shooter game or home finance package, you need to represent numbers some way. You've got high scores or checking account balances to work with, after all. Fortunately, Python has several different types of numbers to fit all of your game or application programming needs.

Introducing the Word Problems Program

This next program uses those dreaded word problems. You know, the kind that always seems to involve two trains leaving different cities at the same time headed in opposite directions... bringing back nightmares of junior high algebra as they're about to collide. Well, fear not. You won't have to solve a single word problem, or even do any math at all. I promise. The computer will do all the work. All you have to do is press the Enter key. The Word Problems program is just an amusing (hopefully) way to explore working with numbers. Check out Figure 2.5 to see a sample run.

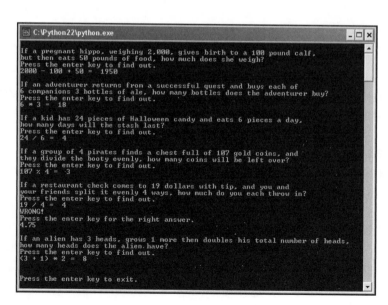

FIGURE 2.5

With Python, you can add, subtract, multiply, divide, and keep track of a pregnant hippo's weight.

The following is the source code for the program:

```
# Word Problems
# Demonstrates numbers and math

print \
"""
If a pregnant hippo, weighing 2,000 pounds, gives birth to a 100 pound calf,
but then eats 50 pounds of food, how much does she weigh?"""
raw_input("Press the enter key to find out.")
print "2000 - 100 + 50 = ",
print 2000 - 100 + 50


print \
"""
If an adventurer returns from a successful quest and buys each of
6 companions 3 bottles of ale, how many bottles does the adventurer buy?"""
raw_input("Press the enter key to find out.")
print "6 * 3 = ",
print 6 * 3


print \
"""
If a kid has 24 pieces of Halloween candy and eats 6 pieces a day,
how many days will the stash last?"""
raw_input("Press the enter key to find out.")
print "24 / 6 = ",
print 24 / 6


print \
"""
If a group of 4 pirates finds a chest full of 107 gold coins, and
they divide the booty evenly, how many coins will be left over?"""
raw_input("Press the enter key to find out.")
print "107 % 4 = ",
print 107 % 4


print \
"""
```

```
If a restaurant check comes to 19 dollars with tip, and you and
your friends split it evenly 4 ways, how much do you each throw in?"""
raw_input("Press the enter key to find out.")
print "19 / 4 = ",
print 19 / 4
print "WRONG!"
raw_input("Press the enter key for the right answer.")
print 19.0 / 4

raw_input("\n\nPress the enter key to exit.")
```

Understanding Numeric Types

The program Word Problems uses numbers. That's obvious. But what may not be obvious is that it uses two different types of numbers. Python allows programmers to use several different types of numbers. The two types used in this program, and probably the most common, are *integers* and *floating-point numbers* (or *floats*). Integers are whole numbers—numbers with no fractional part. Or, another way to think about them is that they can be written without a decimal point. The numbers 1, 27, -100, and 0 are all examples of integers. Floats are numbers with a decimal point, such as 2.376, -99.1, and 1.0.

You might be thinking, "Numbers are numbers. What's the big deal?" But integers and floats can act a little differently under special circumstances, as you'll see.

Using Mathematical Operators

With mathematical operators, you can turn your computer into an expensive calculator. The operators should look pretty familiar. For example, the following line

```
print 2000 - 100 + 50
```

subtracts 100 from 2000 and then adds 50 before printing the result of 1950. Technically, it evaluates the *expression* 2000 - 100 + 50, which evaluates to 1950. An expression is just a sequence of values, joined by operators, that can be simplified to another value.

The line

```
print 6 * 3
```

multiplies 6 by 3 and prints the result of 18.

The line

```
print 24 / 6
```

divides 24 by 6 and prints the result of 4.

Pretty standard stuff. But check out the next calculation:

```
print 107 % 4
```

Okay, using % as a mathematical operator is probably new to you. Used here, the symbol %
stands for modulus, which is just a fancy way of saying, "give me the remainder." So 107 %
4 evaluates to the remainder of 107 / 4, which is 3.

The next calculation might also make you scratch your head. The following line produces a
result of 4:

```
print 19 / 4
```

But if each person puts four dollars in, that's a total of only 16, not 19. And that leaves the
waitress short three bucks. What happened? Well, when Python performs integer division
(where all the numbers involved are integers), the result is always an integer. So, any fractional
part is ignored. If you want floating-point division, or what some people call *true division*, then
at least one of your numbers must be a floating-point number. The following line results
in true division:

```
print 19.0 / 4
```

This line prints the expected 4.75. Now you've done true division and made your waitress
happy.

IN THE REAL WORLD

Python is an evolving language. There's a highly open process for discussing potential
changes and improvements. In fact, there's a list of every proposed enhancement at
http://www.python.org/peps/. One change that is definitely on its way is the end of integer
division. Starting in Python 3.0, all division will be true division. So, beginning in that release,
3 / 4 will be .75 and not 0.

Table 2.2 summarizes mathematical operators for integers, while Table 2.3 summarizes
mathematical operators for floating-point numbers. Take a close look at the results of the
division operator in each table.

TABLE 2.2   MATHEMATICAL OPERATORS WITH INTEGERS

Operator	Description	Example	Evaluates To
*	Multiplication	7 * 3	21
/	Division	7 / 3	2
%	Modulus	7 % 3	1
+	Addition	7 + 3	10
–	Subtraction	7 - 3	4

TABLE 2.3   MATHEMATICAL OPERATORS WITH FLOATING-POINT NUMBERS

Operator	Description	Example	Evaluates To
*	Multiplication	7.0 * 3.0	21.0
/	Division	7.0 / 3.0	2.3333333333333335
%	Modulus	7.0 % 3.0	1.0
+	Addition	7.0 + 3.0	10.0
–	Subtraction	7.0 - 3.0	4.0

TRAP Notice the division entry in Table 2.3. It says that 7.0 divided by 3.0 is 2.3333333333333335. While this is pretty accurate, it's not exact. Computers tend to round floating-point numbers. The results are fine for most purposes. But you should be aware of this when using floats.

UNDERSTANDING VARIABLES

Through variables, you can store and manipulate information, a fundamental aspect of programming. Python lets you create variables to organize and access this information.

Introducing the Greeter Program

Check out Figure 2.6 to see the results of the Greeter program.

From just a screen shot, the program looks like something you could have already written. But within the code lurks the whole, new, powerful concept of variables. Take a look:

```
# Greeter
# Demonstrates the use of a variable
```

```
name = "Larry"

print name

print "Hi, " + name

raw_input("\n\nPress the enter key to exit.")
```

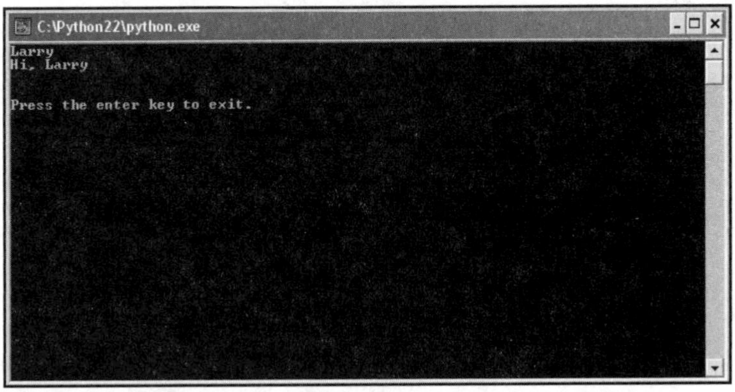

FIGURE 2.6

A shout-out to all
the Larry's of the
world.

Creating Variables

A variable provides a way to label and access information. Instead of having to know exactly where in the computer's memory some information is stored, you use a variable to get at it. It's kind of like calling your friend on his cell phone. You don't have to know where in the city your friend is to reach him. You just press a button and you get him. But before you use a variable, you have to create it, as in the following line:

```
name = "Larry"
```

This line is called an *assignment statement*. It creates a variable called name and assigns it a value so that it references the string "Larry". In general, assignment statements assign a value to a variable. If the variable doesn't exist, like in the case of name, it's created, then assigned a value.

Technically, an assignment statement stores the value on the right side of the equal sign in your computer's memory, while the variable on the left side only refers to the value (and doesn't directly store it). Therefore, Python purists would say that a variable "gets" a value instead of saying that a variable is "assigned" a value. However, I use "gets" and "assigned" interchangeably, depending upon which seems clearest.

You'll learn more about the implications of the way variables refer to values in Chapter 5, in the section, "Understanding Shared References."

Using Variables

Once a variable has been created, it refers to some value. The convenience of a variable is that it can be used just like the value to which it refers. So the line

```
print name
```

prints the string "Larry" just like the statement `print "Larry"` does. And the line

```
print "Hi, " + name
```

concatenates the values "Hi," and "Larry" to create a new string, "Hi, Larry", and prints it out. The results are the same as the results of `print "Hi," + "Larry"`. Basically, I can use `name` instead of "Larry" with the same results.

Naming Variables

Like the proud parent of your program, you pick the names of your variables. For this program, I chose to call my variable `name`, but I could just as easily have used `person`, `guy`, or `alpha7345690876`, and the program would have run exactly the same. There are only a few rules that you have to follow to create legal variable names. Create an illegal one and Python will let you know about it with an error. The following are the two most important rules:

1. A variable name can contain only numbers, letters, and underscores.
2. A variable name can't start with a number.

In addition to the rules for creating *legal* variable names, the following are some guidelines that more experienced programmers follow for creating *good* variable names—because once you've programmed for a while, you know the chasm of difference that exists between a legal variable name and a good one. (I'll give you one guideline right now: Don't ever name a variable `alpha7345690876`.)

- **Choose descriptive names.** Variable names should be clear enough so that another programmer could look at the name and have a good idea what it represents. So, for example, use `score` instead of `s`. (One exception to this rule involves variables used for a brief period. Often, programmers give those variables short names, such as x. But that's fine because by using x, the programmer clearly conveys that the variable represents a quick holding place.)

- **Be consistent.** There are different schools of thought about how to write multiword variable names. Is it `high_score` or `highScore`? I use the underscore style. But it's not important which method you use, as long as you're consistent.

- **Follow the traditions of the language.** Some naming conventions are just traditions. For example, in most languages (Python included) variable names start with a lowercase letter. Another tradition is to avoid using an underscore as the first character of your variable names. Names that begin with an underscore have special meaning in Python.

- **Keep the length in check.** This may seem to go against the first guideline: Choose descriptive names. Isn't `personal_checking_account_balance` a great variable name? Maybe not. Long variable names can lead to problems. They can make statements hard to read. Plus, the longer the variable name, the greater the chance of a typo. As a guideline, try to keep your variable names less than 15 characters.

 TRICK *Self-documenting* code is written in such a way that it's easy to understand what is happening in the program independent of any comments. Choosing good variable names is an excellent step toward this kind of code.

GETTING USER INPUT

After appreciating all that program Greeter has to offer, you may still be thinking, "So what?" Yes, you could write a program that does exactly what Greeter does without going to the trouble of creating any fancy variables. But to do fundamentally important things, including getting, storing, and manipulating user input, you need variables. Check out the next program, which uses input to give a personalized greeting.

Introducing the Personal Greeter Program

The Personal Greeter program adds a single, but very cool, element to the Greeter program: user input. Instead of working with a predefined value, the computer lets the user enter his or her name and then uses it to say Hi. Figure 2.7 shows off the program.

Getting user input isn't very hard. As a result, the code doesn't look much different:

```
# Personal Greeter
# Demonstrates getting user input

name = raw_input("Hi. What's your name? ")
print name
```

```
print "Hi, " + name

raw_input("\n\nPress the enter key to exit.")
```

FIGURE 2.7

Now, name is assigned a string based on whatever the user enters, including "Rupert".

Using the raw_input() Function

The only line that's changed is the assignment statement:

```
name = raw_input("Hi. What's your name? ")
```

The left side of the statement is exactly the same as in the Greeter program. name is created and a value is assigned to it, just like before. But this time, the right side of the assignment statement is a call to the *function* raw_input(). A function is like a mini-program that goes off and does some specific task. The task of raw_input() is to get some text from the user. Sometimes you give a function values to use. You put these values, called *arguments,* between the parentheses. In this case, the one argument passed to raw_input() is the string "Hi. What's your name? ". As you can see from Figure 2.7, raw_input() uses the string to prompt the user. raw_input() waits for the user to enter something. Once the user presses the Enter key, raw_input() returns whatever the user typed, as a string. That's the string that name gets.

If you're still not totally clear on how this works, think of it this way: Using raw_input() is like ordering a pizza. The raw_input() function is like a pizza parlor. You make a call to a pizza parlor to place your order, and you make a call to the raw_input() function to kick it into gear. When you call the pizza parlor, you provide information, such as "pepperoni." When you call the raw_input() function, you pass it the argument, "Hi. What's your name?". After you finish your call to the pizza parlor, the employees get a pepperoni pizza to your door. And after you make your call to raw_input(), the function returns whatever string the user entered.

The rest of the Personal Greeter program works just like the Greeter program. It makes no difference to the computer how name gets its value. So the line

```
print name
```

prints the value of name. The line

```
print "Hi, " + name
```

concatenates the "Hi," and the value of name, and prints this new string out.

At this point, you know enough to understand the last line in all of these console programs. The goal of the last line is to wait for the user to press the Enter key:

```
raw_input("\n\nPress the enter key to exit.")
```

It does exactly that through the raw_input() function. Because I don't care what the user enters, so long as he or she presses the Enter key, I don't assign the return value of raw_input() to a variable like before. It may seem weird to get a value and do nothing with it, but it's my option. If I don't assign the return value to a variable, the computer just ignores it. So once the user presses the Enter key, the program ends and the console window closes.

USING STRING METHODS

Python has a rich set of tools for working with strings. One type of these tools is string methods. String methods allow you to create new strings from old ones. You can do everything from the simple, such as creating a string that's just an all-capital-letters version of the original, to the complex, such as creating a new string that's the result of a series of intricate letter substitutions.

Introducing the Quotation Manipulation Program

According to Mark Twain, "The art of prophecy is very difficult, especially with respect to the future." No one can accurately foretell the future, but it's still amusing to read predictions that pundits have made about technology. A good one is, "I think there is a world market for maybe five computers." This was made by then IBM chairman, Thomas Watson, in 1943. The Quotation Manipulation program that I wrote prints this quote several ways using string methods. (Fortunately, I was able to write this program because I happen to own computer #3.) Take a look at the sample run in Figure 2.8.

The following is the code for the program:

```
# Quotation Manipulation
# Demonstrates string methods
```

```
# quote from IBM Chairman, Thomas Watson, in 1943
quote = "I think there is a world market for maybe five computers."

print "Original quote:"
print quote

print "\nIn uppercase:"
print quote.upper()

print "\nIn lowercase:"
print quote.lower()

print "\nAs a title:"
print quote.title()

print "\nWith a minor replacement:"
print quote.replace("five", "millions of")

print "\nOriginal quote is still:"
print quote

raw_input("\n\nPress the enter key to exit.")
```

Creating New Strings with String Methods

Though there's a new concept at work here, the code is still pretty understandable. Take a look at the line:

```
print quote.upper()
```

You can probably guess what it does: print a version of quote in all uppercase letters.

The line does this through the use of a string method, upper(). A *string method* is like an ability a string has. So, quote has the ability to create a new string, a capitalized version of itself, through its upper() method. When it does this, it returns this new string, and the line becomes equivalent to the following line:

```
print "I THINK THERE IS A WORLD MARKET FOR MAYBE FIVE COMPUTERS."
```

Now, the line of code is never like this, but you can think of it in this way to help you understand how the method works.

You've probably noticed the parentheses in this method call. It should remind you of functions, which you just learned about in this chapter. Methods are similar to functions. The main difference is that a built-in function, such as `raw_input()`, can be called on its own, but a string method has to be called through a particular string. It makes no sense to just type the following:

```
print upper()
```

You kick off a method, or *invoke* it, by adding a dot, followed by the name of the method, followed by a pair of parentheses, after a string value. The parentheses aren't just for show. Just as with functions, you can pass arguments inside them. `upper()` doesn't take any arguments, but you'll see an example of a string method that does with `replace()`.

The line

```
print quote.lower()
```

invokes the `lower()` method of `quote` to create an all-lowercase-letters version, which it returns. Then, that new lowercase string is printed.

The line

```
print quote.title()
```

prints a version of `quote` that's like a title. The `title()` method returns a string where the first letter of each word is capitalized and the rest of the string is in lowercase.

The line

```
print quote.replace("five", "millions of")
```

prints a new string, where every occurrence of `"five"` in quotes is replaced with `"millions of"`.

The method `replace()` needs at least two pieces of information: the old text to be replaced and the new text that replaces it. You separate the two arguments with a comma. You can add an optional third argument, an integer, that tells the method the maximum number of times to make the replacement.

Finally, the program prints `quote` again, with

```
print "\nOriginal quote is still:"
print quote
```

You can see from Figure 2.8 that `quote` hasn't changed. Remember, string methods create a new string. They don't affect the original one. Table 2.4 summarizes the string methods you've just seen, along with a few others.

```
C:\Python22\python.exe                                    _ □ ×
Original quote:
I think there is a world market for maybe five computers.

In uppercase:
I THINK THERE IS A WORLD MARKET FOR MAYBE FIVE COMPUTERS.

In lowercase:
i think there is a world market for maybe five computers.

As a title:
I Think There Is A World Market For Maybe Five Computers.

With a minor replacement:
I think there is a world market for maybe millions of computers.

Original quote is still:
I think there is a world market for maybe five computers.

Press the enter key to exit.
```

FIGURE 2.8

This slightly low guess is printed several ways with the help of string methods.

TABLE 2.4	**USEFUL STRING METHODS**
Method	**Description**
`upper()`	Returns the uppercase version of the string.
`lower()`	Returns the lowercase version of the string.
`swapcase()`	Returns a new string where the case of each letter is switched. Uppercase becomes lowercase and lowercase becomes uppercase.
`capitalize()`	Returns a new string where the first letter is capitalized and the rest are lowercase.
`title()`	Returns a new string where the first letter of each word is capitalized and all others are lowercase.
`strip()`	Returns a string where all the white space (tabs, spaces, and newlines) at the beginning and end is removed.
`replace(old, new [,max])`	Returns a string where occurrences of the string *old* are replaced with the string *new*. The optional *max* limits the number of replacements.

USING THE RIGHT TYPES

You've used three different types so far: strings, integers, and floating-point numbers. It's important to know not only which data types are available to you, but how to work with them. If you don't, you might end up with programs that produce unintended results.

Introducing the Trust Fund Buddy–Bad Program

The idea for the next program was to create a tool for those souls who play all day, living off a generous trust fund. The program is supposed to calculate a grand total for monthly expenditures based on user input. This grand total is meant to help those living beyond any reasonable means stay within budget so they don't ever have to think about getting a real job. But, as you may have guessed from the program's title, Trust Fund Buddy–Bad doesn't work as the programmer intended. Figure 2.9 shows a sample run.

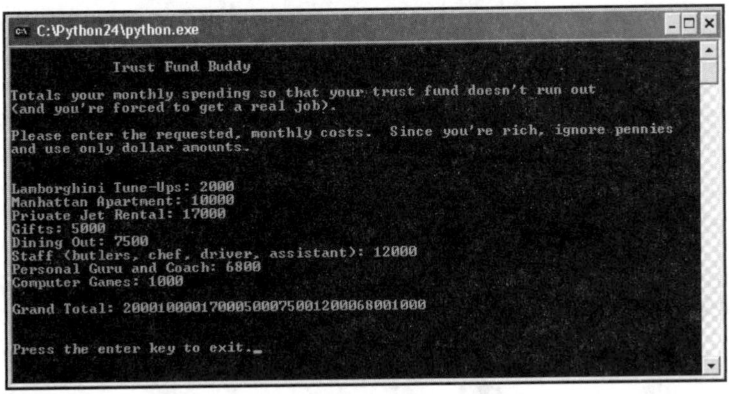

FIGURE 2.9

The monthly total should be high, but not that high. Something is wrong.

All right, the program obviously isn't working correctly. It has a bug. But not a bug that causes it to crash, like the syntax error you saw last chapter. When a program produces unintended results but doesn't crash, it has a *logical error*. Based on what you already know, you might be able to figure out what's happening by looking at the code. Here's the listing:

```
# Trust Fund Buddy - Bad
# Demonstrates a logical error
print \
"""

        Trust Fund Buddy


Totals your monthly spending so that your trust fund doesn't run out
(and you're forced to get a real job).


Please enter the requested, monthly costs. Since you're rich, ignore pennies
and use only dollar amounts.


"""
```

```
car = raw_input("Lamborghini Tune-Ups: ")
rent = raw_input("Manhattan Apartment: ")
jet = raw_input("Private Jet Rental: ")
gifts = raw_input("Gifts: ")
food = raw_input("Dining Out: ")
staff = raw_input("Staff (butlers, chef, driver, assistant): ")
guru = raw_input("Personal Guru and Coach: ")
games = raw_input("Computer Games: ")


total = car + rent + jet + gifts + food + staff + guru + games

print "\nGrand Total: " + total

raw_input("\n\nPress the enter key to exit.")
```

It's okay if you don't see the problem right now. I'll give you one more hint, though. Take a look at the output in Figure 2.9 again. Examine the huge number that the program prints as the grand total. Then look at all the numbers the user entered. Notice any connection? Okay, whether you do or don't, read on.

Tracking Down Logical Errors

Logical errors can be the toughest bugs to fix. Because the program doesn't crash, you don't get the benefit of an error message to offer a clue. You have to observe the behavior of the program and investigate the code.

In this case, the program's output tells the story. The huge number is clearly not the sum of all the numbers the user entered. But, by looking at the numbers, you can see that the grand total printed is a concatenation of all the numbers. How did that happen? Well, if you remember, the raw_input() function returns a string. So each "number" the user enters is treated like a string. Which means that each variable in the program has a string value associated with it. So, the line

```
total = car + rent + jet + gifts + food + staff + guru + games
```

is not adding numbers. It's concatenating strings!

IN THE REAL WORLD

The + symbol works with pairs of strings as well as pairs of integers. Using the same operator for values of different types is called *operator overloading*. Now, "overloading" may sound like a bad thing, but actually it's a good thing. Doesn't it make sense that strings are joined using the plus sign? You immediately understand what it means. Implemented well, operator overloading can make for clearer and more elegant code.

Now that you know the problem, how do you fix it? Somehow those string values need to be converted to numbers. Then the program will work as intended. If only there was some way to do this. Well, as you may have guessed, there is.

CONVERTING VALUES

The solution to the Trust Fund Buddy-Bad program is to convert the string values returned by raw_input() to numeric ones. Because the program works with whole dollar amounts, it makes sense to convert each string to an integer before working with it.

Introducing the Trust Fund Buddy-Good Program

The Trust Fund Buddy-Good program fixes the logical bug in Trust Fund Buddy-Bad. Take a look at the output of the new program in Figure 2.10.

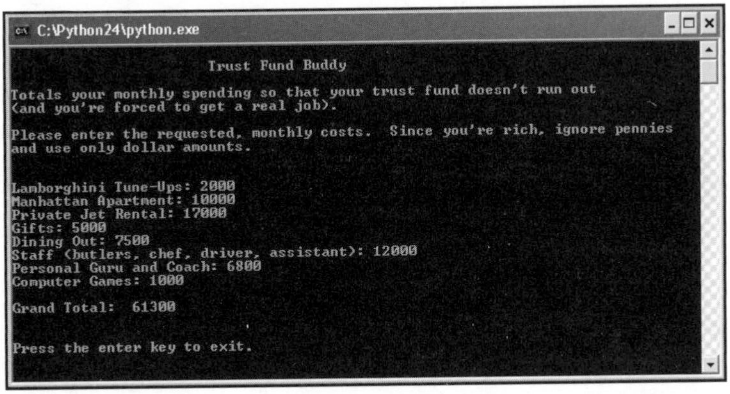

FIGURE 2.10

Ah, 61,300 dollars a month is much more reasonable.

Now the program arrives at the correct total. Here's the code:

```
# Trust Fund Buddy - Good
```

```
# Demonstrates type conversion

print \
"""

                Trust Fund Buddy

Totals your monthly spending so that your trust fund doesn't run out
(and you're forced to get a real job).


Please enter the requested, monthly costs. Since you're rich, ignore pennies
and use only dollar amounts.

"""

car = raw_input("Lamborghini Tune-Ups: ")
car = int(car)

rent = int(raw_input("Manhattan Apartment: "))
jet = int(raw_input("Private Jet Rental: "))
gifts = int(raw_input("Gifts: "))
food = int(raw_input("Dining Out: "))
staff = int(raw_input("Staff (butlers, chef, driver, assistant): "))
guru = int(raw_input("Personal Guru and Coach: ") )
games = int(raw_input("Computer Games: "))

total = car + rent + jet + gifts + food + staff + guru + games

print "\nGrand Total: ", total

raw_input("\n\nPress the enter key to exit.")
```

Converting Strings to Integers

There are several functions that convert between types. The function to convert a value to an integer is demonstrated in the following lines:

```
car = raw_input("Lamborghini Tune-Ups: ")
car = int(car)
```

The first line is just like before. It gets input from the user as a string and assigns that value to car. The second line does the conversion. The function int() takes the string referenced by car and returns an integer version of it. Then, car gets this new integer value.

The next seven lines get and convert the remaining expenditure categories:

```
rent = int(raw_input("Manhattan Apartment: "))
jet = int(raw_input("Private Jet Rental: "))
gifts = int(raw_input("Gifts: "))
food = int(raw_input("Dining Out: "))
staff = int(raw_input("Staff (butlers, chef, driver, assistant): "))
guru = int(raw_input("Personal Guru and Coach: ") )
games = int(raw_input("Computer Games: "))
```

Notice that the assignments are done in just one line now. That's because the two function calls, raw_input() and int(), are nested. *Nesting* function calls means putting one inside the other. This is perfectly fine as long as the return values of the inner function can be used by the outer function. Here, the return value of raw_input() is a string, and a string is a perfectly acceptable type for int() to convert.

In the assignment statement for rent, raw_input() goes out and asks the user how much the rent was. The user enters some text, and that is returned as a string. Then, the program calls the function int() with that string. int() returns the integer the string represented. Then, that integer is assigned to rent. The other six assignment statements work the same way.

There are other functions that convert values to a specific type. Table 2.5 lists several.

TABLE 2.5 SELECTED TYPE CONVERSION FUNCTIONS

Function	Description	Example	Returns
float(x)	Returns a floating-point value by converting x	float("10.0")	10.0
int(x)	Returns an integer value by converting x	int("10")	10
str(x)	Returns a string value by converting x	str(10)	'10'

Using Augmented Assignment Operators

Augmented assignment operators is a mouthful. But the concept is simple. Let's say you want to know the yearly amount the user spends on food. To calculate and assign the yearly amount, you could use the line

```
food = food * 52
```

This line multiplies the value of food by 52 and then assigns the result back to food. You could accomplish the same thing with this line:

```
food *= 52
```

*= is an augmented assignment operator. It also multiplies the value of food by 52 and then assigns the result back to food, but it's shorter than the first version. Because assigning a new value to a variable based on its original value is something that happens a lot in programming, these operators provide a nice shortcut to a common task. There are other augmented assignment operators. Table 2.6 summarizes some useful ones.

TABLE 2.6   USEFUL AUGMENT ASSIGNMENT OPERATORS

Operator	Example	Is Equivalent To
*=	x *= 5	x = x * 5
/=	x /= 5	x = x / 2
%=	x %= 5	x = x % 5
+=	x += 5	x = x + 5
-=	x -= 5	x = x - 5

Printing Strings and Numbers Together

The next line of code

```
print "\nGrand Total: ", total
```

is only slightly different than the corresponding line in the Trust Fund Buddy–Bad program:

```
print "\nGrand Total: " + total
```

But the difference is an important one. In the Trust Fund Buddy–Bad program, the string "\nGrand Total: " and the value of total are joined together by string concatenation through the + operator. That's great because both are strings. However, in the Trust Fund Buddy–Good program, the value of total is an integer. So string concatenation won't work. Instead, the values are listed, separated by a comma. In general, you can list values separated by commas in a print statement to have them all print out together.

BACK TO THE USELESS TRIVIA PROGRAM

You now know everything you need to know to program the project Useless Trivia from the beginning of the chapter. I'll present the program a little differently than the others. Instead of listing the code out in its entirety, I'll go over the program one section at a time.

Creating the Initial Comments

Although comments don't have any effect while the program runs, they are an important part of every project. As always, I begin with a few:

```
# Useless Trivia
#
# Gets personal information from the user and then
# prints true, but useless facts about him or her
```

 TRICK Experienced programmers also use the initial comments area to describe any modifications they make to code over time. This provides a great history of the program right up front. This practice is especially helpful when several programmers have their hands on the same code.

Getting the User Input

Using the raw_input() function, the program gets the user's name, age, and weight:

```
name = raw_input("Hi. What's your name? ")


age = raw_input("And how old are you? ")
age = int(age)


weight = raw_input("Okay, last question. How many pounds do you weigh? ")
weight = int(weight)
```

Remember, raw_input() always returns a string. Because age and weight will be treated as numbers, they must be converted. I broke up this process into two lines for each variable. First, I assigned the string from raw_input() to a variable. Then, I converted that string to an integer and assigned it to the variable again. I could have done both the assignments in one line, but I felt it's clearer this way.

Printing Lowercase and Uppercase Versions of name

The following lines print a version of name in uppercase and a version in lowercase with the help of string methods:

```
print "\nIf poet ee cummings were to email you, he'd address you as", name.lower()
```

```
ee_mad = name.upper()
print "But if ee were mad, he'd call you", ee_mad
```

In the uppercase version, I assigned the value to the variable ee_mad before printing. As you can see from the lowercase version before it, it's not necessary to use a variable. But I think it makes it clearer.

ee cummings, by the way, was an experimental American poet who didn't use uppercase letters. So, if he were alive and e-mailing you, he'd probably use all lowercase letters in your name. But if he were mad, he'd probably make an exception and "shout" via e-mail by addressing you in uppercase.

Calculating dog_years

The user's age in dog years is calculated and printed out:

```
dog_years = age / 7
print "\nDid you know that you're just", dog_years, "in dog years?"
```

It's a common belief that seven human years are equal to one dog year. So, in the first line, I divide age by 7 and assign that value to dog_years. Because 7 and age are both integers, dividing them results in an integer. That works out great since dog years are always expressed as integers.

The next line displays the result.

Calculating seconds

The user's age, in seconds, is calculated and printed in the two following lines:

```
seconds = age * 365 * 24 * 60 * 60
print "But you're also over", seconds, "seconds old."
```

Because there are 365 days in a year, 24 hours in a day, 60 minutes in an hour, and 60 seconds in a minute, age is multiplied by the product of 365 * 24 * 60 * 60. This value is assigned to seconds. The next line displays the result.

Printing name **Five Times**

The program displays the user's name five times in a row using string repetition:

```
called = name * 5
print "\nIf a small child were trying to get your attention, " \
    "your name would become:"
print called
```

The variable `called` is assigned the value of `name`, repeated five times. Then, a message is printed, followed by `called`.

Calculating moon_weight **and** sun_weight

The next four lines calculate and display the user's weight on the moon and sun:

```
moon_weight = weight / 6.0
print "\nDid you know that on the moon you would weigh only", moon_weight, "pounds?"

sun_weight = weight * 27.1
print "But on the sun, you'd weigh", sun_weight, "(but, ah... not for long)."
```

Because the moon has one-sixth the gravitational pull of the earth, `moon_weight` is assigned the value of `weight` divided by `6.0`. I use a floating-point number so that the result is a more accurate floating-point number instead of an integer.

Since the gravitational force on the sun is about `27.1` times stronger than it is here on earth, I multiply `weight` by `27.1` and assign the result to `sun_weight`. Because `27.1` is a floating-point number, `sun_weight` will be a float too.

The other two lines print out messages telling the user about his or her new weights.

Waiting for the User

The last statement waits for the user to press the Enter key:

```
raw_input("\n\nPress the enter key to exit.")
```

SUMMARY

- A string can be defined with either single or double quotes.
- Tripled-quoted strings, defined by three opening quotes and three closing quotes, can span multiple lines.

- An escape sequence, which typically begins with the \ character, is a set of characters that allow you to insert special characters into a string.
- String concatenation is the joining together of two strings to form a new string.
- A value's type determines what you can do with it.
- Two numeric types in Python are integers and floats.
- Integers are whole numbers, with no decimal part.
- Floats are numbers with a decimal part.
- The result of integer division is always an integer.
- The result of floating-point division is always a float.
- A variable represents a value and provides a way to get at information in computer memory.
- An assignment statement assigns a value to a variable and creates the variable, if necessary.
- A function is a named collection of programming code that can receive values, do some work, and return values.
- An argument is a value passed to a function.
- A return value is a value returned from a function upon completion.
- The `raw_input()` function prompts the user for text input and returns what the user entered as a string.
- A method is essentially a function an object has. It represents something an object can do.
- You use dot notation to invoke a method.
- Strings have methods that can return new strings.
- A logical error is an error that doesn't cause a program to crash, but instead produces unintended results.
- Augmented assignment operators provide shorthand for changing the value of a variable based on its original value.
- To print multiple values in a single print statement, separate the values with commas.

REVIEW QUESTIONS

1. Why use the line continuation character if the computer doesn't care how long a line of code is?
2. What does ASCII stand for?

3. Why might you use an escape sequence in a string? Give an example.
4. What's an expression?
5. What's the string concatenation operator?
6. How can integer division lead to unexpected results?
7. What's a floating-point rounding error?
8. How do variables help programmers?
9. What's the difference between a legal variable name and a good variable name?
10. What is self-documenting code?
11. How does having built-in functions, like `raw_input()`, help a programmer?
12. How are arguments and return values different?
13. What's the difference between a function and a method?
14. What is invoking a method?
15. Why is it important to use the right types in your programs?
16. What's an example of a logical error?
17. What is operator overloading and how can it be helpful to a programmer?
18. Why would you want to convert a value of one type to another?
19. How are augmented assignment operators helpful to programmers?
20. What is function nesting?

PROJECTS

1. Create a list of legal and illegal variable names. Describe why each is either legal or illegal. Next, create a list of "good" and "bad" legal variable names. Describe why each is either a good or bad choice.
2. Write a program that allows a user to enter his or her two favorite foods. The program should then print out the name of a new food by joining the original food names together.
3. Write a program that gets two game scores from a user. The program should calculate and display the average as a floating-point number.
4. Write a program where the user enters a restaurant bill total. The program should then display two amounts: a 15-percent tip and a 20-percent tip. (Hint: Don't worry about the number of decimal places displayed).
5. Write a program that produces a personalized adventure about a band of explorers that find a stash of 750 gold pieces. The player should be asked for the number of explorers, the number of explorers lost in battle, and the name of the quest leader. The program should then use the information to fill out a basic adventure story. Here's a sample run of the program where the player entered 17, followed by 13, followed by Dawson:

```
Welcome to Lost Fortune!

Please enter the following for your personalized adventure:

Enter the number of explorers: 17
Enter the number of explorers lost in battle: 13
Enter the name of the quest leader: Dawson

The brave Dawson led 17 adventurers on a quest for gold.
The group fought a band of ogres and lost 13 members.
Only 4 survived.

The party was about to give up when they stumbled upon the
buried fortune of 750 gold pieces. They split the loot and
Dawson kept the extra 2 gold pieces.
```

In addition to using the values that the player provides, the program should calculate the number of remaining explorers after the battle and the number of extra gold pieces that the leader keeps. (Hint: Calculating the extra gold pieces requires an operator that may be new to you.)

## CHAPTER 3

BRANCHING, while LOOPS, AND PROGRAM PLANNING: THE GUESS MY NUMBER GAME

S o far, the programs you've written have had a simple, sequential flow: each statement is executed once, in order, every time. If you were limited to just this type of programming, it would be very difficult, if not impossible, to write complex applications. But in this chapter, you'll learn how to selectively execute certain portions of your code and repeat parts of your program. Specifically, you'll learn to do the following:

- Generate random numbers using `randrange()`
- Use `if` structures to execute code based on a condition
- Use `if-else` structures to make a choice based on a condition
- Use `if-elif-else` structures to make a choice based on several conditions
- Use `while` loops to repeat parts of your program
- Plan your programs using pseudocode

Introducing the Guess My Number Game

The program you'll create in this chapter is the classic number guessing game. For those who missed out on this game in their childhood, the game goes like this: the computer chooses a random number between 1 and 100 and the player tries to guess it in as few attempts as possible. Each time the player enters a guess, the computer tells the player whether the guess is too high, too low, or right on the money. Once the player guesses the number, the game is over. Figure 3.1 shows Guess My Number in action.

```
C:\Python22\python.exe
              Welcome to 'Guess My Number'!

I'm thinking of a number between 1 and 100.
Try to guess it in as few attempts as possible.

Take a guess: 50
Lower...
Take a guess: 25
Lower...
Take a guess: 15
You guessed it!  The number was 15
And it only took you 3 tries!


Press the enter key to quit.
```

Figure 3.1

Got it in only three guesses! Try to beat that.

Generating Random Numbers

As much as users want consistent, predictable results from programs, sometimes what makes the programs exciting is their unpredictability: the sudden change in a computer opponent's strategy, or an alien creature bursting out from an arbitrary door. Random numbers can supply this element of chance or surprise, and Python provides an easy way to generate those random numbers.

TRAP   Python generates random numbers based on a formula, so they are not truly random. This kind of random generation is called pseudorandom and is good enough for most applications (just don't try to start an online casino with it). If you really need truly random numbers, visit http://www.fourmilab.ch/hotbits/. The site generates random numbers based on the natural and unpredictable process of radioactive decay.

Introducing the Craps Roller Program

Craps Roller replicates the dice roll of the fast-paced, casino game of craps. But you don't have to know anything about craps to appreciate the program. Craps Roller just simulates the roll of two six-sided dice. It displays the value of each and their total. To determine the dice values, the program uses a function that generates random numbers. Figure 3.2 shows the program in action.

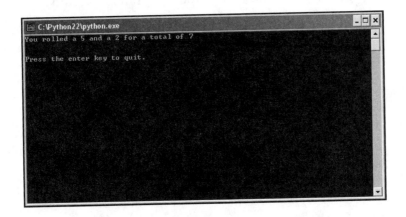

FIGURE 3.2

Ack! I got a total of seven on my first roll, which means I lose.

Here's the code:

```
# Craps Roller
# Demonstrates random number generation

import random

# generate random numbers 1 - 6
die1 = random.randrange(6) + 1
die2 = random.randrange(6) + 1

total = die1 + die2

print "You rolled a", die1, "and a", die2, "for a total of", total

raw_input("\n\nPress the enter key to exit.")
```

Using the import **Statement**

The first line of code in the program introduces the import statement. The statement allows you to import, or load, modules—in this case, the random module:

```
import random
```

Modules are files that contain code meant to be used in other programs. These modules usually group together a collection of programming related to one area. The `random` module contains functions related to generating random numbers and producing random results.

If you think of your program as a construction project, then modules are like special toolkits that you can pull out from the garage when you need them. But instead of going to the shelf and grabbing a powered circular saw, here I imported the `random` module.

Once you import a module, you can use its code. Then, it just becomes a matter of accessing it.

Accessing `randrange()`

The `random` module contains a function, `randrange()`, which produces a random integer. The Craps Roller program accesses `randrange()` through the following function call:

```
random.randrange(6)
```

You'll notice the program doesn't directly call `randrange()`. Instead, it's called with `random.randrange()`, because the program accesses `randrange()` through its module, `random`. In general, you can call a function from an imported module by giving the module name, followed by a period, followed by the function call itself. This method of access is called *dot notation*. Dot notation is like the possessive in English. In English, "Mike's Ferrari" means that it's the Ferrari that belongs to Mike. Using dot notation, `random.randrange()` means the function `randrange()` that belongs to the module `random`. Dot notation can be used to access different elements of imported modules.

Now that you know how to access `randrange()`, you need to know how to use it.

Using `randrange()`

There are several ways to call `randrange()`, but the simplest is to use a single, positive integer argument. Called this way, the function returns a random integer from (and including) 0, up to (but not including) that number. So the call `random.randrange(6)` produces either a 0, 1, 2, 3, 4, or 5. All right, where's the 6? Well, `randrange()` is picking a random number from a group of six numbers—and the list of numbers starts with 0. You may think this is odd, but you'll find that most computer languages start counting at 0 instead of 1. So, I just added 1 to the result to get the right values for a die:

```
die1 = random.randrange(6) + 1
```

Now, `die1` gets either a 1, 2, 3, 4, 5, or 6.

TRAP It's a common mistake to think that the single argument you provide `randrange()` could be returned as a result. It can't. Remember, `randrange()` starts counting at 0, so you'll get back a random number between (and including) 0 and up to one less than the number you provide.

USING THE `if` STRUCTURE

Branching is a fundamental part of computer programming. It basically means making a decision to take one path or another. Through the `if` structure, your programs can branch to a section of code or just skip it, all based on how you've set things up.

Introducing the Password Program

The Password program uses the `if` structure to simulate the login procedure of a highly secure computer server. The program grants the user access if he or she enters the right password. Figures 3.3 and 3.4 show a few sample runs.

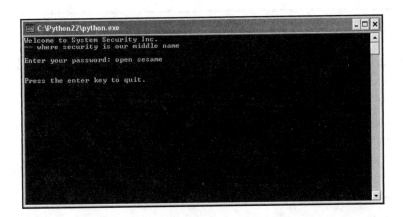

FIGURE 3.3

Ha, you'll never crack the code.

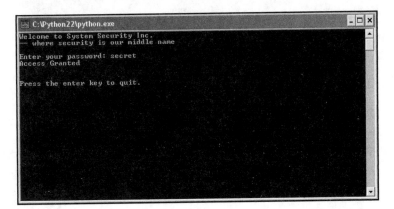

FIGURE 3.4

Guess I should have picked a better password than "secret."

Here is the program code for Password:

```
# Password
# Demonstrates the if structure

print "Welcome to System Security Inc."
print "-- where security is our middle name\n"

password = raw_input("Enter your password: ")

if password == "secret":
    print "Access Granted"

raw_input("\n\nPress the enter key to exit.")
```

IN THE REAL WORLD

While the program Password does a good job of demonstrating the if structure, it's not a good example of how to implement computer security. In fact, anyone could simply examine the source code and discover the "secret" password.

To create a password validation system, a programmer would most likely use some form of *cryptography*. Cryptography, an ancient idea that dates back thousands of years, is used to encode information so that only the intended recipients can understand it. Cryptography is an entire field unto itself, and some computer scientists devote their careers to it.

Examining the if Structure

The key to the program Password is the if structure:

```
if password == "secret":
    print "Access Granted"
```

The if structure is pretty straightforward. You can probably figure out what's happening just by reading the code. If password is equal to "secret", then "Access Granted" is printed and the program continues to the next statement. But, if it isn't equal to "secret", the program does not print the message and continues directly to the next statement following the if structure.

Creating Conditions

All `if` structures have a *condition*. A condition is just an expression that is either true or false. You're already familiar with conditions. They're pretty common in daily life. In fact, almost any statement you make could be viewed as a condition. For example, the statement, "It's 100 degrees outside," could be treated as a condition. It's either true or false.

Python has its own built-in values to represent truth and falsehood. `True` represents true and `False` (drumroll) represents false. A condition can always be evaluated to one of these. In the Password program, the condition used in the `if` structure is `password == "secret"`. It means that `password` is equal to `"secret"`. This condition evaluates to either `True` or `False`, depending on the value of `password`. If the value of `password` is equal to `"secret"`, then the condition is `True`. Otherwise, the condition is `False`.

TRAP   `True` and `False` didn't exist in Python before version 2.2. In earlier versions of Python, it was common to use 1 to represent true and 0 to represent false.

Understanding Comparison Operators

Conditions are often created by comparing values. You can compare values using *comparison operators*. You've already seen one comparison operator by way of the Password program. It's the equal-to comparison operator, written as `==`.

TRAP   The equal-to comparison operator is two equal signs in a row. Using just one equal sign in a condition will result in a syntax error, because one equal sign represents the assignment operator. So, `password = "secret"` is an assignment statement. It assigns a value. And `password == "secret"` is a condition. It evaluates to either `True` or `False`. Even though the assignment operator and the equal-to operator look similar, they are two different things.

In addition to equal-to, there are other comparison operators. Table 3.1 summarizes some useful ones.

Using comparison operators, you can compare any values. If you compare strings, you get results based on alphabetical order. For example, `"apple" < "orange"` is `True` because `"apple"` is alphabetically less than `"orange"` (it comes before it in the dictionary).

Python allows you to compare any values you like, regardless of their type. But just because you can doesn't mean you should. When using comparison operators, it's best to "compare apples to apples and oranges to oranges" and only compare values of the same type, because even though you can create the condition `"orange" < 2`, it doesn't really make much sense. (If you're curious, `"orange" < 2` is `False`.)

TABLE 3.1	COMPARISON OPERATORS		
Operator	**Meaning**	**Sample Condition**	**Evaluates To**
==	equal to	5 == 5	True
!=	not equal to	8 != 5	True
>	greater than	3 > 10	False
<	less than	5 < 8	True
>=	greater than or equal to	5 >= 10	False
<=	less than or equal to	5 <= 5	True

Using Indentation to Create Blocks

You may have noticed that the second line of the `if` structure, `print "Access Granted"`, is indented. By indenting the line, it becomes a *block*. A block is one or more consecutive lines indented by the same amount. Indenting sets lines off not only visually, but logically too. Together, they form a single unit.

Blocks can be used, among other ways, as the last part of an `if` structure. They're the statement or group of statements that gets executed if the condition is `True`. In the Password program, the block is the single statement `print "Access Granted"`.

Because blocks can be as many statements as you like, you could add a special welcome for users who enter the proper password by changing the block in the `if` structure, like so:

```
if password == "secret":
    print "Access Granted"
    print "Welcome! You must be someone very important."
```

Now, users who correctly enter the secret password will see the `Access Granted` followed by `Welcome! You must be someone very important.` And if a user enters something besides `secret`, the user won't see either of the messages.

Indenting to create blocks is not optional. It's the only way to define a block. This is one of Python's more unique features. And believe it or not, it's one of its most controversial.

If you've programmed in another language before, odds are indenting was optional. You could have written every line of code flush left, if you wanted. But required indentation has its benefits. It makes for more consistent and readable code. After a short time, it'll become second nature.

If you haven't programmed before, don't worry about it. By indenting your code, you'll pick up a good programming habit without even realizing it.

There's passionate debate within the Python community about whether to use tabs or spaces (and if spaces, the number to use) for indentation. This is really a question of personal style. But there are two guidelines worth following. First, be consistent. If you indent blocks with two spaces, then always use two spaces. Second, don't mix spaces and tabs. Even though you can line up blocks using a combination of both, this can lead to big headaches later. Common indentation styles include one tab, or two spaces, or (the style the creator of Python uses) four spaces. The choice is yours.

Building Your Own if Structure

You've seen a full example of an if structure, but I want to leave the topic by summarizing how to build your own. You can construct an if structure by using if, followed by a condition, followed by a colon, followed by a block of one or more statements. If the condition evaluates to True, then the statements that make up the block are executed. If the condition evaluates to False, then the program moves on to the next statement after the if structure.

USING THE if-else STRUCTURE

Sometimes you'll want your program to "make a choice" based on a condition: do one thing if the condition is true, do something else if it's false. The if-else structure gives you that power.

Introducing the Granted or Denied Program

The program Password did a good job welcoming a user who entered the correct password, but it didn't do anything if the wrong password was entered. Program Granted or Denied solves this problem by using the if-else structure. Figures 3.5 and 3.6 show off the new-and-improved version.

FIGURE 3.5

The correct password grants the user access, just like before.

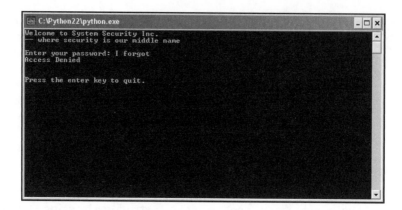

FIGURE 3.6

An incorrect
password
generates the
stinging "Denied"
message.

Here is the code for Granted or Denied:

```
# Granted or Denied
# Demonstrates the if-else structure

print "Welcome to System Security Inc."
print "-- where security is our middle name\n"

password = raw_input("Enter your password: ")

if password == "secret":
    print "Access Granted"
else:
    print "Access Denied"

raw_input("\n\nPress the enter key to exit.")
```

Examining the else Statement

I only made one change from the Password program. I added an else clause to create an if-else structure:

```
if password == "secret":
    print "Access Granted"
else:
    print "Access Denied"
```

If the value of password is equal to "secret", the program prints Access Granted, just like before. But now, thanks to the else statement, the program prints Access Denied otherwise.

In an `if-else` structure, you're guaranteed that exactly one of the code blocks will execute. If the condition is true, then the block immediately following the condition is executed. If the condition is false, then the block immediately after the `else` is executed.

You can create an `else` clause immediately following the `if` block with `else`, followed by a colon, followed by a block of statements. The `else` statement must be in the same block as its corresponding `if`. That is, the `else` and `if` must be indented the same amount; otherwise, your program will generate a nasty error.

USING THE `if-elif-else` STRUCTURE

Choosing from among several possibilities is the job of the `if-elif-else` structure. It's the most powerful and flexible of all the conditional structures. It can be used in multiple ways, but comes in quite handy when you have one variable that you want to compare to a bunch of different values.

Introducing the Mood Computer Program

In the mid-1970s (yes, last century), there was a wildly successful fad product called the Mood Ring. The ring revealed the wearer's mood through a color-changing gem. Well, the Mood Computer program takes the technology to the next level by looking into the psyche of the user and displaying his or her mood. Figure 3.7 reveals my mood while writing this very chapter.

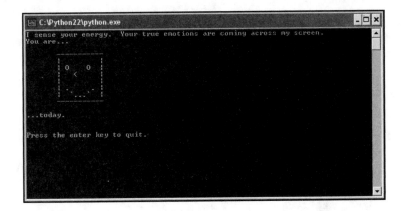

FIGURE 3.7

Looks like I was in a great mood while writing the Mood Computer program.

Okay, the program doesn't really plum the emotional depths of the user through electrodermal impulses transmitted via the keyboard. Instead, Mood Computer generates a random number to choose one of three faces to print through an `if-elif-else` structure. By the way, the Mood Ring didn't really reveal the wearer's emotions either. It was just an LCD that changed colors based on body temperature.

The program code for Mood Computer:

```
# Mood Computer
# Demonstrates the if-elif-else structure

import random

print "I sense your energy. Your true emotions are coming across my screen."
print "You are..."

mood = random.randrange(3)

if mood == 0:
    # happy
    print \
    """

     ----------
    |          |
    | 0    0   |
    |    <     |
    |          |
    | .     .  |
    |  `...`   |
     ----------

    """
elif mood == 1:
    # neutral
    print \
    """
```

```
     --------
    |        |
    |  0   0 |
    |   <    |
    |        |
    | ------ |
    |_____|
           """
elif mood == 2:
    # sad
    print \
    """
     --------
    |        |
    |  0   0 |
    |   <    |
    |        |
    | .'.    |
    |_'   '__|
           """
else:
    print "Illegal mood value! (You must be in a really bad mood)."

print "...today."

raw_input("\n\nPress the enter key to exit.")
```

Examining the `if-elif-else` Structure

An `if-elif-else` structure can contain a whole list of conditions for a program to evaluate. In Mood Computer, the lines containing the different conditions are

- `if mood == 0:`
- `elif mood == 1:`
- `elif mood == 2:`

Notice that you write the first condition using an if clause, but then list the remaining conditions using elif (short for "else if") clauses. elif clauses are constructed just like if clauses. And you can have as many elif clauses as you like.

> Although the if-elif-else structure is flexible enough to test a list of unrelated conditions, it's almost always used to test related ones.

By isolating the conditions, you can see the purpose of the structure: to test mood against three different values. The program first checks to see whether mood is equal to 0. If it is, then the happy face is printed. If not, the program moves to the next condition and checks whether mood is equal to 1. If it is, the neutral face is printed. If not, the program checks whether mood is equal to 2. If so, the sad face is printed.

> An important feature of the if-elif-else structure is that once a condition evaluates to True, the computer executes its corresponding block and exits the structure. This means that at most, only one block executes, even if several conditions evaluate to True. In Mood Computer, that's no big deal. mood can only be equal to a single number, so only one of the conditions can be true. But it's important to be aware of this behavior because it's possible to create structures where more than one condition can be true at the same time. In that case, only the block associated with the first true condition executes.

If none of the preceding conditions for mood turn out to be True, then the final else clause's block runs and Illegal mood value! (You must be in a really bad mood). appears on the screen. This should never happen, since mood will always be either 0, 1, or 2. But I put the clause in there just in case. I didn't have to, though, since the final else clause is optional.

> Even though it's not necessary to use the final else clause, it's a good idea. It works as a catchall for when none of the conditions are True. Even if you think one of your conditions will always be True, you can still use it to catch the "impossible" case, like I did.

You've seen three similar, but progressively more powerful branching structures. For a concise review, check out Table 3.2.

TABLE 3.2   BRANCHING STRUCTURES SUMMARY

Structure	Description
```if <condition>:``` ```<block>```	`if` structure. If `<condition>` is true, `<block>` is executed; otherwise it's skipped.

```if <condition>:```
  ```<block 1>```
```else:```
  ```<block 2>```
	`if-else` structure. If `<condition>` is true, `<block1>` is executed; otherwise `<block2>` is executed.

```if <condition 1>:```
  ```<block 1>```
```elif <condition 2>:```
  ```<block 2>```
    .
    .
    .
```elif <condition N>:```
  ```<block N>```
```else:```
  ```<block N+1>```
	`if-elif-else` structure. The block of the first true condition is executed. If no condition is true, the optional `else` clause's block, `<block N+1>`, is executed.

CREATING while LOOPS

Loops are all around us. Even your shampoo bottle has looping instructions on it: "While your hair is dirty: Rinse. Lather. Repeat." This may seem like a simple idea—while some condition is true, repeat something—but it's a powerful tool in programming. It would come in quite handy, for example, in making a quiz-show game. You might want to tell your program: While there are questions left, keep playing the game. Or, in a banking application, you might want to tell your program: While the user hasn't entered a valid account number, keep asking the user for an account number. The `while` loop lets you do exactly this.

Introducing the Three-Year-Old Simulator Program

In today's fast-paced world, many people don't get to spend the time they'd like with the children in their lives. A busy lawyer might be stuck at the office and not see her small son. A salesman might be on the road and not see his little niece. Well, the Three-Year-Old Simulator solves that problem by reproducing a conversation with a three-year-old child.

The key to mimicking a three-year-old, it turns out, is the `while` loop. Figure 3.8 shows a sample run.

```
C:\Python22\python.exe                                        _ □ ×
              Welcome to the 'Three-Year-Old Simulator'
This program simulates a conversation with a three-year-old child.
Try to stop the madness.

Why?
Why what?
Why?
I don't know.  Why?
Why?
Really, I don't know.
Why?
Please, I don't know.
Why?
Please, stop.
Why?
Please!  I'm begging you to stop.
Why?
Because.
Oh.  Okay.

Press the enter key to exit.
```

As you can see, the program keeps asking `Why?` until the answer, `Because.`, is entered. The code for the program is short:

```python
# Three-Year-Old Simulator
# Demonstrates the while loop

print "\tWelcome to the 'Three-Year-Old Simulator'\n"
print "This program simulates a conversation with a three-year-old child."
print "Try to stop the madness.\n"

response = ""
while response != "Because.":
    response = raw_input("Why?\n")

print "Oh. Okay."

raw_input("\n\nPress the enter key to exit.")
```

Examining the `while` Structure

The loop from the Three-Year-Old Simulator program is just two lines:

```python
while response != "Because.":
    response = raw_input("Why? ")
```

If the format of the `while` loop looks familiar, there's a good reason. It bears a striking resemblance to its cousin, the `if` structure. The only difference is that `if` is replaced by `while`. And the similarities aren't just skin-deep. In both structures, if the condition is true, the block (sometimes call the *loop body* in a loop) is executed. But in the `while` structure, the computer tests the condition and executes the block over and over, until the condition is false. That's why it's called a loop.

In this case, the loop body is just `response = raw_input("Why? ")`, which will continue to execute until the user enters `Because.`. At that point, `response != "Because."` is false and the loop mercifully ends. Then, the program executes the next statement, `print "Oh. Okay."`

Initializing the Sentry Variable

Often, `while` loops are controlled by a *sentry variable*, a variable used in the condition and compared to some other value or values. Like a human sentry, you can think of your sentry variable as a guard, helping form a barrier around the `while` loop's block. In the Three-Year-Old Simulator program, the sentry variable is `response`. It's used in the condition and is compared to the string `"Because."` before the block is executed each time.

It's important to initialize your sentry variable. Most of the time, sentry variables are initialized right before the loop itself. That's what I did with:

```
response = ""
```

 If the sentry variable doesn't have a value when the condition is evaluated, your program will generate an error.

It's usually a good idea to initialize your sentry variables to some type of empty value. I assign `""`, the empty string, to `response`. While I could assign the string `"aardvark"`, and the program would work just the same, it would make the code needlessly confusing.

Checking the Sentry Variable

Make sure that it's possible for the `while` condition to evaluate to `True` at some point; otherwise, the block will *never* run. Take, for example, one minor change to the loop you've been working with:

```
response = "Because."
while response != "Because.":
    response = raw_input("Why? ")
```

Since `response` is equal to `"Because."` right before the loop, the block will never run. The program will act like the loop isn't even there.

Updating the Sentry Variable

Once you've established your condition, initialized your sentry variable, and are sure that under some conditions the loop block will execute, you have yourself a working loop. Next, make sure the loop will end.

If you write a loop that never stops, you've created an *infinite* loop. Welcome to the club. At one time or another, all programmers have accidentally created an infinite loop and watched their program get stuck doing something over and over. Or they see their programs just plain freeze up.

Here's a simple example of an infinite loop:

```
counter = 0
while counter <= 10
    print counter
```

What the programmer probably meant was for the loop to print the numbers from 0 to 10. Unfortunately, what this program does is print 0 forever. The programmer forgot to change `counter`, the sentry variable inside the block. So remember, the values in the condition must be able to change as a result of the code inside the loop block. If they can't ever change, the loop won't end, and you have yourself an infinite loop.

AVOIDING INFINITE LOOPS

One type of infinite loop is where the sentry variable is never updated, like you just saw. But there are more insidious forms of the never-ending loop. Check out the next program. It does change the value of the sentry variable in the loop body. But something is wrong, because the loop never ends. See if you can spot the trouble before I explain what's going on.

Introducing the Losing Battle Program

The Losing Battle program describes the last, valiant fight of a hero overwhelmed by an army of trolls, a scenario you might find in a role-playing game. The program narrates the battle action. It describes the struggle, blow by blow, as the hero defeats a troll, but then takes more damage. In the end, the program always ends with the death of the hero. Or does it? Here's the code:

```
# Losing Battle
# Demonstrates the dreaded infinite loop
```

```
print "Your lone hero is surrounded by a massive army of trolls."
print "Their decaying green bodies stretch out, melting into the horizon."
print "Your hero unsheathes his sword and begins the last fight of his life.\n"


health = 10
trolls = 0
damage = 3

while health != 0:
    trolls += 1
    health = health - damage

    print "Your hero swings and defeats an evil troll, " \
          "but takes", damage, "damage points.\n"

print "Your hero fought valiantly and defeated", trolls, "trolls."
print "But alas, your hero is no more."

raw_input("\n\nPress the enter key to exit.")
```

Figure 3.9 shows a run of the program. This resulted in an infinite loop and I had to stop the process by pressing Ctrl+C, or it would have continued.

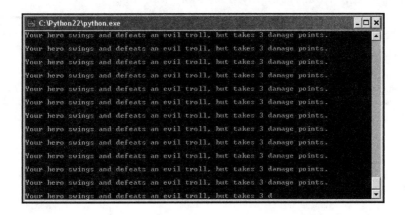

FIGURE 3.9

It seems you have an immortal hero. The only way to end the program was to stop the process.

So, what's going on?

Tracing the Program

Well, it looks like the program has a logical error. A good way to track down this kind of error is to trace your program's execution. *Tracing* means you simulate the running of your program and do exactly what it would do, following every command and keeping track of the values assigned to variables. This way, you can step through the program, understand exactly what is happening at each point, and discover the circumstances that conspire to produce the bug in your code.

The most basic way to trace a program is with old-fashioned pencil and paper. I created columns, one for each variable and condition. So to start, my page looks like this:

health	trolls	damage	health != 0

Right after the condition of the `while` structure is evaluated, my page looks like this:

health	trolls	damage	health != 0
10	0	3	True

Since the condition is `True`, the loop executes for the first time. After one full time through and back up to evaluate the condition again, my trace looks like this:

health	trolls	damage	health != 0
10	0	3	True
7	1	3	True

After a few more times through the loop, my trace looks like:

health	trolls	damage	health != 0
10	0	3	True
7	1	3	True
4	2	3	True
1	3	3	True
-2	4	3	True
-5	5	3	True
-7	6	3	True

I stopped the trace because it seemed like I was in an infinite loop. Because the value of health is negative (and not equal to 0) in the last three lines of the trace, the condition is still True. The problem is, health will never become 0. It will just grow in the negative direction each time the loop executes. As a result, the condition will never become False, and the loop will never end.

Creating Conditions That Can Become False

In addition to making sure values in a while loop's condition change, you should be sure that the condition can eventually evaluate to False; otherwise, you still have an infinite loop on your hands. In the case of the Losing Battle program, the fix is easy. The line with the condition just needs to become

```
while health > 0:
```

Now, if health becomes 0 or negative, the condition evaluates to False and the loop ends. To be sure, you can trace the program using this new condition:

health	trolls	damage	health > 0
10	0	3	True
7	1	3	True
4	2	3	True
1	3	3	True
-2	4	3	False

And the program ends as it should. Figure 3.10 shows how the debugged program runs.

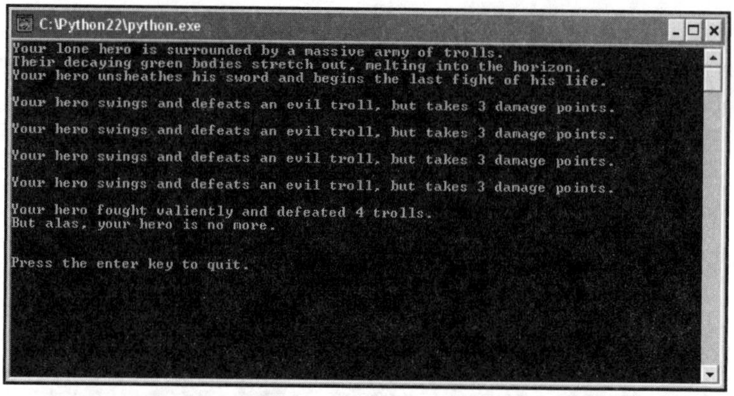

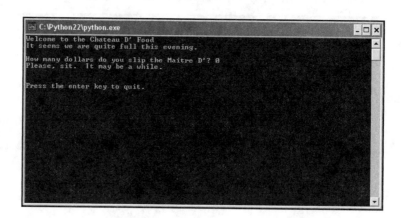

FIGURE 3.10

Now, the program runs correctly, avoiding an infinite loop. Your hero's fate, however, is not as bright.

TREATING VALUES AS CONDITIONS

If I asked you to evaluate 35 + 2 you'd come back quickly with 37. But if I asked you to evaluate 37 as either True or False, you'd probably come back with, "Huh?" But the idea of looking at any value as either True or False is valid in Python. Any value, of any type, can be treated this way. So, 2749, 8.6, "banana", 0, and "" can each be interpreted as True or False. This may seem bizarre, but it's easy. The rules that establish True and False are simple. More importantly, interpreting values this way can make for more elegant conditions.

Introducing the Maitre D' Program

If you haven't been snubbed at a fancy, French restaurant lately, then I have just the program for you. Maitre D' welcomes you to the fine eatery and then asks you how much money you slip your host. If you give zero dollars, then you are rightly ignored. If you give some other amount, then your table is waiting. Figures 3.11 and 3.12 show off the program.

FIGURE 3.11

When you don't tip the maitre d', there are no tables to be found.

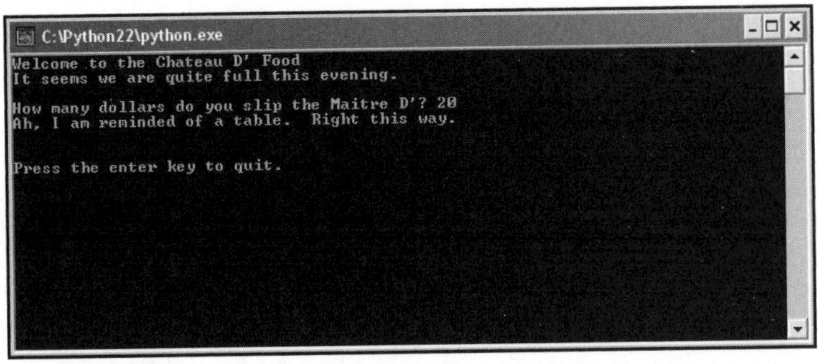

FIGURE 3.12

This time, my money has helped cure the maitre d' of his amnesia.

From watching the program run, you might not be impressed. This seems like something you could have already done. The difference is, there is no comparison operator used in this program. Instead, a value (the amount of money) is treated as a condition. Take a look at the code to see how it works:

```
# Maitre D'
# Demonstrates treating a value as a condition

print "Welcome to the Chateau D' Food"
print "It seems we are quite full this evening.\n"

money = int(raw_input("How many dollars do you slip the Maitre D'? "))

if money:
    print "Ah, I am reminded of a table. Right this way."
else:
    print "Please, sit. It may be a while."

raw_input("\n\nPress the enter key to exit.")
```

Interpreting Any Value as True or False

The new concept is demonstrated in the line:

```
if money:
```

Notice that money is not compared to any other value. money is the condition. When it comes to evaluating numbers, 0 is False and everything else is True. So, the above line is equivalent to

```
if money != 0:
```

The first version is simpler, more elegant, and more intuitive. It reads more naturally and could be translated to "if there is money."

The rules for what makes a value True or False are simple. The basic principal is this: Any empty or zero value is False, everything else is True. So, 0 evaluates to False, but any other number evaluates to True. The empty string, " ", is False, while any other string is True. As you can see, most every value is True. It's only the empty or zero value that's False. You'll find that testing for an empty value is a common thing to do, so this way of treating values can come up a lot in programs.

One last thing to note here is that if you enter a negative dollar amount, the maitre d' will still seat you. Remember, for numbers, only 0 is False. So, all negative numbers are True, just like positive ones.

CREATING INTENTIONAL INFINITE LOOPS

Coming soon after a section called "Avoiding Infinite Loops," you might be more than a bit surprised to see a section about *creating* infinite loops. Aren't infinite loops always a mistake? Well, if a loop were truly infinite—that is, it could never end—then yes, it would be a logical error. But what I call *intentional infinite loops* are infinite loops with an exit condition built into the loop body. The best way to understand an intentional infinite loop is to see an example.

Introducing the Finicky Counter Program

The Finicky Counter program counts from 1 to 10 using an intentional infinite loop. It's finicky because it doesn't like the number 5 and skips it. Figure 3.13 shows a run of the program.

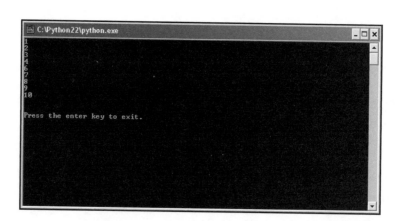

FIGURE 3.13

The number 5 is skipped with a continue statement and the loop ends through a break statement.

Here's the code to the program:

```
# Finicky Counter
# Demonstrates the break and continue statements

count = 0
while True:
    count += 1
    # end loop if count is greater than 10
    if count > 10:
        break
    # skip 5
    if count == 5:
        continue
    print count

raw_input("\n\nPress the enter key to exit.")
```

Using the break **Statement to Exit a Loop**

I set up the loop with:

```
while True:
```

This technically means that the loop will continue forever, unless there is an exit condition in the loop body. Luckily, I put one in:

```
    # end loop if count greater than 10
    if count > 10:
        break
```

Because count is increased by 1 each time the loop body begins, it will eventually reach 11. When it does, the break statement, which means "break out of the loop," is executed and the loop ends.

Using the continue **Statement to Jump Back to the Top of a Loop**

Just before count is printed, I included the lines:

```
    # skip 5
    if count == 5:
        continue
```

The continue statement means "jump back to the top of the loop." At the top of the loop, the while condition is tested and the loop is entered again if it evaluates to True. So when count is equal to 5, the program does not get to the print count statement. Instead it goes right back to the top of the loop, and 5 is skipped and never printed.

Understanding When to Use break and continue

You can use break and continue in any loop you create. They aren't just restricted for use in intentional infinite loops. But they should be used sparingly. Both break and continue make it harder for someone (including you!) to see the flow of a loop and understand under what conditions it ends. Plus, you don't actually need break and continue. Any loop you can write using them can be written without them.

In Python, there are times when an intentional infinite loop can be clearer than a traditional loop. In those few cases, where it's really clunky to write the loop with a regular condition, some programmers use intentional infinite loops.

USING COMPOUND CONDITIONS

So far, you've only seen comparisons where exactly two values are involved. These are called *simple conditions*. This is probably the most common way to create a condition. But you may find yourself wishing for more power. Luckily, you can combine simple conditions together with *logical operators*. Combined, these simple conditions become *compound conditions*. Using compound conditions, your programs can make decisions based on how multiple groups of values compare.

Introducing the Exclusive Network Program

Exclusive clubs are no fun unless you're a member. So, I created the Exclusive Network program. It simulates an elite computer network where only a select few are members. The membership consists of me and several top game designers in the world today (not bad company).

Like real-world computer systems, each person has to enter a username and a password. A member has to enter both his or her username and password, or the member won't be able to log in. With a successful login, the member is personally greeted. Also like real-world systems, everyone has a security level.

Because I'm not a total elitist, guests are allowed to log in. Guests have the lowest security level, though.

Figures 3.14 through 3.16 show off the program.

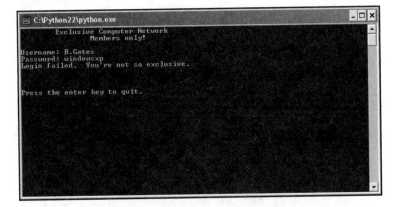

FIGURE 3.14

If you're not a member or a guest, you can't get in.

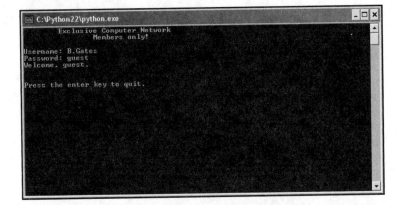

FIGURE 3.15

A guest can log in, but their security level is set quite low.

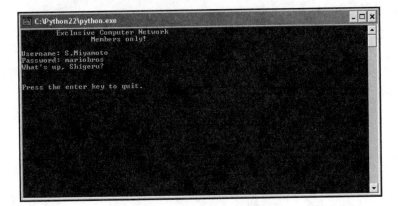

FIGURE 3.16

Looks like one of the guys logged in today.

Here's the code:

```
# Exclusive Network
# Demonstrates logical operators conditions

print "\tExclusive Computer Network"
print "\t\tMembers only!\n"

security = 0

username = ""
while not username:
    username = raw_input("Username: ")

password = ""
while not password:
    password = raw_input("Password: ")

if username == "M.Dawson" and password == "secret":
    print "Hi, Mike."
    security = 5
elif username == "S.Meier" and password == "civilization":
    print "Hey, Sid."
    security = 3
elif username == "S.Miyamoto" and password == "mariobros":
    print "What's up, Shigeru?"
    security = 3
elif username == "W.Wright" and password == "thesims":
    print "How goes it, Will?"
    security = 3
elif username == "guest" or password == "guest":
    print "Welcome, guest."
    security = 1
else:
    print "Login failed. You're not so exclusive.\n"

raw_input("\n\nPress the enter key to exit.")
```

IN THE REAL WORLD

If you really want to implement a private network, you wouldn't write usernames and passwords directly into your code. You'd probably use some type of *database management system* (DBMS). Database management systems allow you to organize, access, and update related information. These systems are powerful and can handle thousands or even millions of pairs of usernames and passwords quickly and securely.

Understanding the not Logical Operator

I wanted to make sure that the user enters something for the username and password. Just pressing the Enter key, which results in the empty string, won't do. I wanted a loop that continues to ask for a username until the user enters something. This is the loop I came up with for getting the username:

```
username = ""
while not username:
    username = raw_input("Username: ")
```

In the `while` condition, I used the logical `not` operator. It works a lot like the word "not." In English, putting the word "not" in front of something creates a new phrase that means the opposite of the old one. In Python, putting `not` in front of a condition creates a new condition that evaluates to the opposite of the old one.

That means `not username` is `True` when `username` is `False`. And `not username` is `False` when `username` is `True`. Here's another way to understand how `not` works:

username	not username
True	False
False	True

Because `username` is initialized to the empty string in the program, it starts out as `False`. That makes `not username` `True` and the loop runs the first time. Then, the program gets a value for `username` from the user. If the user just presses Enter, `username` is the empty string, just as before. And just as before, `not username` is `True` and the loop keeps running. So, as long as the user just hits Enter, the loop keeps running, and the user keeps getting prompted for a username.

But when the user finally enters something, `username` becomes a new string, something other than the empty string. That makes `username` evaluate to `True` and `not username` evaluate to `False`. As a result, the loop ends, just like I wanted.

The program does the same thing for the variable `password`.

Understanding the and **Logical Operator**

If a member wants to log in to this exclusive network, the member has to enter a username and password that are recognized together. If, for example, Sid Meier wants to log in, he has to enter `S.Meier` for his username and `civilization` for his password. If Sid doesn't enter both just that way, he can't log in. `S.Meier` and `mariobros` won't work. Neither will `M.Dawson` and `civilization`. The combination `civilization` and `S.Meier` fails too. The program checks that Sid enters `S.Meier` for his username and `civilization` for his password with the following code:

```
elif username == "S.Meier" and password == "civilization":
```

The line contains a single compound condition made up of two simple conditions. The simple conditions are `username == "S.Meier"` along with `password == "civilization"`. These are just like conditions you've already seen, but they've been joined together by the `and` logical operator to form a larger compound condition, `username == "S.Meier"` and `password == "civilization"`. This compound condition, though longer than you're used to, is still just a condition, which means that it can be either `True` or `False`.

So, when is `username == "S.Meier"` and `password == "civilization"` True, and when is it `False`? Well, just like in English, "and" means both. So, the condition is `True` only if both `username == "S.Meier"` and `password == "civilization"` are `True`; otherwise it's `False`. Here's another way to see how this works:

username == "S.Meier"	password == "civilization"	username == "S.Meier" and password == "civilization"
True	True	True
True	False	False
False	True	False
False	False	False

HINT Put and between two conditions when you want to create a new condition that is true only if both original conditions are true.

So, when Sid enters S.Meier for his username and civilization for his password, the compound condition is true. Sid is then greeted and assigned a security level.

The program, of course, works for others besides Sid Meier. Through an if-elif-else structure, the program checks four different username and password pairs. If a user enters a recognized pair, the member is personally greeted and assigned a security value.

If a member or guest doesn't properly log in, the computer prints a "failed login" message and tells the person that he or she is not so exclusive.

Understanding the or **Logical Operator**

Guests are allowed in the network, too, but with a limited security level. To make it easy for a guest to try the network, all he or she has to do is enter guest for either the username or password. The following lines of code log in a guest:

```
elif username == "guest" or password == "guest":
    print "Welcome, guest."
    security = 1
```

The elif condition, username == "guest" or password == "guest", looks a lot like the other conditions, the ones used for the members. But there's a major difference. The guest condition is created by using the logical or operator.

A compound condition created with an or is True as long as at least one of the simpler conditions is True. Again, the operator works just like in English. "Or" means either, so if either condition is True, the compound condition is True. In this particular case, if username == "guest" is True or if password == "guest" is True, or even if both are True, then username == "guest" or password == "guest" is True; otherwise, it's False. Here's another way to look at how or works:

username == "guest"	password == "guest"	username == "guest" or password == "guest"
True	True	True
True	False	True
False	True	True
False	False	False

PLANNING YOUR PROGRAMS

So far, all the programs you've seen have been pretty simple. The idea of planning any of them formally on paper probably seems like overkill. It's not. Planning your programs, even the small ones, will almost always result in time (and often frustration) saved.

Programming is a lot like construction. So, imagine a contractor building a house for you without a blueprint. Yikes! You're liable to end up with a house that has 12 bathrooms, no windows, and a front door on the second floor. Plus, it will cost you 10 times the estimated price.

Programming is the same way. Without a plan, you'll likely struggle through the process, wasting time. You might even end up with a program that doesn't quite work.

Program planning is so important that there's an entire field of software engineering dedicated to it. But even a beginning programmer can benefit from a few simple planning tools and techniques.

Creating Algorithms with Pseudocode

An *algorithm* is a set of clear, easy-to-follow instructions for accomplishing some task. An algorithm is like an outline for your program. It's something you planned out, before programming, to guide you along as you code.

An algorithm isn't just a goal—it's a concrete list of steps to be followed in order. So, for example, "Be a millionaire" is not really an algorithm. It's more like a goal. But a worthy one. So I wrote the Make a Million Dollars algorithm. Here it is:

if you can think of a new and useful product

> *then that's your product*

otherwise

> *repackage an existing product as your product*

make an infomercial about your product

show the infomercial on TV

charge $100 per unit of your product

sell 10,000 units of your product

There you go. It's a clear series of finite steps that can be followed to achieve the goal.

Algorithms are generally written in something called *pseudocode*, and mine is no exception. Pseudocode falls somewhere between English and a programming language. Anyone who understands English can understand my algorithm. But at the same time, my algorithm should feel vaguely like a program. The first four lines resemble an `if-else` structure, and that's intentional.

Applying Stepwise Refinement to Your Algorithms

Like any outline or plan, your algorithm might not be finished after one draft. Often, algorithms need multiple passes before they can be implemented in code. *Stepwise refinement* is one process used to rewrite algorithms so that they're ready for implementation. Stepwise refinement is pretty simple. Basically, it means "make it more detailed." By taking each step in an algorithm and breaking it down into a series of simpler steps, the algorithm becomes closer to programming code. In stepwise refinement, you keep breaking down each step until you feel that the entire algorithm could be fairly easily translated into a program. As an example, take a step from the Make a Million Dollars algorithm:

create an infomercial about your product

This might seem like too vague a task. How do you create an infomercial? Using stepwise refinement, the single step can be broken down into several others. So, it becomes the following:

write a script for an infomercial about your product

rent a TV studio for a day

hire a production crew

hire an enthusiastic audience

film the infomercial

If you feel that these five steps are clear and achievable, then that part of the algorithm has been thoroughly refined. If you're still unclear about a step, refine it some more. Continue with this process, and you will have a complete algorithm and a million dollars.

RETURNING TO THE GUESS MY NUMBER GAME

The Guess My Number game combines many of the concepts you learned in this chapter. But, more importantly, it represents the first full game that you can use to show off to your friends, family, and members of the opposite sex.

Planning the Program

To plan the game, I wrote some pseudocode first:

pick a random number

while the player hasn't guessed the number

> *let the player guess*

congratulate the player

This isn't a bad first pass, but it's missing some important elements. First, the program needs to tell the player if the guess is too high or too low. Second, the program should keep track of how many guesses the player has made and then tell the player this number at the end of the game.

 HINT It's okay if your first program plan isn't complete. Start planning with the major ideas first, then fill in the gaps until it feels done.

Okay, here's a refinement of my algorithm:

welcome the player to the game and explain it

pick a random number between 1 and 100

ask the player for a guess

set the number of guesses to 1

> *while the player's guess does not equal the number*

>> *if the guess is greater than the number*

>>> *tell the player to guess lower*

>> *otherwise*

>>> *tell the player to guess higher*

>> *get a new guess from the player*

>> *increase the number of guesses by 1*

congratulate the player on guessing the number

let the player know how many guesses it took

Now I feel ready to write the program. Take a look over the next few sections and see how directly pseudocode can be translated into Python.

Creating the Initial Comment Block

Like all good programs, this one begins with a block of comments:

```
# Guess My Number
#
# The computer picks a random number between 1 and 100
# The player tries to guess it and the computer lets
# the player know if the guess is too high, too low
# or right on the money
```

Importing the random Module

To be fun, the program needs to generate a random number. So, I imported the random module:

```
import random
```

Explaining the Game

The game is simple, but a little explanation wouldn't hurt:

```
print "\tWelcome to 'Guess My Number'!"
print "\nI'm thinking of a number between 1 and 100."
print "Try to guess it in as few attempts as possible.\n"
```

Setting the Initial Values

Next, I set all the variables to their initial values:

```
# set the initial values
the_number = random.randrange(100) + 1
guess = int(raw_input("Take a guess: "))
tries = 1
```

the_number represents the number the player has to guess. I assign it a random integer from 1 to 100 with a call to random.randrange(). Next, raw_input() gets the player's first guess. int() converts the guess to an integer. I assign this number to guess. I assign tries, which represents the number of guesses so far, the value 1.

Creating a Guessing Loop

This is the core of the program. The loop executes as long as the player hasn't correctly guessed the computer's number. During the loop, the player's guess is compared to the computer's number. If the guess is higher than the number, Lower. . . is printed; otherwise, Higher. . . is printed. The player enters the next guess, and the number of guesses counter is incremented.

```
# guessing loop
while (guess != the_number):
    if (guess > the_number):
        print "Lower..."
    else:
        print "Higher..."

    guess = int(raw_input("Take a guess: "))
    tries += 1
```

Congratulating the Player

When the player guesses the number, guess is equal to the_number, which means that the loop condition, guess != the_number, is False and the loop ends. At that point, the player needs to be congratulated:

```
print "You guessed it! The number was", the_number
print "And it only took you", tries, "tries!\n"
```

The computer tells the player what the secret number was and how many tries it took the player to guess it.

Waiting for the Player to Quit

As always, the last line waits patiently for the player to press the Enter key:

```
raw_input("\n\nPress the enter key to exit.")
```

SUMMARY

- A module is a file that contains code meant to be used in other programs.
- The import statement provides access to modules.
- Dot notation is a convention used for accessing elements within a hierarchical structure, such as accessing a function from a module.
- The random module contains code for generating random numbers and random events.

- The `randrange()` function generates a random number from within a range.
- `True` and `False` are the two values of type `bool`.
- A condition is an expression that is either `True` or `False`.
- Comparison operators create a condition by comparing two values.
- A block is a section of code indented to form a single unit.
- The `if` statement defines a block of code to be executed if a condition is `True`.
- The optional `else` clause defines a block to be executed when the condition of an `if` statement is `False`.
- The `if-elif-else` structure tests a series of conditions and can execute a block of code.
- The `while` loop repeats a block of code as long as a condition is `True`.
- An infinite loop is a loop that will never end and is considered a logical error.
- Any value can be interpreted as `True` or `False` when used as a condition. Any empty or zero value is `False` while any other value is `True`.
- The `break` statement causes a loop to end immediately.
- The `continue` statement jumps program control to the top of a loop to test the loop condition.
- The `not` logical operator creates a new condition from a simpler condition that evaluates to the opposite of the original.
- The `and` logical operator creates a new condition from two simpler conditions that is `True` only if both simpler conditions are `True`.
- The `or` logical operator creates a condition from two simpler conditions that is `False` only when both simpler conditions are `False`.
- An algorithm is a set of clear, easy-to-follow instructions for accomplishing some task.
- Pseudocode is something between English and a programming language that's used to plan programs.

REVIEW QUESTIONS

1. How can generating random numbers make a game more exciting?
2. What is pseudorandom?
3. How can using modules help a programmer?
4. What is branching?
5. What is the difference between the assignment operator and the equal-to comparison operator?
6. List and name three comparison operators.

7. Must code be indented to form a block?
8. Should you use spaces or tabs to create a block of code? If spaces, how many?
9. Can you use an `else` statement on its own?
10. Can you use an `if-elif-else` structure to test a series of unrelated conditions?
11. How are an `if` statement and a `while` loop similar?
12. What is a sentry variable?
13. What's wrong with an infinite loop?
14. What is tracing and how can it help a programmer fix a bug?
15. Why might a programmer begin a `while` loop with `while True:`?
16. Why should you limit your use of `break` and `continue` statements in loops?
17. What is a compound condition?
18. Why should you plan your programs?
19. Can a computer run a program written in pseudocode?
20. What is stepwise refinement?

PROJECTS

1. Write a program that gets a score from a player and rates it based on the following:

   - Given a score between 0 – 999, the program should display the message, "Nothing to brag about."

   - Given a score between 1000 – 9999, the program should display the message, "Good score."

   - Given a score over 9999, the program should display the message, "Very impressive!"

   - If the score is a negative number, the program should display the message, "That's not a legal score!"

2. Write a program that simulates flipping a coin 100 times and then displays the total number of heads and total number of tails achieved.

3. Modify the Guess My Number program from this chapter so that the player has only five guesses. If the player runs out of guesses, the program should end the game and display an appropriately chastising message.

4. Write the pseudocode for a two-player version of the game Nim. In the game, players take turns removing from 1 to 4 sticks from a pile of 13. The player who picks up the last stick wins the game. Your program should validate the input from the players. This means that the program should continue to ask a player for the number of sticks he or she wishes to take as long as any of the following are true:

- The number of sticks the player asks to take is greater than the number of sticks left.
- The number of sticks the player asks to take is greater than 4, the maximum number that he or she is allowed to take.
- The number of sticks the players asks to take is less than 1, the minimum number that he or she is allowed to take.

5. Write the Nim game program that you planned in Project 4.

for LOOPS, STRINGS, AND TUPLES: THE WORD JUMBLE GAME

You've seen how variables are a great way to access information, but as your programs grow in size and complexity, so can the number of your variables. Keeping track of all of them can become a lot of work. Therefore, in this chapter, you'll learn about the idea of sequences and meet a new type, called the *tuple*, which lets you organize and manipulate information in ordered groups. You'll also see how a type you've already encountered, the string, is really a sequence too. You'll also learn about a new kind of loop that's built just for working with sequences. Specifically, you'll learn how to do the following:

- Construct for loops to move through a sequence
- Use the range() function to create a sequence of numbers
- Treat strings as sequences
- Use tuples to harness the power of sequences
- Use sequence functions and operators
- Index and slice sequences

Introducing the Word Jumble Game

The Word Jumble game, featured in Figure 4.1, utilizes many of the new ideas you'll learn in this chapter.

```
C:\Python22\python.exe                                        _ □ ×
            Welcome to Word Jumble!

    Unscramble the letters to make a word.
(Press the enter key at the prompt to quit.)

The jumble is: dffuitlic

Your guess:
```

FIGURE 4.1

The Word Jumble
game. This jumble
looks "difficult."

This game recreates the typical word jumble you might find in the Sunday paper (you know, that thing people used to get their news from before the Internet). The computer picks a random word from a group and then creates a jumbled version of it, where the letters are in random order. The player has to guess the original word to win the game.

Using for Loops

In the last chapter, you saw one kind of loop, the while loop, which repeats part of your code based on a condition. As long as the condition is true, some code repeats. The for loop also repeats code, but not based on a condition. Instead, the for loop repeats part of a program based on a *sequence*, an ordered list of things. If you've ever written a list of, say, your top 10 favorite movies, then you've created a sequence.

A for loop repeats its loop body for each *element* of the sequence, in order. When it reaches the end of the sequence, the loop ends. As an example, consider your movie list sequence again. A for loop could go through this sequence of movie titles, one at a time, and print each one. But the best way to understand a for loop is to see one in action.

Introducing the Loopy String Program

This program takes a word from the user and prints its letters, in order, on separate lines. Take a look at a sample run in Figure 4.2.

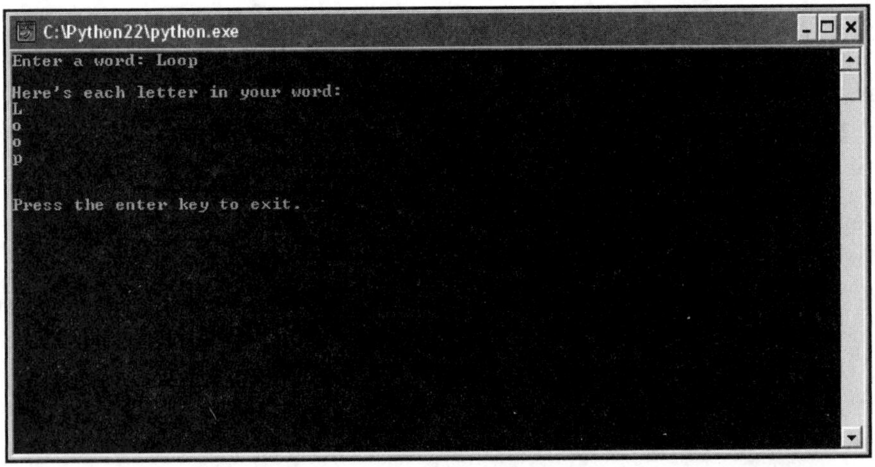

FIGURE 4.2

A for loop goes
through a word
the user enters,
one character at a
time.

This simple program provides a good example of a for loop. Here's the code:

```
# Loopy String
# Demonstrates the for loop with a string

word = raw_input("Enter a word: ")

print "\nHere's each letter in your word:"
for letter in word:
    print letter

raw_input("\n\nPress the enter key to exit.")
```

Understanding for Loops

The new idea in this program is the for loop, which is just the following two short lines:

```
for letter in word:
    print letter
```

Even before you know anything about for loops, the code is pretty clear, but I'll explain exactly how it works. All sequences are made up of elements. A string is a sequence in which each element is one character. In the case of the string "Loop", the first element is the character "L", the second is "o", and so on.

A for loop marches through (or *iterates over*) a sequence one element at a time. In my program, the loop iterates over the string "Loop" one character at a time. A for loop uses a variable that gets each successive element of the sequence. In my loop, letter is the variable that gets each successive character of "Loop". Inside the loop body, the loop can then do something with each successive element. In my loop body, I simply print letter. Now, the variable you use to get each element of the sequence is like any other variable—and if it doesn't exist before the loop, it's created.

So, when my loop begins, letter is created and gets the first character in word, which is "L". Then, in the loop body, the print statement displays L. Next, with the loop body finished, control jumps back to the top of the loop and letter gets the next character in word, which is "o". The computer displays o, and the loop continues until each character in the string "Loop" is displayed.

In the Real World

Most modern languages offer a form of the for loop. However, these loops tend to be more restrictive. The loops generally only allow a counter variable, which must be assigned a number. Then, the counter changes by the same amount each time the loop executes. The ability to loop directly through a sequence makes the Python for loop more flexible than this other, more traditional type of loop.

Creating a for Loop

To create a for loop, you can follow the example in the program. Start with for, followed by a variable for each element, followed by in, followed by the sequence you want to loop through, followed by a colon, and finally, the loop body. That's all there is to it.

COUNTING WITH A for LOOP

When you write a program, you may find that you need to count. In combination with the for loop, you can use Python's range() function to count in all kinds of ways.

Introducing the Counter Program

The Counter program is nothing fancy, but it shows you how to use the range() function to generate lists of numbers. Paired with a for loop, you can use the list to count forward or backward, or even to skip numbers if you like. Take a look at Figure 4.3 to see the results of the program.

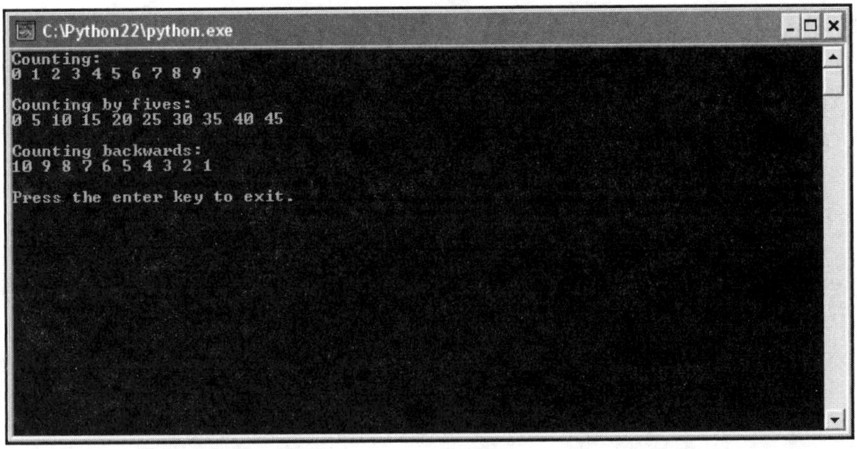

FIGURE 4.3

The range() function and for loop allow you to count forward, by fives, and backward.

Here's the code for the program:

```
# Counter
# Demonstrates the range() function

print "Counting:"
for i in range(10):
    print i,

print "\n\nCounting by fives:"
for i in range(0, 50, 5):
    print i,

print "\n\nCounting backwards:"
for i in range(10, 0, -1):
    print i,

raw_input("\n\nPress the enter key to exit.\n")
```

IN THE REAL WORLD

It's traditional to name generic counter and loop variables i, j, or k. Normally, you want to create descriptive, clear variable names. Believe it or not, i, j, and k are clear to experienced programmers, who know when reading your code that you just need a quick counter variable.

Counting Forward

The first loop in the program counts forward:

```
for i in range(10):
    print i,
```

This `for` loop works just like the `for` loop you saw in the Loopy String program—it loops through a sequence. It just may be hard to tell what the sequence is. The sequence the loop moves through is created by the `range()` function. It creates a sequence of numbers. Give `range()` a positive integer and it will create a sequence starting with 0, up to, but not including, the number you gave it. Take a look at part of an interactive session I ran with IDLE:

```
>>> range(5)
[0, 1, 2, 3, 4]
>>> range(10)
[0, 1, 2, 3, 4, 5, 6, 7, 8, 9]
```

 TRICK Even experienced programmers sometimes forget the way a function or a command works. But instead of guessing, they open an interactive window and experiment. When they get the results they want, they jump back to script mode and use what they learned to continue coding.

Another way to look at this loop is to substitute the results of the `range()` function into the code when you read it. So, when you look at the code, you can imagine that it reads:

```
for i in [0, 1, 2, 3, 4, 5, 6, 7, 8, 9]:
    print i,
```

and that the `range()` function call is replaced with the sequence of numbers it creates. In fact, this loop is a valid one. You can create a list of values by enclosing them in brackets, separated by commas. But don't go off creating a bunch of lists just yet. You'll learn all about lists in Chapter 5, "Lists and Dictionaries: The Hangman Game," I promise.

Counting by Fives

The next loop counts by fives:

```
for i in range(0, 50, 5):
    print i,
```

It does this with a call to `range()` that creates a list of numbers that are multiples of 5. To create a sequence of numbers with `range()`, you can give it the start point, the end point, and the number by which to count. Here, the sequence starts at 0 and goes up by 5 each time to, but not including, 50. I used interactive mode again so that you can see the exact sequence range(0, 50, 5) produces:

```
>>> range(0, 50, 5)
[0, 5, 10, 15, 20, 25, 30, 35, 40, 45]
```

Notice though that the sequence ends at 45. Remember, 50 is the end point, so it's not included. If you wanted to include 50, your end point would have to be greater than 50. So, range(0, 51, 5) would do the trick.

Counting Backwards

The last loop in the program counts backwards:

```
for i in range(10, 0, -1):
    print i,
```

It does this because the last argument in the range() call is −1. This tells the function to go from the start point to the end point by adding −1 each time. This is the same as saying "subtract 1." Again, the end point isn't included, so the loop counts from 10 down to 1 and does not include 0.

 TRICK There's no law that says you have to use the loop variable inside a for loop. You might find that you want to repeat some action a specific number of times. To do this, create a for loop and just ignore the loop variable. For example, let's say I just wanted to print "Hi!" 10 times. The following two lines are all I would need:

```
for i in range(10):
    print "Hi!"
```

USING SEQUENCE OPERATORS AND FUNCTIONS WITH STRINGS

As you just learned, strings are one type of sequence, made up of individual characters. Python offers some useful functions and operators that work with any kind of sequence, including strings. These operators and functions can tell you basic but important things about a sequence, such as how long it is or whether a certain element is in it.

Introducing the Message Analyzer Program

This next program analyzes any message that you enter. It tells you how long the message is and whether it contains the most common letter in the English language (the letter "e"). The program accomplishes this with a new function and operator. Figure 4.4 shows off the program.

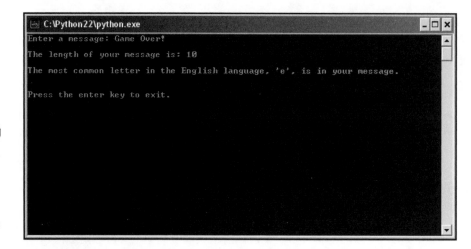

This program uses the len() function and the in operator to produce some information about your message.

Here's the code for the program:

```
# Message Analyzer
# Demonstrates the len() function and the in operator

message = raw_input("Enter a message: ")

print "\nThe length of your message is:", len(message)

print "\nThe most common letter in the English language, 'e',",
if "e" in message:
    print "is in your message."
else:
    print "is not in your message."

raw_input("\n\nPress the enter key to exit.")
```

Using the len() Function

After the program imports the random module and gets the user's message, it prints the message length with

```
print "\nThe length of your message is:", len(message)
```

You can pass any sequence you want to the len() function and it will tell you that sequence's length. A sequence's length is the number of elements it has. Because message has 10 characters in it (you count every character, including the space and exclamation point), it has a length of 10.

Using the in **Operator**

The letter "e" is the most common letter in English. The program uses the following lines to test whether "e" is in the message the user entered:

```
print "\nThe most common letter in the English language, 'e',",
if "e" in message:
    print "is in your message."
else:
    print "is not in your message."
```

The condition in the if statement is "e" in message. If message contains the character "e", it's true. If message doesn't contain "e", it's false. In the sample run, the value of message is "Game Over!", which does contain the character "e". So, the condition "e" in message evaluated to True and the computer printed "is in your message." If the condition had been false (for example, if message had been equal to "Python Programming"), then the computer would have displayed is not in your message. If an element is in a sequence, it's said to be a *member* of the sequence.

You can use in anywhere in your own programs to check whether an element is a member of a sequence. Just put the element you want to check for, followed by in, followed by the sequence. This creates a condition. If the element is a member, the condition is true; otherwise it's false.

INDEXING STRINGS

By using a for loop, you're able to go through a string one character at a time, in order. This is known as *sequential access*, which means you have to go through a sequence one element at a time. Sequential access is like going through a stack of heavy boxes that you can only lift one at a time. To get to the bottom box in a stack of five, you'd have to lift the top box, then the next box, followed by the next box, then one more to finally get to the last box. Wouldn't it be nice to just grab the last box without messing with any of the others? This kind of direct access is called *random access*. Random access allows you to get to any element in a sequence directly. Fortunately, there's a way to randomly access elements of a sequence. It's called *indexing*. Through indexing, you specify a position (or index) number in a sequence and get the element at that position. In the box example, you could get the bottom box directly, by asking for box number five.

Introducing the Random Access Program

The Random Access program uses sequence indexing to directly access random characters in a string. The program picks a random position from the string "index" and prints the letter and the position number. The program does this 10 times to give a good sampling of random positions. Figure 4.5 shows the program in action.

```
C:\Python22\python.exe                                          _ □ ×
The word is:   index

word[ 2 ]        d
word[ 4 ]        x
word[ -1 ]       x
word[ -2 ]       e
word[ 3 ]        e
word[ -5 ]       i
word[ 2 ]        d
word[ 3 ]        e
word[ 0 ]        i
word[ -4 ]       x

Press the enter key to exit.
```

FIGURE 4.5

You can directly access any character in a string through indexing.

The following is the code for the program:

```python
# Random Access
# Demonstrates string indexing

import random

word = "index"
print "The word is: ", word, "\n"

high = len(word)
low = -len(word)

for i in range(10):
    position = random.randrange(low, high)
    print "word[", position, "]\t", word[position]

raw_input("\n\nPress the enter key to exit.")
```

Working with Positive Position Numbers

In this program, one of the first things I do is assign a string value to a variable:

```
word = "index"
```

Nothing new here. But by doing this, I create a sequence (like every time I create a string) where each character has a numbered position. The first letter, "i," is at position 0. (Remember, computers usually start counting from 0.) The second letter, "n," is at position 1. The third letter, "d," is at position 2, and so on.

Accessing an individual character of a string is easy. To access the letter in position 0 from the variable word, you'd just type word[0]. For any other position, you'd just substitute that number. To help cement the idea, take a look at part of an interactive session I had:

```
>>> word = "index"
>>> print word[0]
i
>>> print word[1]
n
>>> print word[2]
d
>>> print word[3]
e
>>> print word[4]
x
```

TRAP Because there are five letters in the string ""index"", you might think that the last letter, "x," would be at position 5. But you'd be wrong. There is no position 5 in this string, because the computer begins counting at 0. Valid positive positions are 0, 1, 2, 3, and 4. Any attempt to access a position 5 will cause an error. Take a look at an interactive session for proof:

```
>>> word = "index"
>>> print word[5]
Traceback (most recent call last):
    File "<pyshell#1>", line 1, in ?
        print word[5]
IndexError: string index out of range
```

Somewhat rudely, the computer is saying there is no position 5. So remember, the last element in a sequence is at the position number of its length minus one.

Working with Negative Position Numbers

Except for the idea that the first letter of a string is at position 0 and not 1, working with positive position numbers seems pretty natural. But there's also a way to access elements of a sequence through negative position numbers. With positive position numbers, your point of reference is the beginning of the sequence. For strings, this means that the first letter is where you start counting. But with negative position numbers, you start counting from the end. For strings, that means you start counting from the last letter and work backward.

The best way to understand how negative position numbers work is to see an example. Take a look at another interactive session I had, again using the string "index":

```
>>> word = "index"
>>> print word[-1]
'x'
>>> print word[-2]
'e'
>>> print word[-3]
'd'
>>> print word[-4]
'n'
>>> print word[-5]
'i'
```

You can see from this session that word[-1] accesses the last letter of "index", the "x." When using negative position numbers, −1 means the last element, the index −2 means the second to the last element, the index −3 means the third to the last element, and so on. Sometimes it makes more sense for your reference point to be the end of a sequence. For those times, you can use negative position numbers.

Figure 4.6 provides a nice way to see the string "index" broken up by position numbers, both positive and negative.

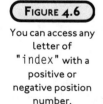

FIGURE 4.6

You can access any letter of "index" with a positive or negative position number.

0	1	2	3	4
i	n	d	e	x
-5	-4	-3	-2	-1

Accessing a Random String Element

It's time to get back to the Random Access program. To access a random letter from the "index", I need to generate random numbers. So, the first thing I did in the program was import the random module:

```
import random
```

Next, I wanted a way to pick any valid position number in word, negative or positive. I wanted my program to be able to generate a random number between –5 and 4, inclusive, because those are all the possible position values of word. Luckily, the random.randrange() function can take two end points and produce a random number from between them. So, I created two end points:

```
high = len(word)
low = -len(word)
```

high gets the value 5, because "index" has five characters in it. The variable low gets the negative value of the length of the word (that's what putting a minus sign in front of a numeric value does). So low gets the value of –5. This represents the range from which I want to grab a random number.

Actually, I want to generate a random number between (and including) -5, up to (but not including) 5. And that's exactly the way the random.randrange() function works. If you pass it two arguments, it will produce a random number from and including the low end point, up to, but not including, the high end point. So in my sample run, the line:

```
position = random.randrange(low, high)
```

produces either –5, –4, –3, –2, –1, 0, 1, 2, 3, or 4. This is exactly what I want, since these are all the possible valid position numbers for the string "index".

Finally, I created a for loop that executes 10 times. In the loop body, the program picks a random position value and prints that position value and corresponding letter:

```
for i in range(10):
    position = random.randrange(low, high)
    print "word[", position, "]\t", word[position]
```

UNDERSTANDING STRING IMMUTABILITY

Sequences fall into one of two categories: mutable or immutable. (Again, more fancy computer jargon.) *Mutable* means changeable. So, a sequence that's a mutable sequence is one that can change. *Immutable* means unchangeable. So, a sequence that's immutable is one that can't change. Strings are immutable sequences, which means that they can't change. So, for example, the string "Game Over!" will always be the string "Game Over!". You can't change it. In fact, you can't change any string you create. Now, you might think from your experience with strings, that I'm totally wrong on this. You might even run an interactive session to prove that you *can* change a string, maybe something resembling this:

```
>>> name = "Chris"
>>> print name
Chris
>>> name = "Jackson"
>>> print name
Jackson
```

You might offer this as proof that you can change a string. After all, you changed the string "Chris" to "Jackson". But, you didn't change any strings in this session. You just created two different strings. First, you created a string "Chris" and assigned it to the variable name. Then, you created another string, "Jackson", and assigned it to name. Now, both "Chris" and "Jackson" are great names, but they're different names and always will be, just as they are different strings and always will be. Take a look at Figure 4.7 for a visual representation of what happened in the interactive session.

FIGURE 4.7

First, name gets the string "Chris", then it gets a different string, "Jackson". But no string values ever change.

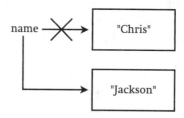

Another way to think about this is to imagine that strings are written in ink on pieces of paper. You can throw out a piece of paper with a string on it and replace it with another piece of paper with a new string on it, but you can't change the words once they've been written.

You might think this is much ado about nothing. So what if a string is immutable? But string immutability does have consequences. Because you can't change a string, you can't assign a new character to a string through indexing. Here's an interactive session to show you what I mean:

```
>>> word = "game"
>>> word[0] = "l"
```

```
Traceback (most recent call last):
    File "<pyshell#1>", line 1, in ?
        word[0] = "l"
TypeError: object doesn't support item assignment
```

In this session, I wanted to change the string "game" to the string "lame" (obviously, I didn't much like the game I was referring to). All I needed to do was change the letter "g" to an "l." So I just assigned "l" to the first position in the string, word[0]. But as you can see, this resulted in a big, fat error. The interpreter even tells me that strings don't support item assignment. (You can't assign a new value to a character in a string.)

But, just because you can't alter a string doesn't mean you can't create new strings from existing ones.

BUILDING A NEW STRING

You've already seen how you can concatenate two strings with the + operator. Sometimes, you may want to build a new string, one character at a time. Because strings are immutable, what you'll really be doing is creating a new string every time you use the concatenation operator.

Introducing the No Vowels Program

This next program, No Vowels, takes a message from the user and prints it, minus any vowels. Figure 4.8 shows the program in action.

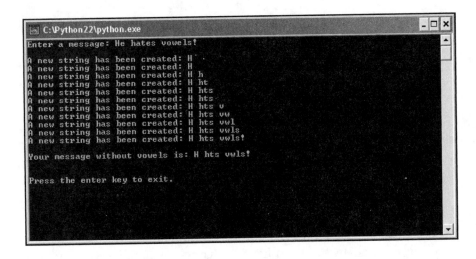

FIGURE 4.8

Using a for loop, new strings are created. The program skips the concatenation operation for any vowels.

The program creates a new string of the original message, without the vowels. Really what it does is create a series of new strings. Here's the code:

```
# No Vowels
# Demonstrates creating new strings with a for loop

message = raw_input("Enter a message: ")
new_message = ""
VOWELS = "aeiou"

print
for letter in message:
    if letter.lower() not in VOWELS:
        new_message += letter
        print "A new string has been created:", new_message

print "\nYour message without vowels is:", new_message

raw_input("\n\nPress the enter key to exit.")
```

Creating Constants

After the program gets the message from the user and creates an empty new message, it creates a string:

```
VOWELS = "aeiou"
```

This variable, VOWELS, gets a string of all the vowels. You probably notice that the variable name is in all caps, contrary to what you have learned: that, traditionally, variable names are in lowercase. Well, I haven't veered from tradition here. In fact, there's a special meaning associated with variable names in all caps. They're called *constants* and refer to values that are not meant to change (their value is constant).

Constants are valuable to programmers in two ways. First, they make programs clearer. In this program, I can use the variable name VOWELS anywhere I need the sequence of vowels, instead of the string "aeiou". Using the variable name instead of the string is clearer. When you see the variable name, you understand what it means, but you might be confused by seeing the odd-looking string itself. Second, constants save retyping (and possibly errors from mistyping). Constants are especially useful if you have a long value, like a very long number or string. Use a constant in programs where you have the same, unchanging value used in multiple places.

You have to be careful when you create constants by making an all-caps variable name. Even though you're saying to yourself and other programmers that this variable will always refer to the same value, there's nothing in Python that will stop you from changing it in your program. This naming practice is simply a convention. So, once you create a variable with a name in all caps, make sure to treat it as unchangeable.

In the Real World

In some programming languages, constants are exactly that. They can't be changed once they're defined. That's the safest way to create and use constants. In Python, though, there isn't a simple way to create true constants of your own.

Creating New Strings from Existing Ones

The real work of the program happens in the loop. The program creates a new message, without any vowels, as the loop runs. Each time through, the computer checks the next letter in the original message. If it's not a vowel, it adds this letter to the new message it's creating. If it is a vowel, the program moves on to the next letter. You know that a program can't literally add a character to a string, so, more precisely, when the program comes across a character that's not a vowel, it concatenates the new message it has so far with this character to create a new string. The code that accomplishes this is:

```
for letter in message:
    if letter.lower() not in VOWELS:
        new_message += letter
        print "A new string has been created:", new_message
```

There are two new ideas in the loop, so let me go over both of them. First, Python is picky when dealing with strings and characters. "A" is not the same as "a". Because VOWELS is assigned a string that contains only lowercase letters, I needed to make sure that I checked only lowercase letters when using the in operator. That's why I used letter.lower().

Often, when you compare two strings, you don't care about the case matching, only the letters. If you ask a player if he or she wants to continue a game, the string "Yes" is as good as the string "yes". Well, in these instances, just make sure to convert both strings to the same case (upper- or lowercase, it doesn't matter) before you compare them.

Here's an example. Let's say I want to compare two strings, name and winner, to see if they are equal, and I don't care about matching the case. I could create the condition:

```
name.lower() == winner.lower()
```

This condition is true whenever name and winner each have the same sequence of characters, regardless of case. So, "Larry" and "larry" are a match. "LARRY" and "larry" are too. Even "LaRrY" and "lArRy" works.

Second, you also might notice that I used the augmented assignment operator, +=, in the program for string concatenation. You saw the augmented assignment operators with numbers, but they also work with strings. So, this line:

```
new_message += letter
```

is exactly the same as:

```
new_message = new_message + letter
```

SLICING STRINGS

Indexing is a useful technique, but you aren't restricted to copying just one element at a time from a sequence. You can make copies of continuous sections of elements (called *slices*). You can copy (or *slice*) one element (just like indexing) or part of a sequence (like, say, the middle three elements). You can even create a slice that is a copy of the entire sequence. So, for strings, that means you can grab anything ranging from a single character, to a group of consecutive characters, to the entire string.

Introducing the Pizza Slicer Program

The Pizza Slicer program lets you slice the string "pizza" any way you want. It's a great, interactive way to help you understand slicing. All you do is enter the starting and ending positions of the slice, and the program displays the results. Figure 4.9 shows off the program.

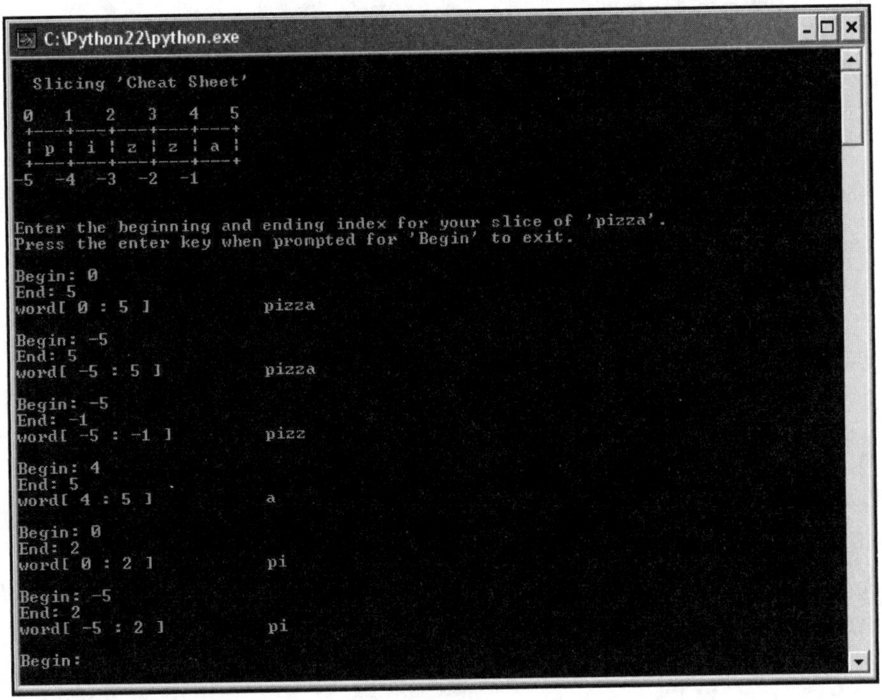

FIGURE 4.9

Fresh, hot slices of "pizza", made just the way you asked. The program also offers a "cheat sheet" so you can visualize how a slice will be created.

Here's the code:

```
# Pizza Slicer
# Demonstrates string slicing

word = "pizza"

print \
"""
    Slicing 'Cheat Sheet'

0 1 2 3 4 5
+--+--+--+--+--+
| p | i | z | z | a |
+--+--+--+--+--+
-5 -4 -3 -2 -1

"""
```

```
print "Enter the beginning and ending index for your slice of 'pizza'."
print "Press the enter key at 'Begin' to exit."


begin = None
while begin != "":
    begin = (raw_input("\nBegin: "))

    if begin:
        begin = int(begin)

        end = int(raw_input("End: "))

        print "word[", begin, ":", end, "]\t\t",
        print word[begin:end]

raw_input("\n\nPress the enter key to exit.")
```

Introducing None

Before you get to the code about slicing, take a look at this line, which introduces a new idea:

```
begin = None
```

The line assigns a special value, called None, to begin. None is Python's way of representing nothing. None makes a good placeholder for a value. It also evaluates to False when treated as a condition. I used it here because I wanted to initialize begin for use in the while loop condition.

Understanding Slicing

Creating a slice is similar to indexing. But instead of using a single position number, you supply a starting position and ending position. Every element between the two points becomes part of the slice. Figure 4.10 shows a way to look at slicing end point numbers for the string "pizza". Notice that it's a slightly different numbering system than the index numbering in Figure 4.6.

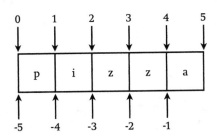

FIGURE 4.10

An example of slicing end point numbers for the string "pizza". You can use any combination of positive and negative end points for your slice.

To specify the end points of a slice, include both in brackets, separated by a colon. Here's a quick interactive session to show you what I mean:

```
>>> word = "pizza"
>>> print word[0:5]
pizza
>>> print word[1:3]
iz
>>> print word[-4:-2]
iz
>>> print word[-4:3]
iz
```

word[0:5] returns the entire string because all its characters are between those two end points. word[1:3] returns the string "iz" because those two characters are between the end points. Just like with indexing, you can use negative numbers. word[-4:-2] also produces the string "iz" because those characters are between the two negative positions. You can also mix and match positive and negative end points. This works just like creating any other slice; the elements between the two position numbers will be in the slice. So, word[-4:3] also produces the string "iz", because they are the two characters between those two end points.

TRAP   If you create an "impossible" slice, where the starting point is bigger than the ending point, such as word[2:1], you won't cause an error. Instead, Python will quietly return an empty sequence. For strings, that means you'll get the empty string. So be careful, because this is probably not the kind of result you're after.

Creating Slices

Inside the loop of Pizza Slicer, the program prints the syntax for creating a slice based on the beginning and ending positions the user entered, through the following line:

```
print "word[", begin, ":", end, "]\t\t",
```

Then, the program prints the actual slice using the variables `begin` and `end`:

```
print word[begin:end]
```

Using Slicing Shorthand

Although you can get every possible slice by specifying two numbers, there are a few slicing shortcuts you can use. You can omit the beginning point for the slice to start the slice at the beginning of the sequence. So, given that `word` has been assigned `"pizza"`, the slice `word[:4]` is exactly the same as `word[0:4]`. You can omit the ending point so that the slice ends with the very last element. So, `word[2:]` is just shorthand for `word[2:5]`. You can even omit both numbers to get a slice that is the entire sequence. So, `word[:]` is shorthand for `word[0:5]`.

Here's an interactive session to back up this proposition:

```
>>> word = "pizza"
>>> word[0:4]
'pizz'
>>> word[:4]
'pizz'
>>> word[2:5]
'zza'
>>> word[2:]
'zza'
>>> word[0:5]
'pizza'
>>> word[:]
'pizza'
```

 TRICK If there's one bit of slicing shorthand you should remember, it's that `[:]` returns a complete copy of a sequence. As you program, you'll find you may need to make a copy of a sequence, and this is a quick and efficient way to do just that.

CREATING TUPLES

Tuples are a type of sequence, like strings. But unlike strings, which can only contain characters, tuples can contain elements of any type. That means you can have a tuple that stores a bunch of high scores for a game, or one that stores a group of employee names. But tuple elements don't have to all be of the same type. You could create a tuple with both strings and numbers, if you wanted. And you don't have to stop at strings and numbers. You can create a tuple that contains a sequence of graphic images, sound files, or even a group of aliens (once you learn how to create these things, which you will in later chapters). Whatever you can assign to a variable, you can group together and store as a sequence in a tuple.

Introducing the Hero's Inventory Program

Hero's Inventory maintains the inventory of a hero from a typical role-playing game. Like most role-playing games ever created, the hero is from a small, insignificant village. His father was, of course, killed by an evil warlord. (What's a quest without a dead father?) And now that the hero has come of age, it's time for him to seek his revenge.

In this program, the hero's inventory is represented by a tuple. The tuple contains strings, one for each item in the hero's possession. The hero starts out with nothing, but then I give him a few items. Figure 4.11 shows the humble beginnings of our hero's journey.

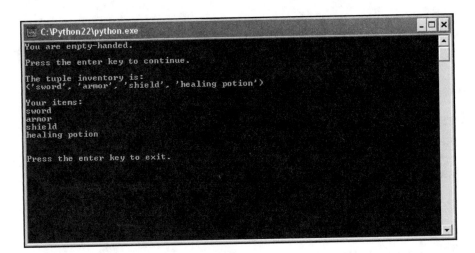

FIGURE 4.11

At first, the hero has no items in his inventory. Then, the program creates a new tuple with string elements, and our hero is stocked.

Here's the code for the program:

```
# Hero's Inventory
# Demonstrates tuple creation

# create an empty tuple
inventory = ()

# treat the tuple as a condition
if not inventory:
    print "You are empty-handed."
```

```
raw_input("\nPress the enter key to continue.")

# create a tuple with some items
inventory = ("sword",
             "armor",
             "shield",
             "healing potion")

# print the tuple
print "\nThe tuple inventory is:\n", inventory

# print each element in the tuple
print "\nYour items:"
for item in inventory:
    print item

raw_input("\n\nPress the enter key to exit.")
```

Creating an Empty Tuple

To create a tuple, you just surround a sequence of values, separated by commas, with parentheses. Even a pair of lone parentheses is a valid (but empty) tuple. I created an empty tuple in the first part of the program to represent that the hero has nothing:

```
inventory = ()
```

It's as simple as that. So in this line, the variable inventory gets an empty tuple.

Treating a Tuple as a Condition

When you learned about conditions, you saw that you could treat any value in Python as a condition. That means you can treat a tuple as a condition, too. And that's what I did in the next lines:

```
if not inventory:
    print "You are empty-handed."
```

As a condition, an empty tuple is False. A tuple with at least one element is True. Because the tuple assigned to inventory is empty, it's False. That means not inventory is True. So the computer prints the string, "You are empty-handed.", just as it should.

Creating a Tuple with Elements

An unarmed hero is a boring hero. So next, I created a new tuple with string elements that represent useful items for our hero. I assigned this new tuple to inventory with the following lines:

```
inventory = ("sword",
             "armor",
             "shield",
             "healing potion")
```

Each element in the tuple is separated by a comma. That makes the first element the string "sword", the next "armor", the next "shield", and the last element "healing potion". So each string is a single element in this tuple.

Also, notice that the tuple spans multiple lines. You can write a tuple in one line or span it across multiple lines like I did, as long as you end each line after a comma. This is one of the few cases where Python lets you break up a statement across multiple lines.

TRICK Make your programs easier to read by creating tuples across multiple lines. You don't have to write exactly one element per line, though. It might make sense to write several on a line. Just end each line at one of the commas separating elements and you'll be fine.

Printing a Tuple

Though a tuple can contain many elements, you can print the entire tuple just like you would any single value. That's what I did in the next line:

```
print "\nThe tuple inventory is:\n", inventory
```

The computer displays all of the elements, surrounded by parentheses.

Looping through a Tuple's Elements

Finally, I wrote a for loop to march through the elements in inventory and print each one individually:

```
print "\nYour items:"
for item in inventory:
    print item
```

This loop prints each element (each string) in inventory on a separate line. This loop looks just like the ones you've seen with strings. In fact, you can use this kind of loop to go through the elements of any sequence.

Even though I created a tuple where all the elements are of the same type (strings in this case), tuples don't have to be filled with values of the same type. A single tuple can just as easily contain strings, integers, and floating-point numbers, for example.

TRAP   Other programming languages offer structures similar to tuples. Some go by the name "arrays" or "vectors." However, those other languages usually restrict the elements of these sequences to just one type. So, for example, you couldn't mix strings and numbers together. Just be aware that these other structures don't usually offer all the flexibility that Python sequences do.

USING TUPLES

Because tuples are simply another kind of sequence, everything you learned about sequences from strings works with tuples. You can get the length of a tuple, print each element with a `for` loop, and use the `in` operator to test whether an element is in a tuple. You can index, slice, and concatenate tuples, too.

Introducing the Hero's Inventory 2.0

Our hero's journey continues. In this program, his inventory is counted, tested, indexed, and sliced. Our hero will also happen upon a chest with items in it (represented by another tuple). Through tuple concatenation, our hero's inventory will be replaced with all of his current items plus the treasure he finds in the chest. Figure 4.12 shows a sample run of the program.

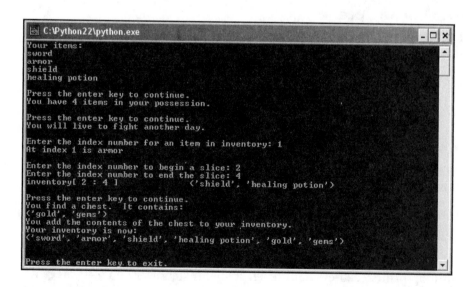

FIGURE 4.12

The hero's inventory is a tuple, which means it can be counted, indexed, sliced, and even concatenated with another tuple.

Because this program is a little long, I'll go through the code one section at a time rather than show you the whole thing at once. But check out the CD to see the program in its entirety.

Setting Up the Program

The first part of the program works just like it did in the previous program, Hero's Inventory. These lines create a tuple and print out each element:

```
# Hero's Inventory 2.0
# Demonstrates tuples

# create a tuple with some items and display with a for loop
inventory = ("sword",
             "armor",
             "shield",
             "healing potion")
print "Your items:"
for item in inventory:
    print item


raw_input("\nPress the enter key to continue.")
```

Using the len() Function with Tuples

The len() function works with tuples just the way it does with strings. If you want to know the length of a tuple, place it inside the parentheses. The function returns the number of elements in the tuple. Empty tuples, or any empty sequences for that matter, have a length of 0. The following lines use the len() function with the tuple:

```
# get the length of a tuple
print "You have", len(inventory), "items in your possession."

raw_input("\nPress the enter key to continue.")
```

Because this tuple has four elements (the four strings: "sword", "armor", "shield", and "healing potion"), the message You have 4 items in your possession. is displayed.

TRAP   Notice that in the tuple inventory, the string "healing potion" is counted as a single element, even though it's two words.

Using the in Operator with Tuples

Just like with strings, you can use the in operator with tuples to test for element membership. And, just like before, the in operator is usually used to create a condition. That's how I used it here:

```
# test for membership with in
if "healing potion" in inventory:
    print "You will live to fight another day."
```

The condition "healing potion" in inventory tests whether the entire string "healing potion" is an element in inventory. Since it is, the message You will live to fight another day. is displayed.

Indexing Tuples

Indexing tuples works like indexing strings. You specify a position number, in brackets, to access a particular element. In the following lines, I let the user choose the index number and then the computer displays the corresponding element:

```
# display one item through an index
index = int(raw_input("\nEnter the index number for an item in inventory: "))
print "At index", index, "is", inventory[index]
```

Figure 4.13 shows this tuple with index numbers.

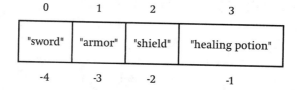

FIGURE 4.13

Each string is a single element in the tuple.

Slicing Tuples

Slicing works just like you saw with strings. You give a beginning and ending position. The result is a tuple containing every element between those two positions.

Just as in the Pizza Slicer program from earlier in this chapter, I let the user pick the beginning and ending position numbers. Then, like before, the program displays the slice:

```
# display a slice
begin = int(raw_input("\nEnter the index number to begin a slice: "))
end = int(raw_input("Enter the index number to end the slice: "))
print "inventory[", begin, ":", end, "]\t\t",
print inventory[begin:end]
raw_input("\nPress the enter key to continue.")
```

Using this tuple as an example, Figure 4.14 provides a visual way to understand tuple slicing.

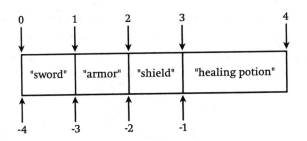

FIGURE 4.14

Slicing positions for tuples are defined between elements, just as they are for strings.

Understanding Tuple Immutability

Like strings, tuples are immutable. That means you can't change a tuple. Here's an interactive session to prove my point:

```
>>> inventory = ("sword", "armor", "shield", "healing potion")
>>> print inventory
('sword', 'armor', 'shield', 'healing potion')
>>> inventory[0] = "battleax"
Traceback (most recent call last):
    File "<pyshell#3>", line 1, in ?
        inventory[0] = "battleax"
TypeError: object doesn't support item assignment
```

Although you can't change tuples, like strings, you can create new tuples from existing ones.

Concatenating Tuples

You can concatenate tuples the same way you concatenate strings. You simply join them together with +, the concatenation operator:

```
# concatenate two tuples
chest = ("gold", "gems")
print "You find a chest. It contains:"
print chest
print "You add the contents of the chest to your inventory."
inventory += chest
print "Your inventory is now:"
print inventory
raw_input("\n\nPress the enter key to exit.")
```

The first thing I did was create a new tuple, chest, with the two string elements "gold" and "gems". Next, I printed chest to show its elements. After that, I used an augmented assignment operator to concatenate inventory with chest and assign the result back to inventory. I did not modify the original tuple assigned to inventory (since that's impossible, because tuples are immutable). Instead, the augmented assignment operator created a brand-new tuple with the elements from inventory and chest and assigned that to inventory.

BACK TO THE WORD JUMBLE GAME

The Word Jumble game combines several new ideas you learned about in this chapter. You can easily modify the program to contain your own list of words to guess.

Setting Up the Program

After my initial comments, I import the random module:

```
# Word Jumble
#
# The computer picks a random word and then "jumbles" it
# The player has to guess the original word

import random
```

Next, I used a tuple to create a sequence of words. Notice that the variable name WORD is in all caps, implying that I'll treat it as a constant.

```
# create a sequence of words to choose from
WORDS = ("python", "jumble", "easy", "difficult", "answer", "xylophone")
```

Next, I use a new function, random.choice(), to grab a random word from WORDS:

```
# pick one word randomly from the sequence
word = random.choice(WORDS)
```

This function is new to you, but it's pretty simple. The computer looks at whatever sequence you give and picks a random element.

Once the computer has chosen a random word, it assigns it to word. This is the word the player will have to guess. Lastly, I assign word to correct, which I'll use later to see if the player makes a correct guess:

```
# create a variable to use later to see if the guess is correct
correct = word
```

Planning the Jumble Creation Section

The next section of code uses the new concepts in the chapter and is the most interesting part of the program. It's the section that actually creates the jumbled word from the original, randomly chosen word.

But, before I wrote any code, I planned out this part of the program in pseudocode (yes, I actually use all that stuff I write about.) Here's my first pass at the algorithm to create a jumbled word from the chosen word:

create an empty jumble word

while the chosen word has letters in it

> *extract a random letter from the chosen word*

> *add the random letter to the jumble word*

Conceptually, this is pretty good, but I have to watch my semantics. Because strings are immutable, I can't actually "extract a random letter" from the string the user entered. But, I can create a new string that doesn't contain the randomly chosen letter. And while I can't "add the random letter" to the jumble word string either, I can create a new string by concatenating the current jumble word with the "extracted" letter.

Creating an Empty Jumble String

The very first part of the algorithm is easy:

```
# create a jumbled version of the word
jumble =""
```

The program creates the empty string and assigns it to `jumble`, which will refer to the final jumbled word.

Setting Up the Loop

The jumble creation process is controlled by a `while` loop. The loop condition is pretty simple, as you can see:

```
while word:
```

I set the loop up this way so that it will continue until `word` is equal to the empty string. This is perfect, because each time the loop executes, the computer creates a new version of `word` with one letter "extracted" and assigns it back to `word`. Eventually, `word` will become the empty string and the jumbling will be done.

Generating a Random Position in word

The first line in the loop body generates a random position in word, based on its length:

```
position = random.randrange(len(word))
```

So, the letter word[position] is the letter that is going to be "extracted" from word and "added to" jumble.

Creating a New Version of jumble

The next line in the loop creates a new version of the string jumble. It becomes equal to its old self, plus the letter word[position].

```
jumble += word[position]
```

Creating a New Version of word

The next line in the loop

```
word = word[:position] + word[(position + 1):]
```

creates a new version of word minus the one letter at position position. Using slicing, the computer creates two new strings from word. The first slice, word[:position], is every letter up to, but not including, word[position]. The next slice, word[(position + 1):], is every letter after word[position]. These two string are joined together and assigned to word, which is now equal to its old self, minus the one letter word[position].

Welcoming the Player

After the jumbled word has been created, the next section of the program welcomes the player to the game and displays the jumbled word to be rearranged:

```
# start the game
print \
"""
            Welcome to Word Jumble!

    Unscramble the letters to make a word.
(Press the enter key at the prompt to quit.)
"""
print "The jumble is:", jumble
```

Getting the Player's Guess

Next, the computer gets the player's guess. The computer keeps asking the player for a guess as long as the player doesn't enter the correct word or press the Enter key at the prompt:

```
guess = raw_input("\nYour guess: ")
guess = guess.lower()
while (guess != correct) and (guess != ""):
    print "Sorry, that's not it."
    guess = raw_input("Your guess: ")
    guess = guess.lower()
```

I made sure to convert `guess` to lowercase since the word the player is trying to guess is in lowercase.

Congratulating the Player

At this point in the program, the player has either correctly guessed the word or quit the game. If the player has guessed the word, then the computer offers its hearty congratulations:

```
if guess == correct:
    print "That's it! You guessed it!\n"
```

Ending the Game

Finally, the program thanks the player for playing the game and ends:

```
print "Thanks for playing."

raw_input("\n\nPress the enter key to exit.")
```

SUMMARY

- A sequence is an ordered list of elements.
- An element is a single item in a sequence.
- A string is a sequence of characters.
- To iterate is to move through a sequence, in order.
- A for loop iterates over a sequence and performs its loop body for each element in the sequence.
- During each iteration of a for loop, the loop variable gets the next element in the sequence.
- In the for loop body, something is usually done with the loop variable.

- The `range()` function returns a sequence of numbers in a range.
- The `len()` function returns the number of elements in a sequence.
- The `in` operator tests for element membership and returns `True` if the element is in the sequence and `False` otherwise.
- Indexing is the process used to access a specific element of a sequence.
- Sequences can be indexed, providing random access to elements based on position numbers.
- Mutable means changeable.
- Immutable means unchangeable.
- Strings are immutable sequences so they can't be changed.
- Constants are values that are not meant to change. By convention, their names are in all uppercase.
- String concatenation is the joining of two strings to create a brand-new string. The concatenation operator, +, can be used to concatenate strings.
- `None` is a value that represents nothing and evaluates to `False` when treated as a condition.
- Slicing is creating a copy of a continuous segment of a sequence.
- A tuple is an immutable sequence of any type.
- The concatenation operator, +, works with tuples just like with strings.

REVIEW QUESTIONS

1. How is a `while` loop different from a `for` loop?
2. Which is better, a `for` loop or a `while` loop?
3. Do experienced programmers ever need to use Python's interactive mode?
4. Is the value `"Am I a string or a sequence?"` a string or a sequence?
5. Does the `len()` function work with more than one type?
6. Does `len()` count the spaces in a string when determining its length?
7. Does the `in` operator work with more than one type?
8. What's the difference between sequential and random access?
9. What's the first position number in a sequence?
10. Using negative position numbers, what's the last element in a sequence?
11. What does it mean for a string to be immutable?
12. If strings are immutable, how does string concatenation work?
13. How can constants be helpful?
14. Are constants truly unchangeable in Python?

15. What is the value None good for?
16. What happens if you create an "impossible" slice, such as name[3:2]?
17. What kinds of elements can you store with a tuple?
18. Must all of the elements stored with a tuple be of the same type?
19. Is an empty tuple valid?
20. What does the function random.choice() do?

PROJECTS

1. Write a program that asks for a phrase and then calculates and displays the number of vowels in the phrase, twice. The first time, your program should calculate the number of vowels in the phrase using a for loop. The second time, your program should use a while loop.

2. Write a program that gets a message from the user and prints the message out backwards.

3. Write a program that prints out a string representation of a random card from a deck of playing cards. The program should use either "A", "2", "3", "4", "5", "6", "7", "8", "9", "10", "J", "Q", or "K" for the value of the card and either "c", "h", "s", or "d" for the suit. So, if the program randomly selects the jack of clubs, it should display Jc. Use one tuple to represent all of the possible card values and another tuple for the possible suits.

4. Write a program that displays all of the cards from a deck of playing cards using the same format as described in Project 3. Again, use one tuple to represent all of the possible card values and another tuple for the possible suits. The program should display:

```
Ac Ah As Ad
2c 2h 2s 2d
3c 3h 3s 3d
4c 4h 4s 4d
5c 5h 5s 5d
6c 6h 6s 6d
7c 7h 7s 7d
8c 8h 8s 8d
9c 9h 9s 9d
10c 10h 10s 10d
Jc Jh Js Jd
Qc Qh Qs Qd
Kc Kh Ks Kd
```

5. Improve the Word Jumble game presented in this chapter so that each word is paired with a hint. If the player enters hint, then the program should display the corresponding hint. Use a new tuple for the hints.

LISTS AND DICTIONARIES:
THE HANGMAN GAME

Tuples are a great way to work with sequences of any type, but their immutability can be limiting. Fortunately, another kind of sequence, the *list*, does everything that the tuple can plus more. That's because lists are mutable. Elements can be added or removed from a list. You can even sort or reverse an entire list. You'll also be introduced to another type, the *dictionary*. Whereas lists work with sequences of information, dictionaries work with pairs of data. Dictionaries, like their real-life counterparts, let you look up one value with another. Specifically in this chapter, you'll learn to do the following:

- Create, index, and slice a list
- Add and delete elements from a list
- Use list methods to append, sort, and reverse a list
- Use nested sequences to represent even more complex information
- Use dictionaries to work with pairs of data
- Add and delete dictionary items

INTRODUCING THE HANGMAN GAME

The final game program for this chapter is the game of Hangman. The computer picks a secret word and the player has to try to guess it, one letter at a time. Each time the player makes an incorrect guess, the computer shows a new image of a figure being hanged. If the player doesn't guess the word in time, the stick figure is a goner. Figures 5.1 through 5.3 show off the game in all its glory.

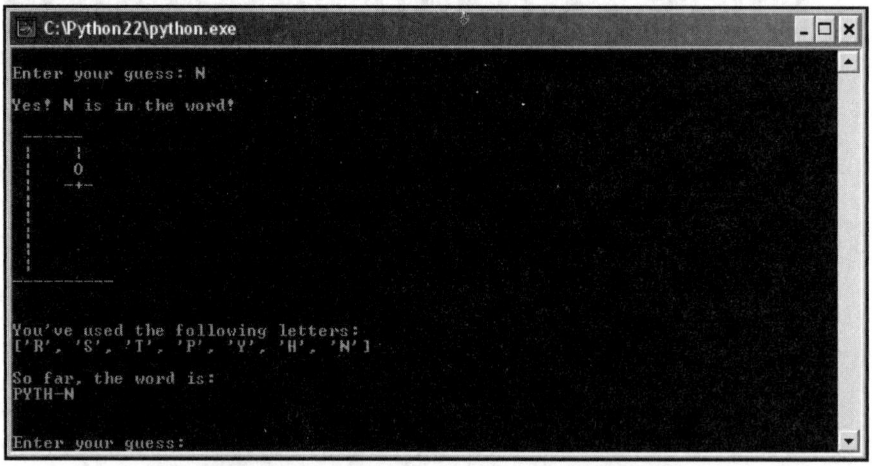

FIGURE 5.1

The Hangman game in action. Hmm...I wonder what the word could be.

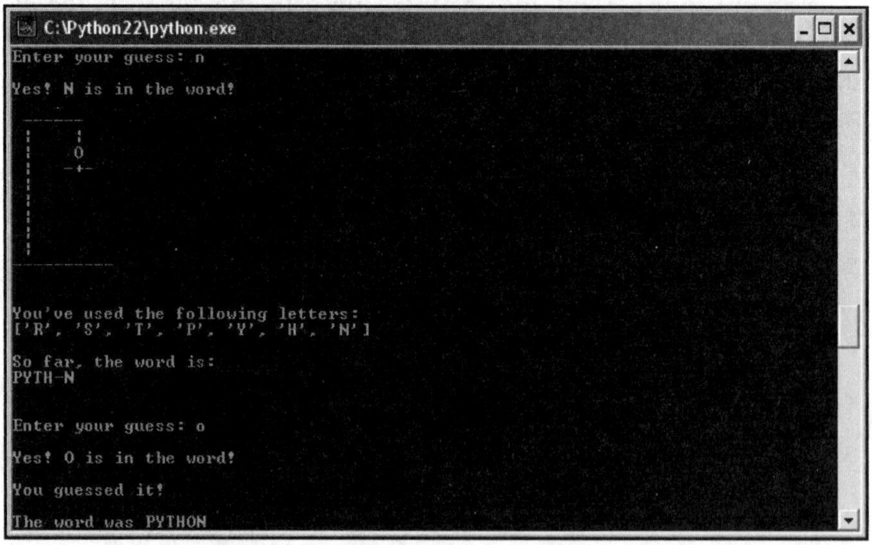

FIGURE 5.2

I won this game!

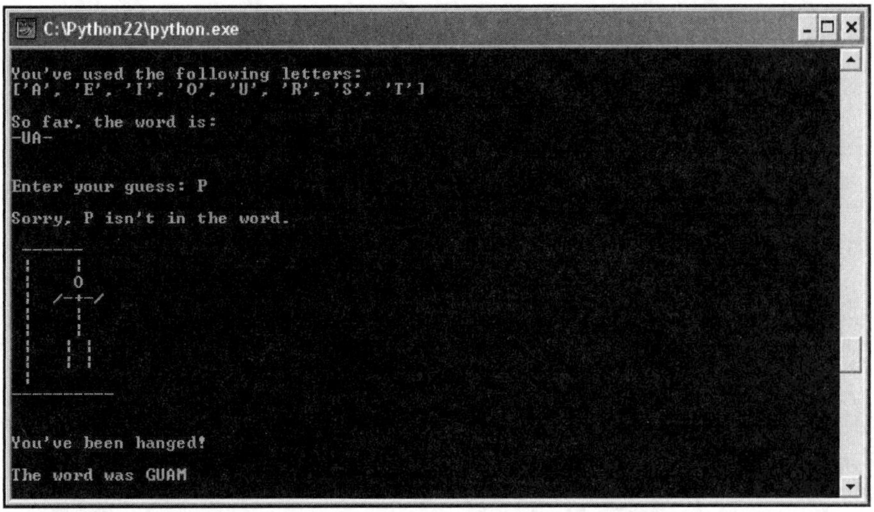

FIGURE 5.3

This game ended
badly, especially
for the little guy
made of text.

Not only is this game fun, but by the end of the chapter, you'll know how to create your own version. You can have a personalized group of secret words, and even update my marginally adequate artwork.

Using Lists

Lists are sequences, just like tuples, but lists are mutable. They can be modified. So, lists can do everything tuples can, plus more. Lists work just like tuples, so everything you learned about tuples is applicable to lists, which makes learning to use them a snap.

Introducing the Hero's Inventory 3.0 Program

This program is based on the Hero's Inventory 2.0 program, introduced in Chapter 4, in the section "Creating Tuples." But instead of using tuples to store the hero's inventory, this program uses lists. The first part of Hero's Inventory 3.0 creates the same results as version 2.0. In fact, the code is almost exactly the same. The only difference is that it uses lists instead of tuples. Figure 5.4 shows off the results of the first part of the program. The second part of the program takes advantage of the mutability of lists and does some brand-new things with sequences. Figure 5.5 shows that part in action.

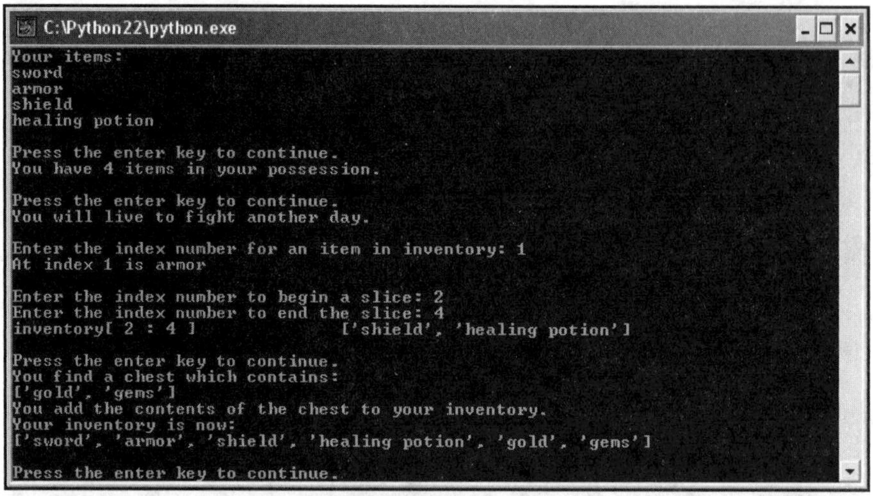

FIGURE 5.4

The hero's inventory is now represented by a list. The results look almost exactly the same as when the inventory was represented by a tuple in Hero's Inventory 2.0.

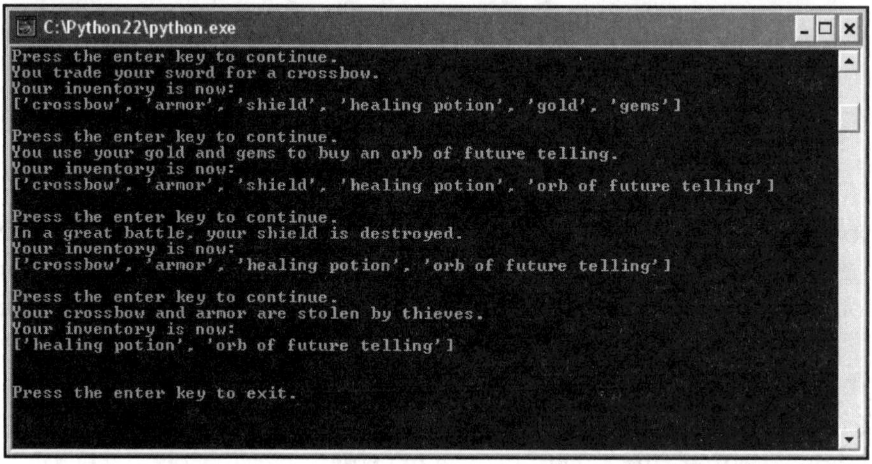

FIGURE 5.5

Because the hero's inventory is represented by a list, items can be added, modified, and deleted.

Creating a List

The first line of the program creates a new list, assigns it to inventory, and prints each element. The last line waits for the user before continuing. This works almost exactly like it did in Hero's Inventory 2.0. The only difference is that I surrounded the elements with square brackets instead of parentheses, to create a list instead of a tuple.

```
# Hero's Inventory
# Demonstrates lists

# create a list with some items and display with a for loop
```

```
inventory = ["sword", "armor", "shield", "healing potion"]
print "Your items:"
for item in inventory:
    print item

raw_input("\nPress the enter key to continue.")
```

Using the `len()` Function with Lists

The following code is exactly the same as the corresponding code in Hero's Inventory 2.0. The `len()` function works the same with lists as it does with tuples.

```
# get the length of a list
print "You have", len(inventory), "items in your possession."

raw_input("\nPress the enter key to continue.")
```

Using the `in` Operator with Lists

Again, the code for this section is exactly the same as in the older version. The `in` operator works the same with lists as it does with tuples.

```
# test for membership with in
if "healing potion" in inventory:
    print "You will live to fight another day."
```

Indexing Lists

Once again, the code is exactly the same as it was with tuples. Indexing a list is the same as indexing a tuple: Just supply the position number of the element you're after in brackets.

```
# display one item through an index
index = int(raw_input("\nEnter the index number for an item in inventory: "))
print "At index", index, "is", inventory[index]
```

Slicing Lists

Would you believe that slicing a list is exactly the same as slicing a tuple? Again, you just supply the two end points, separated by a colon, in brackets:

```
# display a slice
begin = int(raw_input("\nEnter the index number to begin a slice: "))
end = int(raw_input("Enter the index number to end the slice: "))
print "inventory[", begin, ":", end, "]\t\t",
```

```
print inventory[begin:end]

raw_input("\nPress the enter key to continue.")
```

Concatenating Lists

Concatenating lists works the same way concatenating tuples does. The only real difference here is that I created a list (rather than a tuple) and assigned it to chest. This is a small but important difference, because you can only concatenate the same types of sequences.

```
# concatenate two lists
chest = ["gold", "gems"]
print "You find a chest which contains:"
print chest
print "You add the contents of the chest to your inventory."
inventory += chest
print "Your inventory is now:"
print inventory

raw_input("\nPress the enter key to continue.")
```

Understanding List Mutability

At this point, you may be getting a bit tired of reading the phrase "works exactly the same as it did with tuples." So far, with the exception of using brackets instead of parentheses, lists seem no different than tuples. But there is one huge difference between them. Lists are mutable. They can change. As a result, there are many things you can do with lists that you can't do with tuples.

Assigning a New List Element by Index

Because lists are mutable, you can assign an existing element a new value:

```
# assign by index
print "You trade your sword for a crossbow."
inventory[0] = "crossbow"
print "Your inventory is now:"
print inventory

raw_input("\nPress the enter key to continue.")
```

The following line assigns the string "crossbow" to the element in inventory at position 0:

```
inventory[0] = "crossbow"
```

The new string replaces the previous value (which was "sword"). You can see the results when the print statement displays the new version of inventory.

 TRAP You can assign an existing list element a new value with indexing, but you can't create a new element in this way. An attempt to assign a value to a nonexistent element will result in an error.

Assigning a New List Slice

In addition to assigning a new value to a single element, you can assign a new value to a slice. I assigned the list ["orb of future telling"] to the slice inventory[4:6]:

```
# assign by slice
print "You use your gold and gems to buy an orb of future telling."
inventory[4:6] = ["orb of future telling"]
print "Your inventory is now:"
print inventory

raw_input("\nPress the enter key to continue.")
```

This assignment statement replaces the two items inventory[4] and inventory[5] with the string "orb of future telling". Because I assigned a list with one element to a slice with two elements, the length of the list shrunk by one.

Deleting a List Element

You can delete an element from a list with del—simply designate the element after del:

```
# delete an element
print "In a great battle, your shield is destroyed."
del inventory[2]
print "Your inventory is now:"
print inventory

raw_input("\nPress the enter key to continue.")
```

After this code executes, the element that was at position number 2, the string "shield", is removed from inventory. Deleting an element doesn't create a gap in a sequence. The length of the list shrinks by one and all the elements after the deleted one "slide down" one position. So, in this case, there is still an element in position 2, it's just the element that was at position 3.

Deleting a List Slice

You can also delete a slice from a list:

```
# delete a slice
print "Your crossbow and armor are stolen by thieves."
del inventory[:2]
print "Your inventory is now:"
print inventory


raw_input("\n\nPress the enter key to exit.")
```

The following line removes the slice inventory[:2], which is ["crossbow", "armor"], from inventory:

```
del inventory[:2]
```

Just as with deleting an element, the length of the list shrinks and the remaining elements form a new, continuous list, starting from position 0.

USING LIST METHODS

Lists have methods that allow you to manipulate them. Through list methods, you can add an element, remove an element based on its value, sort a list, and even reverse the order of a list.

Introducing the High Scores Program

The High Scores program uses list methods to create and maintain a list of the user's best scores for a computer game. The program uses a simple, menu-driven interface. The user has a few choices. He or she can add a new score, delete a score, sort the scores, or quit the program. Figure 5.6 shows the program in action.

The user chooses
from a menu to
maintain the high
scores list. Behind
the scenes, list
methods do the
bulk of the work.

Setting Up the Program

The setup code for the program is pretty simple. After the initial comments, I create two
variables. scores is a list that will contain the scores. I set it to an empty list to start out.
choice represents the user's choice from the menu. I initialized it to None.

```
# High Scores
# Demonstrates list methods

scores = []
choice = None
```

Displaying the Menu

The while loop is the core of the program. It continues until the user enters 0. The rest of this
code prints the menu and gets the user's choice:

```
while choice != "0":

    print \
    """

    High Scores Keeper
```

```
0 - Exit
1 - Show Scores
2 - Add a Score
3 - Delete a Score
4 - Sort Scores
"""

choice = raw_input("Choice: ")
print
```

Exiting the Program

I first check whether the user wants to quit. If the user enters 0, the computer says "Good-bye."

```
# exit
if choice == "0":
    print "Good-bye."
```

If the user enters 0, then the `while` loop's condition will be false the next time it's tested. The loop will end and so will the program.

Displaying the Scores

If the user enters 1, then this `elif` block executes and the computer displays the scores:

```
# list high-score table
elif choice == "1":
    print "High Scores"
    for score in scores:
        print score
```

Adding a Score

If the user enters 2, the computer asks the user for a new score and assigns it to `score`. The last line uses the `append()` list method to add `score` to the end of `scores`. The list becomes one element longer.

```
# add a score
elif choice == "2":
    score = int(raw_input("What score did you get?: "))
    scores.append(score)
```

Removing a Score

When the user enters 3, the computer gets a score from the user to remove. If the score is in the list, the computer removes the first occurrence of it. If the score isn't in the list, the user is informed.

```
# delete a score
elif choice == "3":
    score = int(raw_input("Delete which score?: "))
    if score in scores:
        scores.remove(score)
    else:
        print score, "isn't in the high scores list."
```

The code first checks to see whether the score is in the list. If it is, the list method `remove()` is invoked. The method goes through the list, starting at position 0, and searches for the value passed to it—in this case, `score`. When the method finds the first occurrence of the value, that element is deleted from the list. If the value is in the list more than once, only the first occurrence is removed. So, only the first occurrence of `score` is removed. You can see how `remove()` is different from `del`. The `remove()` method doesn't delete an element based on a position, but rather on a value.

 TRAP Watch out when you use the `remove()` method. If you try to remove a value that isn't in a list, you'll generate an error.

Sorting the Scores

The scores in the list are in the exact order the user entered them. Normally, you want a high score list to be sorted with the highest scores at the top. To sort the scores, all the user has to do is enter 4:

```
# sort scores
elif choice == "4":
    scores.sort()
```

The `sort()` method sorts the elements in the list. This is great, except that with `sort()`, you end up with the list in ascending order, where the smallest values are first. But what I want is the largest numbers first. I need the reverse of this.

Reversing the Scores

Luckily, there's a reverse() method for lists. It just reverses the list order. This is exactly what I need so that the highest scores will be at the beginning of the list. Before the elif block ends, I use the reverse() method, like so:

```
scores.reverse()    # want the highest number first
```

Now, all the scores are in order, from largest to smallest. Perfect.

Dealing with an Invalid Choice

If the user enters a number that isn't a valid choice, the else clause catches it. The program lets the user know that the choice isn't understood.

```
# some unknown choice
else:
    print "Sorry, but", choice, "isn't a valid choice."
```

Waiting for the User

After the user enters 0 to exit, the loop ends. As always, the program waits for the user:

```
raw_input("\n\nPress the enter key to exit.")
```

You've seen a bunch of useful list methods in action. To get a summary of these methods (plus a few more), take a look at Table 5.1.

TABLE 5.1   SELECTED LIST METHODS

Method	Description
append(*value*)	Adds *value* to end of a list.
sort()	Sorts the elements, smallest value first.
reverse()	Reverses the order of a list.
count(*value*)	Returns the number of occurrences of *value*.
index(*value*)	Returns the first position number where *value* occurs.
insert(*i*, *value*)	Inserts *value* at position *i*.
pop([*i*])	Returns value at position *i* and removes value from the list. Providing the position number *i* is optional. Without it, the last element in the list is removed and returned.
remove(*value*)	Removes the first occurrence of *value* from the list.

Understanding When to Use Tuples Instead of Lists

At this point, you may be thinking, "Why use tuples at all?" It's true that lists can do everything tuples can, plus more. But don't be so quick to dismiss tuples. There is a place for them in your Python programming world. There are a few occasions where tuples make more sense than lists.

- Tuples are faster than lists. Because the computer knows they won't change, tuples can be stored in a way that makes using them faster than using lists. For simple programs, this speed difference won't matter, but in more complex applications with very large sequences of information, it could.

- Tuples' immutability makes them perfect for creating constants because they can't change. Using tuples can add a level of safety and clarity to your code.

- Sometimes tuples are required. In some cases, Python requires immutable values. Okay, you haven't actually seen any of those cases yet, but there is a common situation you'll see when you learn about dictionaries, later in this chapter. Dictionaries require immutable types, so tuples will be essential when creating some kinds of dictionaries.

But, because lists are so flexible, you're probably best off using them rather than tuples the majority of the time.

Using Nested Sequences

Before, I said that lists or tuples can be sequences of anything. If that's true, then lists can contain other lists or tuples, and tuples can contain other tuples or lists. Well, they can, and when they do, they're called *nested sequences*. Nested sequences are sequences inside other sequences. Nested sequences are a great way to organize more complex collections of information.

Although the term sounds like another cryptic piece of computer jargon, I bet you create and use nested sequences all the time. Let me give you an example. Say you're making a holiday shopping list. You start by making a list of names. Under each name, you list a few possible gifts. Well, you've just created a nested sequence: You have a list of names and each name represents a list of gifts. That's all there is to it.

Introducing the High Scores 2.0 Program

The last program, High Scores, uses only scores. But most high score lists store a name along with a score. That's what this new version does. It also has a few other improvements. It automatically sorts the scores and even limits the list to just the top five. Figure 5.7 shows a sample run.

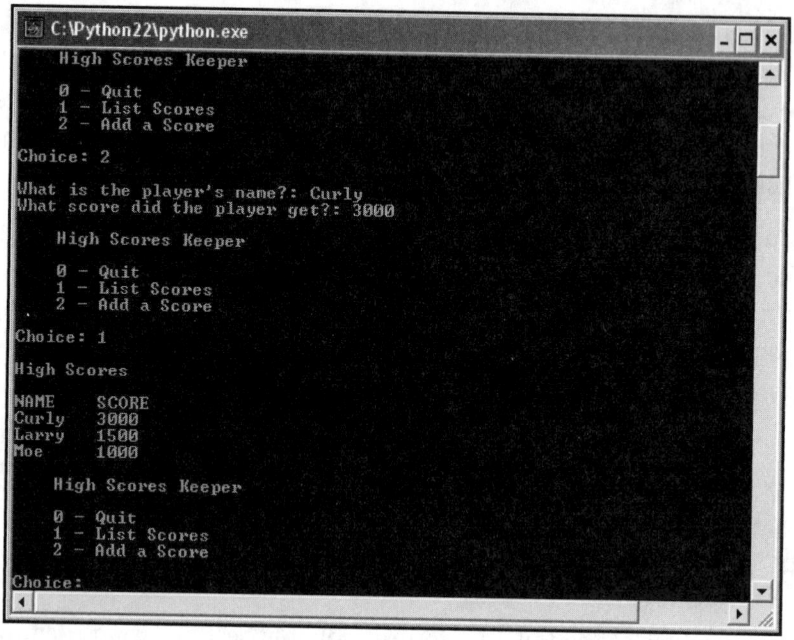

FIGURE 5.7

The new and improved version of High Scores stores a name with a score through nested sequences.

Creating Nested Sequences

You can create a nested list or tuple like always: Type each element, followed by a comma. The difference with nested sequences is that you include entire lists or tuples as elements. Here's an example:

```
>>> nested = ["first", ("second", "third"), ["fourth", "fifth", "sixth"]]
>>> print nested
['first', ('second', 'third'), ['fourth', 'fifth', 'sixth']]
```

So, although you see six strings here, `nested` has only three elements. The first element is the string `"first"`, the second element is the tuple (`"second"`, `"third"`), and the third element is the list [`"fourth"`, `"fifth"`, `"sixth"`].

While you can create a list or tuple with any number of lists and tuples, useful nested sequences often have a consistent pattern. Take a look at the next example:

```
>>> scores = [("Moe", 1000), ("Larry", 1500), ("Curly", 3000)]
>>> print scores
[('Moe', 1000), ('Larry', 1500), ('Curly', 3000)]
```

`scores` is a list with three elements. Each element is a tuple. Each tuple has exactly two elements, a string and a number.

This sequence, by the way, represents a high-score table with names and scores (like a real high score table should have!). In this particular instance, Moe got a score of 1,000; Larry got 1,500; and Curly got a high score of 3,000.

 TRAP Although you can create nested sequences inside nested sequences many times over, as in the following example, this usually isn't a good idea.

```
nested = ("deep", ("deeper", ("deepest", "still deepest")))
```

Things can get confusing quickly. Even experienced programmers rarely use sequences more than a level or two deep. For most programs you'll write, one level of nesting (like the scores list you just saw) is really all you'll need.

Accessing Nested Elements

You access elements of a nested sequence just like any other sequence, through indexing:

```
>>> scores = [("Moe", 1000), ("Larry", 1500), ("Curly", 3000)]
>>> print scores[0]
('Moe', 1000)
>>> print scores[1]
('Larry', 1500)
>>> print scores[2]
('Curly', 3000)
```

Each element is a tuple, so that's exactly what you get when you access one. But what if you want to access one of the elements of one of the tuples? One way is to assign the tuple to a variable and index it, as in:

```
>>> a_score = scores[2]
>>> print a_score
('Curly', 3000)
>>> print a_score[0]
Curly
```

But there's a direct way to access "Curly" right from scores:

```
>>> print scores[2][0]
Curly
```

By supplying two indices with scores[2][0], you're telling the computer to go get the element from scores at position 2 (which is ("Curly", 3000)) and then, from that, to get the element at position 0 (which is "Curly"). You can use this kind of multiple indexing with nested sequences to get directly to a nested element.

Unpacking a Sequence

If you know how many elements are in a sequence, you can assign each to its own variable in a single line of code:

```
>>> name, score = ("Shemp", 175)
>>> print name
Shemp
>>> print score
175
```

This is called *unpacking* and works with any sequence type. Just remember to use the same number of variables as elements in the sequence, because otherwise you'll generate an error.

Setting Up the Program

Just as in the original High Scores program, I set up the variables and `while` loop. As before, if the user enters 0, the computer prints `"Good-bye."`

```
# High Scores 2.0
# Demonstrates nested sequences

scores = []

choice = None
while choice != "0":

    print \
    """
    High Scores Keeper

    0 - Quit
    1 - List Scores
    2 - Add a Score
    """

    choice = raw_input("Choice: ")
    print
    # exit
    if choice == "0":
        print "Good-bye."
```

Displaying the Scores by Accessing Nested Tuples

If the user enters 1, the computer goes through each element in scores and unpacks the score and name into the variables score and name. Then the computer prints them out.

```
# display high-score table
elif choice == "1":
    print "High Scores\n"
    print "NAME\tSCORE"
    for entry in scores:
        score, name = entry
        print name, "\t", score
```

Adding a Score by Appending a Nested Tuple

If the user enters 2, the computer lets the user enter a new score and name. With these two values, the computer creates a tuple, entry. I chose to store the score first in this tuple because I wanted the entries to be sorted by score, then name. Next, the computer appends this new high-score entry to the list. The computer sorts the list and reverses it so that the highest scores are first. The final statement slices and assigns the list so that only the top five scores are kept.

```
# add a score
elif choice == "2":
    name = raw_input("What is the player's name?: ")
    score = int(raw_input("What score did the player get?: "))
    entry = (score, name)
    scores.append(entry)
    scores.sort()
    scores.reverse()        # want the highest number first
    scores = scores[:5]     # keep only top 5 scores
```

Dealing with an Invalid Choice

If the user enters something other than 0, 1, or 2, the else clause catches it. The program lets the user know that the choice wasn't understood.

```
# some unknown choice
else:
    print "Sorry, but", choice, "isn't a valid choice."
```

Waiting for the User

After the user enters 0 to exit, the loop ends and the program waits for the user:

```
raw_input("\n\nPress the enter key to exit.")
```

UNDERSTANDING SHARED REFERENCES

In Chapter 2, you learned that a variable refers to a value. This means that, technically, a variable doesn't store a copy of a value, but just refers to the place in your computer's memory where the value is stored. For example, language = "Python" stores the string "Python" in your computer's memory somewhere and then creates the variable language, which refers to that place in memory. Take a look at Figure 5.8 for a visual representation.

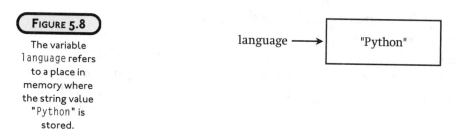

FIGURE 5.8

The variable language refers to a place in memory where the string value "Python" is stored.

To say the variable language stores the string "Python", like a piece of Tupperware stores a chicken leg, is not accurate. In some programming languages, this might be a good analogy, but not in Python. A better way to think about it is like this: A variable refers to a value the same way a person's name refers to a person. It would be wrong (and silly) to say that a person's name "stores" the person. Using a person's name, you can get to a person. Using a variable name, you can get to a value.

So what does all this mean? Well, for immutable values that you've been using, such as numbers, strings, and tuples, it doesn't mean much. But it does mean something for mutable values, like lists. When several variables refer to the same mutable value, they share the same reference. They all refer to the one single copy of that value. And a change to the value through one of the variables results in a change for all the variables, since there is only one shared copy to begin with.

Here's an example to show how this works. Suppose that I'm throwing a hip, happening party with my friends and dignitaries from around the world. (Hey, this is my book. I can make up any example I want.) Different people at the party call me by different names, even though I'm only one person. Let's say that a friend calls me "Mike," a dignitary calls me "Mr. Dawson," and my Pulitzer Prize–winning, supermodel girlfriend, just back from her literacy fundraising world-tour (again, my book, my fictional girlfriend), calls me "Honey." So, all three people refer to me with different names. This is the same way that three variables could all refer to the same list. Here's the beginning of an interactive session to show you what I mean:

```
>>> mike = ["khakis", "dress shirt", "jacket"]
>>> mr_dawson = mike
>>> honey = mike
>>> print mike
['khakis', 'dress shirt', 'jacket']
>>> print mr_dawson
['khakis', 'dress shirt', 'jacket']
>>> print honey
['khakis', 'dress shirt', 'jacket']
```

So, all three variables, mike, mr_dawson, and honey, refer to the same, single list, representing me (or at least what I'm wearing at this party). Figure 5.9 helps drive this idea home.

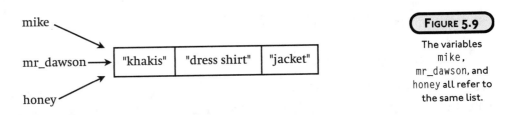

FIGURE 5.9

The variables mike, mr_dawson, and honey all refer to the same list.

This means that a change to the list using any of these three variables will change the list they all refer to. Back at the party, let's say that my girlfriend gets my attention by calling "Honey." She asks me to change my jacket for a red sweater she knitted (yes, she knits, too). I, of course, do what she asks. In my interactive session, this could be expressed as follows:

```
>>> honey[2] = "red sweater"
>>> print honey
['khakis', 'dress shirt', 'red sweater']
```

The results are what you would expect. The element in position number 2 of the list referred to by honey is no longer "jacket", but is now "red sweater".

Now, at the party, if a friend were to get my attention by calling "Mike" or a dignitary were to call me over with "Mr. Dawson," both would see me in my red sweater, even though neither had anything to do with me changing my clothes. The same is true in Python. Even though I changed the value of the element in position number 2 by using the variable honey, that change is reflected by any variable that refers to this list. So, to continue my interactive session:

```
>>> print mike
['khakis', 'dress shirt', 'red sweater']
>>> print mr_dawson
['khakis', 'dress shirt', 'red sweater']
```

The element in position number 2 of the list referred to by mike and mr_dawson is "red sweater". It has to be since there's only one list.

So, the moral of this story is: Be aware of shared references when using mutable values. If you change the value through one variable, it will be changed for all.

However, you can avoid this effect if you make a copy of a list, through slicing. For example:

```
>>> mike = ["khakis", "dress shirt", "jacket"]
>>> honey = mike[:]
>>> honey[2] = "red sweater"
>>> print honey
['khakis', 'dress shirt', 'red sweater']
>>> print mike
['khakis', 'dress shirt', 'jacket']
```

Here, honey is assigned a copy of mike. honey does not refer to the same list. Instead, it refers to a copy. So, a change to honey has no effect on mike. It's like I've been cloned. Now, my girlfriend is dressing my clone in a red sweater, while the original me is still in a jacket. Okay, this party is getting pretty weird with my clone walking around in a red sweater that my fictional girlfriend knitted for me, so I think it's time to end this bizarre yet useful analogy.

One last thing to remember is that sometimes you'll want this shared-reference effect, while other times you won't. Now that you understand how it works, you can control it.

USING DICTIONARIES

By now you probably realize that programmers love to organize information. You saw that lists and tuples let you organize things into sequences. Well, dictionaries let you organize information too, but in a different way. With a dictionary, you don't store information in a sequence; instead, you store it in pairs. It's a lot like an actual dictionary, where each entry is a pair: a word and its definition. When you look up a word, you get its definition. Python dictionaries work the same way: You look up a key and get its *value*.

Introducing the Geek Translator Program

The high-tech world has created many things that impact our lives, including a culture of its own. As the result of technology, new words and concepts have been born. There's a brand-new kind of slang out there, and the Geek Translator is here to help you understand the technophile in your life. The program creates a dictionary with geek terms and definitions. The program not only lets the user look up a term, but also add a term, replace a definition, and delete a term. Figure 5.10 illustrates the program.

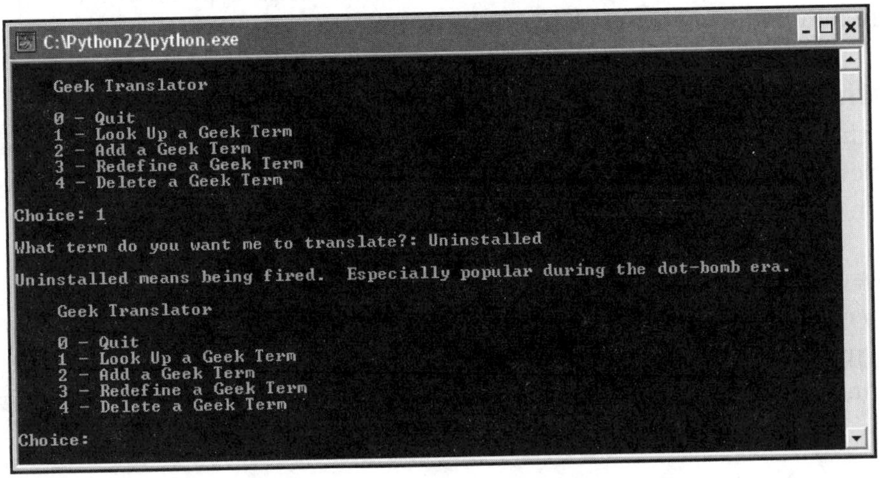

FIGURE 5.10

So "uninstalled" means fired. I was totally 404 on that.

Creating Dictionaries

The first thing I did in the program was create a dictionary of terms and definitions. The geek terms are on the left, and their definitions are on the right.

```
# Geek Translator
# Demonstrates using dictionaries

geek = {"404" : "clueless. From the web error message 404, meaning page not found.",
    "Googling" : "searching the Internet for background information on a person.",
    "Keyboard Plaque" : "the collection of debris found in computer keyboards.",
    "Link Rot" : "the process by which web page links become obsolete.",
    "Percussive Maintenance" :
    "the act of striking an electronic device to make it work.",
    "Uninstalled" : "being fired. Especially popular during the dot-bomb era."}
```

This code creates a dictionary named geek. It consists of six pairs, called *items*. As an example, one of the items is "Keyboard Plaque" : "the collection of debris found in computer keyboards." Each item is made up of a key and a value. The keys are on the left side of the colons. The values are on the right. So, "Keyboard Plaque" is a key, and its value is "the collection of debris found in computer keyboards." The key is literally the "key" to getting the value. That means you could use the key "Keyboard Plaque" to get its value "the collection of debris found in computer keyboards."

To create your own dictionary, follow the pattern I used. Type a key, followed by a colon, followed by the key's value. Use commas to separate all of the key-value pairs, and surround the whole thing with curly brackets. Like tuples and lists, you can either type the whole thing on one line or use separate lines after any of the commas.

Accessing Dictionary Values

The most common thing you'll do with a dictionary is use a key to get its value. There are a few different ways you can do this. I'll show you an example of each in this section, using the interactive interpreter.

Using a Key to Retrieve a Value

The simplest way to retrieve a value from a dictionary is by directly accessing it with a key. To get a key's value, just put the key in brackets, following the name of the dictionary. Here's an interactive session to show you what I mean. (Assume that I've already defined the dictionary geek.)

```
>>> geek["404"]
'clueless. From the web error message 404, meaning page not found.'
>>> geek["Link Rot"]
'the process by which web page links become obsolete.'
```

This looks similar to indexing a sequence, but there's an important difference. When you index a sequence, you use a position number. When you look up a value in a dictionary, you use a key. This is the only direct way to retrieve a value from a dictionary. In fact, dictionaries don't have position numbers at all.

One thing that sometimes trips up beginning programmers is that a value can't be used to get a key in a dictionary. That would be like trying to use a definition to find a word in a real-life dictionary. Real-life dictionaries just aren't set up for that kind of thing, and neither are Python dictionaries. So remember, it's give a key and get a value, only.

TRAP If you try to get a value from a dictionary by directly accessing it with a key that doesn't exist, you'll generate an error:

```
>>> geek["Dancing Baloney"]
Traceback (most recent call last):
    File "<pyshell#3>", line 1, in ?
        geek["Dancing Baloney"]
KeyError: Dancing Baloney
```

Since "Dancing Baloney" isn't a key in the dictionary, this results in an error. ("Dancing Baloney," by the way, means animated graphics and other visual effects that have no substantive value, often used by Web designers to impress clients.)

Testing for a Key with the in Operator Before Retrieving a Value

Because using a nonexistent key can lead to an error, it's usually best not to directly access a dictionary without taking some precautions. One thing you can do is check to see whether a key exists before attempting to retrieve its value. You can check for the existence of a key with the in operator:

```
>>> if "Dancing Baloney" in geek:
        print "I know what Dancing Baloney is."
    else:
        print "I have no idea what Dancing Baloney is."


I have no idea what Dancing Baloney is.
```

Because the dictionary doesn't contain "Dancing Baloney" as a key, the condition "Dancing Baloney" in geek is false. So, the computer says it doesn't know what it is.

You use the in operator with dictionaries much the same way you've used it with lists and tuples. You type the value you're checking for, followed by in, followed by the dictionary. This creates a condition. The condition is true if the key is in the dictionary; otherwise, it's false. This is a handy thing to do before trying to get a value. But remember, in only checks for keys; it can't check for values used this way.

TRAP The in operator didn't work with dictionaries before Python 2.2. If you're using a version of Python before that, you can use the dictionary method has_key() to test for a key in a dictionary. Check out Table 5.2, later in the chapter, for a description of this dictionary method and a few others.

Using the get() Method to Retrieve a Value

There's another way to retrieve a value from a dictionary. You can use the dictionary method get(). The method has a built-in safety net for handling situations where you ask for a value of a key that doesn't exist. If the key doesn't exist, the method returns a default value, which you can define. Take a look at another attempt:

```
>>> print geek.get("Dancing Baloney", "I have no idea.")
I have no idea.
```

By using the get() method here, I was guaranteed to get a value back. If this term was in the dictionary as a key, then I'd get its definition. Since it wasn't, I got back the default value that I defined, the string "I have no idea."

To use the get() method, all you have to do is supply the key you're looking for followed by an optional default value. If the key is in the dictionary, you get its value. If the key isn't in the dictionary, you get the default value. But here's the twist: If you don't supply a default value (it's your option), then you get back None. Here's an example I created without providing a default value:

```
>>> print geek.get("Dancing Baloney")
None
```

Setting Up the Program

Time to get back to the code for the Geek Translator program. After I created the geek dictionary, I implemented the menu system you've seen before, this time with five choices. Like before, if the user chooses 0, the computer says good-bye.

```
choice = None
while choice != "0":

    print \
    """

    Geek Translator

    0 - Quit
    1 - Look Up a Geek Term
    2 - Add a Geek Term
    3 - Redefine a Geek Term
    4 - Delete a Geek Term
    """
```

```
choice = raw_input("Choice: ")
print

# exit
if choice == "0":
    print "Good-bye."
```

Getting a Value

If the user enters 1, the next section asks for a term to look up. The computer checks to see whether the term is in the dictionary. If it is, the program accesses the dictionary, using the term as the key, gets its definition, and prints it out. If the term is not in the dictionary, the computer informs the user.

```
# get a definition
elif choice == "1":
    term = raw_input("What term do you want me to translate?: ")
    if term in geek:
        definition = geek[term]
        print "\n", term, "means", definition
    else:
        print "\nSorry, I don't know", term
```

Adding a Key-Value Pair

Dictionaries are mutable, so you can modify them. If the user enters 2, the next section adds a new term to the dictionary:

```
# add a term-definition pair
elif choice == "2":
    term = raw_input("What term do you want me to add?: ")
    if term not in geek:
        definition = raw_input("What's the definition?: ")
        geek[term] = definition
        print "\n", term, "has been added."
    else:
        print "\nThat term already exists! Try redefining it."
```

The computer asks the user for the new term to add. If the term is not already in the dictionary, the computer gets the definition and adds the pair through the line:

```
geek[term] = definition
```

This creates a new item in geek. The term is the key and the definition is its value. This is exactly how you assign a new item to a dictionary. You use the dictionary, followed by the key, in square brackets, followed by the assignment operator, followed by the key's value.

I wrote the program so that the computer refuses to add a term if it's already in the dictionary. This is a safety measure I created to ensure that the user doesn't accidentally overwrite an existing term. If the user really wants to redefine an existing term, he or she should choose menu option 3.

TRICK A dash of pessimism is a good thing, at least when you're programming. As you saw here, I assumed that the user might try to add a new term without realizing it's already in the dictionary. If I hadn't checked for this, a user could overwrite a term without realizing it. When you're writing your own programs, try to think of things that could go wrong, then try to make sure your program can deal with them. So be a pessimist, just a little bit.

Replacing a Key-Value Pair

If the user enters 3, then the next section replaces an existing key-value pair:

```
# redefine an existing term
elif choice == "3":
    term = raw_input("What term do you want me to redefine?: ")
    if term in geek:
        definition = raw_input("What's the new definition?: ")
        geek[term] = definition
        print "\n", term, "has been redefined."
    else:
        print "\nThat term doesn't exist! Try adding it."
```

To replace a key-value pair, I used the exact same line of code that I used for adding a new pair:

```
geek[term] = definition
```

Python replaces the current value (the definition) with the new one.

TRAP If you assign a value to a dictionary using a key that already exists, Python replaces the current value without complaint. So you have to watch out, because you might overwrite the value of an existing key without realizing it.

Deleting a Key-Value Pair

If the user enters 4, then this elif block runs:

```
# delete a term-definition pair
elif choice == "4":
    term = raw_input("What term do you want me to delete?: ")
    if term in geek:
        del geek[term]
        print "\nOkay, I deleted", term
    else:
        print "\nI can't do that!", term, "doesn't exist in the dictionary."
```

The program asks the user for the geek term to delete. Next, the program checks to see whether the term is actually in the dictionary, with the in operator. If it is, the item is deleted with:

```
del geek[term]
```

This deletes the item with the key term from the dictionary geek. You can delete any item in a dictionary this way. Just put del in front of the dictionary followed by the key of the item you wish to delete in square brackets.

If the geek term doesn't exist in the first place, the else clause executes and the computer lets the user know.

TRAP Trying to delete a dictionary item through a key that doesn't exist will give you an error. It's a smart move to be sure the key you're using exists.

Wrapping Up the Program

The final else clause lets the user know that he or she entered an invalid choice:

```
# some unknown choice
else:
    print "\nSorry, but", choice, "isn't a valid choice."

raw_input("\n\nPress the enter key to exit.")
```

TABLE 5.2	SELECTED DICTIONARY METHODS
Method	**Description**
has_key(*key*)	Returns True if *key* is in the dictionary as a key. Otherwise, it returns False.
get(*key*,[*default*])	Returns the value of *key*. If *key* doesn't exist, then the optional *default* is returned. If *key* doesn't exist and *default* isn't specified, then None is returned.
keys()	Returns a list of all the keys in a dictionary.
values()	Returns a list of all the values in a dictionary.
items()	Returns a list of all the items in a dictionary. Each item is a two-element tuple, where the first element is a key and the second element is the key's value.

Understanding Dictionary Requirements

There are a few things you should keep in mind when creating dictionaries:

- A dictionary can't contain multiple items with the same key. Think again about a real dictionary. It becomes pretty meaningless if you can keep adding the same word with totally new definitions whenever you want.

- A key has to be immutable. It can be a string, a number, or a tuple, which gives you lots of possibilities. A key has to be immutable because, if it weren't, you could sneak into a dictionary later and change its keys, possibly ending up with two identical keys. And you just learned you can't have that!

- Values don't have to be unique. Also, values can be immutable. They can be anything you want.

There's even more you can do with dictionaries. Table 5.2 summarizes some useful methods that can help you get more out of this new type.

BACK TO THE HANGMAN GAME

By putting together all you've learned so far, you can create the Hangman game presented at the beginning of the chapter. This program is much longer than anything you've seen, but don't be intimidated by its size. The code isn't much more complex than that of the other game projects you've worked through. The biggest part of the program is just my modest ASCII art, the eight versions of the stick figured being hanged. The real meat of the program is not much more than a screenful of code.

Setting Up the Program

First things first. As always, I started with opening comments, explaining the program. Next, I imported the `random` module. I'll need the module to pick a random word from a sequence.

```
# Hangman Game
#
# The classic game of Hangman. The computer picks a random word
# and the player tries to guess it, one letter at a time. If the player
# can't guess the word in time, the little stick figure gets hanged.



# imports
import random
```

Creating Constants

Though there are several screenfuls of code in this next section, I only create three constants in all that programming. First, I created the biggest tuple you've seen. It's really just a sequence of eight elements, but each element is a triple-quoted string that spans 12 lines.

Each string is a representation of the gallows where the stick figure is being hanged. Each subsequent string shows a more complete figure. Each time the player guesses incorrectly, the next string is displayed. By the eighth entry, the image is complete and the figure is a goner. If this final string is displayed, the player has lost and the game is over. I assigned this tuple to `HANGMAN`, a variable name in all caps, because I'll be using it as a constant.

```
# constants
HANGMAN = (
"""

 ----
 |   |
 |
 |
 |
 |
 |
 |

----------
""",
```

```
"""

    - - - -
   |    |
   |    0
   |
   |
   |
   |
   |
- - - - - - - - - -
""",
"""

    - - - -
   |    |
   |    0
   |   -+-
   |
   |
   |
   |
- - - - - - - - - -
""",
"""

    - - - -
   |    |
   |    0
   |  /-+-
   |
   |
   |
   |
- - - - - - - - - -
""",
```

```
    """
        - - - -
        |   |
        |   0
        | /-+-/
        |
        |
        |
        |
- - - - - - - - - -
    """,
    """
        - - - -
        |   |
        |   0
        | /-+-/
        |   |
        |
        |
        |
- - - - - - - - - -
    """,
    """
        - - - -
        |   |
        |   0
        | /-+-/
        |   |
        |   |
        | |
        | |
        |
- - - - - - - - - -
    """,
```

```
"""

     - - - -
    |    |
    |    0
    | /-+-/
    |    |
    |    |
    |  | |  |
    |  | |  |
    |
 - - - - - - - - - -
""")
```

Next, I created a constant to represent the maximum number of wrong guesses a player can make before the game is over:

```
MAX_WRONG = len(HANGMAN) - 1
```

The maximum number of incorrect guesses is one less than the length of HANGMAN. This is because the first image, of the empty gallows, is displayed even before the player makes a first guess. So although there are eight images in HANGMAN, the player only gets seven wrong guesses before the game is over.

Finally, I created a tuple containing all of the possible words that the computer can pick from for the player to guess. Feel free to modify the program and make up your own group of words.

```
WORDS = ("OVERUSED", "CLAM", "GUAM", "PUCK", "TAFFETA", "PYTHON")
```

Initializing the Variables

Next, I initialized the variables. I used the random.choice() function to pick a random word from the list of possible words. I assigned this secret word to the variable word.

```
# initialize variables
word = random.choice(WORDS)   # the word to be guessed
```

I created another string, so_far, to represent what the player has guessed so far in the game. The string starts out as just a series of dashes, one for each letter in the word. When the player correctly guesses a letter, the dashes in the positions of that letter are replaced with the letter itself.

```
so_far = "-" * len(word)    # one dash for each letter in word to be guessed
```

I created wrong and assigned it the number 0. wrong keeps track of the number of wrong guesses the player makes.

```
wrong = 0    # number of wrong guesses player has made
```

I created an empty list, used to contain all the letters the player has guessed:

```
used = []  # letters already guessed
```

Creating the Main Loop

I created a loop that continues until either the player has guessed too many wrong letters or the player has guessed all the letters in the word:

```
print "Welcome to Hangman. Good luck!"

while wrong < MAX_WRONG and so_far != word:
    print HANGMAN[wrong]
    print "\nYou've used the following letters:\n", used
    print "\nSo far, the word is:\n", so_far
```

Next, I print the current stick figure, based on the number of wrong guesses the player has made. The more wrong guesses the player has made, the closer the stick figure is to being done in. After that, I display the list of letters that the player has used in this game. And then I show what the partially guessed word looks like so far.

Getting the Player's Guess

I get the player's guess and convert it to uppercase so that it can be found in the secret word (which is in all caps). After that, I make sure that the player hasn't already used this letter. If the player has already guessed this letter, then I make the player enter a new character until he or she enters one that hasn't been used yet. Once the player enters a valid guess, I convert the guess to uppercase and add it to the list of used letters.

```
    guess = raw_input("\n\nEnter your guess: ")
    guess = guess.upper()

    while guess in used:
        print "You've already guessed the letter:", guess
        guess = raw_input("Enter your guess: ")
        guess = guess.upper()

    used.append(guess)
```

Checking the Guess

Next, I check to see whether the guess is in the secret word. If it is, I let the player know. Then I go about creating a new version of so_far to include this new letter in all the places where the letter is in the secret word.

```
if guess in word:
    print "\nYes!", guess, "is in the word!"

    # create a new so_far to include guess
    new = ""
    for i in range(len(word)):
        if guess == word[i]:
            new += guess
        else:
            new += so_far[i]
    so_far = new
```

If the player's guess isn't in the word, then I let the player know and increase the number of wrong guesses by one.

```
else:
    print "\nSorry,", guess, "isn't in the word."
    wrong += 1
```

Ending the Game

At this point, the game is over. If the number of wrong guesses has reached the maximum, the player has lost. In that case, I print the final image of the stick figure. Otherwise, I congratulate the player. In either case, I let the player know what the secret word was.

```
if wrong == MAX_WRONG:
    print HANGMAN[wrong]
    print "\nYou've been hanged!"
else:
    print "\nYou guessed it!"

print "\nThe word was", word

raw_input("\n\nPress the enter key to exit.")
```

SUMMARY

- A list is a mutable sequence of any type.
- You can add or remove list elements or slices.
- The remove() list method removes the first occurrence of a value from a list.
- The sort() list method sorts the elements of a list, in ascending order by default.
- The reverse() list method reverses the order of list elements.
- A nested sequence is a sequence inside another sequence.
- Sequence unpacking is the process of automatically accessing each element of a sequence.
- A shared reference is a reference to an object that has at least one other reference to it.
- A dictionary is a mutable collection of key-value pairs.
- In a dictionary, an item is a key-value pair.
- In a dictionary, a key is an object used to look up another object.
- In a dictionary, a value is an object that is returned when its corresponding key is looked up.
- The dictionary get() method takes a key and returns its corresponding value. If the key isn't found, the method returns a default value.
- The in operator can be used to test if a dictionary contains a specific key.
- A dictionary can't contain multiple items with the same key.
- A dictionary can contain multiple items with the same value.
- Dictionary keys must be immutable.
- Dictionary values can be mutable.

REVIEW QUESTIONS

1. How is a list different from a tuple?
2. Which is better, a list or a tuple?
3. How does object mutability help a programmer?
4. How can object mutability be problematic for a programmer?
5. What happens to a list when you assign a single value to a slice of more than one value?
6. Can you add an element to a list by assigning a value to a non-existent position number?
7. Is it possible to use the list remove() method and generate an error?
8. Can the list remove() method create a gap in a list?

9. Why don't tuples have methods like `remove()` and `append()`?
10. How do you create a nested sequence?
11. What are nested sequences useful for?
12. How deeply should you nest sequences?
13. Do variables store the values you assign to them?
14. How are Python dictionaries like actual dictionaries?
15. Why must dictionary keys be unique?
16. Do dictionary values have to be unique?
17. Why must dictionary keys be immutable?
18. If you want to use a sequence as a dictionary key, what type might you use?
19. What happens if you try to index a dictionary with a non-existent key?
20. What happens if you assign a new value to a dictionary using a key that already exists?

PROJECTS

1. Write a program that gets the names of a player's top-five favorite games. Your program should store the names in a list. Then, the program should display the five game names in the list.

2. Write a program that creates a dictionary to represent the possible exits from a location in an adventure game. The dictionary should represent the following:

   - north leads to the kitchen

   - south leads to the dining room

   - east leads to the entry

   - west leads to the living room

   Your program should prompt the player for a direction and respond with the location that is off in that direction. So, if the player enters `north`, your program should respond with `That direction leads to the kitchen`. If the player enters an invalid direction, your program should ignore the input and ask for another direction. The program should continue to ask for a direction until the player enters `quit`.

3. Improve the Word Jumble game presented in Chapter 4 so that each word is paired with a hint. If the player enters `hint`, then the program should display the corresponding hint. Use a nested sequence to store the words and hints.

4. Write a program in which you manually sort a list of integers from 0 to 9. You can use the following code at the top of your program to generate and randomize the list `unordered`:

```
import random

unordered = range(10)
random.shuffle(unordered)
```

You can use an established method to sort the list called the Selection Sort. Here's the pseudocode for an implementation of the Selection Sort algorithm that removes elements from an original, unordered list and appends them to a new, ordered list:

Create an empty list to hold the ordered elements
While there are still elements in the unordered list
   Set a variable, lowest, to the first element in the unordered list
   For each element in the unordered list
      If the element is lower than lowest
         Assign the value of that element to lowest
   Append lowest to the ordered list
   Remove lowest from the unordered list

An important point to remember is that Python's implementation of list sorting is far more efficient than this implementation of the Selection Sort. So, when you want to sort a list (other than for this project), you should use the built-in `sort()` list method.

5. Write a program that creates a dictionary of son-father pairs—you can use celebrities, fictional characters, or even historical figures for fun. Your program should present the user a menu with three options. The following is an example:

Father Finder

```
0 - Quit
1 - Find a Father
2 - Find a Grandfather
```

- Option 0 should end the program.

- Option 1 should prompt the user for the name of a son. If the dictionary contains the son-father pair, the program should display the father. Otherwise, the program should tell the user it doesn't know who the father is.

- Option 2 should prompt the user for the name of a grandson. If the dictionary contains enough information, the program should display the grandson's grandfather. Otherwise, the program should tell the user it doesn't know who the grandfather is.

The dictionary you create should include several generations so that a grandfather can be found given the name of a grandson.

FUNCTIONS: THE TIC-TAC-TOE GAME

Every program you've written so far has been one large, continuous series of instructions. Once your programs reach a certain size or level of complexity, it becomes hard to work with them this way. Fortunately, there are ways to break up big programs into smaller, manageable chunks of code. In this chapter, you learn one way of doing this by creating your own functions. Specifically, in this chapter, you'll learn to do the following:

- Write your own functions
- Accept values into your functions through parameters
- Return information from your functions through return values
- Work with global variables and constants
- Create a computer opponent that plays a strategy game

INTRODUCING THE TIC-TAC-TOE GAME

In this chapter's final game program, you'll learn how to create a computer opponent using a dash of artificial intelligence (AI). In the game, the player and computer square off in a high-stakes, human-machine showdown of Tic-Tac-Toe. The computer plays a formidable, though not perfect, game, and comes with enough attitude to make any match fun. Figures 6.1 through 6.3 illustrate the gameplay.

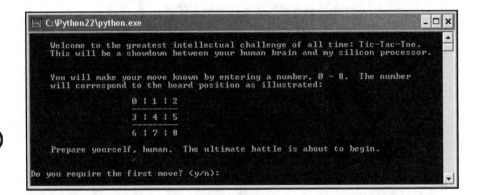

FIGURE 6.1

The computer is full of . . . confidence.

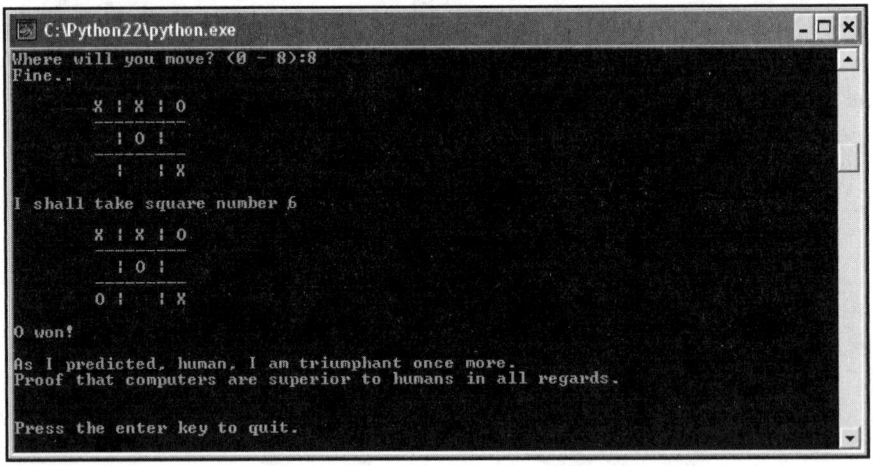

FIGURE 6.2

I did not see that coming. Even with simple programming techniques, the computer makes some pretty good moves.

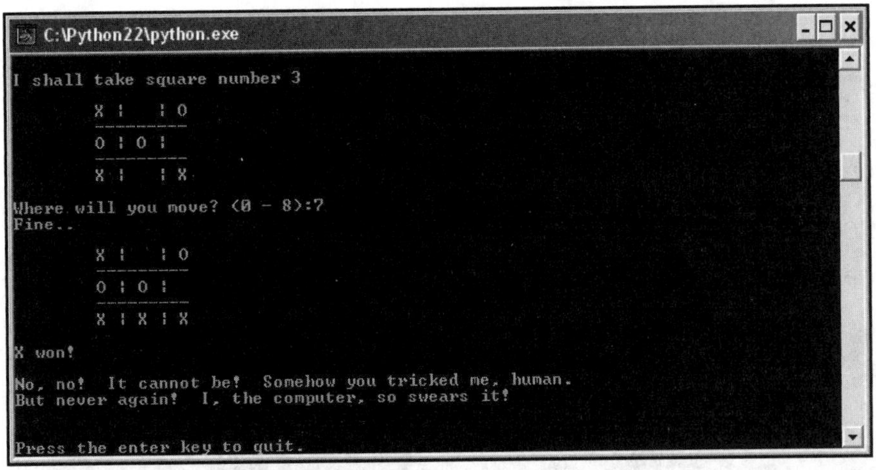

```
C:\Python22\python.exe                                    - □ ×
I shall take square number 3
        X !   ! O
       -----------
        O ! O !
       -----------
        X !   ! X
Where will you move? (0 - 8):7
Fine..
        X !   ! O
       -----------
        O ! O !
       -----------
        X ! X ! X
X won!
No, no! It cannot be!  Somehow you tricked me, human.
But never again!  I, the computer, so swears it!

Press the enter key to quit.
```

FIGURE 6.3

I found the computer's weakness and won this time.

CREATING FUNCTIONS

You've already seen several built-in functions in action, including len() and range(). Well, if these aren't enough for you, Python lets you create functions of your very own. Your functions work just like the ones that come standard with the language. They go off and perform a task and then return control to your program. Creating your own functions offers you many advantages. One of the biggest is that it allows you to break up your code into manageable, bite-sized chunks. Programs that are one long series of instructions with no logical breaks are hard to write, understand, and maintain. Programs that are made up of functions can be much easier to create and work with. Just like the functions you've already met, your new functions should do one job well.

Introducing the Instructions Program

From the screen shots of the Tic-Tac-Toe game, you can probably tell that the computer opponent has a little attitude. It comes across quite clearly in the instructions the computer gives before the game. You'll get a look at the code that produces those instructions in this next program, Instructions. The code is a little different than you might expect. That's because I created a function to display the instructions. I used that same function here in Instructions. Take a look at Figure 6.4 to see a sample run of the program.

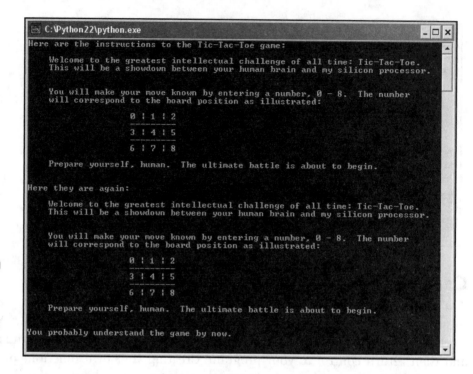

FIGURE 6.4

The instructions
are displayed each
time with just a
single line of code:
a call to a function
I created.

Here's the code:

```
# Instructions
# Demonstrates programmer-created functions

def instructions():
    """Display game instructions."""
    print \
    """
    Welcome to the greatest intellectual challenge of all time: Tic-Tac-Toe.
    This will be a showdown between your human brain and my silicon processor.

    You will make your move known by entering a number, 0 - 8. The number
    will correspond to the board position as illustrated:
```

```
      0 | 1 | 2
      -----------
      3 | 4 | 5
      -----------
      6 | 7 | 8


Prepare yourself, human. The ultimate battle is about to begin. \n
"""

# main
print "Here are the instructions to the Tic-Tac-Toe game:"
instructions()
print "Here they are again:"
instructions()
print "You probably understand the game by now."

raw_input("\n\nPress the enter key to exit.")
```

Defining a Function

I began the definition of my new function with a single line:

```
def instructions():
```

This line tells the computer that the block of code that follows is to be used together as the function instructions(). I'm basically naming this block of statements. This means that whenever I call the function instructions() in this program, the block of code runs.

This line and its block are a *function definition*. They define what the function does, but don't run the function. When the computer sees the function definition, it makes a note that this function exists so it can use it later. It won't actually run the function until it sees a function call for it, later in the program.

To define a function of your own, follow my example. Start with def, followed by your function name, followed by a pair of parentheses, followed by a colon, and then your indented block of statements. To name a function, follow the basic rules for naming variables. Also, try to use a name that conveys what the function produces or does.

Documenting a Function

Functions have a special mechanism that allows you to document them with what's called a *docstring* (or *documentation string*). I created the following docstring for `instructions()`:

```
"""Display game instructions."""
```

A docstring is typically a triple-quoted string and, if you use one, must be the first line in your function. For simple functions, you can do what I did here: write a single sentence that describes what the function does. Functions work just fine without docstrings, but using them is a good idea. It gets you in the habit of commenting your code and makes you describe the function's one well-defined job. Also, a function's docstring can pop up as interactive documentation while you type your call to it in IDLE.

Calling a Programmer-Created Function

Calling a programmer-created function works just like calling a built-in function. Use the name of the function followed by a set of parentheses. I called my new function several times, each time with the line:

```
instructions()
```

This tells the computer to go off and execute the function I defined earlier. So each time I call it, the computer prints the instructions to the game.

Understanding Abstraction

By writing and calling functions, you practice what's known as *abstraction*. Abstraction lets you think about the big picture without worrying about the details. So, in this program, I can just use the function `instructions()` without worrying about the details of displaying the text. All I have to do is call the function with one line of code, and it gets the job done.

You might be surprised where you find abstraction, but people use it all the time. For example, consider two employees at a fast-food place. If one tells the other that he just filled a #3, and "sized it," the other employee knows that the first employee took a customer's order, went to the heat lamps, grabbed a burger, went over to the deep fryer, filled their biggest cardboard container with French fries, went to the soda fountain, grabbed their biggest cup, filled it with soda, gave it all to the customer, took the customer's money, and gave the customer change. Not only would this version be a boring conversation, but it's unnecessary. Both employees understand what it means to fill a #3 and "size it." They don't have to concern themselves with all the details because they're using abstraction.

USING PARAMETERS AND RETURN VALUES

As you've seen with built-in functions, you can provide a function with values and get values back from it. With the len() function, for example, you provide a sequence, and the function returns its length. Your own functions can also receive and return values. This allows your functions to communicate with the rest of your program.

Introducing the Receive and Return Program

I created three functions in the program Receive and Return to show the various combinations of receiving and returning values. One function receives a value. The next function returns a value. And the last function both receives and returns a value. Take a look at Figure 6.5 to see exactly what happens as a result of the program.

FIGURE 6.5

Each function uses a parameter, a return value, or both to communicate with the main part of the program.

Here's the code:

```
# Receive and Return
# Demonstrates parameters and return values

def display(message):
    print message

def give_me_five():
    five = 5
    return five

def ask_yes_no(question):
    """Ask a yes or no question."""
    response = None
    while response not in ("y", "n"):
        response = raw_input(question).lower()
    return response
```

```
# main
display("Here's a message for you.\n")

number = give_me_five()
print "Here's what I got from give_me_five():", number

answer = ask_yes_no("\nPlease enter 'y' or 'n': ")

print "Thanks for entering:", answer

raw_input("\n\nPress the enter key to exit.")
```

Receiving Information through Parameters

The first function I defined, `display()`, receives a value and prints it. It receives a value through its *parameter*. Parameters are essentially variable names inside the parentheses of a function header:

```
def display(message):
```

Parameters catch the values sent to the function from a function call through its arguments. So here, when `display()` is called, `message` is assigned the value provided through the argument `"Here's a message for you.\n"`

In the main part of the program, I call `display()` with:

```
display("Here's a message for you.\n")
```

As a result, `message` gets the string `"Here's a message for you.\n"`. Then, the function runs. `message`, like any parameter, exists inside the function as a variable. So, the line

```
    print message
```

prints the string `"Here's a message for you.\n"`.

If I hadn't passed `message` a value, I would have generated an error. The function `display()` requires exactly one argument value.

Although `display()` has only one parameter, functions can have many. To define a function with multiple parameters, list them out, separated by commas.

Returning Information through Return Values

The next function I wrote, give_me_five(), returns a value. It returns a value through (believe it or not) the return statement:

```
return five
```

When this line runs, the function passes the value of five back to the part of the program that called it, and then ends. A function always ends after it hits a return statement.

It's up to the part of the program that called a function to catch the values it returns and do something with them. Here's the main part of the program, where I called the function:

```
number = give_me_five()
print "Here's what I got from give_me_five():", number
```

I set up a way to catch the return value of the function by assigning the result of the function call to number. So, when the function finishes, number gets the return value of give_me_five(), which is equal to 5. The next line prints number to show that it got the return value okay.

You can pass more than one value back from a function. Just list all the values you want to return, separated by commas.

TRAP Make sure to have enough variables to catch all the return values of a function. If you don't have the right number when you try to assign them, you'll generate an error.

Understanding Encapsulation

You might not see the need for return values when using your own functions. Why not just use the variable five back in the main part of the program? Because you can't. five doesn't exist outside of its function give_me_five(). In fact, no variable you create in a function, including its parameters, can be directly accessed outside its function. This is a good thing and it is called *encapsulation*. Encapsulation helps keep independent code truly separate by hiding or encapsulating the details. That's why you use parameters and return values: to communicate just the information that needs to be exchanged. Plus, you don't have to keep track of variables you create within a function in the rest of your program. As your programs get large, this is a great benefit.

Encapsulation might sound a lot like abstraction. That's because they're closely related. Encapsulation is a principle of abstraction. Abstraction saves you from worrying about the details. Encapsulation hides details from you. As an example, consider a remote control for a TV with volume up and down buttons. When you use a TV remote to change the volume, you're employing abstraction because you don't need to know what happens inside the TV for it to work. Now suppose the TV remote has 10 volume levels. You can get to them all through the remote, but you can't directly access them. That is, you can't get a specific volume number directly. You can only press the up volume and down volume buttons to eventually get to the level you want. The actual volume number is encapsulated and not directly available to you.

 HINT Don't worry if you don't totally get the subtle difference between abstraction and encapsulation right now. They're intertwined concepts, so it can be a little tricky. Plus, you'll get to see them in action again when you learn about software objects and object-oriented programming in Chapters 8 and 9.

Receiving and Returning Values in the Same Function

The final function I wrote, ask_yes_no(), receives one value and returns another. It receives a question and returns a response from the user, either "y" or "n". The function receives the question through its parameter:

```
def ask_yes_no(question):
```

question gets the value of the argument passed to the function. In this case, it's the string, "\nPlease enter 'y' or 'n': ". The next part of the function uses this string to prompt the user for a response:

```
response = None
while response not in ("y", "n"):
    response = raw_input(question).lower()
```

The while loop keeps asking the question until the user enters either y, Y, n, or N. The function always converts the user's entry to lowercase.

Finally, when the user has entered a valid response, the function sends a string back to the part of the program that called it with

```
return response
```

and the function ends.

In the main part of the program, the return value is assigned to answer and printed:

```
answer = ask_yes_no("\nPlease enter 'y' or 'n': ")
print "Thanks for entering:", answer
```

Understanding Software Reuse

Another great thing about functions is that they can easily be reused in other programs. For example, since asking the user a yes or no question is such a common thing to do, you could grab the ask_yes_no() function and use it in another program without doing any extra coding. This type of thing is called *software reuse*. So writing good functions not only saves you time and energy in your current project, but it can also save you effort in future ones!

One way to reuse functions you've written is to copy them into your new program. But there is a better way. You can create your own modules and import your functions into a new program, just like you import standard Python modules and use their functions. You'll learn how to create your own modules and import reusable code you've written in Chapter 9, in the section "Creating Modules."

IN THE REAL WORLD

It's always a waste of time to "reinvent the wheel," so software reuse, using existing software and other project elements in new projects, is a technique that business has taken to heart. Software reuse can do the following:

- **Increase company productivity.** By reusing code and other elements that already exist, companies can get their projects done with less effort.

- **Improve software quality.** If a company already has a tested piece of code, then it can use the code with the knowledge that it's bug-free.

- **Provide consistency across software products.** By using the same user interface, for example, companies can create new software that users feel comfortable with right out of the box.

- **Improve software performance.** Once a company has a good way of doing something through software, using it again not only saves the company the trouble of reinventing the wheel, but it also saves them from the possibility of reinventing a less efficient wheel.

USING KEYWORD ARGUMENTS AND DEFAULT PARAMETER VALUES

Passing values through arguments to parameters allows you to give information to a function. But so far, you've only seen the most basic way to do that. Python allows greater control and flexibility with the way you pass information, through default parameter values and keyword arguments.

Introducing the Birthday Wishes Program

The program Birthday Wishes, a sample run of which is pictured in Figure 6.6, sends birthday greetings through two very similar functions. The first function uses the type of parameters you saw in the last section, called *positional parameters*. The second version of the function uses *default parameter values*. The best way to appreciate the difference is to see examples of them in action.

```
C:\Python22\python.exe                                              _ □ ×
Happy birthday, Jackson !  I hear you're 1 today.
Happy birthday, 1 !  I hear you're Jackson today.
Happy birthday, Jackson !  I hear you're 1 today.
Happy birthday, Jackson !  I hear you're 1 today.
Happy birthday, Jackson !  I hear you're 1 today.
Happy birthday, Katherine !  I hear you're 1 today.
Happy birthday, Jackson !  I hear you're 12 today.
Happy birthday, Katherine !  I hear you're 12 today.
Happy birthday, Katherine !  I hear you're 12 today.

Press the enter key to exit.
```

FIGURE 6.6

Functions can be called in different ways with the flexibility of keyword arguments and default parameter values.

Here's the code for Birthday Wishes:

```python
# Birthday Wishes
# Demonstrates keyword arguments and default parameter values

# positional parameters
def birthday1(name, age):
    print "Happy birthday,", name, "!", " I hear you're", age, "today.\n"

# parameters with default values
def birthday2(name = "Jackson", age = 1):
    print "Happy birthday,", name, "!", "I hear you're", age, "today.\n"


birthday1("Jackson", 1)
birthday1(1, "Jackson")
birthday1(name = "Jackson", age = 1)
birthday1(age = 1, name = "Jackson")
```

```
birthday2()
birthday2(name = "Katherine")
birthday2(age = 12)
birthday2(name = "Katherine", age = 12)
birthday2("Katherine", 12)

raw_input("\n\nPress the enter key to exit.")
```

Using Positional Parameters and Positional Arguments

If you just list out a series of variable names in a function's header, you create positional parameters:

```
def birthday1(name, age):
```

If you call a function with just a series of values, you create positional arguments:

```
birthday1("Jackson", 1)
```

Using positional parameters and positional arguments means that parameters get their values based solely on the position of the values sent. The first parameter gets the first value sent, the second parameter gets the second value sent, and so on.

With this particular function call, it means that name gets "Jackson" and age gets 1. This results in the message: Happy Birthday, Jackson ! I hear you're 1 today. If you switch the positions of two arguments, the parameters get different values. So with the call

```
birthday1(1, "Jackson")
```

name gets the first value, 1, and age gets the second value, "Jackson". As a result, you end up with a message you probably didn't intend: Happy Birthday, 1 ! I hear you're Jackson today.

You've seen this way of creating and calling functions already. But there are other ways to create parameter and argument lists in your programs.

Using Positional Parameters and Keyword Arguments

Positional parameters get values sent to them in order, unless you tell the function otherwise. You can tell the function to assign certain values to specific parameters, regardless of order, if you use keyword arguments. With keyword arguments, you use the actual parameter names from the function header to link a value to a parameter. So, by calling the same function birthday1() with

```
birthday1(name = "Jackson", age = 1)
```

name gets "Jackson" and age gets 1 and the function displays the message Happy Birthday, Jackson ! I hear you're 1 today. This isn't terribly impressive. You could achieve the same results without keyword arguments by just sending these values in this order. But the beauty of keyword arguments is that their order doesn't matter; it's the keywords that link values to parameters. So the call

```
birthday1(age = 1, name = "Jackson")
```

also produces the message Happy Birthday, Jackson ! I hear you're 1 today., even though the values are listed in opposite order.

Keyword arguments let you pass values in any order. But their biggest benefit is clarity. When you see a function call using keyword arguments, you get a much better understanding of what the values represent.

 You can combine keyword arguments and positional arguments in a single function call, but this can get tricky. Once you use a keyword argument, all the remaining arguments in the call must be keyword arguments, too. To keep things simple, try to use all keyword or all positional arguments in your function calls.

Using Default Parameter Values

Finally, you have the option to assign default values to your parameters, values that get assigned to the parameters if no value is passed to them. That's just what I did with the birthday2() function. I made changes in the header only:

```
def birthday2(name = "Jackson", age = 1):
```

This means that if no value is supplied to name, it gets "Jackson". And if no value is supplied for age, it gets 1. So the call

```
birthday2()
```

doesn't generate an error; instead, the default values are assigned to the parameters, and the function displays the message Happy Birthday, Jackson ! I hear you're 1 today.

Once you assign a default value to a parameter in the list, you have to assign default values to all the parameters listed after it. So, this function header is perfectly fine:

```
def monkey_around(bananas = 100, barrel_of = "yes",
                  uncle = "monkey's"):
```

But this isn't:

```
def monkey_around(bananas = 100, barrel_of, uncle):
```

The above header will generate an error.

So far, so good. But you can add a wrinkle here by overriding the default values of any or all the parameters. With the call

```
birthday2(name = "Katherine")
```

the default value of name is overridden. name gets "Katherine", age still gets its default value of 1, and the message Happy Birthday, Katherine ! I hear you're 1 today. is displayed.

With this function call:

```
birthday2(age = 12)
```

the default value of age is overridden. age gets the value of 12. name gets it's default value of "Jackson". And the message Happy Birthday, Jackson ! I hear you're 12 today. is displayed.

With the call

```
birthday2(name = "Katherine", age = 12)
```

both default values are overridden. name gets "Katherine" and age gets 12. The message Happy Birthday, Katherine ! I hear you're 12 today. is displayed.

And with the call

```
birthday2("Katherine", 12)
```

you get the exact same results as you did with the previous call. Both default values are overridden. name gets "Katherine" and age gets 12. And the message Happy Birthday, Katherine ! I hear you're 12 today. is displayed.

Default parameter values are great if you have a function where almost every time it's called, some parameter gets sent the same value. To save programmers using your function the trouble of typing this value every time, you could use a default parameter value instead.

Using Global Variables and Constants

Through the magic of encapsulation, the functions you've seen are all totally sealed off and independent from each other and the main part of your program. The only way to get information into them is through their parameters, and the only way to get information out of them is from their return values. Well, that's not completely true. There is another way that you can share information among parts of your program: through global variables.

Understanding Scopes

Scopes represent different areas of your program that are separate from each other. For example, each function you define has its own scope. That's why the functions you've seen can't directly access each other's variables. A visual representation really helps to gel this idea, so take a look at Figure 6.7.

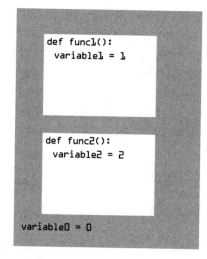

FIGURE 6.7

This simple program has three different scopes: one for each function, plus one for the global scope.

Figure 6.7 shows a program with three different scopes. The first is defined by function `func1()`, the second is defined by function `func2()`, and the third is the global scope (which all programs automatically have). In this program, you're in the global scope when you're not inside any function. The shaded area in the figure represents the global scope. Any variable that you create in the global scope is called a *global variable*, while any variable you create inside a function is called a *local variable* (it's local to that function).

Because `variable1` is defined inside `func1()`, it's a local variable that lives only in the scope of `func1()`. `variable1` can't be accessed from any other scope. So, no command in `func2()` can get at it, and no command in the global space can access or modify it either.

A good way to remember how this works is to think of scopes as houses and encapsulation as tinted windows, giving each house privacy. As a result, you can see anything inside a house if you're in it. But if you're outside a house, you can't see what's inside. This is the way it works with functions. When you're in a function, you have access to all of its variables. But when you're outside a function, like in the global scope, you can't see any of the variables inside a function.

If two variables have the same name inside two separate functions, they're totally different variables with no connection to each other. For example, if I created a variable called `variable2` inside function `func1()`, it would be different and completely separate from the variable named `variable2` in function `func2()`. Because of encapsulation, it would be like they exist in different worlds and have no effect on each other.

Global variables, however, create a little wrinkle in the idea of encapsulation, as you'll see.

Introducing the Global Reach Program

The Global Reach program shows how you can read and even change global variables from inside functions. Figure 6.8 displays the program's results.

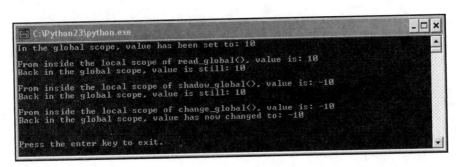

FIGURE 6.8

You can read, shadow, or even change the value of a global variable from inside a function.

Here's the code for the program:

```
# Global Reach
# Demonstrates global variables

def read_global():
    print "From inside the local scope of read_global(), value is:", value

def shadow_global():
    value = -10
    print "From inside the local scope of shadow_global(), value is:", value

def change_global():
    global value
    value = -10
    print "From inside the local scope of change_global(), value is:", value

# main
# value is a global variable because we're in the global scope here
value = 10
print "In the global scope, value has been set to:", value, "\n"

read_global()
print "Back in the global scope, value is still:", value, "\n"

shadow_global()
print "Back in the global scope, value is still:", value, "\n"

change_global()
print "Back in the global scope, value has now changed to:", value

raw_input("\n\nPress the enter key to exit.")
```

Reading a Global Variable from Inside a Function

Although by now you're probably quite comfortable with the idea of encapsulation, I'm going to throw you a little curve ball: You can read the value of a global variable from within any scope in your program. But fear not, this can still work with the concept of houses and tinted windows. Remember, tinted windows keep the houses (or functions) private. But tinted windows also let you see out. So, you can always see outside of a function to the global scope and see the value of a global variable. That's what I did when I created the function `read_global()`. It prints the global variable `value` without a problem.

While you can always read the value of a global variable in any function, you can't change it directly (at least not without asking specifically for that kind of access). So, in `read_global()`, doing something like the following would generate a nasty error:

```
value += 1
```

Back to the houses and tinted glass idea, this means that you can see a global variable from within a function through the tinted window, but you can't touch it because it's outside. So, although you can read the value of a global variable from inside a function, you can't change its value without asking for special access to it.

Shadowing a Global Variable from inside a Function

If you give a variable inside a function the same name as a global variable, you *shadow* the global variable. That is, you hide it with your new variable. It might look like you can change the value of a global variable by doing this, but you only change the local variable you've created. That's what I did in the function `shadow_global()`. When I assigned –10 to `value` with

```
value = -10
```

I didn't change the global version of `value`. Instead, I created a new, local version of `value` inside the function and that got -10. You can see that this is what happened, because when the function finishes, the main program prints out the global version of `value` with

```
print "Back in the global scope, value is still:", value, "\n"
```

and it's still 10.

TRAP It's not a good idea to shadow a global variable inside a function. It can lead to confusion. You might think you're using a global variable when you're really not. Be aware of any global variables in your program and make sure not to use the name anywhere else in your code.

Changing a Global Variable from inside a Function

To gain complete access to a global variable, use the keyword `global` like I did in the function `change_global()`:

```
global value
```

At this point, the function has complete access to `value`. So when I changed it with

```
value = -10
```

the global variable value got -10. When the program prints value again back in the main part of the code with

```
print "Back in the global scope, value has changed to:", value
```

-10 is printed. The global variable was changed from inside the function.

Understanding When to Use Global Variables and Constants

Just because you can, doesn't mean you should. This is a good programming motto. Sometimes things are technically possible, but not good ideas. Using global variables is an example of this. In general, global variables make programs confusing because it can be hard to keep track of their changing values. You should limit your use of them as much as you can.

Global constants (global variables that you treat as constants), on the other hand, can make programs less confusing. For example, say you're writing a business application that calculates someone's taxes. Like a good programmer, you have written a variety of functions in your code, all of which use the somewhat cryptic value .28 as the tax rate. Instead, you could create a global constant called TAX_RATE and set it to .28. Then, in each function, you could replace the number .28 with TAX_RATE. This produces two benefits. It makes your code clearer and it makes changes (like a new tax rate) no sweat.

BACK TO THE TIC-TAC-TOE GAME

The Tic-Tac-Toe game presented at the beginning of the chapter is your most ambitious game program yet. You certainly have all the skills you need to create the game, but instead of jumping straight into the code, I'm going to go through a planning section to help you get the bigger picture and understand how to create a larger program.

Planning the Tic-Tac-Toe Game

If you haven't figured this out by now, I'll bore you with it again: The most important part of programming is planning to program. Without a roadmap, you'll never get to where you want to go (or it'll take you a lot longer as you travel the scenic route).

Writing the Pseudocode

It's back to your favorite language that's not really a language: pseudocode. Because I'll be using functions for most of the tasks in the program, I can afford to think about the program at a pretty general level. Each line of pseudocode should feel like one function call. Then, later, I'll just have to write the functions that the plan implies. Here's the pseudocode:

display the game instructions

determine who goes first

create an empty tic-tac-toe board

display the board

while nobody's won and it's not a tie

    if it's the human's turn

        get the human's move

        update the board with the move

    otherwise

        calculate the computer's move

        update the board with the move

    display the board

    switch turns

congratulate the winner or declare a tie

Representing the Data

All right, I have a good plan, but it is pretty abstract and talks about throwing around different elements that aren't really defined in my mind yet. I see the idea of making a move as placing a piece on a game board. But how exactly am I going to represent the game board? Or a piece? Or a move?

Because I'm going to print the game board on the screen, why not just represent a piece as one character, an "X" or an "O"? An empty piece could just be a space. The board itself should be a list since it's going to change as each player makes a move. There are nine squares on a tic-tac-toe board, so the list should be nine elements long. Each square on the board will correspond to a position in the list that represents the board. Figure 6.9 illustrates what I mean.

FIGURE 6.9

Each square number corresponds to a position in a list that represents the board.

0	1	2
3	4	5
6	7	8

So, each square or position on the board is represented by a number, 0–8. That means the list will be nine elements long and have position numbers 0–8. Because each move indicates a square in which to put a piece, a move is also just a number, 0–8.

The sides the player and computer play could also be represented by "X" and "O", just like a game piece. And a variable to represent the side of the current turn would be either an "X" or an "O".

Creating a List of Functions

The pseudocode inspires the different functions I'll need. I created a list of them, thinking about what they would do, what parameters they would have, and what values they would return. Table 6.1 shows the results of my efforts.

Setting Up the Program

The first thing I did in writing the program was set up some global constants. These are values that more than one function will use. Creating them will make the functions clearer and any changes involving these values easier.

```
# Tic-Tac-Toe
# Plays the game of tic-tac-toe against a human opponent

# global constants
X = "X"
O = "O"
EMPTY = " "
TIE = "TIE"
NUM_SQUARES = 9
```

X is just shorthand for "X", one of the two pieces in the game. O represents "O", the other piece in the game. EMPTY represents an empty square on the board. It's a space because when it's printed, it will look like an empty square. TIE represents a tie game. And NUM_SQUARES is the number of squares on the Tic-Tac-Toe board.

TABLE 6.1   TIC-TAC-TOE FUNCTIONS

Function	Description
display_instruct()	Displays the game instructions.
ask_yes_no(*question*)	Asks a yes or no question. Receives a question. Returns either a "y" or an "n".
ask_number(*question, low, high*)	Asks for a number within a range. Receives a question, a low number, and a high number. Returns a number in the range from *low* to *high*.
pieces()	Determines who goes first. Returns the computer's piece and human's piece.
new_board()	Creates a new, empty game board. Returns a board.
display_board(*board*)	Displays the board on the screen. Receives a board.
legal_moves(*board*)	Creates a list of legal moves. Receives a board. Returns a list of legal moves.
winner(*board*)	Determines the game winner. Receives a board. Returns a piece, "TIE" or None.
human_move(*board, human*)	Gets the human's move from the player. Receives a board and the human's piece. Returns the human's move.
computer_move(*board, computer, human*)	Calculates the computer's move. Receives a board, the computer piece, and the human piece. Returns the computer's move.
next_turn(*turn*)	Switches turns based on the current turn. Receives a piece. Returns a piece.
congrat_winner(*the_winner, computer, human*)	Congratulates the winner or declares a tie. Receives the winning piece, the computer's piece, and the human's piece.

THE display_instruct() FUNCTION

This function displays the game instructions. You've seen it before:

```
def display_instruct():
    """Display game instructions."""
    print \
    """
    Welcome to the greatest intellectual challenge of all time: Tic-Tac-Toe.
    This will be a showdown between your human brain and my silicon processor.
```

```
You will make your move known by entering a number, 0 - 8. The number
will correspond to the board position as illustrated:

                        0 | 1 | 2
                        ---------
                        3 | 4 | 5
                        ---------
                        6 | 7 | 8

Prepare yourself, human. The ultimate battle is about to begin. \n
"""
```

The only thing I did was change the function name for the sake of consistency in the program.

The ask_yes_no() Function

This function asks a yes or no question. It receives a question and returns either a "y" or an "n". You've seen this function before too.

```
def ask_yes_no(question):
    """Ask a yes or no question."""
    response = None
    while response not in ("y", "n"):
        response = raw_input(question).lower()
    return response
```

The ask_number() Function

This function asks for a number within a range. It receives a question, a low number, and a high number. It returns a number within the range specified.

```
def ask_number(question, low, high):
    """Ask for a number within a range."""
    response = None
    while response not in range(low, high):
        response = int(raw_input(question))
    return response
```

The pieces() **Function**

This function asks the player if he or she wants to go first and returns the computer's piece and the human's piece, based on that choice. As the great tradition of Tic-Tac-Toe dictates, the X's go first.

```
def pieces():
    """Determine if player or computer goes first."""
    go_first = ask_yes_no("Do you require the first move? (y/n): ")
    if go_first == "y":
        print "\nThen take the first move. You will need it."
        human = X
        computer = 0
    else:
        print "\nYour bravery will be your undoing... I will go first."
        computer = X
        human = 0
    return computer, human
```

Notice that this function calls another one of my functions, ask_yes_no(). This is perfectly fine. One function can call another.

The new_board() **Function**

This function creates a new board (a list) with all nine elements set to EMPTY and returns it:

```
def new_board():
    """Create new game board."""
    board = []
    for square in range(NUM_SQUARES):
        board.append(EMPTY)
    return board
```

The display_board() **Function**

This function displays the board passed to it. Because each element in the board is either a space, the character "X", or the character "0", the function can print each one. A few other characters on my keyboard are used to draw a decent-looking Tic-Tac-Toe board.

```
def display_board(board):
    """Display game board on screen."""
    print "\n\t", board[0], "|", board[1], "|", board[2]
    print "\t", "-----"
```

```
print "\t", board[3], "|", board[4], "|", board[5]
print "\t", "-------"
print "\t", board[6], "|", board[7], "|", board[8], "\n"
```

The `legal_moves()` Function

This function receives a board and returns a list of legal moves. This function is used by other functions. It's used by the `human_move()` function to make sure that the player chooses a valid move. It's also used by the `computer_move()` function so that the computer can consider only valid moves in its decision making.

A legal move is represented by the number of an empty square. For example, if the center square were open, then 4 would be a legal move. If only the corner squares were open, the list of legal moves would be [0, 2, 6, 8]. (Take a look at Figure 6.9 if you're unclear about this.)

So, this function just loops over the list representing the board. Each time it finds an empty square, it adds that square number to the list of legal moves. Then it returns the list of legal moves.

```
def legal_moves(board):
    """Create list of legal moves."""
    moves = []
    for square in range(NUM_SQUARES):
        if board[square] == EMPTY:
            moves.append(square)
    return moves
```

The `winner()` Function

This function receives a board and returns the winner. There are four possible values for a winner. The function will return either X or O if one of the players has won. If every square is filled and no one has won, it returns TIE. Finally, if no one has won and there is at least one empty square, the function returns None.

The very first thing I do in this function is define a constant called WAYS_TO_WIN, which represents all eight ways to get three in a row. Each way to win is represented by a tuple. Each tuple is a sequence of the three board positions that form a winning three in a row. Take the first tuple in the sequence, (0, 1, 2). This represents the top row: board positions 0, 1, and 2. The next tuple (3, 4, 5) represents the middle row, and so on.

```
def winner(board):
    """Determine the game winner."""
    WAYS_TO_WIN = ((0, 1, 2),
                   (3, 4, 5),
                   (6, 7, 8),
                   (0, 3, 6),
                   (1, 4, 7),
                   (2, 5, 8),
                   (0, 4, 8),
                   (2, 4, 6))
```

Next, I use a for loop to go through each possible way a player can win, to see whether either player has three in a row. The if statement checks to see whether the three squares in question all contain the same value and are not empty. If so, that means that the row has either three X's or 0's in it and somebody has won. The computer assigns one of the pieces in this winning row to winner, returns winner, and ends.

```
for row in WAYS_TO_WIN:
    if board[row[0]] == board[row[1]] == board[row[2]] != EMPTY:
        winner = board[row[0]]
        return winner
```

If neither player has won, then the function continues. Next, it checks to see whether there are any empty squares left on the board. If there aren't any, the game is a tie (because the function has already determined that there is no winner, back in the for loop) and TIE is returned.

```
    if EMPTY not in board:
        return TIE
```

If the game isn't a tie, the function continues. Finally, if neither player has won and the game isn't a tie, there is no winner yet. So, the function returns None.

```
    return None
```

THE human_move() FUNCTION

This next function receives a board and the human's piece. It returns the square number where the player wants to move.

First, the function gets a list of all the legal moves for this board. Then, it continues to ask the user for the square number to which he or she wants to move until that response is in this list of legal moves. Once that happens, the function returns the move.

```
def human_move(board, human):
    """Get human move."""
    legal = legal_moves(board)
    move = None
    while move not in legal:
        move = ask_number("Where will you move? (0 - 8): ", 0, NUM_SQUARES)
        if move not in legal:
            print "\nThat square is already occupied, foolish human. Choose another.\n"
    print "Fine..."
    return move
```

THE computer_move() FUNCTION

The computer_move() function receives the board, the computer's piece, and the human's piece. It returns the computer's move.

TRICK

This is definitely the meatiest function in the program. Knowing it would be, I initially created a short, temporary function that chooses a random but legal move. I wanted time to think about this function, but didn't want to slow the progress of the entire project. So, I dropped in the temporary function and got the game up and running. Later, I came back and plugged in a better function that actually picks moves for a reason.

I had this flexibility because of the modular design afforded by writing with functions. I knew that computer_move() was a totally independent component and could be substituted later, without a problem. In fact, I could even drop a new function in right now, one that chooses even better moves.

I have to be careful here because the board (a list) is mutable and I change it in this function as I search for the best computer move. The problem with this is that any change I make to the board will be reflected in the part of the program that called this function. This is the result of shared references, which you learned about in Chapter 5, in the section "Understanding Shared References." Basically, there's only one copy of the list, and any change I make here changes that single copy. So, the very first thing I do is make my own local copy to work with:

```
def computer_move(board, computer, human):
    """Make computer move."""
    # make a copy to work with since function will be changing list
    board = board[:]
```

HINT

Any time you get a mutable value passed to a function, you have to be careful. If you know you're going to change the value as you work with it, make a copy and use that instead.

TRAP

You might think that changing the board would be a good thing. You could change it so that it contains the new computer move. This way, you don't need to send the board back as a return value.

Changing a mutable parameter directly like this is considered creating a *side effect*. Not all side effects are bad, but this type is generally frowned upon. (I'm frowning right now, just thinking about it.) It's best to communicate with the rest of your program through return values; that way, it's clear exactly what information you're giving back.

Okay, here's the basic strategy I came up with for the computer:

1. If there's a move that allows the computer to win this turn, the computer should choose that move.
2. If there's a move that allows the human to win next turn, the computer should choose that move.
3. Otherwise, the computer should choose the best empty square as its move. The best square is the center. The next best squares are the corners. And the next best squares are the rest.

So next in the code, I define a tuple to represent the best squares, in order:

```
# the best positions to have, in order
BEST_MOVES = (4, 0, 2, 6, 8, 1, 3, 5, 7)
print "I shall take square number",
```

Next, I create a list of all the legal moves. In a loop, I try the computer's piece in each empty square number I got from the legal moves list and check for a win. If the computer can win, then that's the move to make. If that's the case, the function returns that move and ends. Otherwise, I undo the move I just tried and try the next one in the list.

```
# if computer can win, take that move
for move in legal_moves(board):
    board[move] = computer
    if winner(board) == computer:
        print move
        return move
    # done checking this move, undo it
    board[move] = EMPTY
```

If I get to this point in the function, it means the computer can't win on its next move. So, I check to see whether the player can win on his or her next move. The code loops through the list of the legal moves, putting the human's piece in each empty square, checking for a win. If the human can win, then that's the move to take for a block. If this is the case, the function returns the move and ends. Otherwise, I undo the move and try the next legal move in the list.

```
# if human can win, block that move
for move in legal_moves(board):
    board[move] = human
    if winner(board) == human:
        print move
        return move
    # done checking this move, undo it
    board[move] = EMPTY
```

If I get to this point in the function, then neither side can win on its next move. So, I look through the list of best moves and take the first legal one. The computer loops through BEST_MOVES, and as soon as it finds one that's legal, it returns that move.

```
# since no one can win on next move, pick best open square
for move in BEST_MOVES:
    if move in legal_moves(board):
        print move
        return move
```

> ### IN THE REAL WORLD
>
> The Tic-Tac-Toe program considers only the next possible move in the game. Programs that play serious games of strategy, such as Chess, look far deeper into the consequences of individual moves, considering many levels of moves and countermoves. And today's computers can examine a huge number of game positions. Specialized machines, such as IBM's Chess-playing Deep Blue computer, which beat world champion Garry Kasparov, can examine far more. Deep Blue is able to explore over 200,000,000 board positions per second. That sounds quite impressive, until you realize that the total number of board positions in a complete search for Chess is estimated to be over 100,000,000,000,000,000,000,000,000,000,000,000,000,000,000, which means it would take Deep Blue more than 1,585,489,599,188,229 years to look at all those possible positions. (The universe, by the way, is estimated to be only 15,000,000,000 years old.)

THE next_turn() FUNCTION

This function receives the current turn and returns the next turn. A turn represents whose turn it is and is either X or 0.

```
def next_turn(turn):
    """Switch turns."""
    if turn == X:
        return 0
    else:
        return X
```

The function is used to switch turns after one player has made a move.

THE congrat_winner() FUNCTION

This function receives the winner of the game, the computer's piece, and the human's piece. This function is called only when the game is over, so the_winner will be passed either X or 0 if one of the player's has won the game, or TIE if the game ended in a tie.

```
def congrat_winner(the_winner, computer, human):
    """Congratulate the winner."""
    if the_winner != TIE:
        print the_winner, "won!\n"
```

```
        else:
            print "It's a tie!\n"
    if the_winner == computer:
        print "As I predicted, human, I am triumphant once more. \n" \
              "Proof that computers are superior to humans in all regards."

    elif the_winner == human:
        print "No, no! It cannot be! Somehow you tricked me, human. \n" \
              "But never again! I, the computer, so swears it!"

    elif the_winner == TIE:
        print "You were most lucky, human, and somehow managed to tie me. \n" \
              "Celebrate today... for this is the best you will ever achieve."
```

The main() Function

I put the main part of the program into its own function, instead of leaving it at the global level. This encapsulates the main code too. Unless you're writing a short, simple program, it's usually a good idea to encapsulate even the main part of it. If you do put your main code into a function like this, you don't have to call it main(). There's no magic to the name. But it's a pretty common practice, so it's a good idea to use it.

Okay, here's the code for the main part of the program. As you can see, it's almost exactly, line for line, the pseudocode I wrote earlier:

```
def main():
    display_instruct()
    computer, human = pieces()
    turn = X
    board = new_board()
    display_board(board)

    while not winner(board):
        if turn == human:
            move = human_move(board, human)
            board[move] = human
        else:
            move = computer_move(board, computer, human)
            board[move] = computer
        display_board(board)
        turn = next_turn(turn)
```

```
    the_winner = winner(board)
    congrat_winner(the_winner, computer, human)
```

Starting the Program

The next line calls the main function (which in turn calls the other functions) from the global level:

```
# start the program
main()
raw_input("\n\nPress the enter key to quit.")
```

SUMMARY

- A function definition, which begins with the keyword def, defines what a function does.
- A function header is the first line of a function definition.
- A docstring is a triple-quoted string that immediately follows a function header and that documents the function.
- Abstraction is a mechanism that lets you think about the big picture without worrying about the details.
- A parameter is a name in a function header that can receive a value.
- An argument is a value in a function call that's passed to a parameter.
- A return value is a value returned by a function.
- Encapsulation is a technique of keeping independent code separate by hiding the details.
- Variables and parameters created in a function can't be directly accessed outside the function.
- Software reuse is leveraging existing software in a new project.
- Positional parameters are a list of names in a function header.
- Positional arguments are a list of argument values in a function call.
- A keyword argument is an argument passed to a specific parameter using its parameter name.
- A default parameter value is a value that a parameter gets if no value is passed to it.

- Scopes are different areas of a program that are separate from each other.
- A global variable is a variable created in the global scope and that can be accessed in any part of a program.
- A local variable is a variable created in a scope other than the global scope and that can't be accessed outside of its scope.
- Shadowing a global variable is the act of hiding the global variable inside a scope by creating a local variable of the same name.
- You can use the keyword `global` to gain direct access to a global variable from a scope other than the global scope.

REVIEW QUESTIONS

1. How do you define a function in Python?
2. How can using functions make programs easier to read, write, and maintain?
3. Can you call a function before it has been defined?
4. Why should you use docstrings?
5. How can abstraction help a programmer?
6. How are functions and abstraction related?
7. How many parameters can a function have?
8. How many values can be returned from a function?
9. What's the difference between an argument and a parameter?
10. How are functions and encapsulation related?
11. How can software reuse help programmers?
12. What's the difference between a positional argument and a keyword argument?
13. How can keyword arguments help a programmer?
14. How can default parameter values help a programmer?
15. When calling a function, must an argument be passed for every parameter in the function's parameter list?
16. How are functions and scopes related?
17. What's the difference between a local variable and a global variable?
18. Why should you keep the use of global variables to a minimum?
19. How can global constants help a programmer?
20. Why is it considered poor programming practice to shadow a global variable?

PROJECTS

1. Write a program with a function called `rate_score()` that rates a player's score. Your function should have one parameter that receives a score and should return a string based on the score, as follows:

   - If the score your function receives is less than 1000, your function should return `"Nothing to be proud of."`
   - If the score your function receives is greater than or equal to 1000 but less than 10000, your function should return `"Not bad."`
   - If the score your function receives is greater than or equal to 10000, your function should return `"Nice!"`

   Call your function three times—once with a score of 50, once with a score of 5000 and finally once with a score of 50000—and print the return value for each.

2. Improve the program you wrote in Project 1 so that the parameter of function `rate_score()` has a default value of 0. Add a call to `rate_score()` in which you pass no value to the function.

3. Write a program that has two functions: `first()` and `second()`. Function `first()` should print the string `"In function first()"` and then call function `second()`. Function `second()` should print the string `"In function second()"`. In the global scope, you should call function `first()`.

4. Modify the Guess My Number Chapter Project from Chapter 3 by reusing the function `ask_number()` from the Tic-Tac-Toe Chapter Project from this chapter. Replace the code in Guess My Number that asks the player for a guess with a call to `ask_number()`.

5. Rewrite the Word Jumble Chapter Project from Chapter 4 so that the program is separated into the following functions:

   - `instructions()`, which displays instructions to the player. It takes no arguments and returns no values.
   - `random_word()`, which randomly selects the word to be guessed. It takes no arguments and returns the word to be guessed.
   - `jumble()`, which creates a jumble of the word to be guessed. It takes a word and returns a jumbled version of that word.
   - `play()`, which gets the player's guess until the guess is correct or the player quits. It takes the word to be guessed and a jumbled version of that word. It returns no values.
   - `main()`, which calls all of the other functions. It takes no values and returns no values. It should look like this:

```
def main():
 instructions()
 the_word = random_word()
 the_jumble = jumble(word)
 play(the_word, the_jumble)
```

Finally, don't forget to call your `main()` function to play the game.

FILES AND EXCEPTIONS: THE TRIVIA CHALLENGE GAME

Variables provide a great way to store and access information while a program runs, but often, you'll want to save data so that you can retrieve it later. In this chapter, you'll learn to use files for this kind of permanent storage. You'll also learn how to handle errors that your code may generate. Specifically, you'll learn to do the following:

- Read from text files
- Write to text files
- Read and write more complex data with files
- Intercept and handle errors during a program's execution

INTRODUCING THE TRIVIA CHALLENGE GAME

The Trivia Challenge game tests a player's knowledge with a series of multiple-choice questions. The game delivers the questions as a single "episode." The episode I created to show off the program is about the Mafia and is called "An Episode You Can't Refuse." All of the questions relate in some way to the Mafia (although a bit indirectly at times).

The cool thing about the game is that the questions for an episode are stored in a separate file, independent of the game code. This way, it's easy to play different ones. Even better, this means that anyone with a text editor (such as Notepad on Windows machines) can create their own trivia episode about whatever topic they choose—anything from anime to zoology. Figure 7.1 shows the game (and my episode) in action.

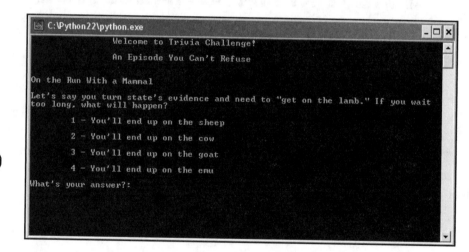

FIGURE 7.1

The player is always presented with four inviting choices. But only one is correct.

READING FROM TEXT FILES

With Python, it's easy to read strings from *plain text files*—files that are made up of only ASCII characters. (Although there are different types of text files, when I use the term "text file," I mean a plain text file.) Text files are a good choice for permanently storing simple information, for a number of reasons. First, text files are cross-platform. A text file on a Windows machine is the same text file on a Mac and is the same text file under UNIX. Second, text files are easy to use. Most operating systems come with basic tools to view and edit them.

Introducing the Read It Program

The Read It program demonstrates several ways you can read strings from a text file. The program demonstrates how to read anything from a single character to the entire file. It also shows several different ways to read one line at a time (probably the most common way you'll access text files). The program reads a simple text file I created on my system using a text editor. Here are the contents of the file:

```
Line 1
This is line 2
That makes this line 3
```

I saved the file with the name read_it.txt and put it in the same directory as the Read It program file for easy access. Figure 7.2 illustrates the program.

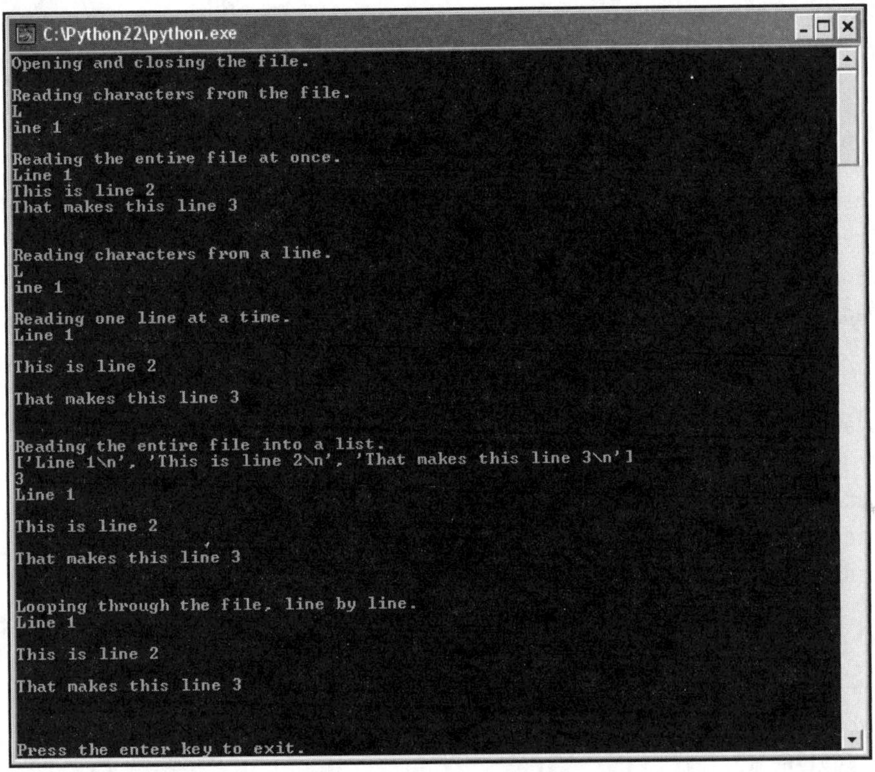

FIGURE 7.2

The file is read using a few different techniques.

Here's the code for the program:

```
# Read It
# Demonstrates reading from a text file

print "Opening and closing the file."
text_file = open("read_it.txt", "r")
```

```
text_file.close()

print "\nReading characters from the file."
text_file = open("read_it.txt", "r")
print text_file.read(1)
print text_file.read(5)
text_file.close()

print "\nReading the entire file at once."
text_file = open("read_it.txt", "r")
whole_thing = text_file.read()
print whole_thing
text_file.close()

print "\nReading characters from a line."
text_file = open("read_it.txt", "r")
print text_file.readline(1)
print text_file.readline(5)
text_file.close()

print "\nReading one line at a time."
text_file = open("read_it.txt", "r")
print text_file.readline()
print text_file.readline()
print text_file.readline()
text_file.close()

print "\nReading the entire file into a list."
text_file = open("read_it.txt", "r")
lines = text_file.readlines()
print lines
print len(lines)
for line in lines:
    print line
text_file.close()

print "\nLooping through the file, line by line."
text_file = open("read_it.txt", "r")
```

```
for line in text_file:
    print line
text_file.close()

raw_input("\n\nPress the enter key to exit.")
```

I'll show you exactly how the code works through an interactive session.

Opening and Closing a Text File

Before you can read from (or write to) a text file, you need to open it. That's the first thing I do in the Read It program:

```
>>> text_file = open("read_it.txt", "r")
```

I use the `open()` function to open a text file and assign the results to `text_file`. In the function call, I provide two string arguments: a file name and an access mode.

The file argument, `"read_it.txt"`, is pretty straightforward. Because I don't include any path information, Python looks in the current directory for the file. I can access a file in any directory by providing the proper path information. For example, on my Windows machine I could provide an absolute path with the string `"C:\Documents and Settings\Owner\Desktop\ read_it.txt"` to access the file `read_it.txt` located on my desktop. This will access the file regardless of the directory from which Read It is run. Or, I could provide a relative path with the string `"data\read_it.txt"` to access the file `read_it.txt` located in the subdirectory `data` of the directory from which Read It is run. In either case, I'm not limited to accessing files from the only directory where Read It is run.

Next, I provide `"r"` for the access mode, which tells Python that I want to open the file for reading. You can open a file for reading, writing, or both. Table 7.1 describes valid access modes.

After opening the file, I access it through the variable `text_file`. There are many useful file methods that I can invoke, but the simplest is `close()`, which closes the file, sealing it off from further reading or writing until the file is opened again. That's what I do next in the program:

```
>>> text_file.close()
```

Whenever you're done with a file, it's good programming practice to close it.

TABLE 7.1	SELECTED FILE ACCESS MODES
Mode	**Description**
"r"	Read from a file. If the file doesn't exist, Python will complain with an error.
"w"	Write to a file. If the file exists, its contents are overwritten. If the file doesn't exist, it's created.
"a"	Append a file. If the file exists, new data is appended to it. If the file doesn't exist, it's created.
"r+"	Read from and write to a file. If the file doesn't exist, Python will complain with an error.
"w+"	Write to and read from a file. If the file exists, its contents are overwritten. If the file doesn't exist, it's created.
"a+"	Append and read from a file. If the file exists, new data is appended to it. If the file doesn't exist, it's created.

Reading Characters from a Text File

For a file to be of any use, you need to do something with its contents between opening and closing it. So next, I open the file and read its contents with the read() file method. read() allows you to read a specified number of characters from a file, which the method returns as a string. After opening the file again, I read and print exactly one character from it:

```
>>> text_file = open("read_it.txt", "r")
>>> print text_file.read(1)
L
```

All I have to do is specify the number of characters between the parentheses. Next, I read and print the next five characters:

```
>>> print text_file.read(5)
ine 1
```

Notice that I read the five characters following the "L". Python remembers where I last left off. It's like the computer puts a bookmark in the file and each subsequent read() begins where the last ended. When you read to the end of a file, subsequent reads return the empty string.

To start back at the beginning of a file, you can close and open it. That's just what I did next:

```
>>> text_file.close()
>>> text_file = open("read_it.txt", "r")
```

If you don't specify the number of characters to be read, Python returns the entire file as a string. Next, I read the entire file, assign the returned string to a variable, and print the variable:

```
>>> whole_thing = text_file.read()
>>> print whole_thing
Line 1
This is line 2
That makes this line 3
```

If a file is small enough, reading the entire thing at once may make sense. Because I've read the entire file, any subsequent reads will just return the empty string. So, I close the file again:

```
>>> text_file.close()
```

Reading Characters from a Line

Often, you'll want to work with one line of a text file at a time. The readline() method lets you read characters from the current line. You just pass the number of characters you want read from the current line, and the method returns them as a string. If you don't pass a number, the method returns the entire line. Once you read all of the characters of a line, the next line becomes the current line. After opening the file again, I read the first character of the current line:

```
>>> text_file = open("read_it.txt", "r")
>>> print text_file.readline(1)
L
```

Then I read the next five characters of the current line:

```
>>> print text_file.readline(5)
ine 1
>>> text_file.close()
```

At this point, readline() may seem no different than read(), but readline() reads characters from the current line only, while read() reads characters from the entire file. Because of this, readline() is usually invoked to read one line of text at a time. In the next few lines of code, I read the file, one line at a time:

```
>>> text_file = open("read_it.txt", "r")
>>> print text_file.readline()
Line 1
```

```
>>> print text_file.readline()
This is line 2

>>> print text_file.readline()
That makes this line 3

>>> text_file.close()
```

Notice that a blank line appears after each line. That's because each line in the text file ends with a newline character ("\n").

Reading All Lines into a List

Another way to work with individual lines of a text file is by using the readlines() method, which reads a text file into a list, where each line of the file becomes a string element in the list. Next, I invoke the readlines() method:

```
>>> text_file = open("read_it.txt", "r")
>>> lines = text_file.readlines()
```

lines now refers to a list with an element for each line in the text file:

```
>>> print lines
['Line 1\n', 'This is line 2\n', 'That makes this line 3\n']
```

lines is like any list. You can find the length of it and even loop through it:

```
>>> print len(lines)
3
>>> for line in lines:
        print line

Line 1

This is line 2

That makes this line 3

>>> text_file.close()
```

Looping through a Text File

Starting in Python 2.2, you can loop directly through the lines of a text file:

```
>>> text_file = open("read_it.txt", "r")
>>> for line in text_file:
        print line

Line 1

This is line 2

That makes this line 3

>>> text_file.close()
```

This technique is the most elegant solution if you want to move through a text file one line at a time.

WRITING TO A TEXT FILE

For text files to be a viable form of storage, you need to be able to get information into them. With Python, it's also a simple matter to write strings to text files. In fact, it's even easier than reading strings from text files, because there are just two basic ways to write to text files.

Introducing the Write It Program

The Write It program creates a text file with the same contents of the read_it.txt file that I used in the Read It program. Actually, the program creates and prints this new file twice, using a different file-writing method each time. Figure 7.3 shows the results of the program.

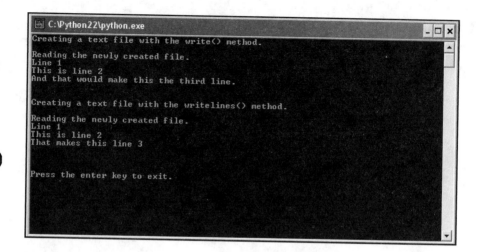

FIGURE 7.3

The same file is
created twice,
each time with a
different file
method.

Writing Strings to a Text File

Just as before, in order to use a file, I have to open it in the correct mode. So, the first thing I do in the program is open a file in write mode:

```
# Write It
# Demonstrates writing to a text file

print "Creating a text file with the write() method."
text_file = open("write_it.txt", "w")
```

The file `write_it.txt` springs into existence as an empty text file just waiting for the program to write to it. If the file `write_it.txt` had already existed, it would have been replaced with a brand-new, empty file and all of its original contents would have been erased.

Next, I use the `write()` file method, which writes a string to the file:

```
text_file.write("Line 1\n")
text_file.write("This is line 2\n")
text_file.write("That makes this line 3\n")
```

The `write()` method does not automatically insert a newline character at the end of a string it writes. You have to put newlines in where you want them. If I had left the three newline characters out of the previous lines of code, the program would write one long line to the file.

Also, you don't have to end every string you write to a file with a newline character. To achieve the same end result, I could just as easily have stuck all three of the previous strings together to form one long string, `"Line 1\n This is line 2\n That makes this line 3\n"`, and written that string to the file with a single `write()` method.

Finally, I close the file:

```
text_file.close()
```

Next, just to prove that the writing worked, I read and print the entire contents of the file:

```
print "\nReading the newly created file."
text_file = open("write_it.txt", "r")
print text_file.read()
text_file.close()
```

Writing a List of Strings to a Text File

Next, I create the same file, using the `writelines()` file method. Like its counterpart, `readlines()`, `writelines()` works with a list of strings. But instead of reading a text file into a list, the method writes a list of strings to a file.

The first thing I do is open the file for writing:

```
print "\nCreating a text file with the writelines() method."
text_file = open("write_it.txt", "w")
```

I open the same file, `write_it.txt`, which means I wipe out the existing file and start with a new, empty one. Next, I create a list of strings to be written, in order, to the file:

```
lines = ["Line 1\n",
    "This is line 2\n",
    "That makes this line 3\n"]
```

Again, I inserted newline characters where I want them in the text file.

Next, I write the entire lists of strings to the file with the `writelines()` method:

```
text_file.writelines(lines)
```

Finally, I close the file:

```
text_file.close()
```

Lastly, I print out the contents of the file to show that the new file is exactly the same as the previous version:

```
print "\nReading the newly created file."
text_file = open("write_it.txt", "r")
```

```
print text_file.read()
text_file.close()

raw_input("\n\nPress the enter key to exit.")
```

You've seen a lot of file read and write methods. Take a look at Table 7.2 for a summary of them.

TABLE 7.2 SELECTED TEXT FILE METHODS		
Method	**Description**
close()	Closes the file. A closed file cannot be read from or written to until opened again.
read([*size*])	Reads *size* characters from a text file and returns them as a string. If size is not specified, the method returns all of the characters from the current position to the end of the file.
readline([*size*])	Reads *size* characters from the current line in a text file and returns them as a string. If size is not specified, the method returns all of the characters from the current position to the end of the line.
readlines()	Reads all of the lines in a text file and returns them as elements in a list.
write(*output*)	Writes the string *output* to a text file.
writelines(*output*)	Writes the strings in the list *output* to a text file.

STORING COMPLEX DATA IN FILES

Text files are convenient because you can read and manipulate them with any text editor, but they're limited to storing a series of characters. Sometimes you may want to store more complex information, such as a list or a dictionary, for example. You could try to convert the contents of these data structures to characters and save them to a file, but Python offers a much better way. You can store more complex data in a file with a single line of code. You can even store a simple database of values in a single file that acts like a dictionary.

Introducing the Pickle It Program

Pickling means to preserve—and that's just what it means in Python. You can pickle a complex piece of data, such as a list or dictionary, and save it in its entirety to a file. Best of all, your hands won't smell like vinegar when you're done.

IN THE REAL WORLD

Other languages can convert complex data for storage in files too, but may not call the process pickling. Instead, these languages may call the process *serialization* or *marshaling*.

The Pickle It program pickles, stores, and retrieves three lists of strings. First, the program stores and retrieves the lists sequentially using a file, much like you've seen with characters in a text file. But then the program stores and retrieves the same three lists so that any list can be randomly accessed. The results of the program are shown in Figure 7.4.

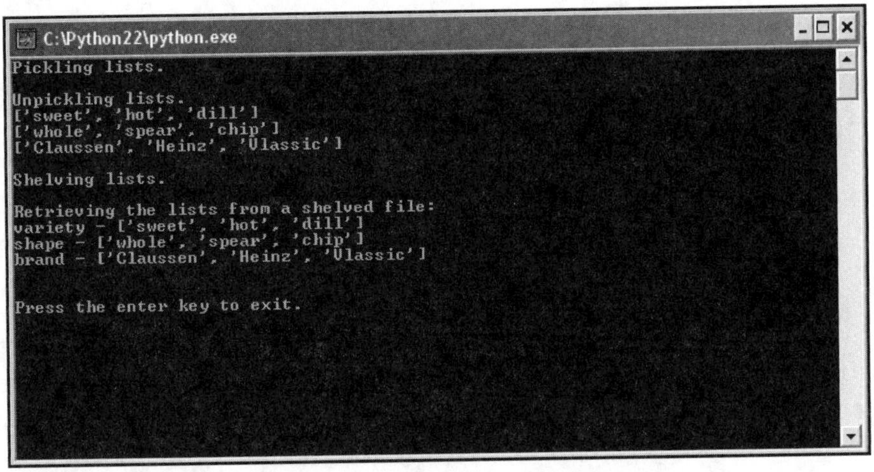

```
C:\Python22\python.exe
Pickling lists.

Unpickling lists.
['sweet', 'hot', 'dill']
['whole', 'spear', 'chip']
['Claussen', 'Heinz', 'Vlassic']

Shelving lists.

Retrieving the lists from a shelved file:
variety - ['sweet', 'hot', 'dill']
shape - ['whole', 'spear', 'chip']
brand - ['Claussen', 'Heinz', 'Vlassic']


Press the enter key to exit.
```

FIGURE 7.4

Each list is written to and read from a file in its entirety.

Pickling Data and Writing It to a File

The first thing I do in the program is import two new modules:

```
# Pickle It
# Demonstrates pickling and shelving data

import cPickle, shelve
```

The cPickle module allows you to pickle and store more complex data in a file. The shelve module allows you to store and randomly access pickled objects in a file.

Python also has a `pickle` module, which works like the `cPickle` module. `pickle` is written in Python while `cPickle` is written in C. Because `cPickle` can be much faster, it's better to use `cPickle` over `pickle` in almost every case.

Pickling is pretty simple. Instead of writing characters to a text file, you can write a pickled object to a file. Pickled objects are stored in files much like characters; you can store and retrieve them sequentially.

In the next section of code, I pickle and store the three lists `variety`, `shape`, and `brand` in the file `pickles1.dat` using the `cPickle.dump()` function. The function requires two arguments: the data to pickle and the file in which to store it.

```
print "Pickling lists."
variety = ["sweet", "hot", "dill"]
shape = ["whole", "spear", "chip"]
brand = ["Claussen", "Heinz", "Vlassic"]
pickle_file = open("pickles1.dat", "w")
cPickle.dump(variety, pickle_file)
cPickle.dump(shape, pickle_file)
cPickle.dump(brand, pickle_file)
pickle_file.close()
```

So, this code pickles the list referred to by `variety` and writes the whole thing as one object to the file `pickles1.dat`. Next, the program pickles the list referred to by `shape` and writes the whole thing as one object to the file. Then, the program pickles the list referred to by `brand` and writes the whole thing as one object to the file. Finally, the program closes the file.

You can pickle a variety of objects, including:

- Numbers
- Strings
- Tuples
- Lists
- Dictionaries

Reading Data from a File and Unpickling It

Next, I retrieve and unpickle the three lists with the `cPickle.load()` function. The function takes one argument: the file from which to load the next pickled object.

```
print "\nUnpickling lists."
pickle_file = open("pickles1.dat", "r")
variety = cPickle.load(pickle_file)
shape = cPickle.load(pickle_file)
brand = cPickle.load(pickle_file)
```

The program reads the first pickled object in the file, unpickles it to produce the list ["sweet", "hot", "dill"], and assigns the list to variety. Next, the program reads the next pickled object from the file, unpickles it to produce the list ["whole", "spear", "chip"], and assigns the list to shape. Finally, the program reads the last pickled object from the file, unpickles it to produce the list ["Claussen", "Heinz", "Vlassic"], and assigns the list to brand.

Finally, I print the unpickled lists to prove that the process worked:

```
print variety, "\n", shape, "\n", brand
pickle_file.close()
```

Table 7.3 describes selected cPickle functions.

TABLE 7.3   SELECTED cPICKLE FUNCTIONS

Function	Description
dump(*object, file,* [,*bin*])	Writes pickled version of *object* to file. If *bin* is True, *object* is written in binary format. If *bin* is False, *object* is written in less efficient, but more human-readable, text format. The default value of *bin* is equal to False.
load(file)	Unpickles and returns the next pickled object in file.

Using a Shelf to Store Pickled Data

Next, I take the idea of pickling one step further by shelving the lists together in a single file. Using the shelve module, I create a shelf that acts like a dictionary, which allows the lists to be accessed randomly.

First, I create a shelf, pickles:

```
print "\nShelving lists."
pickles = shelve.open("pickles2.dat")
```

The shelve.open() function works a lot like the file open() function. However, the shelve.open() function works with a file that stores pickled objects and not characters. In this case, I assigned the resulting shelf to `pickles`, which now acts like a dictionary whose contents are permanently stored in the newly created file `pickles2.dat`.

The `shelve.open()` function requires one argument: a file name. It also takes an optional access mode. If you don't supply an access mode (like I didn't), it defaults to `"c"`. Table 7.4 details access modes for the function.

TABLE 7.4   SHELVE ACCESS MODES

Mode	Description
`"c"`	Open a file for reading or writing. If the file doesn't exist, it's created.
`"n"`	Create a new file for reading or writing. If the file exists, its contents are overwritten.
`"r"`	Read from a file. If the file doesn't exist, Python will complain with an error.
`"w"`	Write to a file. If the file doesn't exist, Python will complain with an error.

Next, I add three lists to the shelf:

```
pickles["variety"] = ["sweet", "hot", "dill"]
pickles ["shape"] = ["whole", "spear", "chip"]
pickles["brand"] = ["Claussen", "Heinz", "Vlassic"]
```

`pickles` works like a dictionary. So, the key `"variety"` is paired with the value `["sweet", "hot", "dill"]`. The key `"shape"` is paired with the value `["whole", "spear", "chip"]`. And the key `"brand"` is paired with the value `["Claussen", "Heinz", "Vlassic"]`. One important thing to note is that a shelf key can only be a string.

Lastly, I invoke the shelf's `sync()` method:

```
pickles.sync() # make sure data is written
```

Python writes changes to a shelf file to a buffer and then periodically writes the buffer to the file. To make sure the file reflects all the changes to a shelf, you can invoke a shelf's `sync()` method. A shelf file is also updated when you close it with its `close()` method.

 While you could simulate a shelf by pickling a dictionary, the `shelve` module is more memory efficient. So, if you need random access to pickled objects, create a shelf.

Using a Shelf to Retrieve Pickled Data

Because a shelf acts like a dictionary, you can retrieve pickled objects from it by supplying a key. Next, I loop through all of the pickled objects in `pickles`, treating it like a dictionary:

```
print "\nRetrieving the lists from a shelved file:"
for key in pickles.keys():
    print key, "-", pickles[key]
```

I loop through a list of keys, which includes `"variety"`, `"shape"` and `"brand"`, printing the key and its value. Finally, I close the file:

```
pickles.close()

raw_input("\n\nPress the enter key to exit.")
```

IN THE REAL WORLD

Pickling and unpickling are good ways to store and retrieve structured information, but more complex information can require even more power and flexibility. Databases and XML are two popular methods for storing and retrieving more complex data, and Python has modules that can interface with either. To learn more, visit the Python language Web site at http://www.python.org.

HANDLING EXCEPTIONS

When Python runs into an error, it stops the current program and displays an error message. More precisely, it raises an *exception*, indicating that, well, something exceptional has occurred. If nothing is done with the exception, Python halts what it's doing and prints an error message detailing the exception.

Here's a simple example of Python raising an exception:

```
>>> num = float(raw_input("Enter a number: "))
Enter a number: Hi!
Traceback (most recent call last):
    File "<pyshell#0>", line 1, in ?
        num = float(raw_input("Enter a number: "))
ValueError: invalid literal for float(): Hi!
```

In this interactive session, Python tries to convert the string "Hi!" to a floating-point number. Since it can't, Python raises an exception and prints the details.

Using Python's exception-handling functionality, you can intercept and handle exceptions so that your program doesn't end abruptly (even if a user enters "Hi!" when you ask for a number). At the very least, you can have your program exit gracefully instead of crashing awkwardly.

Introducing the Handle It Program

The Handle It program opens itself up to errors from user input and then purposely generates a few errors of its own. But instead of halting, the program runs to completion. That's because the program handles the exceptions that are raised. Figure 7.5 shows the program in action.

```
C:\Python22\python.exe                                           _ □ ×
Enter a number: Hi!
Something went wrong!

Enter a number: Hi!
That was not a number!

Attempting to convert None --> Something went wrong!
Attempting to convert Hi! --> Something went wrong!

Attempting to convert None --> I can only convert a string or a number!
Attempting to convert Hi! --> I can only convert a string of digits!
Enter a number: Hi!
That was not a number!  Or as Python would say:
invalid literal for float(): Hi!

Enter a number: 5.6
You entered the number 5.6

Press the enter key to exit.
```

FIGURE 7.5

Although the program can't convert "Hi!" to a number, it doesn't halt when exceptions are raised.

Using a try Statement with an except Clause

The most basic way to handle (or *trap*) exceptions is to use the try statement with an except clause. By using a try statement, you section off some code that could potentially raise an exception. Then, you write an except clause with a block of statements that are executed only if an exception is raised.

The first thing I do in the Handle It program is ask the user for a number. I get a string from the user and then attempt to convert the string to a floating-point number. I use try and except to handle any exceptions that might be raised in the process.

```
# Handle It
# Demonstrates handling exceptions
```

```
# try/except
try:
    num = float(raw_input("Enter a number: "))
except:
    print "Something went wrong!"
```

If the call to `float()` raises an exception (as a result of the user entering an unconvertible string, such as `"Hi!"`, for example), the exception is caught and the user is informed that `Something went wrong!` If no exception is raised, `num` gets the number the user entered and the program skips the `except` clause, continuing with the rest of the code.

Specifying an Exception Type

Different kinds of errors result in different types of exceptions. For example, trying to convert the string `"Hi!"` with `float()` results in a `ValueError` exception because the characters in the string are of the wrong value (they're not digits). There are over two dozen exception types, but Table 7.5 lists a few of the most common ones.

TABLE 7.5   SELECTED EXCEPTION TYPES

Exception Type	Description
IOError	Raised when an I/O operation fails, such as when an attempt is made to open a nonexistent file in read mode.
IndexError	Raised when a sequence is indexed with a number of a nonexistent element.
KeyError	Raised when a dictionary key is not found.
NameError	Raised when a name (of a variable or function, for example) is not found.
SyntaxError	Raised when a syntax error is encountered.
TypeError	Raised when a built-in operation or function is applied to an object of inappropriate type.
ValueError	Raised when a built-in operation or function receives an argument that has the right type but an inappropriate value.
ZeroDivisionError	Raised when the second argument of a division or modulo operation is zero.

The `except` clause lets you specify exactly which type of exceptions it will handle. You just list the specific type of exceptions in parentheses after `except`.

I again ask the user for a number, but this time I specifically trap for a `ValueError`:

```
# specifying exception type
try:
    num = float(raw_input("\nEnter a number: "))
except(ValueError):
    print "That was not a number!"
```

Now, the `print` statement will only execute if a `ValueError` is raised. As a result, I can be even more specific and display the message `That was not a number!` However, if any other exception is raised inside the `try` statement, the `except` clause will not catch it and the program will come to a halt.

It's good programming practice to specify exception types so that you handle each individual case. In fact, it's dangerous to catch all exceptions the way I did in the first `except` clause of the program. Generally, you should avoid that type of catchall.

When should you trap for exceptions? Any point of external interaction with your program is a good place to think about exceptions. It's a good idea to trap for exceptions when opening a file for reading, even if you believe the file already exists. You can also trap for exceptions when you attempt to convert data from an outside source, such as the user.

So, let's say you know you want to trap for an exception, but you're not exactly sure what the exception type is called. Well, here's a shortcut for finding out: Just create the exception. For example, if you know you want to trap for a division-by-zero exception, but you can't remember exactly what the exception type is called, jump into the interpreter and divide a number by zero:

```
>>> 1/0
Traceback (most recent call last):
File "<pyshell#0>", line 1, in ?
    1/0
ZeroDivisionError: integer division or modulo by zero
```

From this interactive session, I can see that the exception is called `ZeroDivisionError`. Fortunately, the interpreter isn't shy about telling you exactly which type of exception you raise.

Handling Multiple Exception Types

A single piece of code can result in different types of exceptions. Fortunately, you can trap for multiple exception types. One way to trap for multiple exception types is to list them in a single `except` clause:

```
# handle multiple exceptions
print
```

```
for value in (None, "Hi!"):
    try:
        print "Attempting to convert", value, "-->",
        print float(value)
    except(TypeError, ValueError):
        print "Something went wrong!"
```

This code tries to convert two different values to a floating-point number. Both fail, but each raises a different exception type. float(None) raises a TypeError because the function can only convert strings and numbers. float("Hi!") raises a ValueError because, although "Hi!" is a string, the characters in the string are of the wrong value (they're not digits). As a result of the except clause, each type of exception is handled.

Another way to catch multiple exceptions is with multiple except clauses. You can list as many as you'd like, following a single try statement:

```
print
for value in (None, "Hi!"):
    try:
        print "Attempting to convert", value, "-->",
        print float(value)
    except(TypeError):
        print "I can only convert a string or a number!"
    except(ValueError):
        print "I can only convert a string of digits!"
```

Now, each exception type has its own block. So when value is None, a TypeError is raised and the string "I can only convert a string or a number!" is printed. When value is "Hi!", a ValueError is raised and the string "I can only convert a string of digits!" is printed.

Using multiple except clauses allows you to define unique reactions to different types of exceptions from the same try block. In this case, I offer a more specific error message by trapping each exception type individually.

Getting an Exception's Argument

When an exception occurs, it may have an associated value, the exception's *argument*. The argument is usually an official message from Python describing the exception. You can receive the argument if you list a variable before the colon in the except statement.

Here, I receive the exception's argument in variable e and print it out along with my regular error message:

```
# get an exception's argument
try:
    num = float(raw_input("\nEnter a number: "))
except(ValueError), e:
    print "That was not a number! Or as Python would say:\n", e
```

Adding an else Clause

You can add a single else clause after all the except clauses in a try statement. The else block executes only if no exception is raised in the try block.

```
# try/except/else
try:
    num = float(raw_input("\nEnter a number: "))
except(ValueError):
    print "That was not a number!"
else:
    print "You entered the number", num


raw_input("\n\nPress the enter key to exit.")
```

In this code, num is printed in the else block only if the assignment statement in the try block doesn't raise an exception. This is perfect because that means num will be printed only if the assignment statement was successful and the variable exists.

BACK TO THE TRIVIA CHALLENGE GAME

With the basics of files and exceptions under your belt, it's time to tackle the Trivia Challenge game presented at the beginning of the chapter. One of the cool things about the program is that it reads a plain text file, so you can create your own trivia game episodes with a text editor and a dash of creativity. As you'll see in the code, the text file the program reads, trivia.txt, needs to be in the same directory as the program file. To create your own episode full of questions, all you need to do is replace this file with one containing your own work.

Understanding the Data File Layout

Before I go over actual code from the game, you should understand exactly how the trivia.txt file is structured. The very first line in the file is the title of the episode. The rest of the file consists of blocks of seven lines for each question. You can have as many blocks (and thus questions) as you like. Here's a generic representation of a block:

```
<category>
<question>
<answer 1>
<answer 2>
<answer 3>
<answer 4>
<correct answer>
<explanation>
```

And here's the beginning of the file I created for the game:

```
An Episode You Can't Refuse
On the Run With a Mammal
Let's say you turn state's evidence and need to "get on the lamb." If you wait /too long,
what will happen?
You'll end up on the sheep
You'll end up on the cow
You'll end up on the goat
You'll end up on the emu
1
A lamb is just a young sheep.
The Godfather Will Get Down With You Now
Let's say you have an audience with the Godfather of Soul. How would it be /smart to
address him?
Mr. Richard
Mr. Domino
Mr. Brown
Mr. Checker
3
James Brown is the Godfather of Soul.
```

To save space, I only show the first 15 lines of the file—two questions' worth. You can take a look at the complete file, `trivia.txt`, on the CD-ROM that's included with this book.

Remember, the very first line in the file, `An Episode You Can't Refuse,` is the episode title for this game. The next seven lines are for the first question. And the next seven lines are for the second question. So, the line `On the Run With a Mammal` is the category of the first question. The category is just a clever way to introduce the next question. The next line, `Let's say you turn state's evidence and need to "get on the lamb." If you wait /too long, what will happen?`, is the first question in the game. The next four lines, `You'll end up on the sheep, You'll end up on the cow, You'll end up on the goat,` and `You'll end up on the emu,` are the four possible answers from which the player will choose. The next line, 1, is the number of the correct answer. So in this case, the correct answer to the question is the first answer, You'll end up on the sheep. The next line, A lamb is just a young sheep., explains why the correct answer is correct. The rest of the questions follow the same pattern.

An important thing to note is that I included a forward slash (/) in two of the lines. I did this to represent a newline since Python does not automatically wrap text when it prints it. When the program reads a line from the text file, it replaces all of the forward slashes with the newline character. You'll see exactly how the program does this when I go over the code.

The open_file() Function

The first thing I do in the program is define the function open_file(), which receives a file name and mode (both strings) and returns a corresponding file object. I use try and except to trap for an IOError exception for input-output errors, which would occur if the file doesn't exist, for example.

If I trap an exception, that means there was a problem opening the trivia file. If this happens, there's no point in continuing the program, so I print an appropriate message and call the sys.exit() function. This function raises an exception that results in the termination of the program. You should only use sys.exit() as a last resort, when you must end a program. Notice that I didn't have to import the sys module to call sys.exit(). That's because the sys module is always available.

```
# Trivia Challenge
# Trivia game that reads a plain text file

def open_file(file_name, mode):
    """Open a file."""
    try:
        the_file = open(file_name, mode)
    except(IOError), e:
        print "Unable to open the file", file_name, "Ending program.\n", e
        raw_input("\n\nPress the enter key to exit.")
        sys.exit()
    else:
        return the_file
```

The next_line() Function

Next, I define the next_line() function, which receives a file object and returns the next line of text from it:

```
def next_line(the_file):
    """Return next line from the trivia file, formatted."""
    line = the_file.readline()
    line = line.replace("/", "\n")
    return line
```

However, I do one small bit of formatting to the line before I return it. I replace all forward slashes with newline characters. I do this because Python does not automatically word wrap printed text. My procedure gives the creator of a trivia text file some formatting control. He or she can indicate where newlines should go so that words don't get split across lines. Take a look at the triva.txt file and the output of the Trivia Challenge game to see this in action. Try removing the forward slashes from the text file and check out the results.

The next_block() Function

The next_block() function reads the next block of lines for one question. It takes a file object and returns four strings and a list of strings. It returns a string for the category, question, correct answer, and explanation. It returns a list of four strings for the possible answers to the question.

```
def next_block(the_file):
    """Return the next block of data from the trivia file."""
    category = next_line(the_file)

    question = next_line(the_file)

    answers = []
    for i in range(4):
        answers.append(next_line(the_file))

    correct = next_line(the_file)
    if correct:
        correct = correct[0]

    explanation = next_line(the_file)

    return category, question, answers, correct, explanation
```

If the end of the file is reached, reading a line returns the empty string. So, when the program comes to the end of `trivia.txt`, category gets the empty string. I check category in the `main()` function of the program. When it becomes the empty string, the game is over.

The `welcome()` Function

The `welcome()` function welcomes the player to the game and announces the episode's title. The function gets the episode title as a string and prints it along with a welcome message.

```
def welcome(title):
    """Welcome the player and get his/her name."""
    print "\t\tWelcome to Trivia Challenge!\n"
    print "\t\t", title, "\n"
```

Setting Up the Game

Next, I create the `main()` function, which houses the main game loop. In the first part of the function, I set up the game by opening the trivia file, getting the title of the episode (the first line of the file), welcoming the player, and setting the player's score to 0.

```
def main():
    trivia_file = open_file("trivia.txt", "r")
    title = next_line(trivia_file)
    welcome(title)
    score = 0
```

Asking a Question

Next, I read the first block of lines for the first question into variables. Then, I start the `while` loop, which will continue to ask questions as long as category is not the empty string. If category is the empty string, that means the end of the trivia file has been reached and the loop won't be entered. I ask a question by printing the category of the question, the question itself, and the four possible answers.

```
# get first block
category, question, answers, correct, explanation = next_block(trivia_file)
while category:
    # ask a question
    print category
    print question
    for i in range(4):
        print "\t", i + 1, "-", answers[i]
```

Getting an Answer

Next, I get the player's answer:

```
# get answer
answer = raw_input("What's your answer?: ")
```

Checking an Answer

Then, I compare the player's answer to the correct answer. If they match, the player is congratulated and his or her score is increased by one. If they don't match, the player is told he or she is wrong. In either case, I then display the explanation, which describes why the correct answer is correct. Lastly, I display the player's current score.

```
# check answer
if answer == correct:
    print "\nRight!",
    score += 1
else:
    print "\nWrong.",
print explanation
print "Score:", score, "\n\n"
```

Getting the Next Question

Then, I call the `next_block()` function and get the block of strings for the next question. If there are no more questions, `category` will get the empty string and the loop won't continue.

```
# get next block
category, question, answers, correct, explanation = next_block(trivia_file)
```

Ending the Game

After the loop, I close the trivia file and display the player's score:

```
trivia_file.close()

print "That was the last question!"
print "You're final score is:", score
```

Starting the main() Function

The last lines of code start main() and kick off the game:

```
main()
raw_input("\n\nPress the enter key to exit.")
```

Summary

- The open() function opens a file and returns a file object.
- You can open a file for reading, writing, or both.
- The close() file object method closes a file.
- The read() file object method reads a specified number of characters from a text file, which are returned as a string.
- The readline() file object method reads a specified number of characters from the current line of a text file, which are returned as a string.
- The readlines() file object method reads an text file and returns a list of strings where each element is a line from the file.
- The write() file object method writes characters to a file.
- The writelines() file object method writes a list of strings to a file.
- Pickling is a process that converts Python objects into a form that can be written to and read from files.
- The cPickle module contains functions that allow you to pickle complex data, like a list, tuple or dictionary, and write them or read them from a file.
- The cPickle.dump() function pickles and writes objects sequentially to a file.
- The cPickle.load() function reads and unpickles objects sequentially from a file.
- A shelf is an object written to a file that acts like a dictionary, providing random access to a group of objects.
- The shelve module contains functions that allow you to work with shelves.
- The shelve.open() function opens a file with pickled objects.
- An exception is raised when there's an error in a program and can be caught (or trapped) and then handled. An exception that's not handled halts a program.
- A try statement sections off a block of code that could raise an exception and is paired with an except clause. When an error occurs in the try statement's block, the exception can be caught by the except clause and the except clause's block is run. If no exception is raised, the except block is skipped.

- Different types of errors raise different types of exceptions.
- An except clause can specify different exception types to handle.
- An exception may have an argument that you can receive as a string, which is usually a message describing the exception.
- After all except clauses in a try block, you can add a single else clause with a block that executes if no exception is raised.

REVIEW QUESTIONS

1. What type of information would best be stored in a text file?
2. What type of information would best be stored in a file using the cPickle module?
3. What are some of the most common Python file access modes?
4. What happens if you try to read past the end of a text file?
5. Why is it important to close a file when you're done with it?
6. Which file object method is better, read() or readline()?
7. How can you read an entire text file with one method call?
8. How can you read one line of a text file with one method call?
9. How can you use a for loop to read the contents of a text file?
10. What are serialization and marshaling?
11. What types of objects can you pickle?
12. What's the difference between the pickle and cPickle modules?
13. What are the shelve access modes?
14. Why create a shelf instead of simply pickling a dictionary?
15. What are some common exception types?
16. How can you handle exceptions of different types that might arise from a block of code?
17. Why should you avoid catch-all exception handling?
18. When should you consider trapping for exceptions?
19. How can you generate the name of an exception?
20. How might you use an exception's argument?

PROJECTS

1. Modify the High Scores 2.0 program from Chapter 5 so that the program loads and saves the high scores as a pickled list in a file called scores.dat. When your program begins, it should attempt to load the pickled list from the file. If scores.dat doesn't exist, your program should use exception handling to avoid ending and display a warning that the file could not be opened. When the user quits, your program should attempt to write the high scores to scores.dat (or create the file if it doesn't exist). If your program is

unable to write to the file (or create it), use exception handling to exit your program gracefully.

2. Modify the High Scores 2.0 program from Chapter 5 so that the program loads and saves the high scores using a text file called `scores.txt`. When your program begins, it should attempt to load the high scores from the file. If `scores.txt` doesn't exist, your program should use exception handling to avoid ending and display a warning that the file could not be opened. When the user quits, your program should attempt to write the high scores to `scores.txt` (or create the file if it doesn't exist). If your program is unable to write to the file (or create it), use exception handling to exit your program gracefully.

3. Modify the Trivia Challenge Chapter Project from this chapter so that each question has its own point value. In addition to modifying the Python code for the game program, you will need to create a new trivia episode file, which you can base on `trivia.txt`, that stores a point value for each question. Call this new episode file `trivia2.txt` and give question one a point value of 5, question two a point value of 10, question three a point value of 15, question four a point value of 20, and question five a point value of 25.

4. Modify your Project 3 program so that it checks the current file directory and displays a list of all the trivia game episode files. The program should allow the player to choose which trivia episode he or she wants to play by selecting one of the files. In order to avoid confusion with other text files, your program should assume that trivia episode files end with the extension `.trv`. (This means, of course, you will need to create at least one trivia episode file with the extension `.trv` to fully test your program). If no trivia episode files exist in the current directory, your program should display a message saying so and exit gracefully.

To complete this project, you will need to use the following code:

```
os.listdir(os.getcwd())
```

The function `os.getcwd()` returns the path of the current working directory as a string while `os.listdir()` takes a directory, in the form of a string, and returns the names of the files in that directory as a list of strings. This means that `os.listdir(os.getcwd())` returns all of the filenames from the current directory as a list of strings. You can use this list to determine the valid trivia episode files in the current directory (any files that have the extension `.trv`). In order to access these operating system functions, you will need to use `import os` at the top of your program.

5. Write your own trivia questions in an episode file for use with the version of the Trivia Challenge game you completed in Project 4. Your new episode file should contain ten questions that test a player's knowledge of Python file handling and exceptions.

SOFTWARE OBJECTS: THE CRITTER CARETAKER PROGRAM

bject-oriented programming (OOP) is a different way of thinking about programming. It's a modern methodology that's been embraced by the software industry and is used in the creation of the majority of new commercial software. The basic building block in OOP is the *software object*—often just called an object. In this chapter, you'll take your first steps toward understanding OOP as you learn about objects. Specifically, you'll learn to do the following:

- Create classes to define objects
- Write methods and create attributes for objects
- Instantiate objects from classes
- Restrict access to an object's attributes
- Work with both new-style and old-style classes

INTRODUCING THE CRITTER CARETAKER PROGRAM

The Critter Caretaker program charges the user with the care of his or her own virtual pet. The user names the critter and is completely responsible for keeping it happy, which is no small task. The user must feed and play with the critter to keep it in a good mood. The user can listen to the critter to learn how the critter is feeling, which can range from happy to mad. Figures 8.1 through 8.3 show off the Critter program.

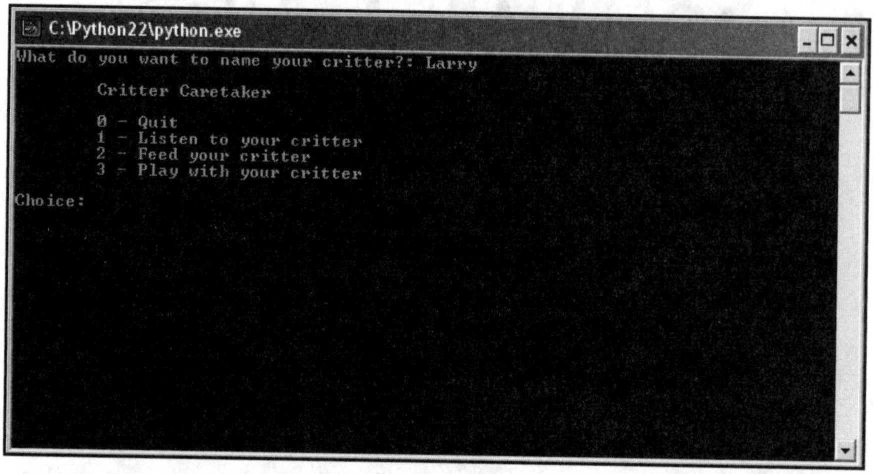

```
C:\Python22\python.exe                                    _ □ ×
What do you want to name your critter?: Larry

        Critter Caretaker

    0 - Quit
    1 - Listen to your critter
    2 - Feed your critter
    3 - Play with your critter

Choice:
```

FIGURE 8.1

You get to name your very own critter.

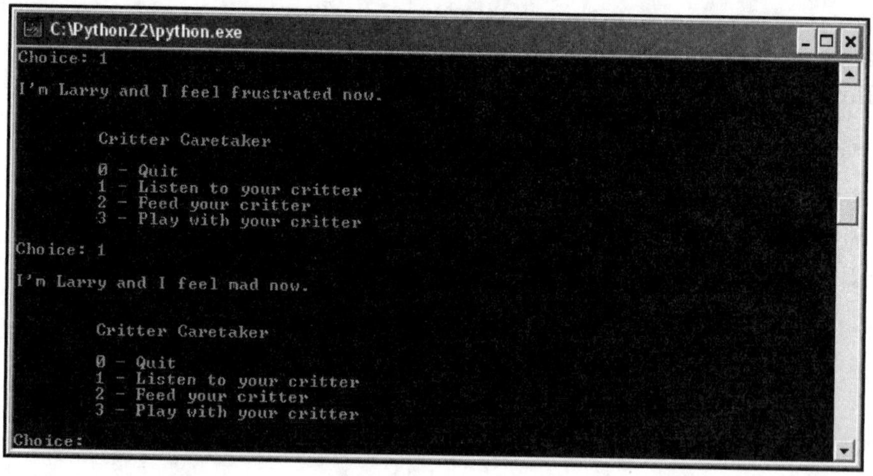

```
C:\Python22\python.exe                                    _ □ ×
Choice: 1

I'm Larry and I feel frustrated now.

        Critter Caretaker

    0 - Quit
    1 - Listen to your critter
    2 - Feed your critter
    3 - Play with your critter

Choice: 1

I'm Larry and I feel mad now.

        Critter Caretaker

    0 - Quit
    1 - Listen to your critter
    2 - Feed your critter
    3 - Play with your critter

Choice:
```

FIGURE 8.2

If you fail to feed or entertain your critter, it will have a mood change for the worse.

```
C:\Python22\python.exe                                    _ □ ×

Choice: 3

Wheee!

        Critter Caretaker

        0 - Quit
        1 - Listen to your critter
        2 - Feed your critter
        3 - Play with your critter

Choice: 1

I'm Larry and I feel happy now.

        Critter Caretaker

        0 - Quit
        1 - Listen to your critter
        2 - Feed your critter
        3 - Play with your critter

Choice:
```

FIGURE 8.3

But with the proper care, your critter will come back to its original, sunny mood.

Though you could create this program without software objects, I created the critter as an object. Ultimately, this makes the program easier to work with and modify. Plus, it allows for painless scaling. Once you've created one critter, it's no sweat to create and manage a dozen. Could a critter farm be far off?

UNDERSTANDING OBJECT-ORIENTED BASICS

OOP has a reputation for being complicated, but I think it's actually simpler than some of the concepts you've already learned. In fact, OOP allows you to represent things in your programs in a way that's more like the real world.

What you often want to represent in your programs—anything from a checking account to an alien spacecraft—are real-life objects. OOP lets you represent these real-life objects as software objects. Like real-life objects, software objects combine characteristics (called *attributes* in OOP-speak) and behaviors (called *methods* in OOP-speak). For example, if you were to create an alien spacecraft object, its attributes could include its location and energy level, while its methods could include its ability to move or fire its weapons.

Objects are created (or *instantiated* in OOP-speak) from a definition called a *class*—programming code that can define attributes and methods. Classes are like blueprints. A class isn't an object, it's a design for one. And just as a foreman can create many houses from the same blueprint, a programmer can create many objects from the same class. As a result, each object (also called an *instance*) instantiated from the same class will have a similar structure. So, if you have a checking account class, you could use it to create multiple checking account objects. And those different objects would each have the same basic structure. Each might have a balance attribute, for example.

But just as you can take two houses built from the same blueprint and decorate them differently, you can have two objects of the same class and give each its own unique set of attribute values. So, you could have one checking account object with a balance attribute of 100 and another with a balance attribute of 1,000,000.

HINT

Don't worry if all this OOP talk isn't crystal clear yet. I just wanted to give you an overview of what objects are all about. Like all new programming concepts, reading about them isn't enough. But after seeing some real Python code that defines classes and creates objects (and coding some on your own), you'll soon "get" OOP.

CREATING CLASSES, METHODS, AND OBJECTS

To build an object, you first need a blueprint, or a class. Classes almost always include methods, things that an object can do. You can create a class without any methods, but that wouldn't be much fun.

Introducing the Simple Critter Program

The Simple Critter program includes your first example of a class written in Python. In it, I define an extremely simple type of critter that can only do one thing: say hi. While this kind of critter might be simple, at least it's polite. The results of the program are pictured in Figure 8.4.

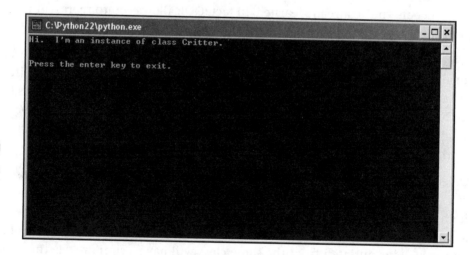

The program is quite short. Here's the code in its entirety:

```
# Simple Critter
# Demonstrates a basic class and object
class Critter(object):
    """A virtual pet"""
    def talk(self):
        print "Hi. I'm an instance of class Critter."

# main
crit = Critter()
crit.talk()

raw_input("\n\nPress the enter key to exit.")
```

Defining a Class

The program starts with a class definition, the blueprint of my first critter. The first line of the definition is the class header:

```
class Critter(object):
```

I used the keyword `class` followed by the class name I chose, `Critter`. You'll notice that my class name begins with a capital letter. Python doesn't require this, but it's the standard convention, so you should begin all your class names with a capital letter.

Next, I told Python to base my class on `object`, a fundamental, built-in type. You can base a new class on `object` or any previously defined class, but that's a topic for Chapter 9, "Object-Oriented Programming: The Blackjack Game." In this chapter, I base all of my classes on `object`.

 TRAP If you're using a version of Python before 2.2, you can't base your classes on `object`. So, to get the programs in this chapter to run, you'll need to remove `(object)` from the class headers. My advice is to use Python 2.2 or later if at all possible. Toward the end of this chapter, I'll explain exactly what's going on in the evolution of Python classes and objects.

The next line is a docstring, which documents the class. A good docstring describes the kind of objects a class can be used to create. My docstring is pretty straightforward:

```
    """A virtual pet"""
```

Defining a Method

The last part of the class defines a method. It looks very much like a function:

```
def talk(self):
    print "Hi. I'm an instance of class Critter."
```

In fact, you can think of methods as functions associated with an object. (You've already seen this with string and list methods, for example.) The talk() method prints the string "Hi. I'm an instance of class Critter."

You'll notice that talk() has one parameter, self (which it doesn't happen to use). Every instance method must have a special first parameter, called self by convention, in its parameter list. It provides a way for a method to refer to the object itself. For now, don't worry about self; you'll see it in action a little later in this chapter.

 TRAP   If you create an instance method without any parameters, you'll generate an error when you invoke it. Remember, all instance methods must have a special first parameter, called self by convention.

Instantiating an Object

After I wrote my class, instantiating a new object took just one line:

```
crit = Critter()
```

This line creates a brand-new object of the Critter class and assigns it to the variable crit. Notice the parentheses after the class name Critter in the assignment statement. It's critical to use them if you want to create a new object.

You can assign a newly instantiated object to a variable with any name. The name doesn't have to be based on the class name. However, you should usually avoid using the same name as the class name in lowercase letters because it could lead to confusion.

Invoking a Method

My new object has a method called talk(). The method is like any other method you've already seen. It's basically a function that belongs to the object. I can invoke this method just like any other, using dot notation:

```
crit.talk()
```

The line invokes the talk() method of the Critter object assigned to crit. The method simply prints the string "Hi. I'm an instance of class Critter."

USING CONSTRUCTORS

You've seen how you can create methods, such as `talk()`, but there's a special method you can write, called a *constructor*, that is automatically invoked right after a new object is created. A constructor method is extremely useful. In fact, you'll often write one for each class you create. The constructor method is usually used to set up the initial attribute values of an object, though I won't use it for that in this program.

Introducing the Constructor Critter Program

The Constructor Critter program defines a new `Critter` class that includes a simple constructor method. The program also shows how easy it is to create multiple objects from the same class. Figure 8.5 shows a sample run of the program.

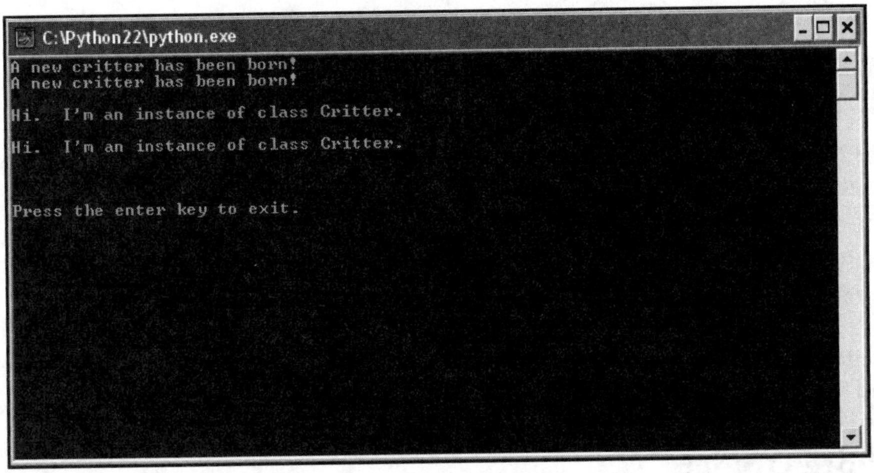

FIGURE 8.5

Two separate
critters are
created. Each
says hi.

Here's the Constructor Critter program code:

```
# Constructor Critter
# Demonstrates constructors

class Critter(object):
    """A virtual pet"""
    def __init__(self):
        print "A new critter has been born!"

    def talk(self):
        print "\nHi. I'm an instance of class Critter."
```

```
# main
crit1 = Critter()
crit2 = Critter()

crit1.talk()
crit2.talk()

raw_input("\n\nPress the enter key to exit.")
```

Creating a Constructor

The first new piece of code in the class definition is the constructor method (also called the *initialization* method):

```
def __init__(self):
    print "A new critter has been born!"
```

Normally, you make up your own method names, but here I used a specific one recognized by Python. By naming the method __init__, I told Python that this is my constructor method. As a constructor method, __init__() is automatically called by any newly created Critter object right after the object springs to life. As you can see from the second line in the method, that means any newly created Critter object automatically announces itself to the world by printing the string "A new critter has been born!"

 HINT Python has a collection of built-in "special methods" whose names begin and end with two underscores, such as __init__, the constructor method.

Creating Multiple Objects

Once you've written a class, creating multiple objects is a snap. In the main part of the program, I create two:

```
# main
crit1 = Critter()
crit2 = Critter()
```

As a result, two objects are created. Just after each is instantiated, it prints "A new critter has been born!" through its constructor method.

Each object is its very own, full-fledged critter. To prove the point, I invoke their talk() methods:

```
crit1.talk()
crit2.talk()
```

Even though these two lines of code print the exact same string, "\nHi. I'm an instance of class Critter.", each is the result of a different object.

Using Attributes

You can have an object's attributes automatically created and initialized just after it's instantiated through its constructor method. This is a big convenience and something you'll do a lot.

Introducing the Attribute Critter Program

The Attribute Critter program creates a new type of object with an attribute, name. The Critter class has a constructor method that creates and initializes name. The program uses the new attribute so that the critter can offer a more personalized greeting. Figure 8.6 shows the program in action.

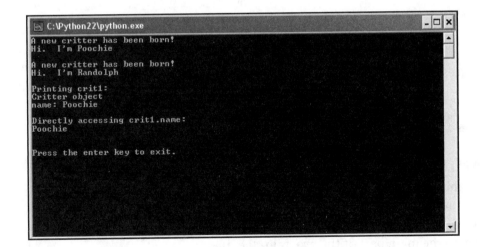

FIGURE 8.6

This time, each Critter object has an attribute name that it uses when it says hi.

The following is the code for the program:

```
# Attribute Critter
# Demonstrates creating and accessing object attributes


class Critter(object):
    """A virtual pet"""
    def __init__(self, name):
```

```
            print "A new critter has been born!"
            self.name = name

    def __str__(self):
        rep = "Critter object\n"
        rep += "name: " + self.name + "\n"
        return rep

    def talk(self):
        print "Hi. I'm", self.name, "\n"
# main
crit1 = Critter("Poochie")
crit1.talk()

crit2 = Critter("Randolph")
crit2.talk()

print "Printing crit1:"
print crit1

print "Directly accessing crit1.name:"
print crit1.name

raw_input("\n\nPress the enter key to exit.")
```

Initializing Attributes

The constructor in this program prints the message "A new critter has been born!" just like the constructor in the Constructor Critter program, but the next line of the method does something new. It creates the attribute name for the new object and sets it to the value of the parameter name. So, in the main part of the program, the line:

```
crit = Critter("Poochie")
```

results in the creation of a new Critter object with an attribute name set to "Poochie". Finally, the object is assigned to crit.

So that you can understand exactly how this works, I'll reveal what the mysterious self parameter is all about. As the first parameter in every method, self automatically receives a reference to the object invoking the method. This means that, through self, a method can get at the object invoking it and access the object's attributes or methods (or even create new attributes for the object).

 HINT You can name the first parameter in a method header something other than self, but you shouldn't. It's the "Pythonic" way to do things, and other programmers will expect it.

So, back in the constructor method, the parameter self automatically receives a reference to the new Critter object while the parameter name receives "Poochie". Then, the line:

```
self.name = name
```

creates the attribute name for the object and sets it to the value of name, which is "Poochie".

Back in the main part of the program, the assignment statement assigns this new object to crit. This means that crit refers to a new object with its own attribute, called name, set to "Poochie". So, a critter has been created with its own name!

The line in the main program:

```
crit2 = Critter("Randolph")
```

kicks off the same basic chain of events. But this time, a new Critter object is created with its own attribute name set to "Randolph". And the object is assigned to crit2.

Accessing Attributes

Attributes aren't any good unless you can use them, so I wrote a more personal talk() method that uses a Critter object's name attribute. Now, when a critter says hi, it introduces itself with its name.

I got my first critter to say hi by invoking its talk() method with:

```
crit1.talk()
```

The talk() method receives the automatically sent reference to the object into its self parameter:

```
def talk(self):
```

Then, the print statement displays the text Hi. I'm Poochie by accessing the attribute name of the object through self.name:

```
print "Hi. I'm", self.name, "\n"
```

The same basic events occur when I then call the method for my second object:

```
crit2.talk()
```

But this time, the `talk()` method displays the text `Hi. I'm Randolph` because the `name` attribute of `crit2` is equal to `"Randolph"`.

By default, you can access and modify an object's attributes outside of its class. In the main part of the program, I directly accessed the `name` attribute of `crit1`:

```
print crit1.name
```

The line prints the string `"Poochie"`. In general, to access an attribute of an object outside the object's class, you can use dot notation. Type the variable name, followed by a dot, followed by the attribute name.

 Usually, you want to avoid directly accessing an object's attributes outside of its class definition. You'll learn more about this later in the chapter, in the section "Understanding Object Encapsulation."

Printing an Object

Normally, if I were to print an object with the code `print crit1`, Python would come back with something like the cryptic:

```
<__main__.Critter object at 0x00A0BA90>
```

This tells me that I've printed a `Critter` object in the main part of my program, but doesn't give me any useful information about the object. However, there is a way to change this. By including the special method `__str__()` in a class definition, you can create a string representation for your objects that will be displayed whenever one is printed. Whatever string you return from the method will be the string that's printed for the object.

The `__str__()` method I wrote returns a string that includes the value of the object's `name` attribute. So, when the following line is executed:

```
print crit1
```

this more useful text appears:

```
Critter object
name: Poochie
```

 Even if you never plan to print an object in your program, creating a `__str__()` method is still not a bad idea. You may find that being able to see the values of an object's attributes helps you understand how a program is working (or not working).

Using Class Attributes and Static Methods

Through attributes, different objects of the same class can each have their own unique values. You could, for example, have 10 different critters running around, each with its own name. But you may have some information that relates not to individual objects, but to the entire class. You might want to, say, keep track of the total number of critters you've created. You could give each `Critter` object an attribute called `total`. But then, whenever a new object is instantiated, you'd have to update every existing object's `total` attribute. This would be a real pain. Fortunately, Python offers a way to create a single value that's associated with a class itself, called a *class attribute*. If a class is like a blueprint, then a class attribute is like a Post-it note stuck to the blueprint. There's only one copy of it, no matter how many things you make from the blueprint.

You might also find that you want a method that's associated with the class; for this, Python offers the *static method*. Because static methods are associated with a class, they're often used to work with class attributes.

Introducing the Classy Critter Program

No, the Classy Critter program doesn't involve a critter that went to finishing school and scoffs at other critters who don't know which fork to use. Instead, the program involves attributes and methods that belong to a class rather than a specific object. The program defines a class attribute that keeps track of the total number of `Critter` objects instantiated. The class also has a static method that displays this number. Figure 8.7 shows the results of the program.

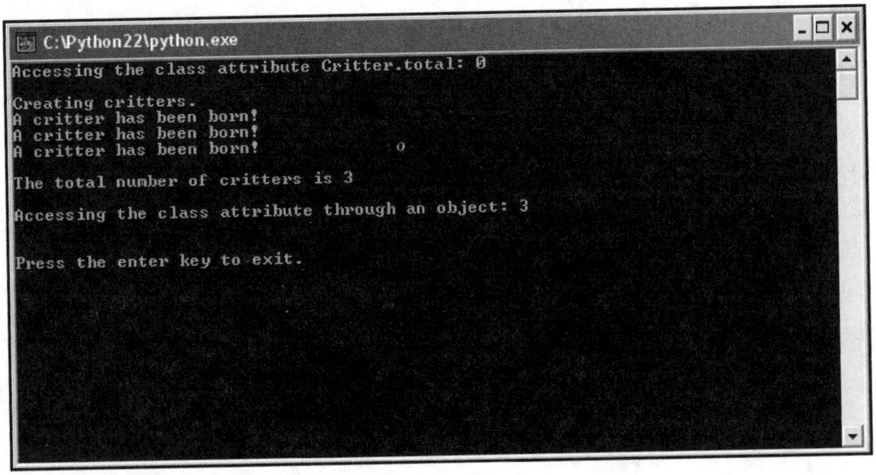

FIGURE 8.7

Critters are being born left and right! The program keeps track of all of them through a single class attribute, which it displays through a static method.

Here's the program listing for Classy Critter:

```
# Classy Critter
# Demonstrates class attributes and static methods

class Critter(object):
    """A virtual pet"""
    total = 0

    def status():
        print "\nThe total number of critters is", Critter.total

    status = staticmethod(status)

    def __init__(self, name):
        print "A critter has been born!"
        self.name = name
        Critter.total += 1

#main
print "Accessing the class attribute Critter.total:",
print Critter.total

print "\nCreating critters."
crit1 = Critter("critter 1")
crit2 = Critter("critter 2")
crit3 = Critter("critter 3")

Critter.status()

print "\nAccessing the class attribute through an object:",
print crit1.total

raw_input("\n\nPress the enter key to exit.")
```

Creating a Class Attribute

The second line in my class definition:

```
total = 0
```

creates a class attribute `total` and assigns 0 to it. Any assignment statement like this—a new variable assigned a value outside of a method—creates a class attribute. The assignment statement is executed only once, when Python first sees the class definition. This means that the class attribute exists even before a single object is created. So, you can use a class attribute without any objects of the class in existence.

Accessing a Class Attribute

Accessing a class attribute is simple. I access the new class attribute in several different places in the program. In the main part of the program, I print it with:

```
print Critter.total
```

In the static method `status()`, I print the value of the `Critter` class attribute `total` with the line:

```
print "\nThe total number of critters is", Critter.total
```

In the constructor method, I increment the value of this class attribute through the line:

```
Critter.total += 1
```

As a result of this line, every time a new object is instantiated, the value of the attribute is incremented by 1.

In general, to access a class attribute, use dot notation. Type the class name, followed by a dot, followed by the attribute name.

Finally, you can access a class attribute through an object of that class. That's just what I did in the main part of the program with the following line:

```
print crit1.total
```

This line prints the value of the class attribute `total` (and not an attribute of the object itself). You can read the value of a class attribute through any object that belongs to that class. So, I could have used `print crit2.total` or `print crit3.total` and gotten the same results in this case.

TRAP Although you can use an object of a class to access a class attribute, you can't assign a new value to a class attribute through an object. If you want to change the value of a class attribute, access it through its class name.

Creating a Static Method

The first method in the class, status(), is a method I wrote to be static. Notice that it doesn't have self in its parameter list. That's because, like all static methods, it's designed to be invoked through a class and not an object. So, the method won't be passed a reference to an object and therefore won't need a parameter, such as self, to receive such a reference. Static methods can certainly have parameters, but I just didn't need any for this one.

The method definition creates a method called status(), but to actually declare it static, I wrote one more line of code:

```
status = staticmethod(status)
```

I passed the staticmethod() function the name of the method I want to be static, status in this case. I assigned the result to status. The name on the left side of the assignment operator is the name that the final static method will have. After this line executes, the class has a static method, status(), which displays the total number of objects created by printing the class attribute total.

TRAP Static methods were introduced in Python 2.2. You can't use them in an earlier version of the language. If you try, you'll get a nasty error message.

Invoking a Static Method

Invoking a static method is simple. With the first line of the main part of the program, I invoke the static method:

```
Critter.status()
```

As you would guess, this displays 0 since no objects have been instantiated. But notice that I'm able to invoke the method without a single object in existence. Because static methods are invoked through a class, no objects of the class need to exist before you can invoke them.

Next, I create three objects. Then, I invoke status() again, which prints a message stating that three critters exist. This works because, during the execution of the constructor method for each object, the class attribute total is increased by 1.

UNDERSTANDING OBJECT ENCAPSULATION

You first learned about the concept of encapsulation with functions in the "Understanding Encapsulation" section of in Chapter 6. You saw that functions are encapsulated and hide the details of their inner workings from the part of your program that calls them (called the *client* of the function). You learned that the client of a well-defined function communicates with the function only through its parameters and return values. In general, objects should be treated the same way. Clients should communicate with objects through method parameters and return values. In general, client code should avoid directly altering the value of an object's attribute.

As always, a concrete example helps. Say, for example, that you had a Checking_Account object with a balance attribute. Let's say your program needs to handle withdrawals from accounts, where a withdrawal decreases an object's balance attribute by some amount. To make a withdrawal, client code could simply subtract a number from the value of balance. This direct access is easy for the client, but can cause problems. The client code may subtract a number so that balance becomes negative, which might be considered unacceptable (especially by the bank). It's much better to have a method called withdraw() that allows a client to request a withdrawal by passing an amount to the method. Then, the object itself can handle the request. If the amount is too large, the object can deal with it, possibly rejecting the transaction. The object keeps itself safe by providing indirect access to its attributes through methods.

USING PRIVATE ATTRIBUTES AND PRIVATE METHODS

By default, all of an object's attributes and methods are *public*, meaning that they can be directly accessed or invoked by a client. To encourage encapsulation, you can define an attribute or method as *private*, meaning that only other methods of the object itself can easily access or invoke it.

Introducing the Private Critter Program

The Private Critter program instantiates an object with both private and public attributes and methods. Figure 8.8 shows a sample run.

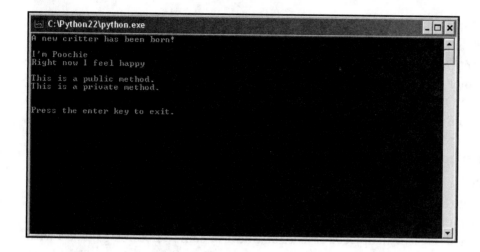

```
A new critter has been born!

I'm Poochie
Right now I feel happy

This is a public method.
This is a private method.

Press the enter key to exit.
```

FIGURE 8.8

The object's private attribute and private method are indirectly accessed.

Creating Private Attributes

To limit the direct access of object attributes by clients, you can use private attributes. In the constructor method, I create two attributes, one public and one private:

```python
# Private Critter
# Demonstrates private variables and methods

class Critter(object):
    """A virtual pet"""
    def __init__(self, name, mood):
        print "A new critter has been born!"
        self.name = name          # public attribute
        self.__mood = mood        # private attribute
```

The two underscore characters that begin the second attribute name tell Python that this is a private attribute. To create a private attribute of your own, just begin the attribute name with two underscores.

Accessing Private Attributes

It's perfectly fine to access an object's private attribute inside the class definition of the object. (Remember, private attributes are meant to discourage client code from directly accessing the attribute.) I access a private attribute in the talk() method:

```python
def talk(self):
    print "\nI'm", self.name
    print "Right now I feel", self.__mood, "\n"
```

This method prints the value of the object's private attribute, which represents a critter's mood.

If I tried to access this attribute outside of the `Critter` class definition, I'd have trouble. Here's an interactive session to show you what I mean:

```
>>> crit = Critter(name = "Poochie", mood = "happy")
A new critter has been born!
>>> print crit.mood
Traceback (most recent call last):
        File "<pyshell#2>", line 1, in ?
        print crit.mood
AttributeError: 'Critter' object has no attribute 'mood'
```

By raising an `AttributeError` exception, Python is saying that `crit` has no attribute `mood`. If you think you can outsmart Python by adding the two leading underscores, you'd be wrong. That's just what I tried in the next part of my interactive session:

```
>>> print crit.__mood
Traceback (most recent call last):
    File "<pyshell#3>", line 1, in ?
        print crit.__mood
AttributeError: 'Critter' object has no attribute '__mood'
```

This also raises an `AttributeError` exception. Python is again saying that the attribute doesn't exist. So does this mean that the value of a private attribute is completely inaccessible outside of its class definition? Well, no. Python hides the attribute through a special naming convention, though it's still technically possible to access the attribute. That's what I did in the next part of my interactive session:

```
>>> print crit._Critter__mood
happy
```

This line prints the value of the elusive private attribute, which in this case is the string `"happy"`.

Because it's possible to access private attributes, you may be thinking: What good are they? Well, defining an attribute or method as private is not about completely preventing access. Rather, it's about preventing inadvertent access. It says that a particular attribute or method is meant only for an object's internal use. So, you should never try to directly access the private attributes or methods of an object from outside of its class definition.

Creating Private Methods

You can create a private method in the same simple way you create a private attribute: by adding two leading underscores to its name. That's just what I do in the next method definition in the class:

```
def __private_method(self):
    print "This is a private method."
```

This is a private method but it can easily be accessed by any other method in the class. Like private attributes, private methods are meant only to be accessed by an object's own methods.

Accessing Private Methods

Just as with private attributes, accessing an object's private methods within its class definition is simple. In the `public_method()` method, I access the class' private method:

```
def public_method(self):
    print "This is a public method."
    self.__private_method()
```

This method prints the string `"This is a public method."` and then invokes the object's private method.

Like private attributes, private methods aren't meant to be directly accessed by clients. Back in my interactive session, I try to access `crit`'s private method:

```
>>> crit.private_method()
Traceback (most recent call last):
    File "<pyshell#6>", line 1, in ?
        crit.private_method()
AttributeError: 'Critter' object has no attribute 'private_method'
```

This attempt raises the familiar `AttributeError` exception. Python is saying that `crit` has no method with this name. Python hides the method through the same special naming convention. If I try again by adding the two leading underscores to the method name, I run into the same error message:

```
>>> crit.__private_method()
Traceback (most recent call last):
    File "<pyshell#7>", line 1, in ?
        crit.__private_method()
AttributeError: 'Critter' object has no attribute '__private_method'
```

However, just as with private attributes, it is technically possible to access private methods from anywhere in a program. Here's the final part of my interactive session as proof:

```
>>> crit._Critter__private_method()
This is a private method.
```

But, as you probably know by now, a client should never attempt to directly access an object's private methods.

Respecting an Object's Privacy

In the main part of the program, I behave myself and don't go prodding into an object's private attributes or methods. Instead, I create an object and invoke its two public methods:

```
# main
crit = Critter(name = "Poochie", mood = "happy")
crit.talk()
crit.public_method()


raw_input("\n\nPress the enter key to exit.")
```

The Critter object's __init__() method, which is automatically called right after the object is created, announces to the world that a new critter has been born. crit's talk() method tells us how the critter is feeling. crit's public_method() method prints the string "This is a public method." and then invokes crit's private method, which prints the string "This is a private method." Finally, the program ends.

Understanding When to Implement Privacy

So now that you know how to use privacy, should you make every attribute in every class private to protect them from the evil outside world? Well, no. Privacy is like a fine spice: Used sparingly, it can greatly improve what you're making. Make private any method you don't want a client to invoke. If it's critical that an attribute never be directly accessed by a client, you can make it private. But keep this to a minimum, as creating private attributes is rare in Python. The philosophy among programmers is to trust that clients will use an object's methods and not directly alter its attributes.

When you write a class:

- Create methods so that clients won't need to directly access an object's attributes.
- Use privacy only for those attributes and methods that are completely internal to the operation of objects.

When you use an object:

- Minimize the direct reading of an object's attributes.
- Avoid directly altering an object's attributes.
- Never directly access an object's private attributes or methods.

Understanding New-Style and Old-Style Classes

Earlier in this chapter, in "Defining a Class," you got a hint that something was afoot in the evolution of classes and objects in the Python language. Beginning in Python 2.2, a new type of class was introduced, called *new-style* classes. A new-style class is a class that is directly or indirectly based on the built-in object introduced in Python 2.2. All of the classes you've seen in this chapter are based on object and are therefore new-style classes. An *old-style* class is a class that is not based on object, directly or indirectly. If you removed the (object) from any of the Critter class headers in this chapter, you'd have an old-style class. To drive the point home, here's an example of a new-style class header:

```
class Critter(object):
```

This is the header of an old-style class:

```
class Critter:
```

Every program you've seen so far in this chapter will work equally well with either new-style or old-style classes. However, new-style classes offer significant improvements over old-style classes. In fact, you'll see one of those improvements at work in the next chapter program, the Property Critter.

HINT

Create new-style classes instead of old-style classes whenever possible. New-style classes can do everything old-style classes can, plus more. Besides, old-style classes will cease to exist beginning in Python 3.0.

Controlling Attribute Access

Sometimes, instead of denying access to an attribute, you may want only to limit access to it. For example, you might have an attribute that you want client code to be able to read, but not change. Python provides a few tools to accomplish this kind of thing, including *properties*. Properties allow you to manage exactly how an attribute is accessed or changed.

Introducing the Property Critter

The Property Critter program allows client code to read a Critter object's attribute that refers to its name, but imposes restrictions when client code attempts to change the attribute's value. If client code tries to assign the attribute the empty string, the program complains and does not allow the change. Figure 8.9 shows the results of the program.

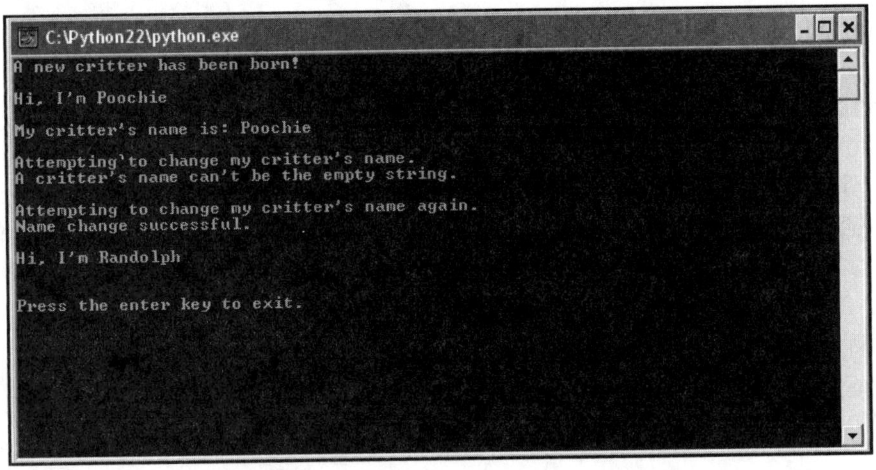

FIGURE 8.9

A property controls access to the Critter object's attribute for its name.

Using Get Methods

One way to control access to an attribute is to create *access methods*—methods that allow indirect access to attributes and often impose some sort of restriction on that access. One type of access method is a *get method*, which gets the value of an attribute. By convention, a get method's name always starts with the word "get." I wrote the simplest form of a get method for the private attribute __name, called get_name(). The method simply returns the value of the private attribute, which represents a critter's name.

```
# Property Critter
# Demonstrates get and set methods and properties

class Critter(object):
    """A virtual pet"""
    def __init__(self, name):
        print "A new critter has been born!"
        self.__name = name

    def get_name(self):
        return self.__name
```

Now, it's easy to get the value of the private attribute through the get method as you can see in this interactive session:

```
>>> crit = Critter("Poochie")
>>> print crit.get_name()
Poochie
```

By creating a get method, you can provide read access to a private attribute.

Using Set Methods

Because I want to allow controlled changes to the name of a critter, I created another type of access method, called a *set method*, which sets an attribute to a value. By convention, a set method's name always starts with the word "set." This new method, set_name(), allows a value to be assigned to the private variable __name; however, it imposes the restriction that the value cannot be the empty string.

```
def set_name(self, new_name):
    if new_name == "":
        print "A critter's name can't be the empty string."
    else:
        self.__name = new_name
        print "Name change successful."
```

If I try to change the name of my critter to the empty string, set_name() won't let me:

```
>>> crit.set_name("")
A critter's name can't be the empty string.
```

However, the method will allow me to set the name to anything else:

```
>>> crit.set_name("Randolph")
Name change successful.
>>> print crit.get_name()
Randolph
```

Using Properties

Properties allow you to harness the power of access methods while hiding the implementation from the client. A property essentially wraps access methods around the consistent and familiar dot notation.

TRAP Properties only work as intended with new-style classes. If you must work with old-style classes, you can control attribute access with the special methods __getattr__() and __setattr__(). You can find out about these methods through the online Python documentation at http://www.python.org/doc.

I use the `property()` function to create a property in the next line of the program:

```
name = property(get_name, set_name)
```

This code creates a property called `name` that allows indirect access to the private attribute __name through the `get_name()` and `set_name()` methods. Notice that the arguments of the `property()` function are the names of the methods, not calls to the methods, so they don't include parentheses.

To create a property, follow my example. Supply the `property()` function with get and set methods to allow controlled access to a private attribute. (You can supply just a get method to create a read-only property.) Finally, make sure to assign the resulting property to an attribute name that client code will use to access the property.

By using the new `name` property, I can get the name of my critter through the familiar dot notation, as you can see in the beginning of this interactive session:

```
>>> print crit.name
Randolph
```

This line of code invokes the `get_name()` method. It has the same effect as the line `print get_name()`, but it maintains the consistent dot-notation format.

I can also set the name of my critter through dot notation:

```
>>> crit.name = "Sammy"
Name change successful.
>>> print crit.name
Sammy
```

This first line of code indirectly invokes the `set_name()` method. It has the same effect as the line `set_name("Sammy")`, but it maintains the consistent dot-notation format.

As before, if I try to make my critter's name the empty string, I can't:

```
>>> crit.name = ""
A critter's name can't be the empty string.
```

The rest of the Property Critter program uses the `name` property to indirectly access the private __name attribute:

```
def talk(self):
    print "\nHi, I'm", self.name
```

As you can see, I access the `name` property in the `talk()` method of the `Critter` class the same way I access it in the main part of the program, through dot notation. You access a property the same way, whether you're in the class definition or in some other part of the program.

Here's the main part of the code, which uses this new `name` property:

```
# main
crit = Critter("Poochie")
crit.talk()

print "\nMy critter's name is:",
print crit.name
print "\nAttempting to change my critter's name."
crit.name = ""
print "\nAttempting to change my critter's name again."
crit.name = "Randolph"

crit.talk()

raw_input("\n\nPress the enter key to exit.")
```

The first line of the section instantiates a new `Critter` object with a private attribute, __name, set to "Poochie". The next line invokes `crit`'s `talk()` method, which uses the object's name property to say hello. Then, I use the object's name property to print out the critter's name. By using `crit.name`, I don't directly access `crit`'s __name attribute; I indirectly invoke the object's `get_name()` method, which returns the value of its private attribute, __name. Next, I attempt to change the critter's name to the empty string, but, by accessing the object's name property, I indirectly invoke its `set_name()` method, which rejects the change. Next, I use the name property to change the critter's name to "Randolph", which `set_name()` allows. Finally, I prove that I made the name change by invoking the object's `talk()` method one last time.

BACK TO THE CRITTER CARETAKER PROGRAM

The final Critter Caretaker program combines parts of classes you've seen throughout this chapter. It also includes the menu system you've worked with that allows the user to interact with his or her very own critter.

The Critter Class

The Critter class is the blueprint for the object that represents the user's critter. The class isn't complicated, and most of it should look quite familiar, but it's a long a enough piece of code that attacking it in pieces makes sense.

The Constructor Method

The constructor method of the class initializes the three public attributes of a Critter object: name, hunger, and boredom. Notice that hunger and boredom both have default values of 0, allowing a critter to start off in a very good mood.

```
# Critter Caretaker
# A virtual pet to care for

class Critter(object):
    """A virtual pet"""
    def __init__(self, name, hunger = 0, boredom = 0):
        self.name = name
        self.hunger = hunger
        self.boredom = boredom
```

I take the more relaxed posture of a Python programmer with this method and leave the attributes at their default public status. I plan to provide all the methods I suspect a client will need, which should encourage the client to interact with a Critter object only through those methods.

The __pass_time() Method

The __pass_time() method is a private method that increases a critter's hunger and boredom levels. It's invoked at the end of each method where the critter does something (eats, plays, or talks) to simulate the passage of time. I made this method private because it should only be invoked by another method of the class. I only see time passing for a critter when it does something (such as eat, play, or talk).

```
    def __pass_time(self):
        self.hunger += 1
        self.boredom += 1
```

The mood Property

The mood property represents a critter's mood. The property is created from a single get method, __get_mood(), making it read-only. __get_mood() adds the values of a Critter object's hunger and boredom attributes. Based on the total, the method returns a string, either "happy", "okay", "frustrated", or "mad".

The interesting thing about the mood property is that it doesn't simply provide access to a private attribute. That's because the string that represents a critter's mood is not stored as part of the Critter object, it's calculated on the fly by __get_mood(). The mood property just passes on the string returned by __get_mood(). To client code, however, mood looks like any other read-only attribute of a Critter object created with a property.

```python
def __get_mood(self):
    unhappiness = self.hunger + self.boredom
    if unhappiness < 5:
        mood = "happy"
    elif 5 <= unhappiness <= 10:
        mood = "okay"
    elif 11 <= unhappiness <= 15:
        mood = "frustrated"
    else:
        mood = "mad"
    return mood


mood = property(__get_mood)
```

The talk() Method

The talk() method announces the critter's mood to the world by accessing the Critter object's mood property. Then, the method invokes __pass_time().

```python
def talk(self):
    print "I'm", self.name, "and I feel", self.mood, "now.\n"
    self.__pass_time()
```

The eat() Method

The eat() method reduces the critter's hunger level by an amount passed to the parameter food. If no value is passed, food gets the default value of 4. The critter's hunger level is kept in check and not allowed to go below 0. Finally, the method invokes __pass_time().

```python
def eat(self, food = 4):
    print "Brruppp. Thank you."
    self.hunger -= food
    if self.hunger < 0:
        self.hunger = 0
    self.__pass_time()
```

The play() Method

The play() method reduces the critter's boredom level by an amount passed to the parameter fun. If no value is passed, fun gets the default value of 4. The critter's boredom level is kept in check and not allowed to go below 0. Finally, the method invokes __pass_time().

```
def play(self, fun = 4):
    print "Wheee!"
    self.boredom -= fun
    if self.boredom < 0:
        self.boredom = 0
    self.__pass_time()
```

Creating the Critter

I put the main part of the program into its own function, main(). At the start of the program, I get the name of the critter from the user. Next, I instantiate a new Critter object. Because I don't supply values for hunger or boredom, the attributes start out at 0, and the critter begins life happy and content.

```
def main():
    crit_name = raw_input("What do you want to name your critter?: ")
    crit = Critter(crit_name)
```

Creating a Menu System

Next, I created the familiar menu system. If the user enters 0, the program ends. If the user enters 1, the object's talk() method is invoked. If the user enters 2, the object's eat() method is invoked. If the user enters 3, the object's play() method is invoked. If the user enters anything else, he or she is told the choice is invalid.

```
choice = None
while choice != "0":
    print \
    """

    Critter Caretaker

    0 - Quit
    1 - Listen to your critter
    2 - Feed your critter
    3 - Play with your critter
    """
```

```
choice = raw_input("Choice: ")
print

# exit
if choice == "0":
    print "Good-bye."

# listen to your critter
elif choice == "1":
    crit.talk()

# feed your critter
elif choice == "2":
    crit.eat()

# play with your critter
elif choice == "3":
    crit.play()

# some unknown choice
else:
    print "\nSorry, but", choice, "isn't a valid choice."
```

Starting the Program

The next line of code calls the main() function and begins the program. The last line waits for the user before ending.

```
main()
("\n\nPress the enter key to exit.")
```

SUMMARY

- Object-oriented Programming (OOP) is a methodology of programming where new types of objects are defined.
- An object is a single software unit that combines attributes and methods.
- An attribute is a "characteristic" of an object, like a variable associated with an object.
- A method is a "behavior" of an object, like a function associated with an object.
- An instance is a single object.

- A class defines the attributes and methods of a kind of object.
- Each instance method must have a special first parameter, called self by convention, which provides a way for a method to refer to the object itself.
- A constructor is a special method, __init__(), that is automatically invoked right after a new object is created and is often used to initialize object attributes.
- The special __str__() method returns a string representation of an object and allows customization of how an object appears when printed.
- A class attribute is a single attribute that's associated with a class itself.
- A static method is a method that's associated with a class itself.
- Client code should communicate with objects through method parameters and return values and should avoid directly altering the values of an object's attributes.
- Objects should update their own attributes and encourage encapsulation by providing indirect access to attributes through methods.
- Public attributes and methods can be directly accessed by client code.
- Private attributes and methods cannot (easily) be directly accessed by client code.
- A new-style class is directly or indirectly based on the built-in object.
- An old-style class is not based on the built-in object, directly or indirectly.
- A get method gets the value of an attribute, which is often private; by convention, its name starts with "get".
- A set method sets an attribute, usually private, to a value; by convention, its name starts with "set".
- A property wraps access methods, such as get and set methods, around dot notation syntax.

REVIEW QUESTIONS

1. How might you use OOP to represent a player in a game? What attributes and methods might a player object have?
2. What does instantiate mean?
3. What naming convention should you use when creating a class and why?
4. For what should you use a docstring in a class?
5. What will happen if you create an instance method without any parameters?
6. Can you name the first parameter of an instance method something other than self?
7. Why is it common to create a constructor method for a class?
8. How might an __str__() method be a useful tool for tracking down programming errors?

9. What are special methods in Python?
10. When would you use a class attribute? Give a specific example.
11. Can you use an object of a class to assign a new value to a class attribute?
12. Are attributes and methods public or private by default?
13. How can you signify that an attribute or method is private?
14. Is it technically possible to access an object's private attributes and methods through the object?
15. Why should only an object update its private attributes?
16. How can you write a class that helps ensure the privacy of its objects?
17. When you use an object, how should you respect its privacy?
18. Why should you create new-style classes instead of old-style classes when possible?
19. What are access methods?
20. How are access methods helpful to programmers?

PROJECTS

1. Modify the Critter Caretaker program from this chapter so that the user specifies how much food he or she feeds the critter and how long he or she plays with the critter, using integer values. These values should affect how quickly a critter's hunger and boredom levels drop. The program should ensure that the user enters values that are greater than zero. Also, add an unlisted menu choice of -1, which displays the exact values of the Critter object's attributes. You should accomplish this by adding an __str__() method to the class and printing the Critter object.

2. Write a program with a class Ship for spaceship objects. The class constructor should create the attributes name and fuel for a new object. The constructor should have a parameter for the ship's name with a default value of "Enterprise" and a parameter for the ship's fuel level, with a default value of 0. If a value of less than 0 is passed to the parameter for the ship's fuel level, the ship's initial fuel level should be set to 0. The class should also have a method, status(), that displays an object's name and fuel values. Your program should instantiate several Ship objects and call their status() methods to test the various aspects of the class constructor.

3. Write a program with a Player class for a player who can carry a limited number of items, represented by strings. The class should define the following attributes:

- name for the player's name.
- max_items for the maximum number of items the player can carry at one time.
- items for the list of items that the player carries.

The class should define the following methods:

- `inventory()` should display the items that the player carries, or a message saying that the player has no items.
- `take()` should have a parameter to receive the item to be added to the player's set of items. The method should add the item to the player's items as long as adding it doesn't exceed the maximum number of items the player can carry; otherwise, the method should display a message saying that the player can't carry any more items.
- `drop()` should have a parameter to receive the item to be removed from the player's set of items. If the item exists in the player's set of items, the method should remove it; otherwise, the method should display a message saying that the player doesn't carry that item.

Your program should instantiate a `Player` object and call its `take()` and `drop()` methods to test the various outcomes.

4. Modify your program from Project 2 by adding two methods to the `Ship` class:

- `move()` should have a parameter to receive the distance for the `ship` to move. If the distance value is less than or equal to the object's `fuel` attribute, then the ship has enough fuel to move. In that case, a message should be displayed reporting the distance the ship moved and the object's `fuel` attribute should be reduced by the distance value. If the distance value is greater than the object's `fuel` attribute, the method should display a message saying that the ship doesn't have enough fuel to move. If the distance value is less than 1, the method should display a message saying that the ship can't move a distance less than 1. In any case, the last thing the method should do is call the object's `status()` method.
- `refuel()` should have a parameter to receive the amount of fuel to add. If the amount to add is greater than or equal to 1, the value should be added to the object's `fuel` attribute and a message saying that the fuel has been added should be displayed. If the amount to add is less than 1, the method should display a message saying that the ship can't be refueled with an amount less than 1. In any case, the last thing the method should do is call the object's `status()` method.

Your program should instantiate a `Ship` object and call its `move()` and `refuel()` methods to test the various outcomes.

5. Write a program that simulates a television with a class `Television`. The class should create the following attributes for a new object:

- __channel for the channel to which the television is tuned
- volume for the volume level of the television
- is_on for whether or not the television is on

The class should define the following methods:

- __init__() should create and initialize an object's three attributes: __channel, volume and is_on
- __str__() should return a string that describes the status of the television; if the television is on, the string should indicate that the television is on and list its channel number and volume level; otherwise, the string should indicate that the television is off
- toggle_power() should turn the television on if it's off or off if it's on
- get_channel() should return the channel number to which the television is tuned
- set_channel() should receive a channel number and change the channel to this number if the television is on and the channel number is between 0 and 499, the minimum and maximum channel values; otherwise, the method should display a message saying why the attempt to change channels was unsuccessful
- raise_volume() should increase the volume level if the television is on and the volume level isn't already 10, the maximum volume level; otherwise, the method should display a message saying why the attempt to raise the volume level was unsuccessful
- lower_volume() should decrease the volume level if the television is on and the volume level isn't already 0, the minimum volume level; otherwise, the method should display a message saying why the attempt to lower the volume level was unsuccessful

The class should define one property:

- channel for the channel to which the television is tuned, using the get_channel() and set_channel() methods

Your program should instantiate an object from the class Television and allow a user to manipulate it through a menu system similar to the one in the Critter Caretaker Chapter program from this chapter. The menu choices should be:

```
0 - Exit
1 - Toggle Power
2 - Change Channel
3 - Raise Volume
4 - Lower Volume
```

The program should display the status of the television each time it presents the menu.

OBJECT-ORIENTED PROGRAMMING: THE BLACKJACK GAME

In the last chapter, you learned about the software object. Almost every program you saw involved a single object. That's a great way to begin to understand how objects work, but the true power of OOP can only be appreciated by seeing a group of objects work together. In this chapter, you'll learn to create multiple objects and define relationships among them so that they can interact. Specifically, you'll learn to do the following:

- Create objects of different classes in the same program
- Allow objects to communicate with each other
- Create more complex objects by combining simpler ones
- Derive new classes from existing ones
- Extend the definition of existing classes
- Override method definitions of existing classes

INTRODUCING THE BLACKJACK GAME

The final game program for this chapter is a simplified version of the card game, Blackjack. The game works like this: Players are dealt cards with point values. Each player tries to reach a total of 21 without going over. Numbered cards count as their face value. An ace counts as either 1 or 11 (whichever is best for the player) and any jack, queen, or king counts as 10.

The computer is the dealer and competes against one to seven players. At the opening of the round, the computer deals all participants (including itself) two cards. Players can see all of their cards, and the computer even displays their total. However, one of the dealer's cards is hidden for the time being.

Next, each player gets a chance to take additional cards. Each player can take one card at a time for as long as the player likes. But if the player's total goes over 21 (known as "busting"), the player loses. If all players bust, the computer reveals its first card and the round is over. Otherwise, play continues. The computer must take additional cards as long as its total is less than 17. If the computer busts, all players who have not themselves busted, win. Otherwise, each remaining player's total is compared with the computer's. If the player's total is greater, the player wins. If the player's total is less, the player loses. If the two totals are the same, the player ties the computer (also known as "pushing"). Figure 9.1 shows off the game.

```
C:\Python22\python.exe
                 Welcome to Blackjack!
How many players? (1 - 7): 2
Enter player name: Larry
Enter player name: Jerry

Larry:   7h      7s      (14)
Jerry:   10d     9h      (19)
Dealer:  XX      3c

Larry, do you want a hit? (Y/N): y
Larry:   7h      7s      2d      (16)

Larry, do you want a hit? (Y/N): y
Larry:   7h      7s      2d      10c     (26)
Larry busts.
Larry loses.

Jerry, do you want a hit? (Y/N): n
Dealer:  10s     3c      (13)
Dealer:  10s     3c      Kh      (23)
Dealer busts.
Jerry wins.

Do you want to play again?:
```

FIGURE 9.1

One player wins,
the other is not so
lucky.

SENDING AND RECEIVING MESSAGES

In a way, an object-oriented program is like an ecosystem and objects are like organisms. To maintain a thriving ecosystem, organisms must interact. The same is true in OOP. To have a useful program, objects must interact in well-defined ways. In OOP-speak, objects interact by *sending messages* to each other. What they do on a practical level is invoke each other's methods.

That may sound a little impolite, but it's actually much more courteous than if an object were to access another object's attributes directly.

Introducing the Alien Blaster Program

The Alien Blaster program simulates an action game where a player blasts an alien. In the program, a hero blasts an invader and the invader dies (but not before giving a grand farewell speech). The program accomplishes this when one object sends another a message. Figure 9.2 shows the results of the program.

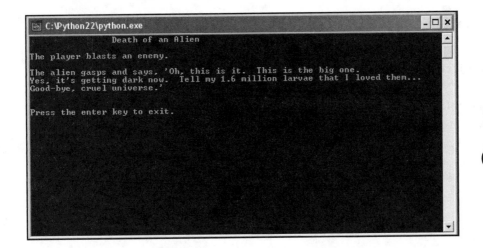

FIGURE 9.2

The battle description is the result of objects exchanging a message.

Technically what happens is that the program instantiates a Player object, hero, and an Alien object, invader. When hero's blast() method is invoked with invader as its argument, hero invokes invader's die() method. In English, this means that when a player blasts an alien, the player sends a message to the alien telling it to die. Figure 9.3 provides a visual representation of the message exchange.

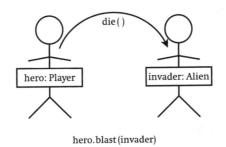

hero.blast(invader)

FIGURE 9.3

hero, a Player object, sends invader, an Alien object, a message.

IN THE REAL WORLD

The diagram I created to show two objects exchanging a message is a pretty simple one. But with many objects and many relationships among them, diagrams like this can become complex. In fact, there are a variety of formal methods for mapping software projects. One of the most popular is the *Unified Modeling Language* (UML), a notational language that is especially useful for visualizing object-oriented systems.

Here's the program listing for Alien Blaster:

```
# Alien Blaster
# Demonstrates object interaction

class Player(object):
    """ A player in a shooter game. """
    def blast(self, enemy):
        print "The player blasts an enemy.\n"
        enemy.die()


class Alien(object):
    """ An alien in a shooter game. """
    def die(self):
        print "The alien gasps and says, 'Oh, this is it. This is the big one. \n" \
                "Yes, it's getting dark now. Tell my 1.6 million larvae that I" \
                "loved them... Good-bye, cruel universe.'"

# main
print "\t\tDeath of an Alien\n"

hero = Player()
invader = Alien()
hero.blast(invader)

raw_input("\n\nPress the enter key to exit.")
```

Sending a Message

Before you can have one object send another object a message, you need two objects! So, I create two in the main part of the program. First, I create a `Player` object and assign it to `hero`. Then, I create an `Alien` object and assign it to `invader`.

The next line of code is where it gets interesting. Through `hero.blast(invader)`, I invoke `hero`'s `blast()` method and pass `invader`—the `Alien` object—as an argument. By examining the definition of `blast()`, you can see that the method accepts the object into its parameter `enemy`. So, when `blast()` executes, `enemy` refers to the `Alien` object. After displaying a message, `blast()` invokes the `Alien` object's `die()` method through `enemy.die()`. Essentially, the `Player` object is sending the `Alien` object a message by invoking its `die()` method.

Receiving a Message

The `Alien` object receives the message from the `Player` object in the form of its `die()` method being invoked. The `Alien` object's `die()` method then displays a melodramatic good-bye.

COMBINING OBJECTS

In the real world, interesting objects are usually made up of other independent objects. For example, a drag racer can be seen as a single object that's composed of individual objects such as a body, tires, and an engine. Other times, you may see an object as a collection of other objects. For example, a zoo can be seen as a collection of animals. Well, you can mimic these kinds of relationships among objects in OOP. You could write a `Drag_Racer` class that has an attribute `engine` that references a `Race_Engine` object. Or, you could write a `Zoo` class that has an attribute `animals` which is a list of different `Animal` objects. Combining objects like this allows you to create more complex objects from simpler ones.

Introducing the Playing Cards Program

The Playing Cards program uses objects to represent individual playing cards that you might use in a game of Blackjack or Go Fish (depending upon your tastes . . . and your tolerance for losing money). The program goes on to represent a hand of cards through an object that is a collection of card objects. Figure 9.4 shows the results of the program.

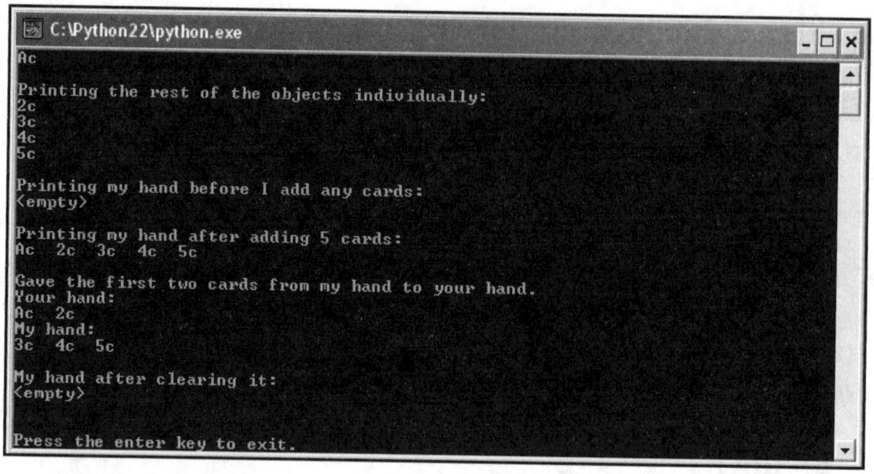

FIGURE 9.4

Each Hand object is
a collection of
Card objects.

Creating the Card Class

The first thing I do in the program is create a Card class for objects that represent playing cards. Here's the code for the Card class:

```python
# Playing Cards
# Demonstrates combining objects

class Card(object):
    """ A playing card. """
    RANKS = ["A", "2", "3", "4", "5", "6", "7",
             "8", "9", "10", "J", "Q", "K"]
    SUITS = ["c", "d", "h", "s"]

    def __init__(self, rank, suit):
        self.rank = rank
        self.suit = suit

    def __str__(self):
        rep = self.rank + self.suit
        return rep
```

Each Card object has a rank attribute, which represents the rank of the card. The possible values are listed in the class attribute RANKS. "A" represents an ace, "2" through "10" represent their corresponding numeric values, "J" represents a jack, "Q" represents a queen, and "K" represents a king.

Each card also has a `suit` attribute, which represents the suit of the card. The possible values for this attribute are listed in the class attribute `SUITS`. "c" represents clubs, "d" means diamonds, "h" stands for hearts, and "s" represents spades. So, an object with the `rank` attribute of "A" and a suit attribute of "d" represents the ace of diamonds.

The special method `__str__()` simply returns the concatenation of the `rank` and `suit` attributes so that an object can be printed.

Creating the Hand Class

The next thing I do in the program is create a `Hand` class for objects, which is a collection of `Card` objects:

```
class Hand(object):
    """ A hand of playing cards. """
    def __init__(self):
        self.cards = []

    def __str__(self):
        if self.cards:
            rep = ""
            for card in self.cards:
                rep += str(card) + " "
        else:
            rep = "<empty>"
        return rep

    def clear(self):
        self.cards = []

    def add(self, card):
        self.cards.append(card)

    def give(self, card, other_hand):
        self.cards.remove(card)
        other_hand.add(card)
```

A new `Hand` object has an attribute `cards` that is intended to be a list of `Card` objects. So each single `Hand` object has an attribute that is a list of possibly many other objects.

The special method __str__() returns a string that represents the entire hand. The method loops through each Card object in the Hand object and concatenates the Card object's string representation. If the Hand object has no Card objects, the string "<empty>" is returned.

The clear() method clears the list of cards by assigning an empty list to an object's cards attribute.

The add() method adds an object to the cards attribute.

The give() method removes an object from the Hand object and appends it to another Hand object by invoking the other Hand object's add() method. Another way to say this is that the first Hand object sends the second Hand object a message to add a Card object.

Using Card Objects

In the main part of the program, I create and print five Card objects:

```
# main
card1 = Card(rank = "A", suit = "c")
print "Printing a Card object:"
print card1

card2 = Card(rank = "2", suit = "c")
card3 = Card(rank = "3", suit = "c")
card4 = Card(rank = "4", suit = "c")
card5 = Card(rank = "5", suit = "c")
print "\nPrinting the rest of the objects individually:"
print card2
print card3
print card4
print card5
```

The first Card object created has a rank attribute equal to "A" and a suit attribute of "c". When I print the object, it's displayed on the screen as Ac. The remaining objects follow the same pattern.

Combining Card Objects Using a Hand Object

Next, I create a Hand object, assign it to my_hand, and print it:

```
my_hand = Hand()
print "\nPrinting my hand before I add any cards:"
print my_hand
```

Because the object's cards attribute is an empty list, printing the object displays the text <empty>.

Next, I add the five Card objects to my_hand and print it again:

```
my_hand.add(card1)
my_hand.add(card2)
my_hand.add(card3)
my_hand.add(card4)
my_hand.add(card5)
print "\nPrinting my hand after adding 5 cards:"
print my_hand
```

This time, the text Ac 2c 3c 4c 5c is displayed.

Then, I create another Hand object, your_hand. Using my_hand's give() method, I transfer the first two cards from my_hand to your_hand. Then, I print both hands:

```
your_hand = Hand()
my_hand.give(card1, your_hand)
my_hand.give(card2, your_hand)
print "\nGave the first two cards from my hand to your hand."
print "Your hand:"
print your_hand
print "My hand:"
print my_hand
```

As you'd expect, your_hand is displayed as Ac 2c while my_hand appears as 3c 4c 5c.

Finally, I invoke my_hand's clear() method and print my_hand one last time:

```
my_hand.clear()
print "\nMy hand after clearing it:"
print my_hand

raw_input("\n\nPress the enter key to exit.")
```

As it should, the text <empty> is displayed.

USING INHERITANCE TO CREATE NEW CLASSES

One of the key elements of OOP is *inheritance*, which allows you to base a new class on an existing one. By doing so, the new class automatically gets (or inherits) all of the methods and attributes of the existing class—it's like getting all of the work that went into writing the existing class for free!

TRAP In Python, it's possible to create a new class that directly inherits from more than one class. This is called *multiple inheritance*. But multiple inheritance is a thorny subject and can get confusing quickly. In fact, several of the most popular modern languages, such as C# and Java, have eliminated multiple inheritance and opted for the simpler, yet still powerful, *single inheritance*—where an object can inherit from only one class. As a beginning programmer, it's best to steer clear of multiple inheritance since it can be more heartache than help.

EXTENDING A CLASS THROUGH INHERITANCE

Inheritance is especially useful when you want to create a more specialized version of an existing class. As you just learned, by inheriting from an existing class, a new class gets all of the methods and attributes of the existing class. But you can also add methods and attributes to the new class to extend what objects of the new class can do.

For example, imagine that your Drag_Racer class defines a drag racer with methods stop() and go(). You could create a new class for a specialized type of drag racer that can clean its windshield (you get a lot of squashed bugs at 250 miles per hour) by basing it on the existing Drag_Racer class. Your new class would automatically inherit stop() and go() from Drag_Racer. So, all you'd have to do is define one new method for cleaning the windshield and the new class would be done.

Introducing the Playing Cards 2.0 Program

The Playing Cards 2.0 program is based on the Playing Cards program. The new version introduces the Deck class to describe a deck of playing cards. However, unlike any other class you've seen, Deck is based on an existing class, Hand. As a result, Deck automatically inherits all of Hand's methods. I create Deck this way because a deck of cards is really like a specialized hand of cards. It's a hand, but with extra behaviors. A deck can do anything that a hand can. It's a collection of cards. It can give a card to another hand, and so on. On top of that, a deck can do a few things that a hand can't. A deck can be shuffled and it can deal cards to multiple hands. The Playing Cards 2.0 program creates a deck that deals cards to two different hands. Figure 9.5 illustrates the results of the program.

The Deck object inherits all of the methods of the Hand class.

Creating a Base Class

I begin the new program like the old version. The first two classes, Card and Hand, are the same as before:

```
# Playing Cards 2.0
# Demonstrates inheritance - class extension

class Card(object):
    """ A playing card. """
    RANKS = ["A", "2", "3", "4", "5", "6", "7",
             "8", "9", "10", "J", "Q", "K"]
    SUITS = ["c", "d", "h", "s"]

    def __init__(self, rank, suit):
        self.rank = rank
        self.suit = suit

    def __str__(self):
        rep = self.rank + self.suit
        return rep
```

```
class Hand(object):
    """ A hand of playing cards. """
    def __init__(self):
        self.cards = []

    def __str__(self):
        if self.cards:
            rep = ""
            for card in self.cards:
                rep += str(card) + "\t"
        else:
            rep = "<empty>"
        return rep

    def clear(self):
        self.cards = []

    def add(self, card):
        self.cards.append(card)

    def give(self, card, other_hand):
        self.cards.remove(card)
        other_hand.add(card)
```

Inheriting from a Base Class

The next thing I do is create the Deck class. You can see from the class header that Deck is based on Hand:

```
class Deck(Hand):
```

Hand is called a *base class* because Deck is based on it. Deck is considered a *derived class* because it derives part of its definition from Hand. As a result of this relationship, Deck inherits all of Hand's methods. So, even if I didn't define a single new method in this class, Deck objects would still have all of the methods defined in Hand:

- __init__()
- __str__()
- clear()
- add()
- give()

If it helps, for this simple example, you can even imagine that you've copied and pasted all of Hand's methods right into Deck because of inheritance.

Extending a Derived Class

You can extend a derived class by defining additional methods in it. That's what I do in the class definition of Deck:

```
""" A deck of playing cards. """
def populate(self):
    for suit in Card.SUITS:
        for rank in Card.RANKS:
            self.add(Card(rank, suit))

def shuffle(self):
    import random
    random.shuffle(self.cards)

def deal(self, hands, per_hand = 1):
    for rounds in range(per_hand):
        for hand in hands:
            if self.cards:
                top_card = self.cards[0]
                self.give(top_card, hand)
            else:
                print "Can't continue deal. Out of cards!"
```

So, in addition to all of the methods that Deck inherits, it has the following new methods:

- populate()
- shuffle()
- deal()

As far as client code is concerned, any Deck method is as valid as any other—whether it's inherited from Hand or defined in Deck. And all of a Deck object's methods are invoked the same way, through dot notation.

Using the Derived Class

The first thing I do in the main part of the program is instantiate a new Deck object:

```
# main
deck1 = Deck()
```

Looking at the class, you'll notice that I don't define a constructor method in Deck. But Deck inherits the Hand constructor, so that method is automatically invoked with the newly created Deck object. As a result, the new Deck object gets a cards attribute which is initialized to an empty list, just as any newly created Hand object would get a similar cards attribute. Finally, the assignment statement assigns the new object to deck1.

Now armed with a new (but empty) deck, I print it:

```
print "Created a new deck."
print "Deck:"
print deck1
```

I didn't define the special __str__() method in Deck either, but again, Deck inherits the method from Hand. Because the deck is empty, the code displays the text <empty>. So far, a deck seems just like a hand. That's because a deck is a specialized type of hand. Remember, a deck can do anything a hand can, plus more.

An empty deck is no fun, so I invoke the object's populate() method, which populates the deck with the traditional 52 cards:

```
deck1.populate()
```

Now the deck has finally done something a hand can't. That's because the populate() method is a new method that I define in the Deck class. The populate() method loops through all of the 52 possible combinations of values of Card.SUITS and Card.RANKS (one for each card in a real deck). For each combination, the method creates a new Card object that it adds to the deck.

Next, I print the deck:

```
print "\nPopulated the deck."
print "Deck:"
print deck1
```

This time, all 52 cards are displayed! But if you look closely, you'll see that they're in an obvious order. To make things interesting, I shuffle the deck:

```
deck1.shuffle()
```

I define the shuffle() method in Deck. It imports the random module and then calls the random.shuffle() function with the object's cards attribute. As you might guess, the random.shuffle() method shuffles a list's elements into a random order. So, all of the elements of cards get shuffled. Perfect.

Now, with the cards in random order, I display the deck again:

```
print "\nShuffled the deck."
print "Deck:"
print deck1
```

Next, I create two Hand objects and put them in a list that I assign to hands:

```
my_hand = Hand()
your_hand = Hand()
hands = [my_hand, your_hand]
```

Then, I deal each hand five cards:

```
deck1.deal(hands, per_hand = 5)
```

The deal() method is a new method I define in Deck. It takes two arguments: a list of hands and the number of cards to deal each hand. The method gives a card from the deck to each hand. If the deck is out of cards, the method prints the message "Can't continue deal. Out of cards!" The method repeats this process for the number of cards to be dealt each hand. So, the previous line of code deals five cards from deck1 to each hand (my_hand and your_hand).

To see the results of the deal, I print each hand and the deck once more:

```
print "\nDealt 5 cards to my hand and your hand."
print "My hand:"
print my_hand
print "Your hand:"
print your_hand
print "Deck:"
print deck1
```

By looking at the output, you can see that each hand has 5 cards and the deck now has only 42.

Finally, I put the deck back to its initial state by clearing it:

```
deck1.clear()
print "\nCleared the deck."
```

And then I print the deck one last time:

```
print "Deck:", deck1
```

ALTERING THE BEHAVIOR OF INHERITED METHODS

You've seen how you can extend a class by adding new methods to a derived class. But you can also redefine how an inherited method of a base class works in a derived class. This is known as *overriding* the method. When you override a base class method, you have two choices. You can create a method with completely new functionality, or you can incorporate the functionality of the base class method that you're overriding.

As an example, take your Drag_Racer class again. Let's say that its stop() method simply applies the racer's brakes. If you want to create a new drag racer class that can stop even more quickly (by releasing a parachute behind the racer), you could derive a new, Parachute_Racer class from Drag_Racer and override its stop() method. You could write the new stop() method so that it invokes the stop() method of the original Drag_Racer class (which applies the racer's brakes) and then defines the action of the racer releasing a parachute.

Introducing the Playing Cards 3.0 Program

The Playing Cards 3.0 program derives two new classes of playing cards from the Card class you've been working with. The first new class defines cards that can't be printed. More precisely, when you print an object of this class, the text <unprintable> is displayed. The next class defines cards that can be either face up or face down. When you print an object of this class, there are two possible results. If the card is face up, it prints out just like an object of the Card class. But if the card is face down, the text XX is displayed. Figure 9.6 shows a sample run of the program.

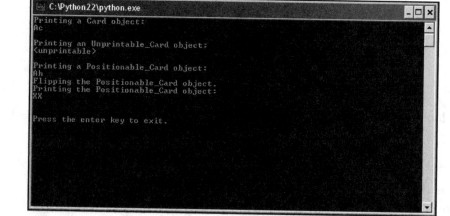

FIGURE 9.6

By overriding the inherited __str__() method, objects of different derived classes are printed out differently.

Creating a Base Class

To derive a new class, you need to start with a base class. For this program, I use the same Card class you've come to know and love:

```
# Playing Cards 3.0
# Demonstrates inheritance - overriding methods

class Card(object):
    """ A playing card. """
    RANKS = ["A", "2", "3", "4", "5", "6", "7",
             "8", "9", "10", "J", "Q", "K"]
    SUITS = ["c", "d", "h", "s"]

    def __init__(self, rank, suit):
        self.rank = rank
        self.suit = suit

    def __str__(self):
        rep = self.rank + self.suit
        return rep
```

Overriding Base Class Methods

Next, I derive a new class for unprintable cards based on Card. The class header looks pretty standard:

```
class Unprintable_Card(Card):
```

From this header, you know that Unprintable_Card inherits all of the methods of Card. But I can change the behavior of an inherited method by defining it in a derived class. And that's just what I did in the remainder of the method definition:

```
    """ A Card that won't reveal its rank or suit when printed. """
    def __str__(self):
        return "<unprintable>"
```

The Unprintable_Card class inherits the __str__() method from Card. But I also define a new __str__() method in Unprintable_Card that overrides (or replaces) the inherited one. Any time you create a method in a derived class with the same name as an inherited method, you override the inherited method in the new class. So, when you print an Unprintable_Card object, the text <unprintable> is displayed.

A derived class has no effect on a base class. A base class doesn't care if you derive a new class from it, or if you override an inherited method in the new class. The base class still functions as it always has. This means that when you print a Card object, it will appear as it always does.

Invoking Base Class Methods

Sometimes when you override the method of a base class, you want to incorporate the inherited method's functionality. For example, I want to create a new type of playing card class based on Card. I want an object of this new class to have an attribute that indicates whether or not the card is face up. This means I need to override the inherited constructor method from Card with a new constructor that creates a face up attribute. However, I also want my new constructor to create and set rank and suit attributes, just like the Card constructor already does. Instead of retyping the code from the Card constructor, I could invoke it from inside my new constructor. Then, it would take care of creating and initializing rank and suit attributes for an object of my new class. Back in the constructor method of my new class, I could add the attribute that indicates whether or not the card is face up. Well, that's exactly the approach I take in the Positionable_Card class:

```
class Positionable_Card(Card):
    """ A Card that can be face up or face down. """
    def __init__(self, rank, suit, face_up = True):
        super(Positionable_Card, self).__init__(rank, suit)
        self.is_face_up = face_up
```

The new function in the constructor, super(), lets you invoke the method of a base class (also called a *superclass*). The line super(Positionable_Card, self).__init__(rank, suit) invokes the __init__() method of Card (the superclass of Positionable_Card). The first argument in the call to super(), Positionable_Card, says that I want to invoke a method of the superclass (or base class) of Positionable_Card, which is Card. The next argument, self, passes a reference to the newly instantiated Positionable_Card object so that Card can get at the object to add the rank and suit attributes to it. The next part of the statement, __init__(rank, suit), tells Python that I want to invoke the constructor method of Card and I want to pass it the values of rank and suit.

TRAP The super() function was introduced in Python 2.2 and only works with new-style classes. If you're using old-style classes, you can still invoke a base class method, you just have to explicitly specify the name of the class. For example, if I want to explicitly invoke the constructor of the Card class in Positionable_Card, I could use this line:

```
Card.__init__(self, rank, suit)
```

But the super() function is better in more complex situations, so use super() whenever possible over this explicit way of calling a base class method.

The next method in Positionable_Card also overrides a method inherited from Card and invokes the overridden method:

```
def __str__(self):
    if self.is_face_up:
        rep = super(Positionable_Card, self).__str__()
    else:
        rep = "XX"
    return rep
```

This __str__() method first checks to see whether an object's face_up attribute is True (which means that the card is face up). If so, the string representation for the card is set to the string returned from Card's __str__() method called with the Positionable_Card object. In other words, if the card is face up, the card prints out like any object of the Card class. However, if the card is not face up, the string representation returned is "XX".

The last method in the class doesn't override an inherited method. It simply extends the definition of this new class:

```
def flip(self):
    self.is_face_up = not self.is_face_up
```

The method flips a card over by toggling the value of an object's face_up attribute. If an object's face_up attribute is True, then invoking the object's flip() method sets the attribute to False. If an object's face_up attribute is False, then invoking the object's flip() method sets the attribute to True.

Using the Derived Classes

In the main part of the program, I create three objects: one from `Card`, another from `Unprintable_Card`, and the last from `Positionable_Card`:

```
#main
card1 = Card("A", "c")
card2 = Unprintable_Card("A", "d")
card3 = Positionable_Card("A", "h")
```

Next, I print the `Card` object:

```
print "Printing a Card object:"
print card1
```

This works just like in previous programs, and the text `Ac` is displayed.

The next thing I do is print an `Unprintable_Card` object:

```
print "\nPrinting an Unprintable_Card object:"
print card2
```

Even though the object has a `rank` attribute set to `"A"` and a `suit` attribute set to `"d"`, printing the object displays the text `<unprintable>` because the `Unprintable_Card` class overrides its inherited `__str__()` method with one that always returns the string `"<unprintable>"`.

The next two lines print a `Positionable_Card` object:

```
print "\nPrinting a Positionable_Card object:"
print card3
```

Because the object's `face_up` attribute is `True`, the object's `__str__()` method invokes `Card`'s `__str__()` method and the text `Ah` is displayed.

Next, I invoke the `Positionable_Card` object's `flip()` method:

```
print "Flipping the Positionable_Card object."
card3.flip()
```

As a result, the object's `face_up` attribute is set to `False`.

The next two lines print the `Positionable_Card` object again:

```
print "Printing the Positionable_Card object:"
print card3

raw_input("\n\nPress the enter key to exit.")
```

This time `XX` is displayed because the object's `face_up` attribute is `False`.

Understanding Polymorphism

Polymorphism is the quality of being able to treat different types of things the same and have those things each react in their own way. Used in the context of OOP, polymorphism means that you can send the same message to objects of different classes related by inheritance and achieve different and appropriate results. For example, Unprintable_Card is derived from Card, and when you invoke the __str__() method of an Unprintable_Card object, you get a different result than when you invoke the __str__() method of a Card object. The result of this polymorphic behavior is that you can print an object even if you don't know whether it's an Unprintable_Card or a Card object. Regardless of the class of the object, when printed, its __str__() method is invoked and the correct string representation of it is displayed.

CREATING MODULES

You first learned about modules in Chapter 3, in the section "Using the import Statement," where you met the random module. But a powerful aspect of Python programming is that you can create, use, and even share your own modules. Creating your own modules provides important benefits.

First, by creating your own modules, you can reuse code, which can save you time and effort. For example, you could reuse the Card, Hand, and Deck classes you've seen so far to create many different types of card games without having to reinvent basic card, deck, and hand functionality every time.

Second, by breaking up a program into logical modules, large programs become easier to manage. So far, the programs you've been working with have been contained in one file. Because they've been pretty short, this is no big deal. But imagine a program that's thousands (or even tens of thousands) of lines long. Working with a program of this size in one massive file would be a real nightmare (professional projects, by the way, can easily get this large.)

Third, by creating modules, you can share your genius. If you create a useful module, you can e-mail it to a friend, who then can use it much like any built-in Python module.

Introducing the Simple Game Program

The Simple Game program, as the name suggests, is simple. The program first asks how many players wish to participate and then proceeds to get each player's name. Finally, the program assigns a random score to each player and displays the results. Not very thrilling, but the point of the program is not the game, but rather how the game works. The program uses a brand-new module with functions and a class that I created. Figure 9.7 displays the results of the program.

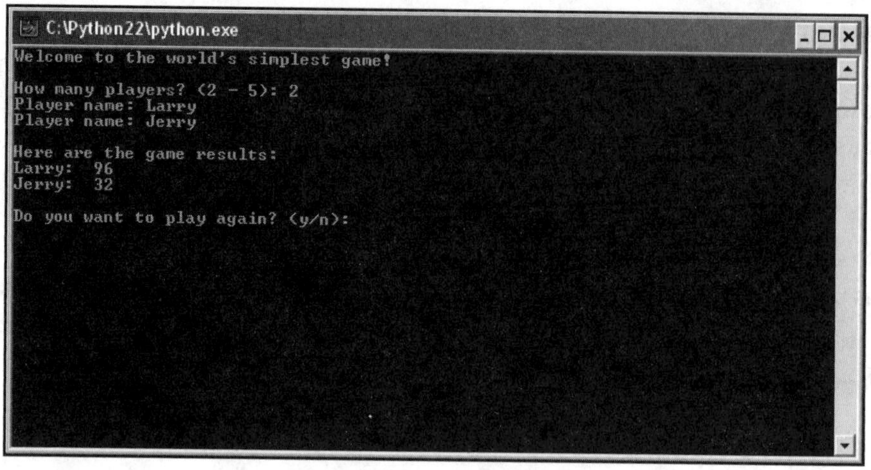

FIGURE 9.7

Several functions and a class used in the program are from a programmer-created module.

Writing Modules

Normally, I'd show you the code for the next program, Simple Game, but in this section, I go over the module I've written that Simple Game uses.

You create a module the same way you write any other Python program. When you create a module, though, you should build a collection of related programming components, such as functions and classes, and store them in a single file to be imported into a new program.

I created a basic module, called games, that contains two functions and a class that might be useful in creating a game. Here's the code:

```python
# Games
# Demonstrates module creation

class Player(object):
    """ A player for a game. """
    def __init__(self, name, score = 0):
        self.name = name
        self.score = score

    def __str__(self):
        rep = self.name + ":\t" + str(self.score)
        return rep

def ask_yes_no(question):
    """Ask a yes or no question."""
```

```
        response = None
        while response not in ("y", "n"):
            response = raw_input(question).lower()
        return response


def ask_number(question, low, high):
    """Ask for a number within a range."""
    response = None
    while response not in range(low, high):
        response = int(raw_input(question))
    return response


if __name__ == "__main__":
    print "You ran this module directly (and did not 'import' it)."
    raw_input("\n\nPress the enter key to exit.")
```

This module is named games because I saved the file with the name games.py. Programmer-created modules are named (and imported) based on their file names.

The bulk of the module is straightforward. The Player class defines an object with two attributes, name and score, which are set in the constructor method. There's only one other method, __str__(), which returns a string representation so that objects can be printed.

You've seen the next two functions, ask_yes_no() and ask_number(), before in Chapter 6, in the "The ask_yes_no() Function" and the "The ask_number() Function" sections.

The next part of the program introduces a new idea, related to modules. The condition of the if statement, __name__ == "__main__", is true if the program is run directly. It's false if the file is imported as a module. So, if the games.py file is run directly, a message is displayed telling the user that the file is meant to be imported and not directly run.

Importing Modules

Now that you've seen the games module, I'll introduce the code of the Simple Game program. The following are the first few lines:

```
# Simple Game
# Demonstrates importing modules

import games, random
```

You import a programmer-created module the same way you import a built-in module, with the import statement. In fact, I import the games module along with the familiar random module in the same import statement.

If a programmer-created module isn't in the same directory as the program that imports it, Python won't be able to find the module. There are ways around this. It's even possible to install a programmer-created module so that it's available system-wide, just like built-in modules, but this requires a special installation procedure that's beyond the scope of this book. So for now, make sure that any module you want to import is in the same directory as the programs that import it.

Using Imported Functions and Classes

I use the imported modules in the remainder of the Simple Game program. After welcoming the players and setting up a simple loop, I ask how many players there will be in the game:

```
print "Welcome to the world's simplest game!\n"

again = None
while again != "n":
    players = []
    num = games.ask_number(question = "How many players? (2 - 5): ",
                           low = 2, high = 5)
```

I get the number of players by calling the ask_number() function from the games module. Just as with other imported modules, to call a function I use dot notation, specifying first the module name followed by the function name.

Next, for each player, I get the player's name and generate a random score between 1 and 100 by calling the randrange() function from the random module. Then, I create a player object using this name and score. Because the Player class is defined in the games module, again I use dot notation and include the module name before the class name. Then, I append this new player object to a list of players.

```
    for i in range(num):
        name = raw_input("Player name: ")
        score = random.randrange(100) + 1
        player = games.Player(name, score)
        players.append(player)
```

Next, I print each player in the game:

```
print "\nHere are the game results:"
for player in players:
    print player
```

Finally, I ask if the players want to play another game. I use the `ask_yes_no()` function from the `games` module to obtain my answer:

```
again = games.ask_yes_no("\nDo you want to play again? (y/n): ")
```

```
raw_input("\n\nPress the enter key to exit.")
```

BACK TO THE BLACKJACK GAME

At this point, you're an expert in using Python classes to create playing cards, hands, and decks. So now it's time to build on that expertise and see how to combine these classes in a larger program to create a complete casino-style card game (tacky green felt not included).

The cards Module

To write the Blackjack game, I created a final `cards` module based on the Playing Cards programs. The `Hand` and `Deck` classes are exactly the same as those in the Playing Cards 2.0 program. The new `Card` class represents the same functionality as the `Positionable_Card` from the Playing Cards 3.0 program. Here's the code for this module, stored in the file `cards.py`:

```
# Cards Module
# Basic classes for a game with playing cards

class Card(object):
    """ A playing card. """
    RANKS = ["A", "2", "3", "4", "5", "6", "7",
            "8", "9", "10", "J", "Q", "K"]
    SUITS = ["c", "d", "h", "s"]
    def __init__(self, rank, suit, face_up = True):
        self.rank = rank
        self.suit = suit
        self.is_face_up = face_up

    def __str__(self):
        if self.is_face_up:
            rep = self.rank + self.suit
        else:
            rep = "XX"
```

```
        return rep

    def flip(self):
        self.is_face_up = not self.is_face_up


class Hand(object):
    """ A hand of playing cards. """
    def __init__(self):
        self.cards = []

    def __str__ (self):
        if self.cards:
            rep = ""
            for card in self.cards:
                rep += str(card) + "\t"
        else:
            rep = "<empty>"
        return rep

    def clear(self):
        self.cards = []

    def add(self, card):
        self.cards.append(card)

    def give(self, card, other_hand):
        self.cards.remove(card)
        other_hand.add(card)


class Deck(Hand):
    """ A deck of playing cards. """
    def populate(self):
        for suit in Card.SUITS:
            for rank in Card.RANKS:
                self.add(Card(rank, suit))

    def shuffle(self):
```

```
        import random
        random.shuffle(self.cards)

    def deal(self, hands, per_hand = 1):
        for rounds in range(per_hand):
            for hand in hands:
                if self.cards:
                    top_card = self.cards[0]
                    self.give(top_card, hand)
                else:
                    print "Can't continue deal. Out of cards!"


if __name__ == "__main__":
    print "This is a module with classes for playing cards."
    raw_input("\n\nPress the enter key to exit.")
```

Designing the Classes

Before you start coding a project with multiple classes, it can help to map them out on paper. You might make a list and include a brief description of each class. Table 9.1 shows my first pass at such a listing for the Blackjack game.

TABLE 9.1 BLACKJACK CLASSES

Class	Base Class	Description
BJ_Card	cards.Card	A Blackjack playing card. Define an attribute value to represent the point value of a card.
BJ_Deck	cards.Deck	A Blackjack deck. A collection of BJ_Card objects.
BJ_Hand	cards.Hand	A Blackjack hand. Define an attribute total to represent the point total of a hand. Define an attribute name to represent the owner of the hand.
BJ_Player	BJ_Hand	A Blackjack player.
BJ_Dealer	BJ_Hand	A Blackjack dealer.
BJ_Game	object	A Blackjack game. Define an attribute deck for a BJ_Deck object. Define an attribute dealer for a BJ_Dealer object. Define an attribute players for a list of BJ_Player objects.

You should try to include all of the classes you think you'll need, but don't worry about making your class descriptions complete, because invariably they won't be (mine aren't). But making such a list should help you get a good overview of the types of objects you'll be working with in your project.

In addition to describing your classes in words, you might want to draw a family tree of sorts to visualize how your classes are related. That's what I did in Figure 9.8.

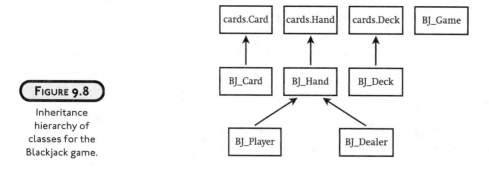

A class hierarchy diagram, like the one in Figure 9.8, can give you a summary view of how you're using inheritance.

Writing Pseudocode for the Game Loop

The next thing I did in planning the game was write some pseudocode for the play of one round. I thought this would help me see how objects would interact. Here's the pseudocode I came up with:

Deal each player and dealer initial two cards

For each player

    While the player asks for a hit and the player is not busted

        Deal the player an additional card

If there are no players still playing

    Show the dealer's two cards

Otherwise

    While the dealer must hit and the dealer is not busted

        Deal the dealer an additional card

> *If the dealer is busted*
>
>> *For each player who is still playing*
>>
>>> *The player wins*
>
> *Otherwise*
>
>> *For each player who is still playing*
>>
>>> *If the player's total is greater than the dealer's total*
>>>
>>>> *The player wins*
>>>
>>> *Otherwise, if the player's total is less than the dealer's total*
>>>
>>>> *The player loses*
>>>
>>> *Otherwise*
>>>
>>>> *The player pushes*

Importing the `cards` and `games` Modules

Now that you've seen the planning, it's time to check out the code. In the first part of the Blackjack program, I import the two modules `cards` and `games`:

```
# Blackjack
# From 1 to 7 players compete against a dealer

import cards, games
```

I created the `games` module, you'll remember, in the Simple Game program, earlier in this chapter.

The `BJ_Card` Class

The `BJ_Card` class extends the definition of what a card is by inheriting from `cards.Card`. In `BJ_Card`, I create a new property, `value`, for the point value of a card:

```
class BJ_Card(cards.Card):
    """ A Blackjack Card. """
    ACE_VALUE = 1

    def get_value(self):
        if self.is_face_up:
            value = BJ_Card.RANKS.index(self.rank) + 1
```

```
            if value > 10:
                value = 10
        else:
            value = None
        return value

    value = property(get_value)
```

The get_value() method returns a number between 1 and 10, which represents the value of a Blackjack card. The first part of the calculation is computed through the expression BJ_Card.RANKS.index(self.rank) + 1. This expression takes the rank attribute of an object (say "6") and finds its corresponding index number in BJ_Card.RANKS through the list method index() (for "6" this would be 5). Finally, 1 is added to the result since the computer starts counting at 0 (this makes the value calculated from "6" the correct 6). However, because rank attributes of "J", "Q", and "K" result in numbers larger than 10, any value greater than 10 is set to 10. If an object's face_up attribute is False, this whole process is avoided and a value of None is returned. Finally, I use the property() function with the get_value() method to create the property value.

The BJ_Deck **Class**

The BJ_Deck class is used to create a deck of Blackjack cards. The class is almost exactly the same as its base class, cards.Deck. The only difference is that I override cards.Deck's populate() method so that a new BJ_Deck object gets populated with BJ_Card objects:

```
class BJ_Deck(cards.Deck):
    """ A Blackjack Deck. """
    def populate(self):
        for suit in BJ_Card.SUITS:
            for rank in BJ_Card.RANKS:
                self.cards.append(BJ_Card(rank, suit))
```

The BJ_Hand **Class**

The BJ_Hand class, based on cards.Hand, is used for Blackjack hands. I override the cards.Hand constructor and add a name attribute to represent the name of the hand owner:

```
class BJ_Hand(cards.Hand):
    """ A Blackjack Hand. """
    def __init__(self, name):
        super(BJ_Hand, self).__init__()
        self.name = name
```

Next, I override the inherited __str__() method to display the total point value of the hand:

```
def __str__(self):
    rep = self.name + ":\t" + super(BJ_Hand, self).__str__()
    if self.total:
        rep += "(" + str(self.total) + ")"
    return rep
```

I concatenate the object's name attribute with the string returned from the cards.Hand__str__() method for the object. Then, if the object's total property isn't None, I concatenate the string representation of the value of total. Finally, I return that string.

Next, I create a property called total, which represents the total point value of a Blackjack hand. If a Blackjack hand has a face-down card in it, then its total property is None. Otherwise, total is calculated by adding the point values of all the cards in the hand.

```
def get_total(self):
    # if a card in the hand has value of None, then total is None
    for card in self.cards:
        if not card.value:
            return None

    # add up card values, treat each Ace as 1
    total = 0
    for card in self.cards:
        total += card.value

    # determine if hand contains an Ace
    contains_ace = False
    for card in self.cards:
        if card.value == BJ_Card.ACE_VALUE:
            contains_ace = True

    # if hand contains Ace and total is low enough, treat Ace as 11
    if contains_ace and total <= 11:
        # add only 10 since we've already added 1 for the Ace
        total += 10

    return total

total = property(get_total)
```

The first part of this method checks to see whether any card in the Blackjack hand has a value attribute equal to None (which would mean that the card is face down). If so, the method returns None. The next part of the method simply sums the point values of all the cards in the hand. The next part determines whether the hand contains an ace. If so, the last part of the method determines whether the card's point value should be 11 or 1. The last line of this section creates the property total.

The last method in BJ_Hand is_busted(). It returns True if the object's total property is greater than 21. Otherwise, it returns False.

```
def is_busted(self):
    return self.total > 21
```

Notice that in this method, I return the result of the condition self.total > 21 instead of assigning the result to a variable and then returning that variable. You can create this kind of return statement with any condition (any expression actually) and it often results in a more elegant method.

This kind of method, which returns either True or False, is pretty common. It's often used (like here) to represent a condition of an object with two possibilities, such as "on" or "off," for example. This type of method almost always has a name that starts with the word "is," as in is_on().

The BJ_Player Class

The BJ_Player class, derived from BJ_Hand, is used for Blackjack players:

```
class BJ_Player(BJ_Hand):
    """ A Blackjack Player. """
    def is_hitting(self):
        response = games.ask_yes_no("\n" + self.name + ", do you want a hit? (Y/N): ")
        return response == "y"

    def bust(self):
        print self.name, "busts."
        self.lose()

    def lose(self):
        print self.name, "loses."

    def win(self):
        print self.name, "wins."
```

```
def push(self):
    print self.name, "pushes."
```

The first method, is_hitting(), returns True if the player wants another hit and returns False if the player doesn't. The bust() method announces that a player busts and invokes the object's lose() method. The lose() method announces that a player loses. The win() method announces that a player wins. And the push() method announces that a player pushes. The bust(), lose(), win(), and push() methods are so simple that you may wonder why they exist. I put them in the class because they form a great skeleton structure to handle the more complex issues that arise when players are allowed to bet.

The BJ_Dealer Class

The BJ_Dealer class, derived from BJ_Hand, is used for the game's Blackjack dealer:

```
class BJ_Dealer(BJ_Hand):
    """ A Blackjack Dealer. """
    def is_hitting(self):
        return self.total < 17

    def bust(self):
        print self.name, "busts."

    def flip_first_card(self):
        first_card = self.cards[0]
        first_card.flip()
```

The first method, is_hitting(), represents whether or not the dealer is taking additional cards. Because a dealer must hit on any hand totaling 17 or less, the method returns True if the object's total property is less than 17; otherwise, it returns False. The bust() method announces that the dealer busts. The flip_first_card() method turns over the dealer's first card.

The BJ_Game Class

The BJ_Game class is used to create a single object that represents a Blackjack game. The class contains the code for the main game loop in its play() method. However, the mechanics of the game are complex enough that I create a few elements outside the method, including an __additional_cards() method that takes care of dealing additional cards to a player, and a still_playing property that returns a list of all players still playing in the round.

The __init__() Method

The constructor receives a list of names and creates a player for each name. The method also creates a dealer and a deck.

```
class BJ_Game(object):
    """ A Blackjack Game. """
    def __init__(self, names):
        self.players = []
        for name in names:
            player = BJ_Player(name)
            self.players.append(player)

        self.dealer = BJ_Dealer("Dealer")

        self.deck = BJ_Deck()
        self.deck.populate()
        self.deck.shuffle()
```

The still_playing Property

The still_playing property returns a list of all the players that are still playing (those that haven't busted this round):

```
    def get_still_playing(self):
        remaining = []
        for player in self.players:
            if not player.is_busted():
                remaining.append(player)
        return remaining

    # list of players still playing (not busted) this round
    still_playing = property(get_still_playing)
```

The __additional_cards() Method

The __additional_cards() method deals additional cards to either a player or the dealer. The method receives an object into its player parameter, which can be either a BJ_Player or BJ_Dealer object. The method continues while the object's is_busted() method returns False and its is_hitting() method returns True. If the object's is_busted() method returns True, then the object's bust() method is invoked.

```
def __additional_cards(self, player):
    while not player.is_busted() and player.is_hitting():
        self.deck.deal([player])
        print player
        if player.is_busted():
            player.bust()
```

Polymorphism is at work here in two method calls. The `player.is_hitting()` method call works equally well whether `player` refers to a `BJ_Player` object or a `BJ_Dealer` object. The `__additional_cards()` method never has to know which type of object it's working with. The same is true in the line `player.bust()`. Since both classes, `BJ_Player` and `BJ_Dealer`, each define their own `bust()` method, the line creates the desired result in either case.

The `play()` Method

The `play()` method is where the game loop is defined. It bears a striking resemblance to the pseudocode I introduced earlier:

```
def play(self):
    # deal initial 2 cards to everyone
    self.deck.deal(self.players + [self.dealer], per_hand = 2)
    self.dealer.flip_first_card() # hide dealer's first card
    for player in self.players:
        print player
    print self.dealer

    # deal additional cards to players
    for player in self.players:
        self.__additional_cards(player)

    self.dealer.flip_first_card() # reveal dealer's first

    if not self.still_playing:
        # since all players have busted, just show the dealer's hand
        print self.dealer
    else:
        # deal additional cards to dealer
        print self.dealer
        self.__additional_cards(self.dealer)
```

```
        if self.dealer.is_busted():
            # everyone still playing wins
            for player in self.still_playing:
                player.win()
        else:
            # compare each player still playing to dealer
            for player in self.still_playing:
                if player.total > self.dealer.total:
                    player.win()
                elif player.total < self.dealer.total:
                    player.lose()
                else:
                    player.push()

    # remove everyone's cards
    for player in self.players:
        player.clear()
    self.dealer.clear()
```

All players and the dealer are dealt the initial two cards. The dealer's first card is flipped to hide its value. Next, all of the hands are displayed. Then, each player is given cards as long as the player requests additional cards and hasn't busted. If all players have busted, the dealer's first card is flipped and the dealer's hand is printed. Otherwise, play continues. The dealer gets cards as long as the dealer's hand total is less than 17. If the dealer busts, all remaining players win. Otherwise, each remaining player's hand is compared with the dealer's. If the player's total is greater than the dealer's, the player wins. If the player's total is less, the player loses. If the two totals are equal, the player pushes.

The main() Function

The main() function gets the names of all the players, puts them in a list, and creates a BJ_Game object, using the list as an argument. Next, the function invokes the object's play() method and will continue to do so until the players no longer want to play.

```
def main():
    print "\t\tWelcome to Blackjack!\n"

    names = []
    number = games.ask_number("How many players? (1 - 7): ", low = 1, high = 8)
    for i in range(number):
```

```
        name = raw_input("Enter player name: ")
        names.append(name)
    print

    game = BJ_Game(names)

    again = None
    while again != "n":
        game.play()
        again = games.ask_yes_no("\nDo you want to play again?: ")
main()
raw_input("\n\nPress the enter key to exit.")
```

SUMMARY

- In object-oriented programming, objects can send messages to each other by invoking each other's methods.
- Objects can be composed of other objects or have collections of objects.
- Inheritance is an aspect of object-oriented programming that allows a new class to be based on an existing one where the new class automatically gets (or inherits) all of the methods and attributes of the existing one.
- Inheritance can be used to create a more specialized version of an existing class.
- A base class is a class upon which another is based; it is inherited from this other class (the derived class).
- A derived class is a class that is based upon another class; it inherits from this other class (a base class).
- Superclass is another name for base class.
- A derived class can define new methods and attributes in addition to the ones that it inherits.
- To override an inherited method is to redefine how the method of a base class works in a derived class.
- When overriding a method, the new definition can have completely different functionality than the original definition or the new definition can incorporate the functionality of the original.
- The super() function aids you in invoking the method of a superclass.

- Polymorphism is an aspect of object-oriented programming that allows you to send the same message to objects of different classes, related by inheritance, and achieve different but appropriate results for each object.
- You can write, import, and even share your own modules.
- You write a module as a collection of related programming components, like functions and classes, in a single Python file.
- Programmer-created modules can be imported the same way that built-in modules can, with an `import` statement.

REVIEW QUESTIONS

1. What's an example of one object sending another object a message?
2. How can the Unified Modeling Language (UML) help you design programs?
3. What's an example of an object that is composed of other objects?
4. What's an example of an object that has a collection of other objects?
5. In the Playing Cards program from this chapter, how does a `Hand` object maintain a collection of `Card` objects?
6. What are some advantages that inheritance provides?
7. Are there any disadvantages to using inheritance?
8. What is the difference between multiple inheritance and single inheritance?
9. Why might you want to extend a class through inheritance? Give a specific example.
10. In the Playing Cards 2.0 program from this chapter, what attribute is inherited by the `Deck` class?
11. How can you tell if a method of an object is derived from a base class?
12. When might you want to override an inherited method? Give a specific example.
13. Why might you want to invoke a method from a base class in a derived class?
14. In the Playing Cards 3.0 program from this chapter, why is the superclass constructor invoked in the `Positionable_Card` constructor?
15. When should you use or avoid the `super()` function?
16. How can polymorphism help a programmer?
17. What are some advantages that being able to write your own modules provides?
18. Why should you include only related programming elements in a single module?
19. Can the `cards` module from this chapter be used for a card game other than blackjack?
20. In the Blackjack Chapter Project from this chapter, what important element of object-oriented programming does the `__additional_cards()` method depend on?

PROJECTS

1. Add some much-needed error checking to the Blackjack game program from this chapter. Before a new round of play begins, make sure that the deck has at least seven cards per human player. If it doesn't, clear, repopulate and reshuffle the deck.

2. Write two classes for weapons in a fantasy role-playing game. The first class, Weapon, a generic class upon which all other weapon classes will be based, should define just one attribute:

   • damage - represents the amount of damage the weapon inflicts when used. It should have a default value of 0.

   The class should define one method:

   • __init__() - accepts a value into a parameter and assigns it to the object's new attribute damage.

   The second class, Sword, should be derived from Weapon and define a single method:

   • swing() - displays the message You swing and inflict XX damage points, where XX is equal to the object's attribute damage.

3. Modify your Project 2 program to include a new class, Crossbow, that's derived from Weapon, which defines the attribute:

   • is_loaded – represents, with a Boolean value, whether or not a crossbow is loaded. It should have a default value of True.

   The class should define the following methods:

   • __init__() - overrides but invokes Weapon's __init__() method; creates and initializes the attribute is_loaded.

   • fire() - tests the object's is_loaded attribute; if True, it displays the message You fire and inflict XX damage points, where XX is equal to the object's attribute damage; otherwise, it displays You must reload before you can fire again!

   • reload() - tests the object's is_loaded attribute; if False, displays the message Loaded! and sets is_loaded to True; otherwise, displays Already loaded!

4. Modify the Alien Blaster program from this chapter so that a player starts with a positive amount of ammunition. Each time a player blasts an alien, the player's ammunition count should be reduced by 1. If the player's ammunition count reaches 0, the player should no longer be able to blast aliens. An alien should start with a positive health value. Each time an alien is blasted, its health should be reduced by 1. When an alien's health drops below 1, it should die. If a player blasts a dead alien, the alien should

complain that it's already dead. Have the player blast the alien multiple times to test the various outcomes.

5. Modify your Project 1 program by giving each player a bankroll of 1,000 dollars. Each player should place a bet for each round of the blackjack game. Keep track of each player's bankroll and remove any player from the game who runs out of money.

GUI DEVELOPMENT:
THE MAD LIB PROGRAM

So far, all the programs you've seen have used plain old text to interact with the user. But there are more sophisticated ways to present and accept information. A graphical user interface (GUI) provides a visual way for a user to interact with the computer. The most popular home operating systems all employ a GUI, making user interactions simpler and more consistent. In this chapter, you'll learn to create GUIs. Specifically, you'll learn to do the following:

- Work with a GUI toolkit
- Create and fill frames
- Create and use buttons
- Create and use text entries and text boxes
- Create and use check buttons
- Create and use radio buttons

INTRODUCING THE MAD LIB PROGRAM

The final program for this chapter, the Mad Lib game, asks for the user's help in creating a story. The user supplies the name of a person, a plural noun, and a verb. The user can also choose from several adjectives and may select one body part. The program takes all of this information and uses it to create a story. Figures 10.1 through 10.3 show off the program. As you can see, the Mad Lib program uses a GUI to interact with the user.

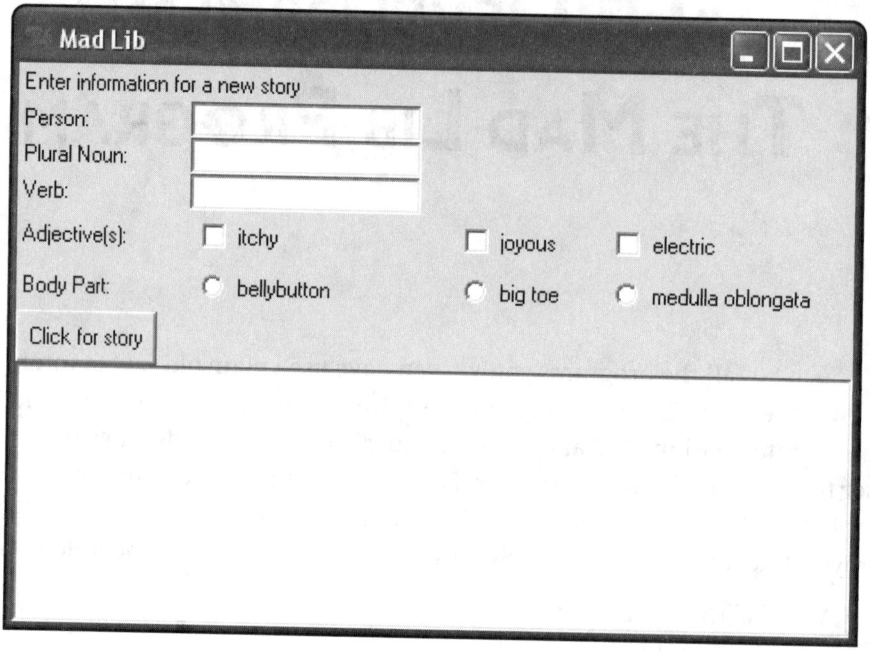

Mad Lib	
Enter information for a new story	
Person:	
Plural Noun:	
Verb:	
Adjective(s): ☐ itchy ☐ joyous ☐ electric	
Body Part: ○ bellybutton ○ big toe ○ medulla oblongata	
Click for story	

FIGURE 10.1

A nicely laid-out GUI awaits the user's creativity.

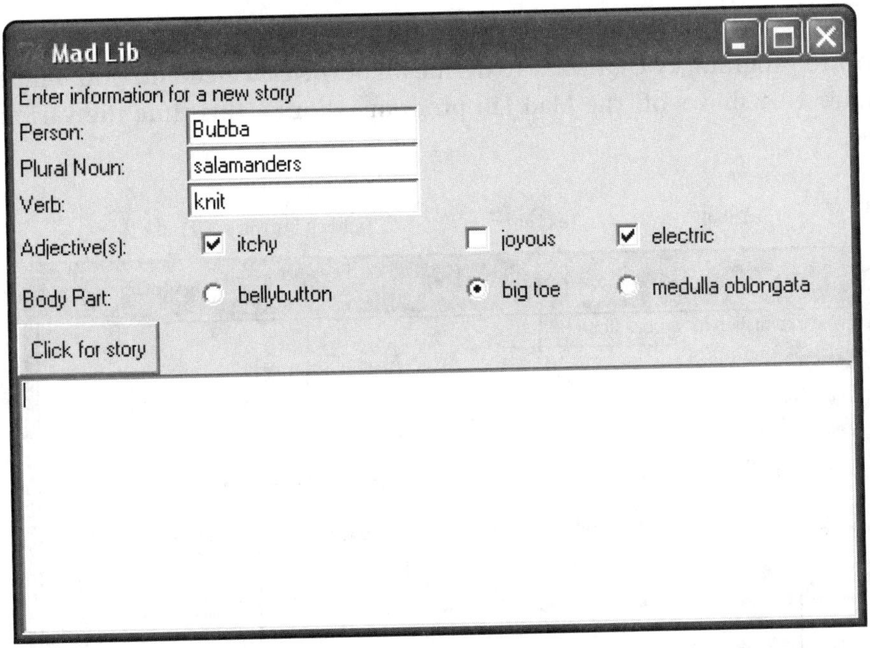

FIGURE 10.2

The user has entered all of the necessary information.

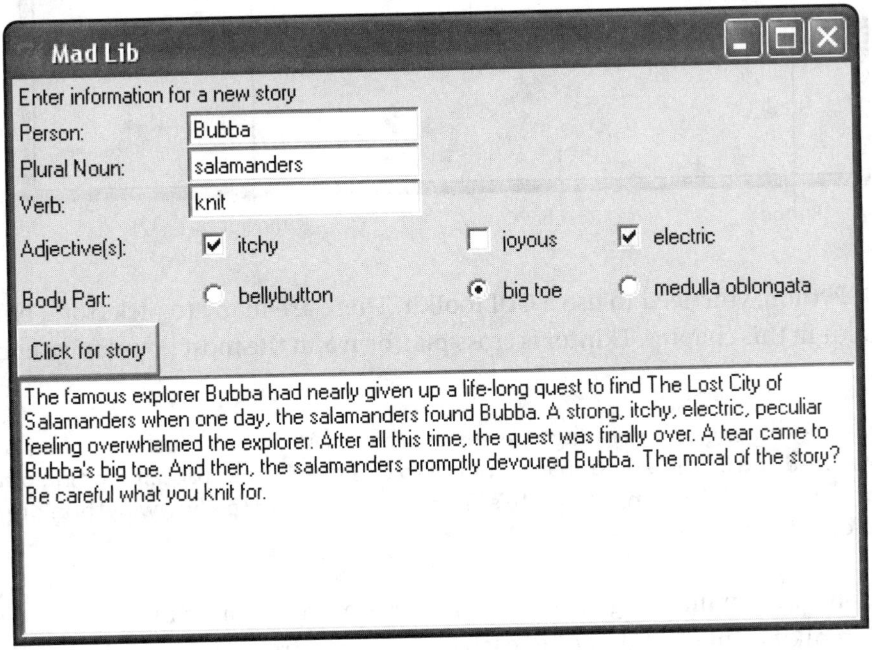

FIGURE 10.3

After clicking the Click for story button, the text box displays the literary masterpiece.

EXAMINING A GUI

Before I describe how to program a GUI, I want to define all of the GUI elements you'll meet in this chapter. Figure 10.4 shows off the Mad Lib program, though this time the various elements are labeled.

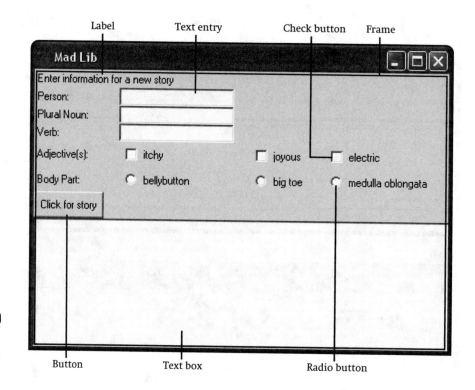

FIGURE 10.4

You'll learn to create all of these GUI elements.

To create a GUI with Python, you need to use a GUI toolkit. There are many to pick from, but I use the Tkinter toolkit in this chapter. Tkinter is cross-platform and the most popular Python GUI toolkit around.

If you're running an operating system other than Windows, you may need to download and install additional software to use the Tkinter toolkit. To find out more, visit the Python Web site's Tkinter page at http://www.python.org/topics/tkinter.

You create GUI elements by instantiating objects from classes of the Tkinter module, which is part of the Tkinter toolkit. Table 10.1 describes each GUI element from Figure 10.4 and lists its corresponding Tkinter class.

There's no need to memorize all of these Tkinter classes. I just want to give you an overview of the classes that you learn about in this chapter.

TABLE 10.1 SELECTED GUI ELEMENTS

Element	Tkinter Class	Description
Frame	Frame	Holds other GUI elements
Label	Label	Displays uneditable text or icons
Button	Button	Performs an action when the user activates it
Text entry	Entry	Accepts and displays one line of text
Text box	Text	Accepts and displays multiple lines of text
Check button	Checkbutton	Allows the user to select or not select an option
Radio button	Radiobutton	Allows, as a group, the user to select one option from several

UNDERSTANDING EVENT-DRIVEN PROGRAMMING

GUI programs are traditionally *event-driven*, meaning they respond to actions regardless of the order in which they occur. Event-driven programming is a somewhat different way of thinking about coding. But don't worry, because if you've ever used a GUI before (such as a Web browser), then you've already worked within an event-driven system.

To better understand the event-driven way, think about the Mad Lib game from this chapter. If you were to write a similar program with your current Python skills, you'd probably ask the user a series of questions with the raw_input() function. You might ask for the name of a person, followed by a plural noun, followed by a verb, and so on. As a result, the user would have to provide each piece of information in order. But, if you were to write the program in an event-driven way, say with a GUI, the user could enter the information in any order. Also, the timing of when the program actually generates the story would be up to the user as well.

When you write an event-driven program, you *bind* (associate) *events* (things that can happen involving the program's objects) with *event handlers* (code that runs when the events occur). As a concrete example, think about the Mad Lib program again. When the user clicks the Click for story button (the event), the program invokes a method that displays the story (the event handler). In order for this to happen, I have to associate the button click with the story-telling method (I bind the two with each other).

By defining all of your objects, events, and event handlers, you establish how your program works. Then, you kick off the program by entering an *event loop*, where the program waits for the events that you've described to occur. When any of those events do occur, the program handles them, just as you've laid out.

Don't worry if this somewhat different way of thinking about programming isn't completely clear yet. After seeing a few working examples, you'll understand how to devise event-driven programs of your own.

USING A ROOT WINDOW

The foundation of your GUI program is its root window, upon which you add all other GUI elements. If you think of your GUI as a tree, then the root window is, well, the root. Your tree can branch out in all directions, but every part of it is, directly or indirectly, anchored by the root.

Introducing the Simple GUI Program

The Simple GUI program creates about the simplest GUI possible: a single window. Figure 10.5 shows the results of the program.

FIGURE 10.5

The program creates only a lone window. Hey, you have to start somewhere.

Running a Tkinter program directly from IDLE will cause either your program or IDLE to lock up. The simplest solution is to run your Tkinter program directly. In Windows, you can do this simply by double-clicking your program's icon.

Although you can run a Tkinter program by double-clicking its icon, you'll have a problem if the program contains an error—your console window will close before you can read the error message. Under Windows, you can create a batch file that runs your program and pauses once the program ends, keeping the console window open so you can see any error messages. For example, if your program is simple_gui.py, just create a batch file comprised of the two lines:

```
simple_gui.py
pause
```

Then run the batch file by double-clicking its icon.

To create a batch file:

1. Open a text editor such as Notepad (not Word or WordPad).
2. Type your text.
3. Save the file with a `.bat` extension (such as `simple_gui.bat`) and make sure there is no `.txt` extension after the `.bat`.

I've created batch files for all of the programs in this chapter. They're available on the CD-ROM along with the chapter programs.

In addition to the window pictured in Figure 10.5, Simple GUI may generate another window (depending upon your operating system): the familiar console window, pictured in Figure 10.6.

FIGURE 10.6

A GUI program can generate a console window too.

Although you may think that this console window is just an eyesore, marring your otherwise perfect GUI, don't be so quick to dismiss it. The console window can provide valuable feedback if (and when) your Tkinter program produces errors. Also, don't close the console window, because that will close your GUI program along with it.

TRICK   Once you get your GUI programming running perfectly, you may want to suppress its accompanying console window. On a Windows machine, the easiest way to do this is to change the extension of your program from `py` to `pyw`.

Importing the Tkinter **Module**

Finally, it's time to get your hands dirty with some code! The first thing I do in the Simple GUI program is import the Tkinter module:

```
# Simple GUI
# Demonstrates creating a window

from Tkinter import *
```

The previous code imports all of Tkinter directly into the program's global scope. Normally, you want to avoid doing something like this; however, a few modules, such as Tkinter, are designed to be imported in this way. You'll see just how this helps in the next line of code.

Creating a Root Window

To create a root window, I instantiate an object of the Tkinter class Tk:

```
# create the root window
root = Tk()
```

Notice, though, that I didn't have to prefix the module name, Tkinter, to the class name, Tk. In fact, I can now directly access any part of the Tkinter module without having to use the module name. Since most Tkinter programs involve many references to classes and constants in the module, this saves a lot of typing and makes code easier to read.

TRAP You can have only one root window in a Tkinter program. If you create more than one, you're bound to freeze up your program as both root windows fight for control.

Modifying a Root Window

Next, I modify the root window using a few of its methods:

```
# modify the window
root.title("Simple GUI")
root.geometry("200x100")
```

The title() method sets the title of the root window. All you have to do is pass the title you want displayed as a string. I set the title so that the text Simple GUI appears in the window's title bar.

The geometry() method sets the size of the root window. The method takes a string (and not integers) that represents the window's width and height, separated by the "x" character. I set the window's width to 200 and its height to 100.

Entering a Root Window's Event Loop

Finally, I start up the window's event loop by invoking root's `mainloop()` method:

```
# kick off the window's event loop
root.mainloop()
```

As a result, the window stays open, waiting to handle events. Because I haven't defined any events, the window doesn't do much. But it is a full-fledged window that you can resize, minimize, and close. Feel free to give it a test drive.

USING LABELS

GUI elements are called *widgets* (short for "window gadgets"). Probably the simplest widget is the `Label` widget, which is uneditable text or icons (or both). A label widget labels part of a GUI. It's often used to label other widgets. Unlike most other widgets, labels aren't interactive. A user can't click on a label. (All right, a user can, but the label won't do anything.) Still, labels are important and you'll probably use at least one every time you create a GUI.

Introducing the Labeler Program

The Labeler program creates a root window and adds a label to it. The label widget simply declares that it is a label. Figure 10.7 illustrates the program.

Setting Up the Program

First, I set up the Labeler program by importing `Tkinter` and creating a root window:

```
# Labeler
# Demonstrates a label

from Tkinter import *

# create the root window
root = Tk()
root.title("Labeler")
root.geometry("200x50")
```

Creating a Frame

A Frame is a widget that can hold other widgets (such as Label widgets). A frame is like the cork in a corkboard; you use it as a base on which to place other things. So, I create a new frame:

```
# create a frame in the window to hold other widgets
app = Frame(root)
```

Any time you create a new widget, you must pass its *master* (the thing that will contain the widget) to the constructor of the new object. Here, I pass root to the Frame constructor. As a result, the new frame is placed inside the root window.

Next, I invoke the grid() method of the new object:

```
app.grid()
```

grid() is a method that all widgets have. It's associated with a *layout manager,* which lets you arrange widgets. To keep things simple, I save the discussion of layout managers for a bit later in this chapter.

Creating a Label

I create a Label widget by instantiating an object of the Label class:

```
# create a label in the frame
lbl = Label(app, text = "I'm a label!")
```

By passing app to the Label object's constructor, I make the frame that app refers to the master of the Label widget. As a result, the label is placed in the frame.

Widgets have options that you can set. Many of these options affect how the widget appears. By passing the string "I'm a label!" to the text parameter, I set the widget's text option to that string. As a result, the text I'm a label! appears when the label is displayed.

Next, I invoke the object's grid() method:

```
lbl.grid()
```

This ensures that the label will be visible.

Entering the Root Window's Event Loop

Last, but not least, I invoke the root window's event loop to start up the GUI:

```
# kick off the window's event loop
root.mainloop()
```

USING BUTTONS

A Button widget can be activated by the user to perform some action. Since you already know how to create labels, learning how to create buttons will be pretty easy.

Introducing the Lazy Buttons Program

In the Lazy Buttons program, I create several buttons that don't do anything when activated. This is sort of like installing a new light fixture before wiring it. The fixture is put into place, but not yet functional. Figure 10.8 illustrates the program.

FIGURE 10.8

You can click these lazy buttons all you want; they won't do a thing.

Setting Up the Program

First, I set up the program by importing Tkinter and creating a root window and a frame:

```
# Lazy Buttons
# Demonstrates creating buttons

from Tkinter import *

# create a root window
root = Tk()
root.title("Lazy Buttons")
root.geometry("200x85")

# create a frame in the window to hold other widgets
app = Frame(root)
app.grid()
```

Creating Buttons

You create a Button widget by instantiating an object of the Button class. That's what I did in the next lines:

```
# create a button in the frame
bttn1 = Button(app, text = "I do nothing!")
bttn1.grid()
```

These lines create a new button with the text I do nothing! The button's master is the frame I created earlier, which means that the button is placed in the frame.

The Tkinter module offers flexibility when it comes to creating, defining, and altering widgets. You can create a widget and set all of its options in one line (like I've been doing), or you can create a widget and set or alter its options later. I'll show you what I mean with the next button. First, I create a new button:

```
# create a second button in the frame
bttn2 = Button(app)
bttn2.grid()
```

Notice though that the only value I pass to the object's constructor is app, the button's master. So, all I've done is add a blank button to the frame. However, I can fix that. I can modify a widget after I create it, using the object's configure() method:

```
bttn2.configure(text = "Me too!")
```

This line sets the text option of the button to the string "Me too!", which puts the text Me too! on the button.

You can use a widget's configure() method for any widget option (and any type of widget). You can even use the method to change an option that you've already set.

Next, I create a third button:

```
# create a third button in the frame
bttn3 = Button(app)
bttn3.grid()
```

Then, I set the button's text option, using a different interface:

```
bttn3["text"] = "Same here!"
```

I access the button's text option through a dictionary-like interface. I set the text option to the string "Same here!", which puts the text Same here! on the button. When you set the value of an option using this type of dictionary-style access, the key for the option is the name of the option as a string.

Entering the Root Window's Event Loop

As always, I invoke the root window's event loop to start up the GUI:

```
# kick off the window's event loop
root.mainloop()
```

CREATING A GUI USING A CLASS

As you've learned in other chapters, organizing your code into classes can make your programming life a lot easier. It's often beneficial to write larger GUI programs by defining your own classes. So next, I show you how to write a GUI program by organizing the code with a class.

Introducing the Lazy Buttons 2 Program

The Lazy Buttons 2 program is simply the Lazy Buttons program rewritten using a class. The program appears exactly the same to the user, but behind the scenes I've done some restructuring. Figure 10.9 shows the ever-so-familiar program in action.

FIGURE 10.9

It's déjà vu all over again. The program looks the same as its predecessor even though there are significant changes under the hood.

Importing the Tkinter Module

Though there are significant structural changes to the program, importing the GUI module is still the same:

```
# Lazy Buttons 2
# Demonstrates using a class with Tkinter

from Tkinter import *
```

Defining the Application **Class**

Next, I create a new class, Application, based on Frame:

```
class Application(Frame):
    """ A GUI application with three buttons. """
```

Instead of instantiating a Frame object, I'll end up instantiating an Application object to hold all of the buttons. This works because an Application object is just a specialized type of Frame object.

Defining a Constructor Method

Next, I define Application's constructor:

```
def __init__(self, master):
    """ Initialize the Frame. """
    Frame.__init__(self, master)
    self.grid()
    self.create_widgets()
```

Because an Application object is just a specialized kind of Frame object, I initialize it through Frame's constructor. I pass along the Application object's master, so it gets properly set as the master. Finally, I invoke the Application object's create_widgets() method, which I define next.

TRAP   Given the way Frame is defined, I'm unable to use the super() function to call a Frame method inside my Application class. Instead, I call Frame methods explicitly inside my class.

Defining a Method to Create the Widgets

I define a method that creates all three buttons, create_widgets():

```
def create_widgets(self):
    """Create three buttons that do nothing. """
    # create first button
    self.bttn1 = Button(self, text = "I do nothing!")
    self.bttn1.grid()

    # create second button
    self.bttn2 = Button(self)
    self.bttn2.grid()
    self.bttn2.configure(text = "Me too!")
```

```
# create third button
self.bttn3 = Button(self)
self.bttn3.grid()
self.bttn3["text"] = "Same here!"
```

The code looks pretty similar to the code that creates the buttons in the original Lazy Buttons program. An important difference is that `bttn1`, `bttn2`, and `bttn3` are attributes of an `Application` object. Another important difference is that I use `self` as the master for the buttons so that the `Application` object is their master.

Creating the `Application` Object

In the main section of code, I create a root window and give it a title and a proper size:

```
# main
root = Tk()
root.title("Lazy Buttons 2")
root.geometry("200x85")
```

Then, I instantiate an `Application` object with the root window as its master:

```
app = Application(root)
```

This code creates an `Application` object with the root window as its master. The `Application` object's constructor invokes the object's `create_widgets()` method. This method then creates the three buttons, with the `Application` object as their master.

Finally, I invoke the root window's event loop to kick off the GUI and keep it running:

```
root.mainloop()
```

BINDING WIDGETS AND EVENT HANDLERS

So far, the GUI programs you've seen don't do a whole lot. That's because there's no code associated with the activation of their widgets. Again, these widgets are like light fixtures that have been installed, but not connected to electrical wiring. Well, now it's time to get the electricity flowing; or in the case of GUI programming, it's time to write event handlers and bind them with events.

Introducing the Click Counter Program

The Click Counter program has a button that does something: It displays the number of times the user has clicked it. Technically, the button's event handler takes care of updating the click count and changing the text on the button. Figure 10.10 shows off the program.

FIGURE 10.10

The button's
event handler
updates the
number of times
the button is
clicked.

Setting Up the Program

As my traditional first step, I import the GUI module:

```
# Click Counter
# Demonstrates binding an event with an event handler

from Tkinter import *
```

Next, I start the Application class definition:

```
class Application(Frame):
    """ GUI application which counts button clicks. """
    def __init__(self, master):
        """ Initialize the frame. """
        Frame.__init__(self, master)
        self.grid()
        self.bttn_clicks = 0    # the number of button clicks
        self.create_widget()
```

You've seen most of this code before. The new line is self.bttn_clicks = 0, which creates an object attribute to keep track of the number of times the user clicks the button.

Binding the Event Handler

In the create_widget() method, I create a single button:

```
    def create_widget(self):
        """ Create button which displays number of clicks. """
        self.bttn = Button(self)
        self.bttn["text"] = "Total Clicks: 0"
        self.bttn["command"] = self.update_count
        self.bttn.grid()
```

I set the Button widget's command option to the update_count() method. As a result, when the user clicks the button, the method gets invoked. Technically, what I've done is bind an event (the clicking of Button widget) to an event handler (the update_count() method).

In general, you set a widget's command option to bind the activation of the widget with an event handler.

Creating the Event Handler

Next, I write the update_count() method, which handles the event of the button being clicked:

```
def update_count(self):
    """Increase click count and display new total. """
    self.bttn_clicks += 1
    self.bttn["text"] = "Total Clicks: " + str(self.bttn_clicks)
```

This method increments the total number of button clicks and then changes the text of the button to reflect the new total. That's all it takes to get a button to do something useful (or almost useful).

Wrapping Up the Program

The main part of the code should be pretty familiar to you by now:

```
# main
root = Tk()
root.title("Click Counter")
root.geometry("200x50")

app = Application(root)

root.mainloop()
```

I create a root window and set its title and dimensions. Then I instantiate a new Application object with the root window as its master. Lastly, I start up the root window's event loop to bring the GUI to life on the screen.

USING Text AND Entry WIDGETS AND THE Grid LAYOUT MANAGER

In GUI programming, there will be times where you'll want a user to enter some text. Other times, you may want to display text to the user. For both of these occasions, you can use text-based widgets. I introduce you to two kinds. The Entry widget is good for one line of text, while the Text widget is great for multiline blocks of text. You can read the contents of either of these widget types to get user input. You can also insert text into them to provide the user with feedback.

Once you start throwing a bunch of widgets into a frame, you need a way to organize them. So far, I've used the Grid layout manager, but in only the most limited way. The Grid layout manager offers you a lot more control over the way your GUI looks. The manager lets you place widgets at specific locations by treating a frame as a grid.

Introducing the Longevity Program

The Longevity program reveals the secret to living to the ripe old age of 100, if the user enters the secret password (the highly secure "secret"). The user enters the password in the text entry and then clicks the Submit button. If the password is correct, the program displays the key to longevity in the text box. Figures 10.11 and 10.12 show off the program.

FIGURE 10.11

If the user fails to enter the correct password, the program politely refuses to divulge its secret.

FIGURE 10.12

Given the correct password, the program shares its invaluable knowledge to long life.

Setting Up the Program

I set up the program just like the last few:

```
# Longevity
# Demonstrates text and entry widgets, and the Grid layout manager

from Tkinter import *

class Application(Frame):
    """ GUI application which can reveal the secret of longevity. """
    def __init__(self, master):
        """ Initialize the frame. """
        Frame.__init__(self, master)
        self.grid()
        self.create_widgets()
```

I import the Tkinter module and start to define the Application class. In the constructor method, I initialize the new Application object, make sure it will be visible, and invoke the object's create_widgets() method.

Placing a Widget with the Grid Layout Manager

Next, I start the create_widgets() method and create a label that provides instructions to the user:

```
    def create_widgets(self):
        """ Create button, text, and entry widgets. """
        # create instruction label
        self.inst_lbl = Label(self,
                text = "Enter password for the secret of longevity")
```

So far, nothing new. But in the next line, I use the Grid layout manager to be specific about the placement of this label:

```
        self.inst_lbl.grid(row = 0, column = 0, columnspan = 2, sticky = W)
```

A widget object's grid() method can take values for many different parameters, but I only use four of them: row, column, columnspan, and sticky.

The row and column parameters take integers and define where an object is placed within its master widget. In this program, you can imagine the frame in the root window as a grid, divided into rows and columns. At each row and column intersection is a cell, where you can place a widget. Figure 10.13 illustrates the placement of nine `Button` widgets, in nine different cells, using row and column numbers.

Grid Layout		
row = 0 column = 0	row = 0 column = 1	row = 0 column = 2
row = 1 column = 0	row = 1 column = 1	row = 1 column = 2
row = 2 column = 0	row = 2 column = 1	row = 2 column = 2

For my `Label` widget, I pass 0 to `row` and 0 to `column`, which puts the label in the upper-left corner of the frame.

If a widget is very wide (like the long instruction `Label` widget I have in this program), you may want to allow the widget to span more than one cell so that your other widgets are correctly spaced. The `columnspan` parameter lets you span a widget over more than one column. I pass 2 to this parameter to allow the long label to span two columns. This means that the label takes up two cells, one at row 0, column 0, and the other at row 0, column 1. (You can also use the `rowspan` parameter to allow a widget to span more than one row.)

Even after you've established which cell (or cells) a widget occupies, you have the flexibility to justify the widget within the cell (or cells) by using the parameter `sticky`, which takes directions as values, including N, S, E, and W. A widget is moved to the quadrant of the cell (or cells) that corresponds to the direction. Because I pass W to `sticky` for the `Label` object, the label is forced to the west (left). Another way to say this is that the label is left-justified in its cells.

Next, I create a label that appears in the next row, left-justified:

```
# create label for password
self.pw_lbl = Label(self, text = "Password: ")
self.pw_lbl.grid(row = 1, column = 0, sticky = W)
```

Creating an `Entry` **Widget**

Next, I create a new type of widget, an `Entry` widget:

```
# create entry widget to accept password
self.pw_ent = Entry(self)
```

This code creates a text entry where the user can enter a password.

I position the Entry widget so that it's in the cell next to the password label:

```
self.pw_ent.grid(row = 1, column = 1, sticky = W)
```

Then, I create a button that lets the user submit his or her password:

```
# create submit button
self.submit_bttn = Button(self, text = "Submit", command = self.reveal)
```

I bind the activation of the button with the reveal() method, which reveals the longevity secret, if the user has entered the correct password.

I place the button in the next row, all the way to the left:

```
self.submit_bttn.grid(row = 2, column = 0, sticky = W)
```

Creating a Text **Widget**

Next, I create a new type of widget, a Text widget:

```
# create text widget to display message
self.secret_txt = Text(self, width = 35, height = 5, wrap = WORD)
```

I pass values to width and height to set the dimensions of the text box. Then I pass a value to the parameter wrap, which determines how text in the box is wrapped. Possible values for the parameter are WORD, CHAR, and NONE. WORD, the value I use for this Text widget, wraps entire words when you reach the right edge of the text box. CHAR wraps characters, meaning that when you get to the right edge of the text box, the next characters simply appear on the following line. NONE means no wrapping. As a result, you can only write text on the first line of the text box.

Next, I set the text box so that it's on the next row and spans two columns:

```
self.secret_txt.grid(row = 3, column = 0, columnspan = 2, sticky = W)
```

Getting and Inserting Text with Text-Based Widgets

Next, I write the reveal() method, which tests to see whether the user has entered the correct password. If so, the method displays the secret to a long life. Otherwise, the user is told that the password is incorrect.

The first thing I do is get the text in the Entry widget by invoking its get() method:

```
def reveal(self):
    """ Display message based on password. """
    contents = self.pw_ent.get()
```

The get() method returns the text in the widget. Both Entry and Text objects have a get() method.

I check to see whether the text is equal to "secret". If so, I set message to the string describing the secret to living to 100. Otherwise, I set message to the string that tells the user that he or she entered the wrong password.

```
if contents == "secret":
    message = "Here's the secret to living to 100: live to 99 " \
            "and then be VERY careful."
else:
    message = "That's not the correct password, so I can't share " \
            "the secret with you."
```

Now that I've got the string that I want to show to the user, I need to insert it into the Text widget. First, I delete any text already in the Text widget by invoking its delete() method:

```
self.secret_txt.delete(0.0, END)
```

The delete() method can delete text from text-based widgets. The method can take a single index, or a beginning and an ending point. You pass floating-point numbers to represent a row and column number pair where the digits to the left of the decimal point are the row numbers and the digits to the right of the decimal point are the column numbers. For example, in the previous line of code, I pass 0.0 as the starting point, meaning that the method should delete text starting at row 0, column 0 (the absolute beginning) of the text box.

Tkinter provides several constants to help out with this type of method, such as END, which means the end of the text. So, this previous line of code deletes everything from the first position in the text box to the end. Both Text and Entry widgets have a delete() method.

Next, I insert the string I want to display into the Text widget:

```
self.secret_txt.insert(0.0, message)
```

The insert() method can insert a string into a text-based widget. The method takes an insertion position and a string. In the previous line of code, I pass 0.0 as the insertion position, meaning the method should start inserting at row 0, column 0. I pass message as the second value, so that the appropriate message shows up in the text box. Both Text and Entry widgets have an insert() method.

Wrapping Up the Program

To wrap up the program, I create a root window and set its title and dimensions. Then I create a new `Application` object with the root window as its master. Finally, I begin the application by starting the window's event loop.

```
# main
root = Tk()
root.title("Longevity")
root.geometry("250x150")

app = Application(root)

root.mainloop()
```

USING CHECK BUTTONS

Check buttons allow a user to select any number of choices from a group. While this gives the user a lot of flexibility, it actually gives the programmer greater control by limiting to a specific list what the user can choose.

Introducing the Movie Chooser Program

The Movie Chooser program lets the user choose his or her favorite movie types from a list of three: comedy, drama, and romance. Because the program uses check buttons, the user can select as many (or as few) as he or she wants. The program displays the results of the user's selections in a text box. Figure 10.14 shows off the program.

FIGURE 10.14

The results of the user's selections show up in the text box.

Setting Up the Program

I set up the Movie Chooser program by importing Tkinter and starting my Application class definition:

```
# Movie Chooser
# Demonstrates check buttons

from Tkinter import *

class Application(Frame):
    """ GUI Application for favorite movie types. """
    def __init__(self, master):
        Frame.__init__(self, master)
        self.grid()
        self.create_widgets()
```

Allowing a Widget's Master to Be Its Only Reference

Next, I create a label that describes the program:

```
    def create_widgets(self):
        """ Create widgets for movie type choices. """
        # create description label
        Label(self,
              text = "Choose your favorite movie types"
              ).grid(row = 0, column = 0, sticky = W)
```

There's one important difference between this label and others I've created: I don't assign the resulting Label object to a variable. Normally, this would be a big mistake, rendering the object useless because it wouldn't be connected to the program in any way. But with Tkinter, a Label object is connected to the program, like all GUI elements, by its master. What this means is that if I know I won't need to directly access a widget, then I don't need to assign the object to a variable. The main benefit of this approach is shorter, cleaner code.

So far, I've been pretty conservative, always assigning each new widget to a variable. But in this case, I know that I'm not going to need to access this label, so I don't assign the Label object to a variable. Instead, I let its master maintain the only reference to it.

Next, I create another label in much the same way:

```
        # create instruction label
        Label(self,
              text = "Select all that apply:"
              ).grid(row = 1, column = 0, sticky = W)
```

This label provides instructions, telling the user that he or she can select as many movie types as apply.

Creating Check Buttons

Next, I create the check buttons, one for each movie type. I first tackle the Comedy check button.

Every check button needs a special object associated with it that automatically reflects the check button's status. The special object must be an instance of the BooleanVar class from the Tkinter module. So, before I create the Comedy check button, I instantiate a BooleanVar object and assign it to a new object attribute, likes_comedy:

```
# create Comedy check button
self.likes_comedy = BooleanVar()
```

IN THE REAL WORLD

A Boolean variable is a special kind of variable that can be only true or false. Programmers often call such a variable simply a "Boolean." The term is always capitalized because it's derived from the name of the English mathematician George Boole.

Next, I create the check button itself:

```
Checkbutton(self,
            text = "Comedy",
            variable = self.likes_comedy,
            command = self.update_text
            ).grid(row = 2, column = 0, sticky = W)
```

This code creates a new check button with the text Comedy. By passing self.likes_comedy to the parameter variable, I associate the check button's status (selected or unchecked) with the likes_comedy attribute. By passing self.update_text() to the parameter command, I bind the activation of the check button with the update_text() method. This means that whenever the user selects or clears the check button, the update_text() method is invoked. Finally, I place the check button on the next row, all the way to the left.

Notice that I don't assign the resulting Checkbutton object to a variable. This is fine, because what I really care about is the status of the button, which I can access from the likes_comedy attribute.

I create the next two check buttons in the same way:

```
# create Drama check button
self.likes_drama = BooleanVar()
Checkbutton(self,
            text = "Drama",
            variable = self.likes_drama,
            command = self.update_text
            ).grid(row = 3, column = 0, sticky = W)

# create Romance check button
self.likes_romance = BooleanVar()
Checkbutton(self,
            text = "Romance",
            variable = self.likes_romance,
            command = self.update_text
            ).grid(row = 4, column = 0, sticky = W)
```

So, whenever the user selects or clears the Drama or Romance check buttons, the update_text() method is invoked. And even though I don't assign the resulting Checkbutton objects to any variables, I can always see the status of the Drama check button through the likes_drama attribute, and I can always see the status of the Romance check button through the likes_romance attribute.

Finally, I create the text box that I use to show the results of the user's selections:

```
# create text field to display results
self.results_txt = Text(self, width = 40, height = 5, wrap = WORD)
self.results_txt.grid(row = 5, column = 0, columnspan = 3)
```

Getting the Status of a Check Button

Next, I write the update_text() method, which updates the text box to reflect the check buttons the user has selected:

```
def update_text(self):
    """ Update text widget and display user's favorite movie types. """
    likes = ""
```

```
if self.likes_comedy.get():
    likes += "You like comedic movies.\n"

if self.likes_drama.get():
    likes += "You like dramatic movies.\n"

if self.likes_romance.get():
    likes += "You like romantic movies."

self.results_txt.delete(0.0, END)
self.results_txt.insert(0.0, likes)
```

You can't access the value of a `BooleanVar` object directly. Instead, you must invoke the object's `get()` method. In the previous code, I use the `get()` method of the `BooleanVar` object referenced by `likes_comedy` to get the object's value. If the value evaluates to true, that means the Comedy check button is selected, and I add the string `"You like comedic movies.\n"` to the string I'm building to display in the text box. I perform similar operations based on the status of the Drama and Romance check buttons. Finally, I delete all of the text in the text box and then insert the new string, `likes`, which I just built.

Wrapping Up the Program

I finish the program with the familiar main section. I create a root window and a new `Application` object with the root window as its master. Then, I start the window's event loop.

```
# main
root = Tk()
root.title("Movie Chooser")
app = Application(root)
root.mainloop()
```

USING RADIO BUTTONS

Radio buttons are a lot like check buttons, except that radio buttons only allow one button in a group to be selected at once. This is great if you want the user to make a single selection from a group of choices. Because radio buttons have so much in common with check buttons, learning to use them is pretty straightforward.

Introducing the Movie Chooser 2 Program

The Movie Chooser 2 program is like the Movie Chooser program. The user is presented with three different movie types from which to select. The difference is that the Movie Chooser 2 program uses radio buttons instead of check buttons so the user can select only one movie type. This is perfect because the program asks the user for his or her favorite type of movie. Figure 10.15 shows off the program.

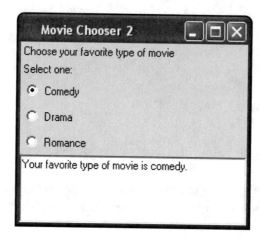

Setting Up the Program

I start the program by importing the Tkinter module:

```
# Movie Chooser 2
# Demonstrates radio buttons

from Tkinter import *
```

Next, I write the Application class. I define its constructor, which initializes a new Application object:

```
class Application(Frame):
    """ GUI Application for favorite movie type. """
    def __init__(self, master):
        """ Initialize Frame. """
        Frame.__init__(self, master)
        self.grid()
        self.create_widgets()
```

Then, I create labels that give the user instructions:

```
    def create_widgets(self):
        """ Create widgets for movie type choices. """
```

```
# create description label
Label(self,
        text = "Choose your favorite type of movie"
        ).grid(row = 0, column = 0, sticky = W)

# create instruction label
Label(self,
        text = "Select one:"
        ).grid(row = 1, column = 0, sticky = W)
```

Creating Radio Buttons

Because only one radio button in a group can be selected at one time, there's no need for each radio button to have its own status variable, as required for check buttons. Instead, a group of radio buttons share one special object that reflects which of the radio buttons is selected. This object must be an instance of the StringVar class from the Tkinter module, which allows a string to be stored and retrieved. So, before I create the radio buttons themselves, I create a single StringVar object for all of the radio buttons to share and then I assign it to the attribute favorite:

```
# create variable for single, favorite type of movie
self.favorite = StringVar()
```

Next, I create the Comedy radio button:

```
# create Comedy radio button
Radiobutton(self,
            text = "Comedy",
            variable = self.favorite,
            value = "comedy.",
            command = self.update_text
            ).grid(row = 2, column = 0, sticky = W)
```

A radio button's variable option defines the StringVar associated with the radio button, while a radio button's value option defines the string to be stored by the StringVar when the radio button is selected. So, by setting this radio button's variable option to self.favorite and its value option to "comedy.", I'm saying that when the Comedy radio button is selected, the StringVar referenced by self.favorite should store the string "comedy."

Next, I create the other two radio buttons:

```
# create Drama radio button
Radiobutton(self,
            text = "Drama",
            variable = self.favorite,
            value = "drama.",
            command = self.update_text
            ).grid(row = 3, column = 0, sticky = W)

# create Romance radio button
Radiobutton(self,
            text = "Romance",
            variable = self.favorite,
            value = "romance.",
            command = self.update_text
            ).grid(row = 4, column = 0, sticky = W)
```

By setting the Drama radio button's `variable` option to `self.favorite` and its `value` option to "drama.", I'm saying that when the Drama radio button is selected, the `StringVar` referenced by `self.favorite` should store the string "drama."

And by setting the Romance radio button's `variable` option to `self.favorite` and its `value` option to "romance.", I'm saying that when the Romance radio button is selected, the `StringVar` referenced by `self.favorite` should store the string "romance."

Next, I create the text box to display the results of the user's selection:

```
# create text field to display result
self.results_txt = Text(self, width = 40, height = 5, wrap = WORD)
self.results_txt.grid(row = 5, column = 0, columnspan = 3)
```

Getting a Value from a Group of Radio Buttons

Getting a value from a group of radio buttons is as simple as invoking the `get()` method of the `StringVar` object that they all share:

```
def update_text(self):
    """ Update text area and display user's favorite movie type. """
    message = "Your favorite type of movie is "
    message += self.favorite.get()
```

When the Comedy radio button is selected, `self.favorite.get()` returns "comedy."; when the Drama radio button is selected, `self.favorite.get()` returns "drama."; and when the Romance radio button is selected, `self.favorite.get()` returns "romance."

Next, I delete any text that may be in the text box and insert the string I just created, which declares the user's favorite movie type:

```
self.results_txt.delete(0.0, END)
self.results_txt.insert(0.0, message)
```

Wrapping Up the Program

I wrap up the program by creating a root window and a new Application object. Then, I begin the root window's event loop to start up the GUI.

```
# main
root = Tk()
root.title("Movie Chooser 2")
app = Application(root)
root.mainloop()
```

BACK TO THE MAD LIB PROGRAM

Now that you've seen a nice variety of widgets used in isolation, it's time to combine them in one larger GUI. I don't introduce any new concepts in the Mad Lib program, so I don't comment too much on the code.

Importing the Tkinter Module

As you probably know by now, you have to import the Tkinter module before you can use it:

```
# Mad Lib
# Create a story based on user input

from Tkinter import *
```

The Application Class's Constructor Method

Like all other Application class constructors before it, this one initializes the newly created Application object and invokes its create_widgets() method:

```
class Application(Frame):
    """ GUI application that creates a story based on user input. """
    def __init__(self, master):
        """ Initialize Frame. """
        Frame.__init__(self, master)
        self.grid()
        self.create_widgets()
```

The Application Class's create_widgets() Method

This class creates all of the widgets in the GUI. The only new thing I do is create all three radio buttons in a loop, by moving through a list of strings for each radio button's text and value options:

```python
def create_widgets(self):
    """ Create widgets to get story information and to display story. """
    # create instruction label
    Label(self,
          text = "Enter information for a new story"
          ).grid(row = 0, column = 0, columnspan = 2, sticky = W)

    # create a label and text entry for the name of a person
    Label(self,
          text = "Person: "
          ).grid(row = 1, column = 0, sticky = W)
    self.person_ent = Entry(self)
    self.person_ent.grid(row = 1, column = 1, sticky = W)

    # create a label and text entry for a plural noun
    Label(self,
          text = "Plural Noun:"
          ).grid(row = 2, column = 0, sticky = W)
    self.noun_ent = Entry(self)
    self.noun_ent.grid(row = 2, column = 1, sticky = W)

    # create a label and text entry for a verb
    Label(self,
          text = "Verb:"
          ).grid(row = 3, column = 0, sticky = W)
    self.verb_ent = Entry(self)
    self.verb_ent.grid(row = 3, column = 1, sticky = W)

    # create a label for adjectives check buttons
    Label(self,
          text = "Adjective(s):"
          ).grid(row = 4, column = 0, sticky = W)
```

```
# create itchy check button
self.is_itchy = BooleanVar()
Checkbutton(self,
            text = "itchy",
            variable = self.is_itchy
            ).grid(row = 4, column = 1, sticky = W)

# create joyous check button
self.is_joyous = BooleanVar()
Checkbutton(self,
            text = "joyous",
            variable = self.is_joyous
            ).grid(row = 4, column = 2, sticky = W)

# create electric check button
self.is_electric = BooleanVar()
Checkbutton(self,
            text = "electric",
            variable = self.is_electric
            ).grid(row = 4, column = 3, sticky = W)

# create a label for body parts radio buttons
Label(self,
      text = "Body Part:"
      ).grid(row = 5, column = 0, sticky = W)

# create variable for single body part
self.body_part = StringVar()

# create body part radio buttons
body_parts = ["bellybutton", "big toe", "medulla oblongata"]
column = 1
for part in body_parts:
    Radiobutton(self,
                text = part,
                variable = self.body_part,
                value = part
                ).grid(row = 5, column = column, sticky = W)
    column += 1
# create a submit button
```

```
Button(self,
        text = "Click for story",
        command = self.tell_story
        ).grid(row = 6, column = 0, sticky = W)

self.story_txt = Text(self, width = 75, height = 10, wrap = WORD)
self.story_txt.grid(row = 7, column = 0, columnspan = 4)
```

The Application Class's tell_story() Method

In this method, I get the values the user has entered and use them to create the one long string for the story. Then, I delete any text in the text box and insert the new string to show the user the story he or she created.

```
def tell_story(self):
    """ Fill text box with new story based on user input. """
    # get values from the GUI
    person = self.person_ent.get()
    noun = self.noun_ent.get()
    verb = self.verb_ent.get()
    adjectives = ""
    if self.is_itchy.get():
        adjectives += "itchy, "
    if self.is_joyous.get():
        adjectives += "joyous, "
    if self.is_electric.get():
        adjectives += "electric, "
    body_part = self.body_part.get()

    # create the story
    story = "The famous explorer "
    story += person
    story += " had nearly given up a life-long quest to find The Lost City of "
    story += noun.title()
    story += " when one day, the "
    story += noun
    story += " found "
    story += person + ". "
    story += "A strong, "
```

```
story += adjectives
story += "peculiar feeling overwhelmed the explorer. "
story += "After all this time, the quest was finally over. A tear came to "
story += person + "'s "
story += body_part + ". "
story += "And then, the "
story += noun
story += " promptly devoured "
story += person + ". "
story += "The moral of the story? Be careful what you "
story += verb
story += " for."

# display the story
self.story_txt.delete(0.0, END)
self.story_txt.insert(0.0, story)
```

The Main Part of the Program

You've seen this code more than a few times before. I create a root window and an `Application` instance. Then, I start the whole GUI up by invoking root's `mainloop()` method.

```
# main
root = Tk()
root.title("Mad Lib")
app = Application(root)
root.mainloop()
```

SUMMARY

- A GUI is a graphical user interface.
- A widget, short for window gadget, is a GUI element.
- A layout manager controls the arrangement of widgets in a GUI.
- A frame is a widget that can hold other widgets.
- A label widget can display uneditable text or icons.
- A button widget can perform an action when activated.
- A text entry widget can accept and display a single line of text.
- A text box widget can accept and display multiple lines of text.

- A group of check button widgets allow the user to select multiple options from a set of options.
- A group of radio button widgets allow the user to select one option from a set of options.
- An event-driven program responds to actions regardless of the order in which they occur.
- An event is something that happens involving a program's objects.
- An event handler is code that runs when a specific event occurs.
- To bind is to associate an event with an event handler.
- An event loop checks for events and, based on them, calls the appropriate event handlers.
- Tkinter is a GUI module.
- You create a root window, the foundation of a GUI program, by instantiating an object of the Tk class.
- A Label object represents a label widget.
- A Frame object represents a frame widget.
- A Button object represents a button widget.
- An Entry object represents a text entry widget.
- A Text object represents a text box widget.
- A Checkbutton object represents a check button widget.
- A Radiobutton object represents a radio button widget.

REVIEW QUESTIONS

1. How is event-driven programming different from the type of programming you've been doing so far?
2. What Tk object method sets the title of a window?
3. What Tk object method sets the size of a window?
4. What Tk object method starts the object's event loop?
5. What widget option provides access to the text of a text-based widget?
6. What widget method sets a widget's options?
7. Besides using a method to set a widget's options, how else can you access its options?
8. What widget option can you use to bind the activation of a widget with an event handler?
9. What widget method facilitates the placement of a widget in the grid layout manager?
10. What widget method returns text from a text-based widget?
11. What widget method removes text from a text-based widget?

12. What widget method inserts text into a text-based widget?
13. Does a widget object always need to be assigned to a variable? Why or why not?
14. What is a BooleanVar object?
15. How can you test whether or not a check button is checked or unchecked?
16. What Checkbutton object option takes a function or method to be called when the check button is checked or unchecked?
17. What is a StringVar object?
18. What Radiobutton object option takes a StringVar object?
19. How can you test which radio button in a group is selected?
20. What StringVar object method returns the string referenced by the object?

Projects

1. Write a program with a button that changes its background color when clicked. Use the widget option bg to change the color of the button's background. The bg option takes a color as a string. Your button should cycle through the following colors, which are defined in the Tkinter module:

    - "blue"
    - "green"
    - "orange"
    - "red"
    - "yellow"

2. Write a program with a frame that has a three-by-three grid of buttons, as pictured in Figure 10.13. Each button should be labeled with its row and column number.
3. Write a program where the player takes on the computer in a no-holds-barred game of Rock, Paper, Scissors. The GUI should have an appropriate label at the top. It should allow the player to select his or her weapon of choice—either rock, paper or scissors. The program should have a fight button that, when clicked, has the computer select either rock, paper or scissors at random and displays the results of the battle.
4. Write a program that lets the user order a hamburger just the way he or she wants it. The GUI should allow the user to enter his or her name. It should also allow the user to select any combination of the following toppings: cheese, lettuce, onion, tomato, pickles, mustard, mayo, and ketchup. The program should have the user select either a white or wheat bun. When the user clicks an order button, the program should display a message in a text box that details the burger the user created based on his or her selections.
5. Write a program with a GUI that has a text entry widget for a user to enter a password and a button to submit the password. If the submitted password is equal to "secret"

then the program should generate an information message dialog with a message saying that the password is correct. If the submitted password is not equal to "secret" then the program should generate an error message dialog with a message saying that the password is incorrect.

The tkMessageBox module provides functions for generating message dialogs. To import the module in your program, use:

```
from tkMessageBox import *
```

The showinfo function from the tkMessageBox module generates an information message dialog. You pass a string to the function's title parameter for the dialog's title and a string to the function's message parameter for the dialog's message. The showerror function from the tkMessageBox module generates an error message dialog. You pass a string to the function's title parameter for the dialog's title and a string to the function's message parameter for the dialog's message.

CHAPTER 11

GRAPHICS: THE PIZZA PANIC GAME

The majority of programs you've seen so far have focused on presenting text, but today people expect rich visual content from their programs, regardless of the application. In this chapter, you'll learn how to use graphics with the help of a few multimedia modules designed for writing games in Python. Specifically, you'll learn to do the following:

- Create a graphics window
- Create and manipulate sprites
- Display text in a graphics window
- Test for collisions between sprites
- Handle mouse input
- Control a computer opponent

INTRODUCING THE PIZZA PANIC GAME

The final game program for this chapter, the Pizza Panic game, involves a crazy chef, a deep-dish pan, and a bunch of flying pizzas. Here's the scenario: After being pushed over the edge by one too many finicky diners, the chef at the local pizza parlor has taken to the rooftop and is madly flinging pizzas to their doom. Of course, the pizzas must be saved. Using the mouse, the player controls a pan that he or she maneuvers to catch the falling pizzas. The player's score increases with every pizza caught, but, once a pie hits the ground, the game is over. Figures 11.1 and 11.2 show the game in action.

FIGURE 11.1

The player must catch the falling pizzas.

FIGURE 11.2

Once the player misses a pizza, the game is over.

INTRODUCING THE pygame AND livewires PACKAGES

pygame and livewires are sets of modules (called *packages*) that give Python programmers access to a wide range of multimedia classes. With these classes, you can create programs with graphics, sound effects, music, and animation. The packages also allow input from a variety of devices, including the mouse and keyboard. With these packages, you won't have to worry about the low-level hardware details, like what kind of graphics card the player has—or whether he or she has a graphics card at all. Instead, you can concentrate on the program logic and get to writing games quickly.

pygame is the secret weapon in your media arsenal. Written by Pete Shinners, the package allows you to write impressive multimedia programs in Python. Because the package is so powerful, however, it can be a bit overwhelming for the new programmer.

livewires, written by a group of educators in the United Kingdom, was designed to take advantage of the power of pygame while reducing the complexity for the programmer. livewires provides a simpler way to get started programming games with graphics and sound. And even though you won't directly access pygame, it will still be there, working hard behind the scenes.

You need to install both pygame and livewires before you can run the programs presented in this chapter. Fortunately, Windows versions of both are included on the CD-ROM that came with this book. Just follow the installation instructions that accompany the packages.

TRAP Although you're welcome to visit the Web site of the LiveWires organization at http://www.livewires.org.uk/python/, be aware that the livewires package included on this book's CD-ROM is a modified version of the package that LiveWires created. I updated the package to make it even easier for new programmers to use. And don't worry—I've included a modified version of the documentation in Appendix A.

If you want to learn more about pygame, visit its Web site at http://www.pygame.org.

CREATING A GRAPHICS WINDOW

Before you can display any graphics, you must first create a graphics window—your blank canvas on which to display text and images.

Introducing the New Graphics Window Program

Creating a graphics window with the livewires package is a snap. The New Graphics Window program creates an empty graphics window in just a few lines of code. Figure 11.3 shows the results of the program.

FIGURE 11.3

My first graphics window. Not much, but it's mine.

TRAP Just as with a program that uses Tkinter to create a new window, you shouldn't run a livewires program from IDLE. If you're using Windows, create a batch file that runs your Python program and then pauses. To review writing such a batch file, see Chapter 10, in the section "Introducing the Simple GUI Program."

Importing the games Module

The livewires package is made up of several important modules, including games, which contains a group of classes for game programming. You can import a specific module of a package by using the from statement. To import a module, use from, followed by a package name, followed by import, followed by a module name (or a list of module names separated by commas).

The first thing I do in the program is import the games module of the livewires package:

```
# New Graphics Window
# Demonstrates creating a graphics window


from livewires import games
```

As a result, I can use games like any other module I import. To get an overview of the games module, check out Table 11.1, which lists useful games objects, and Table 11.2, which lists useful games classes.

TABLE 11.1   USEFUL games MODULE OBJECTS

Object	Description
screen	Provides access to the graphics screen—the region on which graphics objects may exist, move, and interact.
mouse	Provides access to the mouse.
keyboard	Provides access to the keyboard.

TABLE 11.2   USEFUL games MODULE CLASSES

Class	Description
Sprite	For graphics objects that can be displayed on the graphics screen.
Text	A subclass of Sprite. For text objects displayed on the graphics screen.
Message	A subclass of Text. For text objects displayed on the graphics screen that disappear after a set period of time.

Initializing the Graphics Screen

Next, I initialize the graphics screen:

```
games.init(screen_width = 640, screen_height = 480, fps = 50)
```

When you call the `games init()` function, you create a new graphics screen. The width of the screen is determined by the value you pass `screen_width`, while (drumroll, please) the height of the screen is determined by the value you pass `screen_height`. The screen dimensions are measured in *pixels*—single points in a graphics area. The value you pass `fps` (short for "frames per second") is the number of times the screen will update itself every second.

Starting the Main Loop

The final line in the program is

```
games.screen.mainloop()
```

`screen` is the `games` object that represents the graphics screen. `mainloop()` is the workhorse of `screen` and updates the graphics window, redrawing everything `fps` times per second. So, this last line keeps the graphics window open and updates the screen 50 times per second. Check out Table 11.3 for a few `screen` properties. For a list of useful `screen` methods, see Table 11.4.

TABLE 11.3 USEFUL screen PROPERTIES

Property	Description
width	Width of screen.
height	Height of screen.
fps	Frames per second screen is updated.
background	Background image of screen.
all objects	List of all the sprites on the screen.
event_grab	Boolean that determines if input is grabbed to screen. True for input grabbed to screen. False for input not grabbed to screen.

TABLE 11.4 USEFUL screen METHODS

Method	Description
add(*sprite*)	Adds *sprite*, a Sprite object (or an object of a Sprite subclass), to the graphics screen.
clear()	Removes all sprites from the graphics screen.
mainloop()	Starts the graphics screen's main loop.
quit()	Closes the graphics window.

SETTING A BACKGROUND IMAGE

A blank screen is all well and good, if your goal is to create the world's most boring program. Fortunately, the `screen` object has a property for its background image.

Introducing the Background Image Program

The Background Image program is just a modification of the New Graphics Window program. I add a background image to the graphics screen, shown in Figure 11.4.

FIGURE 11.4

By using the `background` property of the `screen` object, I apply a background image to the graphics window.

To create the Background Image program, I add two lines to the New Graphics Window program, just before invoking `mainloop()`. Here's the code in its entirety:

```
# Background Image
# Demonstrates setting the background image of a graphics screen

from livewires import games

games.init(screen_width = 640, screen_height = 480, fps = 50)
```

```
wall_image = games.load_image("wall.jpg", transparent = False)
games.screen.background = wall_image

games.screen.mainloop()
```

Loading an Image

Before you can do anything with an image, such as set it as the background of a graphics screen, you have to load the image into memory to create an image object. I load an image by adding the following line right after I initialize the graphics window:

```
wall_image = games.load_image("wall.jpg", transparent = False)
```

This calls the `games load_image()` function, which loads the image stored in the file `wall.jpg` into memory and assigns the resulting image object to `wall_image`.

Make sure that any file you want your Python program to access is associated with the correct path information, as you learned in Chapter 7, in the section "Opening and Closing a Text File." The simplest file management solution, and the one I use here, is to store image files in the same folder with the program that loads them. If you follow this method, you won't need to worry about path information at all.

The `load_image()` function takes two arguments: a string for the file name of the image and `True` or `False` for `transparent`. I'll go over exactly what `transparent` means a bit later in this chapter. For now, just remember this rule: Always load a background image with `transparent = False`.

You'll notice that I load a JPEG image for the background in this program. However, you're not restricted to JPEGs when using the `load_image()` function. It works just as well with many other image file types, including BMP, GIF, PNG, PCX, and TGA.

Setting the Background

In order to set an image object as the screen background, you just need to use the `screen` background property. I add the following line right after I load the image:

```
games.screen.background = wall_image
```

This sets the background of the screen to the image object `wall_image`.

When the program encounters `mainloop()`, it keeps the graphics window open with its new background image for all to see.

Understanding the Graphics Coordinate System

So far, I've created several graphics screens, each time with a width of 640 and a height of 480, but I haven't said much about them beyond that. Now we'll take a closer look at the screen and its coordinate system.

You can think of a graphics screen as a grid, 640 columns across by 480 rows down. Each intersection of a column and a row is a location on the screen, a single point or pixel. When you talk about a specific point on the screen, you give two coordinates: an x, which represents the column, and a y, which represents the row. You start counting coordinates from the upper-left corner of the screen. So, the upper-leftmost point is where the x-coordinate is 0 and the y-coordinate is 0, which you write as the pair (0,0). As you move to the right, the x values increase. As you move down the screen, the y values increase. That makes the point in the lower-right corner 639,479. Figure 11.5 gives a visual representation of the graphics screen coordinate system.

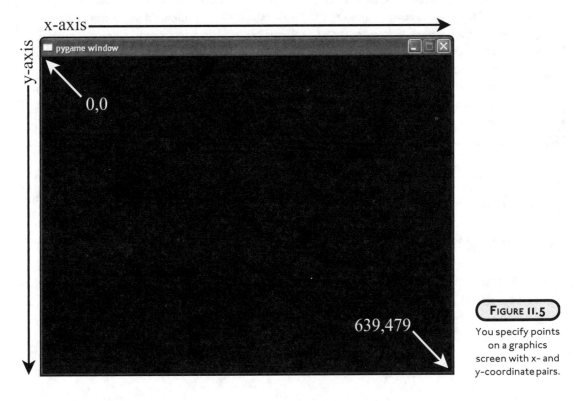

Figure 11.5

You specify points on a graphics screen with x- and y-coordinate pairs.

You can place graphics objects, such as the image of a pizza or the red-colored text "Game Over," on the screen using the coordinate system. The center of a graphics object is placed at the specified coordinates. You'll see exactly how this works in the next program.

Displaying a Sprite

Background images can spruce up a plain graphics screen, but even a breathtaking background is still just a static image. A graphics screen with only a background image is like an empty stage. What you need are some actors. Enter the sprite.

A *sprite* is a graphics object with an image that can make programs really come alive. Sprites are used in games, entertainment software, presentations, and all over the Web. In fact, you've already seen examples of sprites in the Pizza Panic game. The crazy chef, pan, and pizzas are all sprites.

In the Real World

Sprites aren't just for games. There are plenty of places in non-entertainment software where they're used...or misused. In fact, you probably know the most infamous sprite in application software history, Clippy the Office Assistant—the animated paperclip meant to give helpful suggestions in Microsoft Office. However, many people found Clippy obtrusive and irritating. One major online publication even ran an article entitled "Kill Clippy!" Well, Microsoft finally saw the light. Starting in Office XP, Clippy is no longer installed by default. A user must request him (and if a user requests him, he or she deserves him). So, while graphics can make a program more interesting, remember: Use your sprite powers for good instead of evil.

While it would be cool to see a bunch of sprites flying around and crashing into each other, I start with the first step: displaying a single, nonmoving sprite.

Introducing the Pizza Sprite Program

In the Pizza Sprite program, I create a graphics window and set a background image, just like before. Following this step, however, I create a pizza sprite right in the middle of the screen. Figure 11.6 shows the results of the program.

FIGURE 11.6

The pizza image is not part of the background, but an independent object of the Sprite class.

The Pizza Sprite program is just a modification of the Background Image program. I add only three lines to get the new sprite on the screen, just before invoking `mainloop()`. Here's the code for the program in its entirety:

```
# Pizza Sprite
# Demonstrates creating a sprite

from livewires import games

games.init(screen_width = 640, screen_height = 480, fps = 50)

wall_image = games.load_image("wall.jpg", transparent = False)
games.screen.background = wall_image

pizza_image = games.load_image("pizza.bmp")
pizza = games.Sprite(image = pizza_image, x = 320, y = 240)
games.screen.add(pizza)

games.screen.mainloop()
```

Loading an Image for a Sprite

First, I load a pizza image into memory to create an image object:

```
pizza_image = games.load_image("pizza.bmp")
```

You'll notice one small difference in the way I load a background image. This time, I didn't include a value for `transparent`. The default value is `True`, so the image is loaded with transparency on.

When an image is loaded with transparency on, it's displayed on a graphics screen so that the background image shows through its transparent parts. This is great for irregular sprites that aren't perfect rectangles and sprites with "holes" in them, like, say, a Swiss cheese sprite.

The parts of an image that are transparent are defined by their color. If an image is loaded with transparency on, then the color of the point at the upper-left corner of the image is its transparent color. All parts of the image that are this transparent color will allow the background of the screen to show through. Figure 11.7 shows a Swiss cheese sprite on a solid white background, ready to take advantage of transparency.

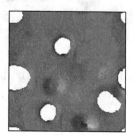

| FIGURE 11.7 |

A cheesy sprite, drawn on a solid-color background to take advantage of transparency.

If I load this Swiss cheese image with transparency on, every part that is pure white (the color taken from the pixel in the image's upper-left corner) will be transparent when the sprite is displayed on a graphics screen. The background image will show through these transparent parts. Figure 11.8 shows how the image looks when loaded with transparency on and off.

As a general rule, you'll want to create your sprite image on a solid color that is not used in any other part of the image.

TRAP Make sure your sprite image doesn't also contain the color you're using for transparency. Otherwise, those parts of the sprite will become transparent too, making your sprite look like it has small holes or tears in it as the background image of the graphics screen shows through.

FIGURE 11.8

On the left, the image is loaded with transparency on. On the right, the same image is loaded with transparency off.

Creating a Sprite

Next, I create a pizza sprite:

```
pizza = games.Sprite(image = pizza_image, x = 320, y = 240)
```

A new `Sprite` object is created with the image of a pizza and x- and y-coordinates of (320,240), which puts it right in the middle of the screen. The new object is then assigned to `pizza`.

Adding a Sprite to the Screen

After you create a sprite, you need to add it to the screen so it can be seen and updated, which is exactly what I do in the next line:

```
games.screen.add(pizza)
```

The `add()` method simply adds a sprite to the graphics screen.

You don't need to be an artist to create graphics for your games. As you see in this chapter, I make up for my utter lack of artistic ability with a modern piece of technology: my digital camera. If you have access to a digital camera, you can create some great images for your projects. In fact, that's how I created all of the graphics for the Pizza Panic game. The brick wall is the back of a friend's house. For the pizza, I ordered delivery one night. And the chef is my brave, brave friend, Dave.

While this is a great technique, an important thing to remember is that, if you take a picture of a person or object, you don't necessarily own the image—obviously, some things are trademarked or copyrighted. Using a digital camera, however, is a great way to capture generic images while infusing your programs with a unique, photorealistic style.

Table 11.5 lists useful `Sprite` properties and Table 11.6 lists useful `Sprite` methods.

TABLE 11.5 USEFUL Sprite PROPERTIES

Property	Description
angle	Facing in degrees.
x	x-coordinate.
y	y-coordinate.
dx	x velocity.
dy	y velocity.
left	x-coordinate of left sprite edge.
right	x-coordinate of right sprite edge.
top	y-coordinate of top sprite edge.
bottom	y-coordinate of bottom sprite edge.
image	Image object of sprite.
overlapping_sprites	List of other objects that overlap sprite.
is_collideable	Whether or not sprite is collideable. True means sprite will register in collisions. False means sprite will not show up in collisions.

TABLE 11.6 USEFUL Sprite METHODS

Method	Description
update()	Updates sprite. Automatically called every mainloop() cycle.
destroy()	Removes sprite from the screen.

DISPLAYING TEXT

Whether you need to show off the numbers for a sales presentation or the number of aliens obliterated, there are times when you'll want to display text on a graphics screen. The games module contains a class that allows you to do just that, aptly named Text.

Introducing the Big Score Program

Displaying text on the graphics screen is just a matter of creating an object of the Text class. The Big Score program is a modification of the Background Image program. I display a score in the upper-right corner of the screen, just like in many classic arcade games. Figure 11.9 shows the results.

FIGURE 11.9

The impressively high score is displayed after a Text object is instantiated.

Here's the code for the program in its entirety:

```
# Big Score
# Demonstrates displaying text on a graphics screen

from livewires import games, color
```

```
games.init(screen_width = 640, screen_height = 480, fps = 50)

wall_image = games.load_image("wall.jpg", transparent = False)
games.screen.background = wall_image

score = games.Text(value = 1756521,
                    size = 60,
                    color = color.black,
                    x = 550,
                    y = 30)
games.screen.add(score)

games.screen.mainloop()
```

Importing the color **Module**

The livewires package contains another module, color, which defines a set of constants that represent different colors. These colors can be used with certain graphics objects, including any Text or Message object. For a complete list of predefined colors, see the livewires documentation in Appendix A.

To choose from a group of possible colors, I import the color module by replacing the import line at the top of the program with:

```
from livewires import games, color
```

Both the color and games modules are loaded from the livewires package.

Creating a Text **Object**

A Text object represents text on the graphics screen. Just before I invoke mainloop(), I create a Text object and assign it to score:

```
score = games.Text(value = 1756521,
                    size = 60,
                    color = color.black,
                    x = 550,
                    y = 30)
```

I pass the integer 1756521 to text so that the characters that make up the number will be displayed. (A Text object will be displayed as the string representation of whatever you pass value.) Then I pass 60 to size, which represents the height of the text in pixels, so the font is nice and big to match the score. I pass color the constant color.black from the color module to make the text—you guessed it—black. I pass 550 to x and 30 to y, placing the center of the object at the coordinates (550,30). This puts the text in the upper-right corner of the graphics window.

Adding a Text **Object to the Screen**

In the next line of code, I add the new object to the screen so it will be displayed:

```
games.screen.add(score)
```

Once mainloop() is invoked, the graphics window is displayed along with score.

Since Text is a subclass of Sprite, Text inherits all of Sprite's properties, attributes, and methods. Table 11.7 lists two additional Text properties that the class defines.

TABLE 11.7 ADDITIONAL Text PROPERTIES	
Property	**Description**
value	Value to be displayed as text.
color	Color of text.

DISPLAYING A MESSAGE

You may want to display some text on the screen for only a brief period of time. You might want to show a message saying "All records have been updated" or "Attack Wave Seven Complete!" The games class Message is perfect for creating temporary messages just like these.

Introducing the You Won Program

The You Won program is a modified version of the Background Image program. I instantiate a Message object right before invoking mainloop() to display the text "You won!" in big, red letters. The message is displayed for about five seconds and then the program ends. Figure 11.10 illustrates the program.

FIGURE 11.10

Ah, the thrill of
victory.

Here's the code for the program:

```
# You Won
# Demonstrates displaying a message

from livewires import games, color

games.init(screen_width = 640, screen_height = 480, fps = 50)

wall_image = games.load_image("wall.jpg", transparent = False)
games.screen.background = wall_image

won_message = games.Message(value = "You won!",
                            size = 100,
                            color = color.red,
                            x = games.screen.width/2,
                            y = games.screen.height/2,
                            lifetime = 250,
                            after_death = games.screen.quit)
games.screen.add(won_message)

games.screen.mainloop()
```

Importing the `color` Module

`Message` objects, like `Text` objects, have a `color` property. To choose from a group of possible colors, I import the `color` module by replacing the `import` line at the top of the program with:

```
from livewires import games, color
```

Creating a `Message` Object

Messages are created from the `games` class `Message`. A message is a special kind of `Text` object that destroys itself after a set period of time. A message can also specify a method or a function to be executed after the object destroys itself.

The constructor method for `Message` takes all of the values you saw with `Text`, but adds two more: `lifetime` and `after_death`. `lifetime` takes an integer value that represents how long the message should be displayed, measured in `mainloop()` cycles. `after_death` can be passed a method or function to be executed after the `Message` object destroys itself. The default value for `after_death` is `None`, so a value isn't required.

I create this `Message` object right before I invoke `mainloop()`:

```
won_message = games.Message(value = "You won!",
                            size = 100,
                            color = color.red,
                            x = games.screen.width/2,
                            y = games.screen.height/2,
                            lifetime = 250,
                            after_death = games.screen.quit)
```

This creates the message "You Won!" in big, red letters at the center of the screen for about five seconds, after which the program ends.

This code instantiates a new `Message` object with a `lifetime` attribute set to 250. This means that the object will live for about five seconds, because `mainloop()` runs at 50 frames per second. After the five seconds, `games.screen.quit()` is called, since I pass that method's name to `after_death`. At that point, the screen and all of its associated objects are destroyed and the program ends.

 Make sure to pass `after_death` just the name of the function or method you want called after the `Message` object disappears. Don't include a set of parentheses after the name.

Using the Screen's Width and Height

The screen object has a width property, which represents the width of the graphics screen, and a height property, which represents the height of the graphics screen. Sometimes it's clearer to use these properties rather than literal integers when you specify a location on the screen.

I use these properties when I pass values for the location of the new Message object, with x = games.screen.width/2, and y = games.screen.height/2. By setting the x-coordinate to half of the screen width and the y-coordinate to half of the screen height, I put the object right in the middle of the screen. You can use this technique to put an object in the middle of the graphics screen, independent of the actual screen width and height.

Adding a Message Object to the Screen

In the next line of code, I add the new object to the screen so it will be displayed:

```
games.screen.add(won_message)
```

Message is a subclass of Text. This means that Message inherits all of Text's properties, attributes, and methods. Table 11.8 lists two additional Message attributes.

TABLE 11.8   ADDITIONAL Message ATTRIBUTES

Attributes	Description
lifetime	Number of mainloop() cycles before object destroys itself. 0 means never destroy itself. The default value is 0.
after_death	Function or method to be run after object destroys itself. The default value is None.

MOVING SPRITES

Moving images are the essence of most games—most forms of entertainment, for that matter. With sprites, going from stationary to moving is easy. Sprite objects have properties that allow them to move around a graphics screen.

Introducing the Moving Pizza Program

This new program is a modification of the Pizza Sprite program. In this program, the pizza moves down and to the right. All I need to do is change a few lines of code to get the pizza to move. That's the power of sprites. Figure 11.11 illustrates the program.

FIGURE 11.11

The pizza moves down and to the right in the direction of the arrow.

Here's the code for the program:

```
# Moving Pizza
# Demonstrates sprite velocities

from livewires import games

games.init(screen_width = 640, screen_height = 480, fps = 50)

wall_image = games.load_image("wall.jpg", transparent = False)
games.screen.background = wall_image

pizza_image = games.load_image("pizza.bmp")
the_pizza = games.Sprite(image = pizza_image,
                         x = games.screen.width/2,
                         y = games.screen.height/2,
                         dx = 1,
                         dy = 1)
games.screen.add(the_pizza)

games.screen.mainloop()
```

Setting a Sprite's Velocity Values

All I have to do is modify the code that creates a new sprite by providing additional values for dx and dy to the constructor method:

```
the_pizza = games.Sprite(image = pizza_image,
                         x = games.screen.width/2,
                         y = games.screen.height/2,
                         dx = 1,
                         dy = 1)
```

Every object based on Sprite has dx and dy properties for the object's velocity along the x and y axes, respectively. ("d," by the way, stands for "delta," which means a change.) So, dx is the change in the object's x-coordinate and dy is the change in the object's y-coordinate each time screen is updated by mainloop(). A positive value for dx moves the sprite to the right, while a negative value moves it to the left. A positive value for dy moves the sprite down, while a negative value moves it up.

Back in the Pizza Sprite program, I didn't pass any values for dx or dy. Although the sprite in that program did have dx and dy properties, they both had the default value of 0.

Since I pass 1 to dx and 1 to dy, every time the graphics window is updated by mainloop(), the pizza's x-coordinate is increased by 1 and its y-coordinate is increased by 1, moving the sprite right and down.

DEALING WITH SCREEN BOUNDARIES

If you watch the Moving Pizza program run for any length of time, you may notice that once the pizza hits a screen boundary, it keeps going. In fact, it disappears out of sight.

Whenever you set a sprite in motion, you should create a mechanism to deal with the graphics window's boundaries. You have a few choices. A moving sprite could simply stop when it reaches the edge of the screen. It could die in, say, a fiery explosion. It could bounce, like a giant rubber ball. It could even wrap around the screen so that, just as it disappears off one edge, it reappears on the opposite. What seems to make the most sense for a pizza? Bouncing, of course.

The Bouncing Pizza Program

When I say that a sprite "bounces" off the edges of the graphics window, I mean that when it reaches a screen boundary, it should reverse the velocity component that was moving it toward that boundary. So, if the bouncing pizza sprite reaches the top or bottom screen edge, it should reverse its dy property. When it reaches the sides of the screen, it should reverse its dx. Figure 11.12 illustrates the Bouncing Pizza program.

FIGURE 11.12

Though you can't tell here, the pizza bounces around, following the path of the arrow.

Setting Up the Program

I begin as I would with any other graphics program:

```
# Bouncing Pizza
# Demonstrates dealing with screen boundaries

from livewires import games

games.init(screen_width = 640, screen_height = 480, fps = 50)
```

As before, the previous lines give me access to the games module and create the graphics screen.

Deriving a New Class from Sprite

For the first time, I want a sprite to do something it isn't programmed to do: bounce. So, I need to derive a new class from Sprite. Since I want a bouncing pizza, I call the new class Pizza:

```
class Pizza(games.Sprite):
    """ A bouncing pizza. """
```

Overriding the update() Method

I need to add just a single method to the Pizza class to turn a moving pizza into a bouncing one. Every time the graphics window is updated by mainloop(), the following two things happen:

- Each sprite's position is updated based on its dx and dy properties.
- Each sprite's update() method is called.

Every Sprite object has an update() method; it just does nothing by default. So, by overriding update() in Pizza, I get the perfect place to put code that will handle screen boundary checking.

```python
def update(self):
    """ Reverse a velocity component if edge of screen reached. """
    if self.right > games.screen.width or self.left < 0:
        self.dx = -self.dx

    if self.bottom > games.screen.height or self.top < 0:
        self.dy = -self.dy
```

In the method, I check to see if the sprite is about to go beyond the screen limits in any direction. If so, I reverse the responsible velocity.

If the object's right property, which represents the x-coordinate of its right edge, is greater than games.screen.width, then the pizza is about to go off the right edge into oblivion. If the object's left property, which represents the x-coordinate of its left edge, is less than 0, then the pizza is headed off the screen to the left. In either case, I simply reverse dx, the pizza's horizontal velocity, to "bounce" the pizza off the screen boundary.

If the object's bottom property, which represents the y-coordinate of its bottom edge, is greater than games.screen.height, then the pizza is about to go off the bottom edge into oblivion. If the object's top property, which represents the y-coordinate of its top edge, is less than 0, then the pizza is headed off the top of the screen. In either case, I simply reverse dy, the pizza's vertical velocity, to "bounce" the pizza off the screen boundary.

Wrapping Up the Program

Since I define a class in the program, I thought I'd organize the rest of the code into a function:

```python
def main():
    wall_image = games.load_image("wall.jpg", transparent = False)
    games.screen.background = wall_image
```

```
    pizza_image = games.load_image("pizza.bmp")
    the_pizza = Pizza(image = pizza_image,
                      x = games.screen.width/2,
                      y = games.screen.height/2,
                      dx = 1,
                      dy = 1)
    games.screen.add(the_pizza)

    games.screen.mainloop()

# kick it off!
main()
```

You've seen the bulk of this code before. One important difference is that I created an object from my new `Pizza` class instead of `Sprite`. Because of this, the object's `update()` method checks for screen boundaries and reverses the velocities when necessary for a pizza that bounces!

HANDLING MOUSE INPUT

Although you've seen a lot of what the `livewires` package has to offer, you haven't seen the main ingredient of interactivity: user input. One of the most common ways to get input from a user is through the mouse. `livewires` offers an object to let you do just that.

Introducing the Moving Pan Program

The `mouse` object from the `games` module gives you access to the mouse. The object has properties that make reading the mouse position on the graphics screen a piece of cake. With these properties, I create the Moving Pan program, which allows a user to drag a pan sprite across the screen as he or she moves the mouse. The results of the program are displayed in Figure 11.13.

Setting Up the Program

The following code should look remarkably familiar:

```
# Moving Pan
# Demonstrates mouse input

from livewires import games

games.init(screen_width = 640, screen_height = 480, fps = 50)
```

As before, I import `games` and initialize the graphics screen. The `init()` method also creates the `mouse` object I'll use to read the mouse position.

FIGURE 11.13

The pan sprite follows the mouse around the graphics screen.

Reading Mouse X- and Y-Coordinates

Next, I create `Pan` for the pan sprite:

```
class Pan(games.Sprite):
    """ A pan controlled by the mouse. """
    def update(self):
        """ Move to mouse coordinates. """
        self.x = games.mouse.x
        self.y = games.mouse.y
```

Like a `Sprite` object, the `mouse` object has an `x` property for its x-coordinate and a `y` property for its y-coordinate. With them, I can read the current mouse location on the graphics screen.

In the `update()` method, I assign the `Pan` object's `x` property the value of the `mouse` object's `x` property. Then I assign the `Pan` object's `y` property the value of the `mouse` object's `y` property. This moves the pan to the current location of the mouse pointer.

Next, I write a `main()` function that contains the type of code you've seen before that sets the background image and creates sprite objects:

```
def main():
    wall_image = games.load_image("wall.jpg", transparent = False)
    games.screen.background = wall_image

    pan_image = games.load_image("pan.bmp")
    the_pan = Pan(image = pan_image,
                    x = games.mouse.x,
                    y = games.mouse.y)
    games.screen.add(the_pan)
```

By passing `games.mouse.x` to `x` and `games.mouse.y` to `y`, the `Pan` object starts off at the mouse coordinates.

Setting Mouse Pointer Visibility

Next in `main()`, I use the `mouse` object's `is_visible` property to set the visibility of the mouse pointer.

```
    games.mouse.is_visible = False
```

Setting the property to `True` means the mouse pointer will be visible, while setting it to `False` means the pointer will not be visible. Since I don't want the pointer sitting on top of the pan image, I set the property to `False`.

Grabbing Input to the Graphics Window

Next in `main()`, I use the `screen` object's `event_grab` property to grab all of the input to the graphics screen:

```
    games.screen.event_grab = True
```

Setting the property to `True` means that all input will be focused on the graphics screen. The benefit of this is that the mouse won't leave the graphics window. Setting the property to `False` means that all input is not focused on the graphics screen and that the mouse pointer can leave the graphics window.

 HINT   If you grab all of the input to the graphics screen, you won't be able to close the graphics window with the mouse. However, you can always close the window by pressing the Escape key.

Wrapping Up the Program

Finally, I wrap up `main()` as before and invoke `mainloop()` to make sure everything on the screen is updated.

```
games.screen.mainloop()
```

```
# kick it off!
main()
```

Check out Table 11.9 for a summary of a few useful `mouse` properties.

TABLE 11.9	USEFUL mouse PROPERTIES
Property	**Description**
x	x-coordinate of mouse pointer.
y	y-coordinate of mouse pointer.
is_visible	Boolean value for setting visibility of mouse pointer. True is visible while False is not visible. Default value is True.

DETECTING COLLISIONS

In most games, when two things collide, there's a clear result. It can be as simple as a 2-D character running into a boundary that won't let him pass, or as spectacular as a 3-D scene where an asteroid tears through the hull of a massive mother ship. Either way, there's a need to detect when objects collide.

Introducing the Slippery Pizza Program

The Slippery Pizza program is an extension of the Moving Pan program. In the Slippery Pizza program, the user controls a pan with the mouse, just like in the Moving Pan program. This time, however, there's a pizza sprite on the screen. The user can move the pan toward the pizza, but as soon as he or she reaches it, the slippery pizza moves to a new, random screen location. Figures 11.14 and 11.15 show the program in action.

FIGURE 11.14

The player almost reaches the pizza.

FIGURE 11.15

The slippery pizza gets away again.

Setting Up the Program

The initial code is taken from the Moving Pan program, with one minor addition:

```
# Slippery Pizza Program
# Demonstrates testing for sprite collisions

from livewires import games
import random


games.init(screen_width = 640, screen_height = 480, fps = 50)
```

The one new thing I do is import our old friend the random module. This allows me to generate a new, random location for the pizza sprite after the collision.

Detecting Collisions

I create a new Pan class by adding some code for the collision detection:

```
class Pan(games.Sprite):
    """ A pan controlled by the mouse. """
    def update(self):
        """ Move to mouse position. """
        self.x = games.mouse.x
        self.y = games.mouse.y
        self.check_collide()

    def check_collide(self):
        """ Check for collision with pizza. """
        for pizza in self.overlapping_sprites:
            pizza.handle_collide()
```

In the last line of update(), I invoke the Pan method check_collide(). The check_collide() method loops through the Pan object's overlapping_sprites property—a list of all of the objects that overlap it. Each object that overlaps the pan has its handle_collide() method called. Basically, the pan is telling any object that overlaps it to handle the collision.

Handling Collisions

Next, I create a new Pizza class:

```
class Pizza(games.Sprite):
    """ A slippery pizza. """
```

```
def handle_collide(self):
    """ Move to a random screen location. """
    self.x = random.randrange(games.screen.width)
    self.y = random.randrange(games.screen.height)
```

I write just one method, `handle_collide()`, which generates random screen coordinates and moves the `Pizza` object to this new location.

Wrapping Up the Program

Here's the `main()` function:

```
def main():
    wall_image = games.load_image("wall.jpg", transparent = False)
    games.screen.background = wall_image

    pizza_image = games.load_image("pizza.bmp")
    pizza_x = random.randrange(games.screen.width)
    pizza_y = random.randrange(games.screen.height)
    the_pizza = Pizza(image = pizza_image, x = pizza_x, y = pizza_y)
    games.screen.add(the_pizza)

    pan_image = games.load_image("pan.bmp")
    the_pan = Pan(image = pan_image,
                  x = games.mouse.x,
                  y = games.mouse.y)
    games.screen.add(the_pan)

    games.mouse.is_visible = False

    games.screen.event_grab = True

    games.screen.mainloop()

# kick it off!
main()
```

As always, I set a background image. Then, I create two objects: a `Pizza` object and a `Pan` object. I generate a random set of screen coordinates for the pizza and place the pan at the mouse coordinates. I set the mouse pointer to invisible and grab all input to the game window. Then, I invoke `mainloop()`. Finally, I kick everything off by calling `main()`.

BACK TO THE PIZZA PANIC GAME

Now that you've gotten a taste of what the livewires multimedia package can do, it's time to create the Pizza Panic game introduced at the beginning of the chapter. Much of the code for the game can be taken directly from the example programs. However, I'll also introduce a few new concepts.

Setting Up the Program

As in all of the programs in this chapter, I begin by importing modules and initializing the graphics screen:

```
# Pizza Panic
# Player must catch falling pizzas before they hit the ground

from livewires import games, color
import random


games.init(screen_width = 640, screen_height = 480, fps = 50)
```

To do any graphics work, I need to import games, while color gives me access to the set of predefined colors. I import random so that the crazy chef seems more lifelike when he makes his choices. Finally, I call games init() to initialize the graphics screen and to give me access to the games mouse object.

The Pan Class

The Pan class is a blueprint for the pan sprite that the player controls with the mouse. However, the pan will only move left and right. I'll go through the class, one section at a time.

Loading the Pan Image

I do something a little different in the beginning of this class: I load a sprite image and assign it to a class variable, image. I do this because Pizza Panic has several classes, and loading an image in its corresponding class definition is cleaner than loading all of the images in the program's main() function.

```
class Pan(games.Sprite):
    """
    A pan controlled by player to catch falling pizzas.
    """
    image = games.load_image("pan.bmp")
```

The __init__() Method

Next, I write the constructor to initialize a new Pan object:

```
def __init__(self, y = 450):
    """ Initialize Pan object and create Text object for score. """
    super(Pan, self).__init__(image = Pan.image,
                              x = games.mouse.x,
                              bottom = games.screen.height)

    self.score = games.Text(value = 0, size = 25, color = color.black,
                            top = 5, right = games.screen.width - 10)
    games.screen.add(self.score)
```

I use the super() function to make sure that the Sprite init() method is called. Then, I define an attribute score—a Text object—for the player's score, which begins at 0. Of course, I remember to add the new Text object to the screen so it's displayed.

The update() Method

This method moves the player's pan:

```
def update(self):
    """ Move to mouse x position. """
    self.x = games.mouse.x

    if self.left < 0:
        self.left = 0

    if self.right > games.screen.width:
        self.right = games.screen.width

    self.check_catch()
```

The method assigns the mouse x-coordinate to the Pan object's x-coordinate, allowing the player to move the pan left and right with the mouse.

Next, I use the object's left property to check whether its left edge is less than 0—meaning that part of the pan is beyond the left edge of the graphics window. If it is, I set the left edge to 0 so that the pan is displayed at the left edge of the window.

Then, I use the object's right property to check whether its right edge is greater than games.screen.width—meaning that part of the pan is beyond the right edge of the graphics window. If it is, I set the right edge to games.screen.width so that the pan is displayed at the right edge of the window.

Finally, I invoke the object's check_catch() method.

The check_catch() **Method**

This method checks whether the player has caught any of the falling pizzas:

```
def check_catch(self):
    """ Check if catch pizzas. """
    for pizza in self.overlapping_sprites:
        self.score.value += 10
        self.score.right = games.screen.width - 10
        pizza.handle_caught()
```

For each object that overlaps the pan, the method increases the player's score by 10 and invokes the handle_caught() method of the overlapping sprite.

The Pizza **Class**

This class is for the falling pizzas that the player must catch:

```
class Pizza(games.Sprite):
    """
    A pizza which falls to the ground.
    """
    image = games.load_image("pizza.bmp")
    speed = 1
```

I define two class variables: image for the pizza image and speed for the pizzas' falling speed. I set speed to 1 so that the pizzas fall at a fairly slow speed. I use both class variables in the Pizza constructor method, as you'll soon see.

The __init__() **Method**

This method initializes a new Pizza object:

```
def __init__(self, x, y = 90):
    """ Initialize a Pizza object. """
    super(Pizza, self).__init__(image = Pizza.image,
                                x = x, y = y,
                                dy = Pizza.speed)
```

All I do in this method is call the constructor of the super class of Pizza. Note that I set the default value for y to 90, which puts each new pizza right at the chef's chest level.

The update() Method

This method handles screen boundary checking:

```
def update(self):
    """ Check if bottom edge has reached screen bottom. """
    if self.bottom > games.screen.height:
        self.end_game()
        self.destroy()
```

All this method does is check whether a pizza has reached the bottom of the screen. If it has, the method invokes the object's end_game() method and then the object removes itself from the screen.

The handle_caught() Method

Remember, this method is invoked by the Pan object when the Pizza object collides with it:

```
def handle_caught(self):
    """ Destroy self if caught. """
    self.destroy()
```

When a pizza collides with a pan, the pizza is considered "caught" and simply ceases to exist. So, the Pizza object invokes its own destroy() method and the pizza literally disappears.

The end_game() Method

This method ends the game. It's invoked when a pizza reaches the bottom of the screen.

```
def end_game(self):
    """ End the game. """
    end_message = games.Message(value = "Game Over",
                                size = 90,
                                color = color.red,
                                x = games.screen.width/2,
                                y = games.screen.height/2,
                                lifetime = 5 * games.screen.fps,
                                after_death = games.screen.quit)
    games.screen.add(end_message)
```

The code creates a Message object that declares that the game is over. After about five seconds, the message disappears and the graphics window closes, ending the game.

TRAP

The end_game() method is called whenever a pizza reaches the bottom of the screen. However, since the "Game Over" message lasts about five seconds, it's possible for another pizza to reach the bottom of the screen before the graphics window closes—resulting in multiple "Game Over" messages.

In Chapter 12, you'll see how to create an object to represent the game itself, which could keep track of whether or not the game is over and prevent something like multiple "Game Over" messages from being created.

The Chef **Class**

The Chef class is used to create the crazy chef who throws the pizzas off the restaurant rooftop.

```
class Chef(games.Sprite):
    """
    A chef which moves left and right, dropping pizzas.
    """
    image = games.load_image("chef.bmp")
```

I define a class attribute, image, for the chef image.

The __init__() **Method**

Here's the constructor method:

```
    def __init__(self, y = 55, speed = 2, odds_change = 200):
        """ Initialize the Chef object. """
        super(Chef, self).__init__(image = Chef.image,
                                   x = games.screen.width / 2,
                                   y = y,
                                   dx = speed)

        self.odds_change = odds_change
        self.time_til_drop = 0
```

First, I call the constructor of the superclass of Chef. I pass image the class attribute Chef.image. I pass x a value that puts the chef right in the middle of the screen. For y, the default value of 55 puts the chef right on top of the brick wall. dx is passed speed, which determines the chef's horizontal velocity as he moves along the rooftop. The default value is 2.

The method also creates two object attributes: odds_change and time_til_drop. odds_change is an integer that represents the odds that the chef will change his direction. For example, if `odds_change` is 200, then there's a one in 200 chance that every time the chef moves, he'll reverse direction. You'll see how this works in the `update()` method of the class.

`time_til_drop` is an integer that represents the amount of time, in `mainloop()` cycles, until the chef drops his next pizza. I set it to 0 initially, meaning that when a `Chef` object springs to life, it should immediately drop a pizza. You'll see how `time_til_drop` works in the `check_drop()` method.

The `update()` Method

This method defines the rules for how the chef decides to slide back and forth along the rooftop:

```
def update(self):
    """ Determine if direction needs to be reversed. """
    if self.left < 0 or self.right > games.screen.width:
        self.dx = -self.dx
    elif random.randrange(self.odds_change) == 0:
        self.dx = -self.dx


    self.check_drop()
```

A chef slides along the rooftop in one direction until he either reaches the edge of the screen or "decides" at random to switch directions. The beginning of this method checks to see whether the chef has moved beyond the left or right edge of the graphics window. If he has, then he reverses direction with the code the `self.dx = -self.dx`. Otherwise, the chef has a one in `odds_change` chance of changing direction.

Regardless of whether or not the chef changes direction, the last thing the method does is invoke the `Chef` object's `check_drop()` method.

The `check_drop()` Method

This method is invoked every `mainloop()` cycle, but that doesn't mean a new pizza is dropped 50 times a second!

```
def check_drop(self):
    """ Decrease countdown or drop pizza and reset countdown. """
    if self.time_til_drop > 0:
        self.time_til_drop -= 1
    else:
        new_pizza = Pizza(x = self.x)
        games.screen.add(new_pizza)
```

```
    # set buffer to approx 30% of pizza height, regardless of pizza speed
    self.time_til_drop = int(new_pizza.height * 1.3 / Pizza.speed) + 1
```

time_til_drop represents a countdown for our chef. If time_til_drop is greater than 0, then 1 is subtracted from it. Otherwise, a new Pizza object is created and time_til_drop is reset.

In creating a new pizza, I pass the Chef object's x-coordinate to the Pizza constructor so that the new pizza sprite begins at the same location as the chef sprite.

The new value of time_til_drop is determined by the height of the pizza sprite image and the speed at which the pizzas are falling. Since the pizza image is 50 pixels high, the formula provides a nice 15 pixel-sized gap between each pie, independent of the falling speed.

The main() Function

The main() function creates objects and starts up the game:

```
def main():
    """ Play the game. """
    wall_image = games.load_image("wall.jpg", transparent = False)
    games.screen.background = wall_image

    the_chef = Chef()
    games.screen.add(the_chef)

    the_pan = Pan()
    games.screen.add(the_pan)

    games.mouse.is_visible = False

    games.screen.event_grab = True
    games.screen.mainloop()

# start it up!
main()
```

First, I set the brick wall as the background. I create a chef and a pan. Then, I set the mouse pointer to invisible and grab all of the input so the mouse pointer can't leave the graphics window. I invoke mainloop() to begin the game. Finally, I call main() to kick it all off!

SUMMARY

- A package is a set of modules.
- A pixel is a single point in a graphics area.
- pygame and livewires are packages that give Python programmers access to a wide range of multimedia functionality.
- games is a module from the livewires package that contains objects, functions, and classes for writing 2D games.
- The games.init() function creates a new graphics screen.
- The games.load_image() function loads an image stored in a graphics file and returns an image object.
- color is a module from the livewires package that defines a set of constants for colors.
- screen is a games module object that provides access to the graphics screen.
- The screen object has properties for width, height, background, and update rate, among others.
- The screen object has methods to add an object, remove all objects, begin its main loop, and quit, among others.
- mouse is a games module object that provides access to the mouse.
- The mouse object has properties for the x-coordinate and the y-coordinate of the mouse pointer as well as a property for mouse pointer visibility.
- Sprite is a class in the games module for graphics objects that can be displayed on the graphics screen.
- A Sprite object has properties for its image, location, speed, orientation, and overlapping objects, among others.
- A Sprite object has methods for updating itself and destroying itself, among others.
- Text is a subclass of Sprite from the games module for text displayed on the graphics screen.
- A Text object has properties for value, color, location, speed, orientation, and overlapping objects, among others.
- Message is a subclass of Text from the games module for text displayed on the graphics screen that disappears after a set period of time.
- A Message object has properties for value, color, location, speed, orientation, overlapping objects, and lifetime, among others.

REVIEW QUESTIONS

1. Why shouldn't you run a graphics program through IDLE?
2. Why should you create a batch file to run your graphics programs?
3. What file types does the `load_image()` function work with?
4. How do you set the background of the graphics screen?
5. What is a graphics coordinate system?
6. In a graphics coordinate system, what does the x-axis represent?
7. In a graphics coordinate system, what does the y-axis represent?
8. How can you determine the coordinates for the middle of the graphics screen?
9. What is image transparency?
10. What is a transparent color?
11. How is loading an image for a `Sprite` object different from loading an image for the background?
12. How does the `load_image()` function determine the transparent color for an image?
13. What is a potential pitfall of the way the `load_image()` function determines the transparent color for an image?
14. How do you ensure that a `Sprite` object will be drawn on the screen?
15. What does a Sprite's `update()` method do?
16. How are `Text` and `Message` objects similar and different?
17. How can you determine the approximate number of seconds a `Message` object will stay on the screen?
18. Why shouldn't you include a set of parentheses when you pass a method or function name to the `after_death` parameter of the `Message` constructor?
19. How does the `screen` object's `fps` property affect the speed of moving sprites?
20. What's a drawback of grabbing all input to the graphics screen?

PROJECTS

1. Avalanche is a 2D game with a chef who must avoid falling rocks. If the chef is hit by a rock, a big red "Game Over" message appears and the game is over. The game begins with only one falling rock, but every time a rock reaches the ground, two new rocks drop from the sky. The player controls the chef at the bottom of the screen with the mouse and may move him left or right. Write the Avalanche program design. List each class you think you'll need in your game program, along with a brief description. Within each class description, detail any attributes and methods. Finally, include pseudocode for a `main()` method.

2. Write the Avalanche game program you designed in Project 1.

3. Modify the Avalanche game program you wrote in Project 2. Give the chef a health level that's displayed in the upper-right corner of the screen. It should have a starting value of 10. When the chef is hit by a falling rock, his health level should decrease by 1 and the rock should fall from the sky again. When the chef's health level is 0 or less, the game should end.

4. Crazy Pong is a twist on the classic game of Pong. In Crazy Pong, the player controls a paddle on the left side of the screen, using the mouse to move up and down. When a bouncing ball hits the paddle, it's deflected and the player scores a point. Once a ball gets past the paddle though, the game is over. The twist with Crazy Pong (and what makes it crazy) is that when a ball hits the paddle, a new ball is created—and all balls must be kept in play or the game ends. Write the Crazy Pong program design. List each class you think you'll need in your game program, along with a brief description. Within each class description, detail any attributes and methods. Finally, include pseudocode for a main() method.

5. Write the Crazy Pong game program you designed in Project 4.

SOUND, ANIMATION, AND PROGRAM DEVELOPMENT: THE ASTROCRASH GAME

I n this chapter, you'll expand your multimedia programming skills to include sound and animation. You'll also see how to write a large program in stages. Specifically, you'll learn to do the following:

- Read the keyboard
- Play sound files
- Play music files
- Create animations
- Develop a program by writing progressively more complete versions of it

INTRODUCING THE ASTROCRASH GAME

The final game program for this chapter, the Astrocrash game, is my version of the classic arcade game Asteroids. In Astrocrash, the player controls a ship in a moving field of deadly asteroids. The ship can rotate and thrust forward—most importantly, though, it can fire missiles at the asteroids to destroy them. The player, however, has some work cut out for him or her as large- and medium-sized asteroids break apart into two smaller asteroids when destroyed. And just when the player manages to obliterate all of the asteroids, a new, larger wave appears. The player's score increases with every asteroid he or she destroys, but once the player's ship collides with a floating space rock, the game is over. Figures 12.1 and 12.2 show the game in action.

FIGURE 12.1

The player controls a spaceship and blasts asteroids to increase his or her score. (Nebula image is in the public domain. Credit: NASA, The Hubble Heritage Team—AURA/ STScI)

FIGURE 12.2

If an asteroid hits the player's ship, the game is over.

READING THE KEYBOARD

You already know how to get strings from the user through the raw_input() function, but reading the keyboard for individual keystrokes is another matter. Fortunately, there's a new object from the games module that lets you do just this.

Introducing the Read Key Program

The Read Key program displays the ship on the nebula background. The user can move the ship around with different keystrokes. When the user presses the W key, the ship moves up. When the user presses the S key, the ship moves down. When the user presses the A key, the ship moves left. When the user presses the D key, the ship moves right. The user can also press multiple keys simultaneously for a combined effect. For example, when the user presses the W and D keys simultaneously, the ship moves diagonally, up and to the right. The program is illustrated in Figure 12.3.

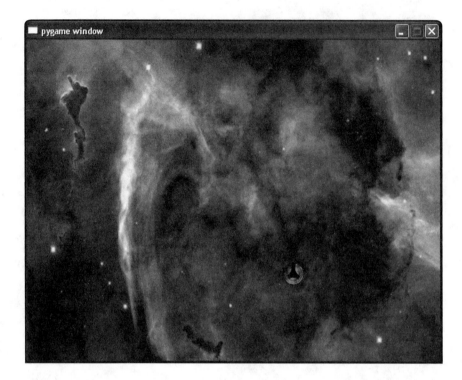

FIGURE 12.3

The ship moves
around the screen
based on
keystrokes.

Setting Up the Program

As I do with all programs that use the livewires package, I start by importing the modules I
need and calling the initialization method:

```
# Read Key
# Demonstrates reading the keyboard

from livewires import games

games.init(screen_width = 640, screen_height = 480, fps = 50)
```

Testing for Keystrokes

Next, I write a class for the ship. In the update() method, I check for keystrokes and change
the position of the ship accordingly.

```
class Ship(games.Sprite):
    """ A moving ship. """
    def update(self):
        """ Move ship based on keys pressed. """
```

```
if games.keyboard.is_pressed(games.K_w):
    self.y -= 1
if games.keyboard.is_pressed(games.K_s):
    self.y += 1
if games.keyboard.is_pressed(games.K_a):
    self.x -= 1
if games.keyboard.is_pressed(games.K_d):
    self.x += 1
```

I use the new keyboard object from the games module. You can use the object to test for specific keypresses. I invoke the object's is_pressed() method, which returns True if the key being tested for is pressed, and False if not.

I use the is_pressed() method in a series of if statements to test whether any of the four keys—W, S, A, or D—is being pressed. If the W key is pressed, I decrease the object's y property by 1, moving the sprite up the screen by one pixel. If the S key is pressed, I increase the object's y property by 1, moving the sprite down the screen. If the A key is pressed, I decrease the object's x property by 1, moving the sprite left. If the D key is pressed, I increase the object's x property by 1, moving the sprite right.

Since multiple calls to is_pressed() can read simultaneous keypresses, the user can hold down multiple keys for a combined effect. For example, if a user holds down the D and S keys at the same time, the ship moves down and to the right because each time update() executes the Ship object adds one to its x-coordinate and one to its y-coordinate.

The games module has a set of constants that represent keys that you can use as an argument in is_pressed(). In this program, I use the games.K_w constant for the W key; games.K_s for the S key; games.K_a for the A key; and games.K_d for the D key. The naming of these constants is pretty intuitive. Here's a quick way to figure out the name of most key constants:

- All keyboard constants begin with games.K_.
- For alphabetic keys, add the key letter, in lowercase, to the end of the constant name. For example, the constant for the A key is games.K_a.
- For numeric keys, add the key number to the end of the constant name. For example, the constant for the 1 key is games.K_1.
- For other keys, you can often add their name, in all capital letters, to the end of the constant name. For example, the constant for the spacebar is games.K_SPACE.

For a complete list of keyboard constants, see the livewires documentation in Appendix A.

Wrapping Up the Program

Finally, I write the familiar `main()` function. I load the nebula background image, create a ship in the middle of the screen, and kick everything off by invoking `mainloop()`.

```
def main():
    nebula_image = games.load_image("nebula.jpg", transparent = False)
    games.screen.background = nebula_image

    ship_image = games.load_image("ship.bmp")
    the_ship = Ship(image = ship_image,
                    x = games.screen.width/2,
                    y = games.screen.height/2)
    games.screen.add(the_ship)

    games.screen.mainloop()

main()
```

ROTATING A SPRITE

In Chapter 11, you learned how to move sprites around the screen, but `livewires` lets you rotate them as well. You rotate a sprite through one of its properties.

Introducing the Rotate Sprite Program

In the Rotate Sprite program, the user can rotate the spacecraft using the keyboard. If the user presses the Right Arrow key, the ship rotates clockwise. If the user presses the Left Arrow key, the ship rotates counterclockwise. If the user presses the 1 key, the ship jumps to a rotation of 0 degrees. If the user presses the 2 key, the ship jumps to a rotation of 90 degrees. If the user presses the 3 key, the ship jumps to a rotation of 180 degrees. If the user presses the 4 key, the ship jumps to a rotation of 270 degrees. Figure 12.4 displays the program.

FIGURE 12.4

The ship can rotate clockwise, rotate counterclockwise, or jump to a predetermined angle.

Here's the code for the program:

```
# Rotate Sprite
# Demonstrates rotating a sprite

from livewires import games

games.init(screen_width = 640, screen_height = 480, fps = 50)

class Ship(games.Sprite):
    """ A rotating ship. """
    def update(self):
        """ Rotate based on keys pressed. """
        if games.keyboard.is_pressed(games.K_RIGHT):
            self.angle += 1
        if games.keyboard.is_pressed(games.K_LEFT):
            self.angle -= 1

        if games.keyboard.is_pressed(games.K_1):
```

```
            self.angle = 0
        if games.keyboard.is_pressed(games.K_2):
            self.angle = 90
        if games.keyboard.is_pressed(games.K_3):
            self.angle = 180
        if games.keyboard.is_pressed(games.K_4):
            self.angle = 270

def main():
    nebula_image = games.load_image("nebula.jpg", transparent = False)
    games.screen.background = nebula_image

    ship_image = games.load_image("ship.bmp")
    the_ship = Ship(image = ship_image,
                    x = games.screen.width/2,
                    y = games.screen.height/2)
    games.screen.add(the_ship)

    games.screen.mainloop()

main()
```

Using a Sprite's angle Property

The new element in the program is the angle property, which represents a sprite's facing in degrees. You can add to or subtract from the property, or you can simply assign a new value to it to change the facing of a sprite.

In the update() method, I first check whether the Right Arrow key is pressed. If it is, I add one to the object's angle property, which rotates the sprite by one degree clockwise. Next, I check whether the Left Arrow key is pressed. If it is, I subtract one from the property, rotating the sprite one degree counterclockwise.

The next set of lines rotates the ship directly to a specific angle by assigning a new value to the angle property. When the user presses the 1 key, the code assigns 0 to angle and the sprite jumps to a rotation of 0 degrees (its starting orientation). When the user presses the 2 key, the code assigns 90 to angle and the sprite jumps to a rotation of 90 degrees. When the user presses the 3 key, the code assigns 180 to angle and the sprite jumps to a rotation of 180 degrees. Finally, when the user presses the 4 key, the code assigns 270 to angle and the sprite jumps to a rotation of 270 degrees.

CREATING AN ANIMATION

Moving and rotating sprites adds excitement to a game, but animation really makes a game come to life. Fortunately, the games module contains a class for animations, aptly named Animation.

Introducing the Explosion Program

The Explosion program creates an explosion animation in the middle of a graphics screen. The animation plays continuously so that you can get a good look at it. When you're done appreciating the cool effect, you can end the program by closing the graphics window. Figure 12.5 shows a snapshot of the program in action.

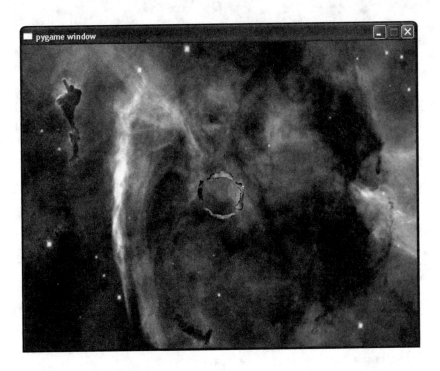

FIGURE 12.5

Although it's hard to tell from a still image, an explosion animates at the center of the graphics window.

Examining the Explosion Images

An animation is a sequence of images (also called *frames*) displayed in succession. I created a sequence of nine images that, when displayed in succession, resembles a fiery explosion. Figure 12.6 displays all nine images.

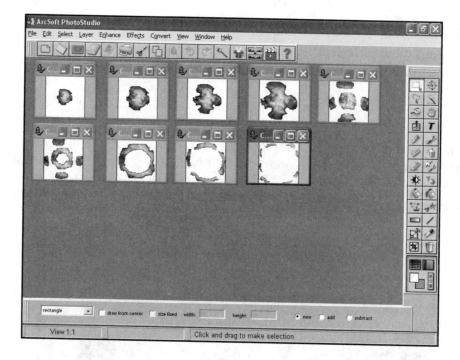

Setting Up the Program

As always, the initial code imports the modules I need and calls the initialization method:

```
# Explosion
# Demonstrates creating an animation

from livewires import games

games.init(screen_width = 640, screen_height = 480, fps = 50)
```

Then, I set the background of the graphics screen:

```
nebula_image = games.load_image("nebula.jpg", transparent = 0)
games.screen.background = nebula_image
```

Creating a List of Image Files

The constructor of the Animation class takes a list of image file names or a list of image objects for the sequence of images to display. So, next, I create a list of image file names, which corresponds to the images shown in Figure 12.6.

```
explosion_files = ["explosion1.bmp",
                   "explosion2.bmp",
                   "explosion3.bmp",
                   "explosion4.bmp",
                   "explosion5.bmp",
                   "explosion6.bmp",
                   "explosion7.bmp",
                   "explosion8.bmp",
                   "explosion9.bmp"]
```

Creating an Animation Object

Finally, I create an Animation object and add it to the screen:

```
explosion = games.Animation(images = explosion_files,
                            x = games.screen.width/2,
                            y = games.screen.height/2,
                            n_repeats = 0,
                            repeat_interval = 5)
games.screen.add(explosion)
```

The Animation class is derived from Sprite, so it inherits all of Sprite's attributes, properties and methods. Like all sprites, you can supply x- and y-coordinates to define where an animation will be located. In the previous code, I supply coordinates to the class constructor so that the animation is created at the center of the screen.

An animation is different from a sprite in that it has a list of images that it cycles through. So, you must supply a list of image file names as strings or a list of image objects for the images to be displayed. I supply a list of strings for the image file names, explosion_files, to images.

An object's n_repeats attribute represents how many times the animation (as a sequence of all of its images) is displayed. A value of 0 means that the animation will loop forever. The default value of n_repeats is 0. Since I pass 0 to n_repeats, the explosion animation will cycle forever (or at least until you close the graphics window).

An object's repeat_interval attribute represents the delay between successive images. A higher number means a longer delay between frames, resulting in a slower animation. A lower number represents a shorter delay, producing a faster animation. I pass repeat_interval the value 5 to get the speed I think is right for a convincing explosion.

Last but not least, I kick off the program by invoking the `screen` object's `mainloop()` method:

```
games.screen.mainloop()
```

WORKING WITH SOUND AND MUSIC

Sound and music add another sensory dimension to your programs. Loading, playing, looping, and stopping sound and music are easy to do with the `games` module. While people might argue about the difference between sound and music, there's no such argument when it comes to `livewires`, where there's a clear distinction between the two.

Introducing the Sound and Music Program

The Sound and Music program allows the user to play, loop, and stop the missile sound effect and the theme music from the Astrocrash game. The user can even play both at the same time. Figure 12.7 shows the program running (but, unfortunately, doesn't make a sound).

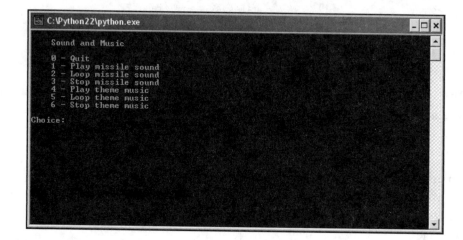

FIGURE 12.7

The program lets the user play a sound and some music.

 HINT When you run the program, you'll want to minimize the graphics window so you can work directly with the menu in the console window.

Working with Sounds

You can create a sound object for use in a program by loading a WAV file. The WAV format is great for sound effects because it can be used to encode whatever you record with a microphone.

Loading a Sound

First, I set up the program as always:

```
# Sound and Music
# Demonstrates playing sound and music files

from livewires import games

games.init(screen_width = 640, screen_height = 480, fps = 50)
```

Then, I load a WAV file by using the games function load_sound().

```
# load a sound file
missile_sound = games.load_sound("missile.wav")
```

The function takes a string for the name of the sound file to be loaded. I load the file missile.wav and assign the resulting sound object to missile.

 TRAP   You can only load WAV files with the load_sound() function.

Next, I load the music file:

```
# load the music file
games.music.load("theme.mid")
```

I'll save the music discussion until after I finish demonstrating sounds.

Playing a Sound

Next, I write the menu system that you first saw in Chapter 5:

```
choice = None
while choice != "0":

    print \
    """
    Sound and Music

    0 - Quit
    1 - Play missile sound
    2 - Loop missile sound
```

```
3 - Stop missile sound
4 - Play theme music
5 - Loop theme music
6 - Stop theme music
"""

choice = raw_input("Choice: ")
print

# exit
if choice == "0":
    print "Good-bye."
```

If the user enters 0, the program says good-bye and then exits.

The following code handles the case in which a user enters 1:

```
# play missile sound
elif choice == "1":
    missile_sound.play()
    print "Playing missile sound."
```

To play the sound once, I invoke the sound object's `play()` method. When a sound plays, it takes up one of the eight available sound channels. To play a sound, you need at least one open sound channel. Once all eight sound channels are in use, invoking a sound object's `play()` method has no effect.

If you invoke the `play()` method of a sound object that's already playing, the sound will start playing on another sound channel, if one is available.

Looping a Sound

You can loop a sound by passing the number of additional times you want the sound played to the object's `play()` method. For example, if you pass 3 to `play()`, the corresponding sound will play four times (its initial playing plus three additional times). You can loop a sound forever by passing -1 to `play()`.

The following code handles the case when a user enters 2:

```
# loop missile sound
elif choice == "2":
    loop = int(raw_input("Loop how many extra times? (-1 = forever): "))
    missile_sound.play(loop)
    print "Looping missile sound."
```

In this section of code, I get the number of additional times the user wants to hear the missile sound and then I pass that value to the sound object's play() method.

Stopping a Sound

You stop a sound object from playing by invoking its stop() method. This stops the particular sound on all channels that it's playing. If you invoke the stop() method of a sound object that's not currently playing, you'll find livewires is forgiving and won't complain with an error.

If the user enters 3, the following code stops the missile sound (if it's playing):

```
# stop missile sound
elif choice == "3":
    missile_sound.stop()
    print "Stopping missile sound."
```

Working with Music

In livewires, music is handled somewhat differently than sound. First, there is only one music channel, so only one file can be designated as the current music file at any given time. However, the music channel is more flexible than the sound channels. The music channel accepts many different types of sound files, including WAV, MP3, OGG, and MIDI. Finally, since there is only one music channel, you don't create a new object for each music file. Instead, you access a single object to load, play, and stop music.

Loading Music

You saw the code for loading the music file in the section "Loading a Sound." The code accesses music from games. It's through the object music from the games module that you're able to load, play, and stop the single music track.

The code I used to load the music track, games.music.load("theme.mid"), sets the current music to the MIDI file theme.mid. You load a music file by invoking the music object's load() method and passing it the music file name as a string.

You have only one available music track. So, if you load a new music file, it replaces the current one.

Playing Music

The following code handles the case in which the user enters 4:

```
# play theme music
elif choice == "4":
    games.music.play()
    print "Playing theme music."
```

As a result, the computer plays the music file that I loaded, `theme.mid`. If you don't pass any values to `games.music.play()`, the music plays once.

Looping Music

You can loop the music by passing the number of additional times you want the music played to `play()`. For example, if you pass 3 to `games.music.play()`, the music will play four times (its initial playing plus an additional three times). You can loop a music file forever by passing -1 to the function.

The following code handles the case when a user enters 5:

```
# loop theme music
elif choice == "5":
    loop = int(raw_input("Loop how many extra times? (-1 = forever): "))
    games.music.play(loop)
    print "Looping theme music."
```

In this section of code, I get the number of additional times the user wants to hear the theme music and then I pass that value to `play()`.

Stopping Music

If the user enters 6, the following code stops the music (if it's playing):

```
# stop theme music
elif choice == "6":
    games.music.stop()
    print "Stopping theme music."
```

You can stop the current music from playing by calling `games.music.stop()`, which is what I do here. If you call the method while there is no music playing, `livewires` is forgiving and won't complain with an error.

Wrapping Up the Program

Finally, I wrap up the program by handling an invalid choice and waiting for the user:

```
# some unknown choice
else:
    print "\nSorry, but", choice, "isn't a valid choice."

raw_input("\n\nPress the enter key to exit.")
```

PLANNING THE ASTROCRASH GAME

It's time to return to the chapter project: the Astrocrash game. I plan to write progressively more complete versions of the game until it's done, but I still feel I need to list a few details of the program, including the game's major features, a few necessary classes, and the multimedia assets required.

Game Features

Although my game is based on a classic video game that I know well (and learned about the hard way, one quarter at a time), it's still a good idea to write out a list of features:

- The ship should rotate and thrust forward based on keystrokes from the player.
- The ship should fire missiles based on a keystroke from the player.
- Asteroids should float at different velocities on the screen. Smaller asteroids should generally have higher velocities than larger ones.
- The ship, any missiles, and any asteroids should "wrap around" the screen—if they move beyond a screen boundary, they should appear at the opposite boundary.
- If a missile hits another object on the screen, it should destroy the other object and itself in a nice, fiery explosion.
- If the ship hits any other object on the screen, it should destroy the other object and itself in a nice, fiery explosion.
- If the ship is destroyed, the game is over.
- If a large asteroid is destroyed, two new, medium-sized asteroids should be produced. If a medium-sized asteroid is destroyed, two new, small asteroids should be produced. If a small asteroid is destroyed, no new asteroids should be produced.
- Every time a player destroys an asteroid, his or her score should increase. Smaller asteroids should be worth more points than larger ones.
- The player's score should be displayed in the upper-right corner of the screen.
- Once all of the asteroids have been destroyed, a new, larger wave of asteroids should be created.

I will leave out a few features of the original to keep the game simple.

Game Classes

Next, I make a list of the classes that I think I need:

- `Ship`
- `Missile`
- `Asteroid`
- `Explosion`

I know a few things about these classes already. `Ship`, `Missile`, and `Asteroid` will be derived from `games.Sprite`, while `Explosion` will be derived from `games.Animation`. I also know that this list could change as I put theory into practice and code the game.

Game Assets

Since the game includes sound, music, sprites, and animation, I know I need to create some multimedia files. Here's the list I came up with:

- An image file for the ship
- An image file for the missiles
- Three image files, one for each size of asteroid
- A series of image files for an explosion
- A sound file for the thrusting of the ship
- A sound file for the firing of a missile
- A sound file for the explosion of an object
- A music file for the theme

CREATING ASTEROIDS

Since the game involves deadly asteroids, I thought I'd start with them. Although this seems like the best first step to me, it may not to another programmer—and that's fine. You could certainly start with a different first step, such as getting the player's ship on the screen. There's no one right first step. The important thing to do is define and complete "bite-sized" programs that build on each other, working your way toward the completed project.

The Astrocrash01 Program

The Astrocrash01 program creates a graphics window, sets the nebula background, and spawns eight asteroids at random locations. The velocity of each asteroid is also randomly calculated, but smaller asteroids have the potential to move faster than larger ones. Figure 12.8 shows the program in action.

FIGURE 12.8

A field of moving asteroids is the foundation of the game.

Setting Up the Program

The program starts like most others:

```
# Astrocrash01
# Get asteroids moving on the screen

import random
from livewires import games

games.init(screen_width = 640, screen_height = 480, fps = 50)
```

I import the random module to generate random x- and y-coordinates for the asteroids.

The Asteroid Class

The Asteroid class is used for creating moving asteroids:

```
class Asteroid(games.Sprite):
    """ An asteroid which floats across the screen. """
    SMALL = 1
    MEDIUM = 2
    LARGE = 3
```

```
images = {SMALL : games.load_image("asteroid_small.bmp"),
          MEDIUM : games.load_image("asteroid_med.bmp"),
          LARGE : games.load_image("asteroid_big.bmp") }

SPEED = 2
```

The first thing I do is define class constants for the three different asteroid sizes: SMALL, MEDIUM, and LARGE. Then I create a dictionary with the sizes and corresponding asteroid image objects. This way, I can use a size constant to look up the corresponding image object. Finally, I create a class constant, SPEED, that I'll use as a base to calculate the random speed of each asteroid.

The __init()__ Method

Next, I tackle the constructor method:

```
def __init__(self, x, y, size):
    """ Initialize asteroid sprite. """
    super(Asteroid, self).__init__(
        image = Asteroid.images[size],
        x = x, y = y,
        dx = random.choice([1, -1]) * Asteroid.SPEED * random.random()/size,
        dy = random.choice([1, -1]) * Asteroid.SPEED * random.random()/size)

    self.size = size
```

The value passed to size represents the size of the asteroid and should be one of the size constants Asteroid.SMALL, Asteroid.MEDIUM, or Asteroid.LARGE. Based on size, the correct image for the new asteroid is retrieved and then passed along to Sprite's constructor (since Sprite is the superclass of Asteroid). The x and y values passed to Asteroid for the location of the new space rock are also passed on to Sprite's constructor.

The Asteroid constructor generates random values for the new object's velocity components and passes those off to Sprite's constructor. The velocity components are random, but smaller asteroids have the potential to move faster than larger ones. Finally, the Asteroid constructor creates and initializes the object's size attribute.

The update() Method

The update() method keeps an asteroid in play by wrapping it around the screen:

```
def update(self):
    """ Wrap around screen. """
    if self.top > games.screen.height:
        self.bottom = 0

    if self.bottom < 0:
        self.top = games.screen.height

    if self.left > games.screen.width:
        self.right = 0

    if self.right < 0:
        self.left = games.screen.width
```

The main() Function

Finally, the main() function sets the nebula background and creates eight asteroids at random screen locations:

```
def main():
    # establish background
    nebula_image = games.load_image("nebula.jpg")
    games.screen.background = nebula_image

    # create 8 asteroids
    for i in range(8):
        x = random.randrange(games.screen.width)
        y = random.randrange(games.screen.height)
        size = random.choice([Asteroid.SMALL, Asteroid.MEDIUM, Asteroid.LARGE])
        new_asteroid = Asteroid(x = x, y = y, size = size)
        games.screen.add(new_asteroid)

    games.screen.mainloop()

# kick it off!
main()
```

ROTATING THE SHIP

For my next task, I introduce the player's ship. My modest goal is to allow a user to rotate the ship with the arrow keys. I plan to attack the other ship functions later.

The Astrocrash02 Program

The Astrocrash02 program extends Astrocrash01. In the new version, I create a ship at the center of the screen that the player can rotate. If the player presses the Right Arrow key, the ship rotates clockwise. If the player presses the Left Arrow key, the ship rotates counterclockwise. Figure 12.9 shows the program in action.

FIGURE 12.9

The player's ship is now part of the action.

The Ship Class

The main thing I have to do is write a Ship class for the player's ship:

```
class Ship(games.Sprite):
    """ The player's ship. """
    image = games.load_image("ship.bmp")
    ROTATION_STEP = 3
```

```
def update(self):
    """ Rotate based on keys pressed. """
    if games.keyboard.is_pressed(games.K_LEFT):
        self.angle -= Ship.ROTATION_STEP
    if games.keyboard.is_pressed(games.K_RIGHT):
        self.angle += Ship.ROTATION_STEP
```

This class is similar to the Rotate Sprite program from earlier in this chapter, but there are some differences. First, I load the image of the ship and assign the resulting image object to the class variable image. Second, I use the class constant ROTATION_STEP for the number of degrees by which the ship rotates.

Instantiating a Ship Object

The last thing I do in this new version of the game is instantiate a Ship object and add it to the screen. I create the new ship in main():

```
# create the ship
the_ship = Ship(image = Ship.image,
                x = games.screen.width/2,
                y = games.screen.height/2)
games.screen.add(the_ship)
```

MOVING THE SHIP

In the next version of the program, I get the ship moving. The player can press the Up Arrow key to engage the ship's engine. This applies thrust to the ship in the direction the ship is facing. Since there's no friction, the ship keeps moving based on all of the thrust the player applies to it.

The Astrocrash03 Program

When the player engages the ship's engine, the Astrocrash03 program changes the velocity of the ship based on the ship's angle (and produces an appropriate sound effect, too). Figure 12.10 illustrates the program.

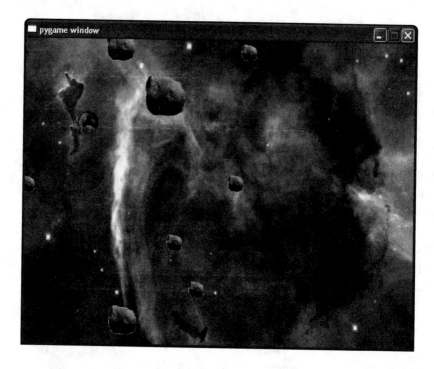

FIGURE 12.10

The ship can now move around the screen.

Importing the math **Module**

The first thing I do is import a new module at the top of the program:

```
import math, random
```

The math module contains a bunch of mathematical functions and constants, but don't let that scare you. I use only a few in this program.

Adding Ship **Class Variable and Constant**

I create a class constant, VELOCITY_STEP, for altering the ship's velocity:

```
VELOCITY_STEP = .03
```

A higher number would make the ship accelerate faster, while a lower number would make the ship accelerate more slowly.

I also add a new class variable, sound, for the thrusting sound of the ship:

```
sound = games.load_sound("thrust.wav")
```

Modifying Ship's update() Method

Next, I add code to the end of Ship's update() method to get the ship moving. I check to see whether the player is pressing the Up Arrow key. If so, I play the thrusting sound:

```
# apply thrust based on up arrow key
if games.keyboard.is_pressed(games.K_UP):
    Ship.sound.play()
```

Now, when the player presses the Up Arrow key, I need to alter the ship's velocity components (the Ship object's dx and dy). So, given the angle of the ship, how can I figure out how much to change each velocity component? Well, the answer is trigonometry. Wait, don't slam this book shut and run as fast as your legs can carry you, screaming incoherently. As promised, I use only two mathematical functions in a few lines of code to figure this out.

To start the process, I get the angle of the ship, converted to radians:

```
# change velocity components based on ship's angle
angle = self.angle * math.pi / 180 # convert to radians
```

A radian is just a measure of rotation, like a degree. Python's math module expects angles in radians (while livewires works with degrees) so that's why I need to make the conversion. In the calculation, I use the math module constant pi, which represents the number pi.

Now that I've got the ship's angle in radians, I can figure out how much to change each velocity component using the math module's sin() and cos() functions, which calculate an angle's sine and cosine. The following lines calculate the object's new dx and dy values:

```
self.dx += Ship.VELOCITY_STEP * math.sin(angle)
self.dy += Ship.VELOCITY_STEP * -math.cos(angle)
```

Basically, math.sin(angle) represents the percent of the thrust that should be applied to the ship's velocity in the x direction, while the -math.cos(angle) represents the percent of the thrust that should be applied to the ship's velocity in the y direction.

All that's left to do is handle the screen boundaries. I use the same strategy as I did with the asteroids: The ship should wrap around the screen. In fact, I copy and paste the code from Asteroid's update() method to the end of Ship's update() method:

```
# wrap the ship around screen
if self.top > games.screen.height:
    self.bottom = 0
```

```
if self.bottom < 0:
    self.top = games.screen.height

if self.left > games.screen.width:
    self.right = 0

if self.right < 0:
    self.left = games.screen.width
```

Although this works, copying and pasting large portions of code is usually a sign of poor design. I'll revisit this code later and find a more elegant solution.

 Repeated chunks of code bloat programs and make them harder to maintain. When you see repeated code, it's often time for a new function or class. Think about how you might consolidate the code into one place and call or invoke it from the parts of your program where the repeated code currently lives.

FIRING MISSILES

Next, I enable the ship to fire missiles. When the player presses the spacebar, a missile fires from the ship's cannon and flies off in the direction the ship is facing. The missile should destroy anything it hits—but to keep things simple, I save the fun of destruction for another version of the program.

The Astrocrash04 Program

The Astrocrash04 program allows the player to fire missiles by pressing the spacebar, but there's a problem. If the player holds down the spacebar, a stream of missiles pours out of the ship, at a rate of about 50 per second. I need to limit the missile fire rate, but I leave that issue for the next version of the game. Figure 12.11 shows off the Astrocrash04 program, warts and all.

Modifying Ship's update() Method

I modify Ship's update() method by adding code so that a ship can fire missiles. If the player presses the spacebar, a new missile is created:

```
# fire missile if spacebar pressed
if games.keyboard.is_pressed(games.K_SPACE):
    new_missile = Missile(self.x, self.y, self.angle)
    games.screen.add(new_missile)
```

Of course, in order to instantiate a new object from `Missile(self.x, self.y, self.angle)`, I need to write a little something...like a `Missile` class.

The `Missile` Class

I write the `Missile` class for the missiles that the ship fires. I start by creating class variables and class constants:

```
class Missile(games.Sprite):
    """ A missile launched by the player's ship. """
    image = games.load_image("missile.bmp")
    sound = games.load_sound("missile.wav")
    BUFFER = 40
    VELOCITY_FACTOR = 7
    LIFETIME = 40
```

`image` is for the image of a missile—a solid, red circle. `sound` is for the sound effect of a missile launching. `BUFFER` represents the distance from the ship that a new missile is created (so that the missile isn't created on top of the ship). `VELOCITY_FACTOR` affects how fast the missile travels. Finally, LIFETIME represents how long the missile exists before it disappears (so that a missile won't float around the screen forever).

The __init__() Method

I start the class constructor with the following lines:

```
def __init__(self, ship_x, ship_y, ship_angle):
    """ Initialize missile sprite. """
```

It may surprise you that the constructor for a missile requires values for the ship's x- and y-coordinates and the ship's angle, which are accepted into the ship_x, ship_y, and ship_angle parameters. The method needs these values so that it can determine two things: exactly where the missile first appears and its velocity components. Where the missile is created depends upon where the ship is located, and how the missile travels depends upon the angle of the ship.

Next, I play the missile-firing sound effect:

```
Missile.sound.play()
```

Then, I perform some calculations to figure out the new missile's starting location:

```
# convert to radians
angle = ship_angle * math.pi / 180

# calculate missile's starting position
buffer_x = Missile.BUFFER * math.sin(angle)
buffer_y = Missile.BUFFER * -math.cos(angle)
x = ship_x + buffer_x
y = ship_y + buffer_y
```

I get the angle of the ship, converted to radians. Then, I calculate the missile's starting x- and y-coordinates, based on the angle of the ship and the Missile.BUFFER. The resulting x and y values place the missile right in front of the ship's cannon.

Next, I calculate the missile's velocity components. I use the same type of calculations as I did in the Ship class:

```
# calculate missile's velocity components
dx = Missile.VELOCITY_FACTOR * math.sin(angle)
dy = Missile.VELOCITY_FACTOR * -math.cos(angle)
```

I invoke the `Sprite` constructor for the object:

```
# create the missile
super(Missile, self).__init__(image = Missile.image,
                              x = x, y = y,
                              dx = dx, dy = dy)
```

Finally, I give the `Missile` object a `lifetime` attribute so that the object won't be around forever.

```
self.lifetime = Missile.LIFETIME
```

The `update()` Method

Next, I write the `update()` method. Here's the first part:

```
def update(self):
    """ Move the missile. """
    # if lifetime is up, destroy the missile
    self.lifetime -= 1
    if self.lifetime == 0:
        self.destroy()
```

This code just counts down the life of the missile. `lifetime` is decremented. When it reaches 0, the `Missile` object destroys itself.

In the second part of `update()`, I include the familiar code to wrap the missile around the screen:

```
# wrap the missile around screen
if self.top > games.screen.height:
    self.bottom = 0

if self.bottom < 0:
    self.top = games.screen.height

if self.left > games.screen.width:
    self.right = 0

if self.right < 0:
    self.left = games.screen.width
```

I see that the preceding code is now repeated three different times in my program. I'll definitely be consolidating it later.

CONTROLLING THE MISSILE FIRE RATE

As you saw in the last program, the ship can fire about 50 missiles per second. Even for a player who wants to win, this is a bit much. So in this next version, I put a limit on the missile fire rate.

The Astrocrash05 Program

The Astrocrash05 program limits the missile fire rate by creating a countdown that forces a delay between missile firings. Once the countdown ends, the player is able to fire another missile. Figure 12.12 illustrates the program.

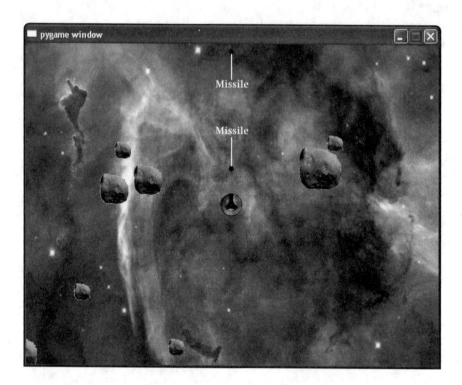

Adding a Ship Class Constant

My first step in forcing a delay between missile firings is to add a class constant to Ship:

```
MISSILE_DELAY = 25
```

MISSILE_DELAY represents the delay a player must wait between missile firings. I'll use it to reset a countdown that forces the player to wait.

Creating Ship's Constructor Method

Next, I create a constructor method for the class:

```
def __init__(self, x, y):
    """ Initialize ship sprite. """
    super(Ship, self).__init__(image = Ship.image, x = x, y = y)
    self.missile_wait = 0
```

The method accepts values for the x- and y-coordinates of the new ship and passes those off to the superclass of Ship, games.Sprite. The next line gives the new object an attribute named missile_wait. I use missile_wait to count down the delay until the player can fire the next missile.

Modifying Ship's update() Method

I add some code to Ship's update() method that decrements an object's missile_wait, counting it down to 0.

```
# if waiting until the ship can fire next, decrease wait
if self.missile_wait > 0:
    self.missile_wait -= 1
```

Then I change the missile firing code from the last version of the game to the following lines:

```
# fire missile if spacebar pressed and missile wait is over
if games.keyboard.is_pressed(games.K_SPACE) and self.missile_wait == 0:
    new_missile = Missile(self.x, self.y, self.angle)
    games.screen.add(new_missile)
    self.missile_wait = Ship.MISSILE_DELAY
```

Now, when the player presses the spacebar, the countdown must be complete (missile_wait must be 0) before the ship will fire a new missile. Once a missile is fired, I reset missile_wait to MISSILE_DELAY to begin the countdown again.

HANDLING COLLISIONS

So far, the player can move the ship around the field of asteroids and even fire missiles, but none of the objects interact. I change all of that in this next version of the game. When a missile collides with any other object, it destroys that other object and itself. When the ship collides with any other object, it destroys the other object and itself. Asteroids will be passive in this system, since I don't want overlapping asteroids to destroy each other.

The Astrocrash06 Program

The Astrocrash06 program achieves all of the necessary collision detection with the Sprite overlapping_sprites property. I also have to handle the destruction of asteroids in a special way because, when large- and medium-sized asteroids are destroyed, two new but smaller asteroids are created.

 Because the asteroids are initially generated at random locations, it's possible for one to be created on top of the player's ship, destroying the ship just as the program begins. I can live with this inconvenience for now, but I'll have to solve this issue in the final game.

Figure 12.13 shows the program in action.

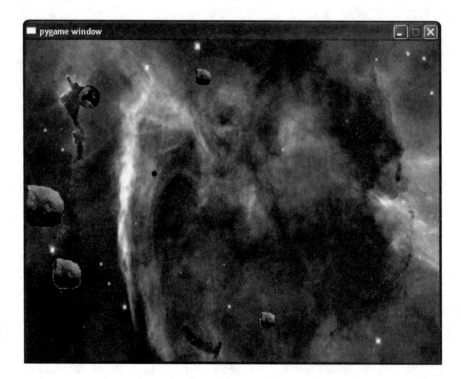

Modifying Missile's update() Method

I add the following code to the end of Missile's update() method:

```
# check if missile overlaps any other object
if self.overlapping_sprites:
    for sprite in self.overlapping_sprites:
        sprite.die()
    self.die()
```

If a missile overlaps any other objects, the other objects and the missile all have their die() methods called. die() is a new method I'll be adding to Asteroid, Ship, and Missile.

Adding Missile's die() Method

Missile, like any class in this version of the game, needs a die() method. The method is about as simple as it gets:

```
def die(self):
    """ Destroy the missile. """
    self.destroy()
```

When a Missile object's die() method is invoked, the object destroys itself.

Modifying Ship's update() Method

I add the following code to the end of the Ship's update() method:

```
# check if ship overlaps any other object
if self.overlapping_sprites:
    for sprite in self.overlapping_sprites:
        sprite.die()
    self.die()
```

If the ship overlaps any other objects, the other objects and the ship all have their die() method called. Notice that this exact code also appears in Missile's update() method. Again, when you see duplicate code, you should think about how to consolidate it. In the next version of the game, I'll get rid of this and other redundant code.

Adding Ship's die() Method

This method is the same as Missile's die() method:

```
def die(self):
    """ Destroy ship. """
    self.destroy()
```

When a Ship object's die() method is invoked, the object destroys itself.

Adding an Asteroid **Class Constant**

I add one class constant to Asteroid:

```
SPAWN = 2
```

SPAWN is the number of new asteroids that an asteroid spawns when it's destroyed.

Adding Asteroid's die() **Method**

Asteroid's die() method is more involved than the others:

```
def die(self):
    """ Destroy asteroid. """
    # if asteroid isn't small, replace with two smaller asteroids
    if self.size != Asteroid.SMALL:
        for i in range(Asteroid.SPAWN):
            new_asteroid = Asteroid(x = self.x,
                                    y = self.y,
                                    size = self.size - 1)
            games.screen.add(new_asteroid)
    self.destroy()
```

The wrinkle I add is that the Asteroid.die() method has the potential to create new Asteroid objects. The method checks to see whether the asteroid being destroyed isn't small. If it's not, two new asteroids, one size smaller, are created at the current asteroid's location. Whether or not new asteroids are created, the current asteroid destroys itself and the method ends.

ADDING EXPLOSIONS

In the previous version of the game, the player could destroy asteroids by firing missiles at them, but the destruction felt a bit hollow. So next I add explosions to the game.

The Astrocrash07 Program

In the Astrocrash07 program, I write a new class for animated explosions based on games.Animation. I also do some work behind the scenes, consolidating redundant code. Even though the player won't appreciate these additional changes, they're important nonetheless. Figure 12.14 shows the new program in action.

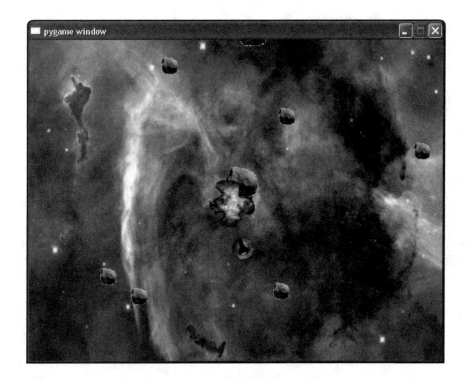

FIGURE 12.14

All of the
destruction in the
game is now
accompanied by
fiery explosions.

The Wrapper **Class**

I start with the behind-the-scenes work. I create a new class, Wrapper, based on games.Sprite.

The update() **Method**

Wrapper has an update() method that automatically wraps an object around the screen:

```
class Wrapper(games.Sprite):
    """ A sprite that wraps around the screen. """
    def update(self):
        """ Wrap sprite around screen. """
        if self.top > games.screen.height:
            self.bottom = 0

        if self.bottom < 0:
            self.top = games.screen.height

        if self.left > games.screen.width:
            self.right = 0

        if self.right < 0:
            self.left = games.screen.width
```

You've seen this code several times already. It wraps a sprite around the screen. Now, if I base the other classes in the game on Wrapper, its update() method can keep instances of those other classes on the screen—and the code only has to exist in one place!

The die() Method

I finish the class up with a die() method that destroys the object:

```
def die(self):
    """ Destroy self. """
    self.destroy()
```

The Collider Class

Next, I take on more redundant code. I notice that both Ship and Missile share the same collision-handling instructions, so I create a new class, Collider (based on Wrapper), for objects that wrap around the screen and that can collide with other objects.

The update() Method

Here's the update() method that handles collisions:

```
class Collider(Wrapper):
    """ A Wrapper that can collide with another object. """
    def update(self):
        """ Check for overlapping sprites. """
        super(Collider, self).update()

        if self.overlapping_sprites:
            for sprite in self.overlapping_sprites:
                sprite.die()
            self.die()
```

The first thing I do in Collider's update() method is invoke its superclass's update() method (which is Wrapper's update() method) to keep the object on the screen. Then I check for collisions. If the object overlaps any others, I call the die() method for the other objects and then the object's own die() method.

The die() Method

Next, I have a die() method for the class, since all Collider objects will do the same thing when they die—create an explosion and destroy themselves:

```
def die(self):
    """ Destroy self and leave explosion behind. """
    new_explosion = Explosion(x = self.x, y = self.y)
    games.screen.add(new_explosion)
    self.destroy()
```

In this method, I create an Explosion object. Explosion is a new class whose objects are explosion animations. You'll see the class in its full glory soon.

Modifying the Asteroid Class

I modify Asteroid so that the class is based on Wrapper:

```
class Asteroid(Wrapper):
```

Asteroid now inherits update() from Wrapper, so I cut Asteroid's own update() method. The redundant code is starting to disappear!

The only other thing I do in this class is change the last line of Asteroid's die() method. I replace self.die() with the line:

```
        super(Asteroid, self).die()
```

Now, if I ever change Wrapper's die() method, Asteroid will automatically reap the benefits.

Modifying the Ship Class

I modify Ship so that the class is based on Collider:

```
class Ship(Collider):
```

In Ship's update() method, I add the line:

```
    super(Ship, self).update()
```

I can now cut several more pieces of redundant code. Since Collider's update() method handles collisions, I cut the collision detection code from Ship's update() method. Since Collider's update() method invokes Wrapper's update() method, I cut the screen wrapping code from Ship's update() method, too. I also cut Ship's die() method, as the class inherits Collider's version.

Modifying the Missile **Class**

In modifying the Missile class, I change its class header so that the class is based on Collider:

```
class Missile(Collider):
```

In Missile's update() method, I add the line:

```
        super(Missile, self).update()
```

Just as with Ship, I can now cut redundant code from Missile. Since Collider's update() method handles collisions, I cut the collision detection code from Missile's update() method. Since Collider's update() method invokes Wrapper's update() method, I cut the screen wrapping code from Missile's update() method, too. I also cut Missile's die() method, as the class inherits Collider's version.

To help you understand the changes I describe, feel free to check out the complete code for all versions of Astrocrash on the CD-ROM that came with this book.

The Explosion **Class**

Since I want to create animated explosions, I write an Explosion class based on games.Animation.

```
class Explosion(games.Animation):
    """ Explosion animation. """
    sound = games.load_sound("explosion.wav")
    explosion_files = ["explosion1.bmp",
                       "explosion2.bmp",
                       "explosion3.bmp",
                       "explosion4.bmp",
                       "explosion5.bmp",
                       "explosion6.bmp",
                       "explosion7.bmp",
                       "explosion8.bmp",
                       "explosion9.bmp"]
```

I define the class variable, sound, for the sound effect of an explosion. I define a class variable, images, for the list of image file names for the nine frames of the explosion animation.

Next, I write the Explosion constructor.

```
def __init__(self, x, y):
    super(Explosion, self).__init__(images = Explosion.images,
                                    x = x, y = y,
                                    repeat_interval = 4, n_repeats = 1,
                                    is_collideable = False)
    Explosion.sound.play()
```

In the Explosion constructor, I accept values into the x and y parameters, which represent the screen coordinates for the explosion. When I invoke a superclass constructor (the games.Animation constructor), I pass these values to x and y so that the animation is created right where I want it. To the superclass constructor, I also pass images the list of image file names, Explosion.images. I pass to n_repeats the value 1 so that the animation plays just once. I pass to repeat_interval the value 4 so that the speed of the animation looks right. I pass is_collideable the value False so that the explosion animation doesn't count as a collision for other sprites that might happen to overlap it.

Finally, I play the explosion sound effect with Explosion.sound.play().

 TRICK   Remember, you can pass the games.Animation constructor either a list of file names or a list of image objects for the frames of animation.

ADDING LEVELS, SCOREKEEPING, AND THEME MUSIC

The game needs just a few more things to feel complete. For my final pass, I add levels—meaning that when a player destroys all of the asteroids on the screen, a new, more plentiful batch appears. I also add scorekeeping functionality and tense theme music to round out the game experience.

The Astrocrash08 Program

In addition to levels, scorekeeping, and theme music, I add some code that may be less obvious to the player but is still important to complete the program. Figure 12.15 shows off my final version of the game.

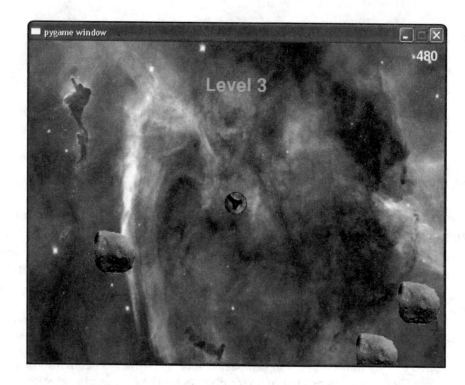

FIGURE 12.15

The final touches let the game continue as long as the player's Astrocrash skills allow.

Importing the color Module

The first addition is simple enough. Along with games, I import color from livewires:

```
from livewires import games, color
```

I need the color module so that the "Game Over" message can be displayed in a nice, bright red color.

The Game Class

Toward the end of the program, I add the Game class—a new class for an object that represents the game itself. Now, creating an object to represent the game may seem like an odd idea at first, but it makes sense the more you think about it. The game itself could certainly be an object with methods like play() to start the game, advance() to move the game to the next level, and end() to end the game.

The design decision to represent the game as an object makes it easy for other objects to send the game messages. For example, as the last remaining asteroid in a level is destroyed, the asteroid could send the game a message to advance to the next level. Or, just as the ship is destroyed, it could send the game a message to end.

As I go through the class, you'll notice that much of the code that was in main() has been incorporated into Game.

The __init__() Method

The first thing I do in the Game class is define a constructor:

```
class Game(object):
    """ The game itself. """
    def __init__(self):
        """ Initialize Game object. """
        # set level
        self.level = 0

        # load sound for level advance
        self.sound = games.load_sound("level.wav")

        # create score
        self.score = games.Text(value = 0,
                                size = 30,
                                color = color.white,
                                top = 5,
                                right = games.screen.width - 10,
                                is_collideable = False)
        games.screen.add(self.score)

        # create player's ship
        self.ship = Ship(game = self,
                         x = games.screen.width/2,
                         y = games.screen.height/2)
        games.screen.add(self.ship)
```

level is an attribute for the current game level number. sound is an attribute for the level-advance sound effect. score is an attribute for the game score—it's a text object that appears in the upper-right corner of the screen. The object's is_collideable property is False, which means that the score won't register in any collisions—so the player's ship won't "crash into" the score and explode! Finally, ship is an attribute for the player's ship.

The play() Method

Next, I define the play() method, which starts up the game.

```python
def play(self):
    """ Play the game. """
    # begin theme music
    games.music.load("theme.mid")
    games.music.play(-1)

    # load and set background
    nebula_image = games.load_image("nebula.jpg")
    games.screen.background = nebula_image

    # advance to level 1
    self.advance()

    # start play
    games.screen.mainloop()
```

The method loads the theme music and plays it so that it will loop forever. It loads the nebula image and sets it as the background. Then the method calls the Game object's own advance() method, which advances the game to the next level. (You'll see what the advance() method is all about next.) Finally, play() invokes games.screen.mainloop() to kick off the whole game!

The advance() Method

The advance() method advances the game to the next level. It increments the level number, creates a new wave of asteroids, displays the level number briefly on the screen, and plays the level-advance sound.

The first thing I do in the method is simple enough—I increase the level number:

```python
def advance(self):
    """ Advance to the next game level. """
    self.level += 1
```

The meat of the method is next: creating the new wave of asteroids. Each level starts with the number of asteroids equal to the level number. So, the first level starts with only one asteroid, the second with two, and so on. Now, creating a bunch of asteroids is easy, but I need to make sure that no new asteroid is created right on top of the ship. Otherwise, the ship will explode just as the new level begins.

```
# amount of space around ship to preserve when creating asteroids
BUFFER = 150

# create new asteroids
for i in range(self.level):
    # calculate an x and y at least BUFFER distance from the ship

    # choose minimum distance along x-axis and y-axis
    x_min = random.randrange(BUFFER)
    y_min = BUFFER - x_min

    # choose distance along x-axis and y-axis based on minimum distance
    x_distance = random.randrange(x_min, games.screen.width - x_min)
    y_distance = random.randrange(y_min, games.screen.height - y_min)

    # calculate location based on distance
    x = self.ship.x + x_distance
    y = self.ship.y + y_distance

    # wrap around screen, if necessary
    x %= games.screen.width
    y %= games.screen.height

    # create the asteroid
    new_asteroid = Asteroid(game = self,
                            x = x, y = y,
                            size = Asteroid.LARGE)
    games.screen.add(new_asteroid)
```

BUFFER is a constant for the amount of safe space I want around the ship.

Next, I start a loop. In each iteration, I create one new asteroid at a safe distance from the ship.

x_min is the minimum distance the new asteroid should be from the ship along the x-axis, while y_min is the minimum distance that the new asteroid should be from the ship along the y-axis. I add variation by using the random module, but x_min and y_min will always total BUFFER.

x_distance is the distance from the ship for the new asteroid along the x-axis. It is a randomly selected number that ensures that the new asteroid will be at least x_min distance from the ship. y_distance is the distance from the ship for the new asteroid along the y-axis. It is a randomly selected number that ensures that the new asteroid will be at least y_min distance from the ship.

x is the x-coordinate for the new asteroid. I calculate it by adding the value of the x-coordinate of the ship to x_distance. Then I make sure x won't put the asteroid off the screen by "wrapping it around" the screen with the modulus operator. y is the y-coordinate for the new asteroid. I calculate it by adding the value of the y-coordinate of the ship to y_distance. Next, I make sure y won't put the asteroid off the screen by "wrapping it around" the screen with the modulus operator. Then, I use x and y to create the brand-new asteroid.

Notice that there's a new parameter in the Asteroid constructor, game. Remember, since each asteroid needs to be able to call a method of the Game object, each Asteroid object needs a reference to the Game object. So, I pass self to the parameter game, which the Asteroid constructor will use as an attribute for the game.

The last thing I do in advance() is display the new level number and play the level-advance sound:

```
# display level number
level_message = games.Message(value = "Level " + str(self.level),
                              size = 40,
                              color = color.yellow,
                              x = games.screen.width/2,
                              y = games.screen.width/10,
                              lifetime = 3 * games.screen.fps,
                              is_collideable = False)
games.screen.add(level_message)

# play new level sound (except at first level)
if self.level > 1:
    self.sound.play()
```

The end() Method

The end() method displays the message "Game Over" in the middle of the screen in big, red letters for about five seconds. After that, the game ends and the graphics screen closes.

```
def end(self):
    """ End the game. """
    # show 'Game Over' for 5 seconds
    end_message = games.Message(value = "Game Over",
                                size = 90,
                                color = color.red,
                                x = games.screen.width/2,
                                y = games.screen.height/2,
                                lifetime = 5 * games.screen.fps,
                                after_death = games.screen.quit,
                                is_collideable = False)
    games.screen.add(end_message)
```

Adding an Asteroid Class Variable and Constant

I make a few changes in the Asteroid class, related to adding levels and keeping score. I add a class constant, POINTS:

```
POINTS = 30
```

The constant will act as a base value for the number of points an asteroid is worth. The actual point value will be modified according to the size of the asteroid—smaller asteroids will be worth more than larger ones.

In order to change levels, the program needs to know when all of the asteroids on the current level are destroyed. So, I keep track of the total number of asteroids with a new class variable, total, which I define toward the beginning of the class:

```
total = 0
```

Modifying Asteroid's Constructor Method

In the constructor, I add a line to increment Asteroid.total:

```
Asteroid.total += 1
```

Now, I want any asteroid to be able to send the Game object a message, so I give each Asteroid object a reference to the Game object. I accept the Game object in the Asteroid constructor by creating a new parameter:

```
def __init__(self, game, x, y, size):
```

The game parameter accepts the Game object, which I then use to create an attribute for the new Asteroid object:

```
self.game = game
```

So, each new Asteroid object has an attribute game that is a reference to the game itself. Through game, an Asteroid object can call a method of the Game object, such as advance().

Modifying Asteroid's die() Method

I make a few additions to Asteroid's die() method. First, I decrement Asteroid.total:

```
Asteroid.total -= 1
```

Next, I increase the score based on Asteroid.POINTS and the size of the asteroid (smaller asteroids are worth more than larger ones). I also make sure the score is always flush right, so I reset the score's right property to be ten pixels from the right edge of the screen.

```
self.game.score.value += Asteroid.POINTS / self.size
self.game.score.right = games.screen.width - 10
```

When I create each of the two new asteroids, I need to pass a reference to the Game object, which I do by modifying the first line of the call to the Asteroid constructor:

```
new_asteroid = Asteroid(game = self.game,
```

Toward the end of Asteroid's die() method, I test Asteroid.total to see if all the asteroids have been destroyed. If so, the final asteroid invokes the Game object's advance() method, which advances the game to the next level and creates a new group of asteroids.

```
# if all asteroids are gone, advance to next level
if Asteroid.total == 0:
    self.game.advance()
```

Adding a Ship Class Constant

I make several additions to the Ship class. I create a class constant, VELOCITY_MAX, which I use to limit the maximum velocity of the player's ship:

```
VELOCITY_MAX = 3
```

Modifying Ship's Constructor Method

Like an Asteroid object, a Ship object needs to have access to the Game object so it can invoke a Game object method. Just as I did with Asteroid, I modify the Ship's constructor:

```
def __init__(self, game, x, y):
```

The new parameter, game, accepts the Game object, which I then use to create an attribute for the Ship object:

```
self.game = game
```

So, each Ship object has an attribute game that is a reference to the game itself. Through game, a Ship object can call a method of the Game object, like end().

Modifying Ship's update() Method

In Ship's update() method, I cap the individual velocity components of a Ship object, dx and dy, using the class constant MAX_VELOCITY:

```
# cap velocity in each direction
self.dx = min(max(self.dx, -Ship.VELOCITY_MAX), Ship.VELOCITY_MAX)
self.dy = min(max(self.dy, -Ship.VELOCITY_MAX), Ship.VELOCITY_MAX)
```

The code ensures that dx and dy will never be less than -Ship.VELOCITY_MAX and never greater than Ship.VELOCITY_MAX. I use the min() and max() functions to accomplish this. min() returns the minimum of two numbers, while max() returns the maximum of two numbers. I cap the ship's speed to avoid several potential problems, including the ship running into its own missiles.

Adding Ship's die() Method

When the player's ship is destroyed, the game is over. I add a die() method to Ship that invokes the Game object's end() method to end the game.

```
def die(self):
    """ Destroy ship and end the game. """
    self.game.end()
    super(Ship, self).die()
```

The `main()` Function

Now that I have a `Game` class, the `main()` function becomes quite short. All I do in this function is create a `Game` object and invoke the object's `play()` method to put the game in action.

```python
def main():
    astrocrash = Game()
    astrocrash.play()


# kick it off!
main()
```

SUMMARY

- `keyboard` is a `games` module object that provides access to the keyboard.
- The `keyboard.is_pressed()` method tests if a specific key is being pressed. It accepts a constant representing a specific key and returns `True` if the corresponding key is being pressed, `False` otherwise.
- The `games` module defines a set of key constants that can be passed to `keyboard.is_pressed()`.
- `Sprite` objects have an `angle` property that represents an object's orientation in degrees.
- `Animation` is a subclass of `Sprite` from the `games` module for graphics objects that are a series of images shown in succession.
- An `Animation` object has properties for a set of images to cycle through, current image, speed, orientation, and overlapping objects, among others.
- The `games.load_sound()` function loads a sound stored in a WAV file and returns a sound object.
- A sound object has a `play()` method that plays the sound. If an integer is passed to the method, the sound is played its initial time plus the number of times equal to the integer. If -1 is passed, the sound loops indefinitely.
- A sound object has a `stop()` method that stops the sound if it's currently playing.
- `music` is a `games` module object that provides access to a single music track.
- The `music` object has a `load()` method that loads a music track, stored in a sound file, as the current music track.
- The `music` object has a `play()` method that plays the currently loaded music track. If an integer is passed to the method, the music track is played its initial time plus the number of times equal to the integer. If -1 is passed, the track loops indefinitely.

- The `music` object has a `stop()` method that stops the currently playing music track.
- After sketching out a design, writing progressively more complete versions of the game until it's done is one strategy for programming a large project.
- The Astrocrash game is based on a classic arcade game where players blast asteroids to score points.
- The Astrocrash01 program creates a graphics window, sets the nebula background, and spawns eight asteroids at random locations.
- The Astrocrash02 program creates a ship at the center of the screen that the player can rotate.
- The Astrocrash03 program allows the player to apply thrust to the ship, which changes the velocity of the craft based on its angle.
- The Astrocrash04 program allows the player to fire missiles, but results in a problem where the firing rate is too rapid.
- The Astrocrash05 program fixes the problem in Astrocrash04 by limiting the missile fire rate.
- The Astrocrash06 program implements collision detection. It handles the destruction of asteroids in a special way since when large- and medium-sized asteroids are destroyed, two new but smaller asteroids are created.
- The Astrocrash07 program adds animated explosions. In addition, it consolidates redundant code.
- The Astrocrash08 program adds levels, scorekeeping, and theme music.

Review Questions

1. How is the `keyboard.is_pressed()` method similar to and different from the `raw_input()` function?
2. What's the naming convention for key constants in the `games` module?
3. What are the two valid values that you can pass the `images` parameter of the `Animation` class constructor?
4. What does an `Animation` object's `n_repeats` attribute represent?
5. What does an `Animation` object's `repeat_interval` attribute represent?
6. How many different music tracks can be loaded at one time with the `livewires` game engine?
7. How many different sound objects can be loaded at any one time with the `livewires` game engine?

8. What's a sound channel?
9. How many different sound channels does the livewires game engine have?
10. What happens if you invoke a sound object's play() method while all eight sound channels are already in use?
11. What happens if you invoke a sound object's play() method when the sound the object represents is already playing?
12. What are some advantages to writing a large program by coding progressively more complete versions of it?
13. In the Astrocrash01 program, was it the best choice to begin by programming a field of asteroids?
14. In the Astrocrash01 program, will a larger asteroid always move more slowly than a smaller asteroid?
15. What are radians and why does the Astrocrash03 program use them?
16. What causes the ship to fire too rapidly in the Astrocrash04 program?
17. How does the Astrocrash05 program solve the problem of the rapid fire rate in Astrocrash04?
18. In the Astrocrash06 program, what's a potential problem caused by asteroids being created at random locations on the screen?
19. In the Astrocrash07 program, how do the Wrapper and Collider classes improve the code?
20. In the Astrocrash08 program, how does adding a Game class improve the code?

PROJECTS

1. Crazy Pong 2.0 is a new version of the Crazy Pong game described in Chapter 11, "Graphics: The Pizza Panic Game," Project 4. In this new version of the game, the player's paddle can change among three sizes: small, medium, and large. The paddle starts out at medium size. The paddle changes sizes depending upon the type of ball that strikes it. There are three types of balls in the game:

   • Bounce Ball: This type of ball is colored blue and behaves just as blue-colored ones from the original Crazy Pong game; when one strikes the player's paddle, it bounces off and the score increases by one. When one of these balls gets past the player, the game is over.

   • Shrink Ball: This type of ball is colored red. When one strikes the player's paddle, it can decrease the paddle's size. If the paddle's size is large, it becomes medium. If the paddle's size is medium, it becomes small. If the paddle's size is small, it remains small. If a shrink ball passes the paddle, it disappears and play continues.

- Growth Ball: This type of ball is colored green. When one strikes the player's paddle, it can increase the paddle's size. If the paddle's size is small, it becomes medium. If the paddle's size is medium, it becomes large. If the paddle's size is large, it remains large. If a growth ball passes the paddle, it disappears and play continues.

When a new ball is created, it has an equal chance of being a Bounce Ball, Shrink Ball, or Growth Ball.

Write the Crazy Pong 2.0 program design. List each class you think you'll need in your game program, along with a brief description. Within each class description, detail any attributes and methods. Also, outline your main() method. In designing your program, create one class for each ball type: Bounce_Ball, Shrink_Ball, and Growth_Ball. These classes should each be derived from a new base class called Ball that contains the functionality common to all ball types.

2. Write the Crazy Pong 2 game program you designed in Project 1.

3. Swarm is a 2D game with a ship that must shoot missiles at giant space flies that angrily flap their wings as they descend from the sky. If a fly reaches the bottom of the screen, it reappears at the top. If a fly is hit by a missile (or the ship), it dies in a fiery explosion. If the ship is hit by a fly, a big red "Game Over" message appears and the game is over. The game begins with only five deadly flies, but every time one is destroyed, two new flies take its place and descend from above. The player controls the ship at the bottom of the screen with the keyboard. The player can press the left arrow key to move the ship left and the right arrow key to move right. The player can press the spacebar to fire a missile. Every time a fly is destroyed, the player's score, displayed in the upper-right corner of the screen, increases by 30. Write the Swarm program design. List each class you think you'll need in your game program, along with a brief description. Within each class description, detail any attributes and methods. Also, outline your main() method.

4. Write the Swarm game program you designed in Project 3.

5. Modify the Swarm game program you wrote in Project 4 by adding the concept of waves. Instead of the death of a fly generating two new ones, the destruction of one group (or wave) of flies should generate a new, larger wave. The game should begin with a first wave of three flies. Once all three are destroyed, a second wave of six flies should be generated. After the second wave is destroyed, a new wave of nine flies should be created, and so on. Each wave should be announced with a message on the screen and a new wave sound effect should be played for the second wave and beyond.

livewires REFERENCE

This appendix includes almost everything you ever wanted to know about the modified version of the livewires package but were afraid to ask. I do leave out some portions for simplicity—if you want the ultimate "documentation," you can always check out the source code of the livewires modules themselves. On a Windows machine, if you installed Python in the default directory, you should find the modules in the C:\Python23\Lib\site-packages\livewires folder.

THE livewires PACKAGE

The livewires package is a set of modules for writing games with graphics, sound, and animation. Table A.1 lists two modules. The livewires package requires the pygame multimedia package.

TABLE A.1	LIVEWIRES MODULES
Module	**Description**
games	Defines functions and classes that make writing games easier.
color	Contains a set of color constants.

games CLASSES

games contains a group of classes and functions for game programming. Table A.2 describes the classes.

TABLE A.2	GAMES CLASSES
Class	**Description**
Screen	An object of this class represents a graphics screen.
Sprite	An object of this class has an image and can be displayed on a graphics screen.
Text	An object of this class represents text on the graphics screen. Text is a subclass of Sprite.
Message	An object of this class represents a message, which disappears after a set period of time, on the graphics screen. Message is a subclass of Text.
Animation	An object of this class represents a series of images shown in succession on a graphics screen. Animation is a subclass of Sprite.
Mouse	An object of this class provides access to the mouse.
Keyboard	An object of this class provides access to the keyboard.
Music	An object of this class provides access to the music channel.

The Screen Class

A Screen object represents the graphics screen. The games.init() function creates a Screen object, screen, that represents the graphics screen. Generally, you should use screen instead of instantiating your own object from Screen. Table A.3 describes Screen properties, while Table A.4 details Screen methods.

TABLE A.3   SCREEN PROPERTIES

Property	Description
width	Width of screen.
height	Height of screen.
fps	Number of times per second screen is updated.
background	Background image of screen.
all_objects	List of all sprites on the screen.
event_grab	Boolean that determines if input is grabbed to screen. True for input grabbed to screen. False for input not grabbed to screen.

TABLE A.4   SCREEN METHODS

Method	Description
get_width()	Returns width of screen.
get_height()	Returns height of screen.
get_fps()	Returns the number of times per second screen is updated.
get_background()	Returns the background image of screen.
set_background(*new_background*)	Sets the background image of screen to *new_background*.
get_all_objects()	Returns list of all the sprites on the screen.
get_event_grab()	Returns the status of the input being grabbed to screen. True for input grabbed to screen. False for input not grabbed to screen.
set_event_grab(*new_status*)	Sets the status of input being grabbed to screen to new_status. True for input grabbed to screen. False for input not grabbed to screen.
add(*sprite*)	Adds *sprite*, a Sprite object (or an object of a Sprite subclass), to the graphics screen.
remove(*sprite*)	Removes *sprite*, a Sprite object (or an object of a Sprite subclass), from the graphics screen.
clear()	Removes all sprites from the graphics screen.
mainloop()	Starts the graphics screen's main loop.
quit()	Closes the graphics window.

The Sprite **Class**

A Sprite object has an image and can be displayed on a graphics screen. Table A.5 describes Sprite properties, while Table A.6 details Sprite methods.

TABLE A.5   SPRITE PROPERTIES

Property	Description
image	Image object of sprite.
width	Width of sprite image.
height	Height of sprite image.
angle	Facing in degrees.
x	x-coordinate.
y	y-coordinate.
position	Position of sprite. A two-element tuple that contains the x-coordinate and the y-coordinate of the object.
top	y-coordinate of top sprite edge.
bottom	y-coordinate of bottom sprite edge.
left	x-coordinate of left sprite edge.
right	x-coordinate of right sprite edge.
dx	x velocity.
dy	y velocity.
velocity	Velocity of sprite. A two-element tuple that contains the x velocity and the y velocity of the object.
overlapping_sprites	List of other objects that overlap sprite.
is_collideable	Whether or not sprite is collideable. True means sprite will register in collisions. False means sprite will not show up in collisions.
interval	Determines the object's tick() interval.

TABLE A.6   SPRITE METHODS

Method	Description
__init__(*image* [, *angle*] [, *x*] [, *y*] [, *top*] [, *bottom*] [, *left*] [, *right*] [, *dx*] [, *dy*] [, *interval*][, *is_collideable*])	Initializes new sprite. *image* has no default value, so one must be passed to it. *angle*, *x*, *y*, *dx*, and *dy* all have the default value of 0. *top*, *bottom*, *left*, and *right* have the default value of None. *interval* has a default value of 1. *is_collideable* has a default value of True.

`get_image()`	Returns the sprite's image object.
`set_image(new_image)`	Sets the sprite's image object to *new_image*.
`get_height()`	Returns the height of the sprite's image.
`get_width()`	Returns the width of the sprite's image.
`get_angle()`	Returns the sprite's current angle in degrees.
`set_angle(new_angle)`	Sets the sprite's angle to *new_angle*.
`get_x()`	Returns sprite's x-coordinate.
`set_x(new_x)`	Sets sprite's x-coordinate to *new_x*.
`get_y()`	Returns the object's y-coordinate.
`set_y(new_y)`	Sets sprite's y-coordinate to *new_y*.
`get_position()`	Returns the sprite's x- and y-coordinates as a two-element tuple.
`set_position(new_position)`	Sets the sprite's x- and y-coordinates to the two-element tuple *new_position*.
`get_top()`	Returns the y-coordinate of the sprite's top edge.
`set_top(new_top)`	Sets the y-coordinate of sprite's top edge to *new_top*.
`get_bottom()`	Returns the y-coordinate of the sprite's bottom edge.
`set_bottom(new_bottom)`	Sets the y-coordinate of sprite's bottom edge to *new_bottom*.
`get_left()`	Returns the x-coordinate of the object's left edge.
`set_left(new_left)`	Sets the x-coordinate of sprite's left edge to *new_left*.
`get_right()`	Returns the x-coordinate of the object's right edge.
`set_right(new_right)`	Sets the x-coordinate of sprite's right edge to *new_right*.
`get_dx()`	Returns the sprite's x velocity.
`set_dx(new_dx)`	Sets the sprite's x velocity to *new_dx*.
`get_dy()`	Returns the sprite's y velocity.
`set_dy(new_dy)`	Sets the sprite's y velocity to *new_dy*.
`get_velocity()`	Returns the sprite's x velocity and the y velocity as a two-element tuple.
`set_velocity(new_velocity)`	Sets the sprite's x velocity and the y velocity to the two-element tuple *new_velocity*.
`get_overlapping_sprites()`	Returns a list of all collideable sprites that overlap with the object.
`overlaps(other)`	Returns True if object overlaps with *other* and False otherwise. Returns False if either object's is_collideable attribute is False.
`get_is_collideable()`	Returns the status of whether or not sprite is collideable. True means sprite registers in collisions. False means sprite does not show up in collisions.
`set_is_collideable(new_status)`	Sets the status of whether or not sprite is collideable to *new_status*. True means sprite registers in collisions. False means sprite does not show up in collisions.

`get_interval()`	Returns the sprite's `tick()` interval.
`set_interval(`*new_interval*`)`	Sets the sprite's `tick()` interval to *new_interval*.
`update()`	Updates sprite. Does nothing by default. Automatically called every `mainloop()` cycle. You might override this method in a subclass of `Sprite`.
`tick()`	Executes every `interval mainloop()` cycles. It does nothing by default. You might override this method in a subclass of `Sprite`.
`destroy()`	Removes sprite from the screen.

The Text Class

Text is a subclass of Sprite. A Text object represents text on the graphics screen. Text of course inherits Sprite's attributes, properties, and methods. Table A.7 describes additional Text properties, while Table A.8 details additional Text methods.

TABLE A.7 TEXT PROPERTIES

Property	Description
value	Value displayed as text.
size	Size of text.
color	Color of text. Can be set with a value from `color` module.

TABLE A.8 TEXT METHODS

Method	Description
`__init__(`*value, size, color* `[,` *angle]* `[,` *x]* `[,` *y]* `[,` *top]* `[,` *bottom]* `[,` *left]* `[,` *right]* `[,` *dx]* `[,` *dy]* `[,` *interval]* `[,` *is_collideable]*`)`	Initializes new object. *value* is the value to be displayed as text. *size* is the size of the text. *color* is the color of the text. *angle, x, y, dx,* and *dy* all have the default value of 0. *top, bottom, left,* and *right* have the default value of None. *interval* has a default value of 1. *is_collideable* has a default value of True.

```
get_value()                  Returns the value displayed as text.
set_value(new_value)         Sets the value displayed as text to new_value.
get_size()                   Returns the size of the text.
set_size(new_size)           Sets the size of the text to new_size.
get_color()                  Returns the color of the text.
set_color(new_color)         Sets the color of the text to new_color. Can be set with a value
                             from color module.
```

The Text class uses *text*, *size*, and *color* to create an image object that represents the text that is displayed.

The Message **Class**

Message is a subclass of Text. A Message object represents a message on the graphics screen that disappears after a set period of time. A Message object can also specify an event to occur after it disappears.

Message inherits Text's attributes, properties, and methods. A Message object, however, has a new attribute, *after_death*, for code to be executed after the object disappears. It can be assigned a function or method name, for example.

Message defines a new __init__() method: __init__(*value, size, color* [, *angle*] [, *x*] [, *y*] [, *top*] [, *bottom*] [, *left*] [, *right*] [, *dx*] [, *dy*] [, *lifetime*] [, *is_collideable*] [, *after_death*]). The method initializes a new object. *value* is the value to be displayed as text. *size* is the size of the text. *color* is the color of the text. *angle*, *x*, *y*, *dx*, and *dy* all have the default value of 0. *top*, *bottom*, *left*, and *right* have the default value of None. *lifetime* represents how long the message appears on the screen in mainloop() cycles before it destroys itself. If it is given a value of 0, then the object is not set to destroy itself. *lifetime* has a default value of 0. *is_collideable* has a default value of True. *after_death* has a default value of None.

 The value of the *lifetime* parameter is simply assigned to the Message object's *interval* property. A Message object has no *lifetime* attribute or property.

The Animation **Class**

The Animation class is a subclass of Sprite. An Animation object represents a series of images shown in succession. Animation inherits Sprite's attributes, properties, and methods. Animation defines additional attributes, described in Table A.9.

TABLE A.9	ANIMATION ATTRIBUTES

Attribute	Description
images	List of image objects.
n_repeats	Number of times the complete animation cycle should repeat. A value of 0 means repeat forever. The default value is 0.

Animation defines a new __init__() method: __init__(*images* [, *angle*] [, *x*] [, *y*] [, *top*] [, *bottom*] [, *left*] [, *right*] [, *dx*] [, *dy*] [, *repeat_interval*] [, *n_repeats*] [, *is_collideable*]). The method initializes a new object. *images* can be passed either a list of image objects or file names as strings from which to create image objects. *angle*, *x*, *y*, *dx*, and *dy* all have the default value of 0. *top*, *bottom*, *left*, and *right* have the default value of None. *repeat_interval* determines the object's tick() interval and therefore the speed of the animation. The default value is 1. *n_repeats* has a default value of 0. *is_collideable* has a default value of True.

> The value of the *repeat_interval* parameter is simply assigned to the Animation object's *interval* property. An Animation object has no *repeat_interval* attribute or property.

The Mouse **Class**

A Mouse object provides access to the mouse. The games.init() function creates a Mouse object, mouse, for use in reading the mouse position and testing for button presses. Generally, you should use mouse instead of instantiating your own object from Mouse. Table A.10 describes Mouse properties, while Table A.11 details Mouse methods.

TABLE A.10	MOUSE PROPERTIES

Property	Description
x	x-coordinate of mouse pointer.
y	y-coordinate of mouse pointer.
position	Position of the mouse pointer. A two-element tuple that contains the x-coordinate and the y- coordinate of mouse pointer.
is_visible	Boolean value for visibility of mouse pointer. True is visible, while False is not visible. Default value is True.

TABLE A.11   MOUSE METHODS

Method	Description
get_x()	Returns the x-coordinate of mouse pointer.
set_x(*new_x*)	Sets the x-coordinate of the mouse pointer to *new_x*.
get_y()	Returns the y-coordinate of mouse pointer.
set_y(*new_y*)	Sets the x-coordinate of the mouse pointer to *new_y*.
get_position()	Returns the mouse pointer's x- and y-coordinates as a two-element tuple.
set_position(*new_position*)	Sets the mouse pointer's x- and y-coordinates to the two-element tuple *new_position*.
set_is_visible(*new_visibility*)	Sets the visibility of the mouse pointer. If *new_visibility* is True, pointer is visible; if *new_visibility* is False, the pointer is not visible.
is_pressed(*button_number*)	Tests for a button press. Returns True if mouse button button_number is pressed; otherwise, returns False.

The Keyboard Class

A Keyboard object provides access to the keyboard. The games.init() function creates a Keyboard object, keyboard, for use in testing for keypresses. Generally, you should use keyboard instead of instantiating your own object from Keyboard.

The class has a single method, is_pressed(*key*), which returns True if the key being tested for, *key*, is pressed, and False if it is not. The games module defines constants that represent keys that you can use as an argument for this method. The constants are listed in this appendix, in the section "games Constants."

The Music class

A Music object provides access to the single music channel, allowing you to load, play, and stop a music file. The games.init() function creates a Music object, music, for accessing the music channel. Generally, you should use music instead of instantiating your own object from Music.

The music channel accepts many different types of files, including WAV, MP3, OGG, and MIDI. Table A.12 lists Music's methods.

TABLE A.12	MUSIC METHODS
Method	**Description**
load(*filename*)	Loads the file named in the string *filename* into the music channel, replacing any currently loaded music file.
play([*loop*])	Plays the music loaded in the music channel *loop* number of times in addition to its initial playing. A value of -1 means loop forever. The default value of *loop* is 0.
fadeout(*millisec*)	Fades out the currently playing music in *millisec* milliseconds.
stop()	Stops the music playing on the music channel.

games FUNCTIONS

The games module defines functions for working with images and sound. They are described in Table A.13.

TABLE A.13	GAMES FUNCTIONS
Function	**Description**
init([*screen_width*,] [*screen_height*,] [*fps*])	Initializes the graphics screen with width *screen_width*, height *screen_height* that updates itself *fps* times per second. Creates the object screen from Screen, which provides access to the game screen. Creates the object mouse from Mouse, which provides access to the player's mouse. Creates the object keyboard from Keyboard, which provides access to the player's keyboard. Creates music from Music, which provides access to the single music channel.
load_image(*filename* [, *transparent*])	Returns an image object loaded from the file named in the string *filename* and sets transparency if *transparent* is True. The default value of *transparent* is True.

`scale_image(image, x_scale [, y_scale])`	Returns a new image object scaled in the x direction by a factor of *x_scale* and in the y direction by a factor of *y_scale*. If no value is passed to *y_scale*, then the image is scaled by a factor of *x_scale* in both directions. The original image *image* is unchanged.
`load_sound(filename)`	Returns a sound object from a WAV file named in the string *filename*.

The sound object returned by `load_sound()` has several methods available to it, which are listed in Table A.14.

TABLE A.14   SOUND OBJECT METHODS

Method	Description
`play([loop])`	Plays the sound *loop* number of times in addition to its initial playing. A value of -1 means loop forever. The default value of *loop* is 0.
`fadeout(millisec)`	Fades out the sound in *millisec* milliseconds.
`stop()`	Stops the sound on all channels.

games CONSTANTS

The `games` module defines a set of constants for keyboard keys. The complete list is in Table A.15.

TABLE A.15   GAMES KEY CONSTANTS

Constant	Key	Constant	Key
K_BACKSPACE	Backspace	K_HASH	Hash Mark
K_TAB	Tab	K_DOLLAR	Dollar Sign
K_RETURN	Return	K_AMPERSAND	Ampersand
K_PAUSE	Pause	K_QUOTE	Single Quote
K_ESCAPE	Escape	K_LEFTPAREN	Left Parenthesis
K_SPACE	Spacebar	K_RIGHTPAREN	Right Parenthesis
K_EXCLAIM	Exclamation Point	K_ASTERISK	Asterisk
K_QUOTEDBL	Double Quote	K_PLUS	Plus Sign

K_COMMA	Comma	K_p	P
K_MINUS	Minus Sign	K_q	Q
K_PERIOD	Period	K_r	R
K_SLASH	Forward Slash	K_s	S
K_0	0	K_t	T
K_1	1	K_u	U
K_2	2	K_v	V
K_3	3	K_w	W
K_4	4	K_x	X
K_5	5	K_y	Y
K_6	6	K_z	Z
K_7	7	K_DELETE	Delete
K_8	8	K_KP0	Keypad 0
K_9	9	K_KP1	Keypad 1
K_COLON	Colon	K_KP2	Keypad 2
K_SEMICOLON	Semicolon	K_KP3	Keypad 3
K_LESS	Less-Than Sign	K_KP4	Keypad 4
K_EQUALS	Equals Sign	K_KP5	Keypad 5
K_GREATER	Greater-Than Sign	K_KP6	Keypad 6
K_QUESTION	Question Mark	K_KP7	Keypad 7
K_AT	At Symbol	K_KP8	Keypad 8
K_LEFTBRACKET	Left Bracket	K_KP9	Keypad 9
K_BACKSLASH	Backslash	K_KP_PERIOD	Keypad Period
K_RIGHTBRACKET	Right Bracket	K_KP_DIVIDE	Keypad Divide
K_CARET	Caret	K_KP_MULTIPLY	Keypad Multiply
K_UNDERSCORE	Underscore	K_KP_MINUS	Keypad Minus
K_a	A	K_KP_PLUS	Keypad Plus
K_b	B	K_KP_ENTER	Keypad Enter
K_c	C	K_KP_EQUALS	Keypad Equals
K_d	D	K_UP	Up Arrow
K_e	E	K_DOWN	Down Arrow
K_f	F	K_RIGHT	Right Arrow
K_g	G	K_LEFT	Left Arrow
K_h	H	K_INSERT	Insert
K_i	I	K_HOME	Home
K_j	J	K_END	End
K_k	K	K_PAGEUP	Page Up
K_l	L	K_PAGEDOWN	Page Down
K_m	M	K_F1	F1
K_n	N	K_F2	F2
K_o	O	K_F3	F3

K_F4	F4	K_RSHIFT	Right Shift
K_F5	F5	K_LSHIFT	Left Shift
K_F6	F6	K_RCTRL	Right Ctrl
K_F7	F7	K_LCTRL	Left Ctrl
K_F8	F8	K_RALT	Right Alt
K_F9	F9	K_LALT	Left Alt
K_F10	F10	K_LSUPER	Left Windows
K_F11	F11	K_RSUPER	Right Windows
K_F12	F12	K_HELP	Help
K_NUMLOCK	Num Lock	K_PRINT	Print Screen
K_CAPSLOCK	Caps Lock	K_BREAK	Break
K_SCROLLOCK	Scroll Lock		

color MODULE CONSTANTS

The color module provides some constants that you can use anywhere the games module wants a color. The constants are

- red
- green
- blue
- black
- white
- dark_red
- dark_green
- dark_blue
- dark_gray
- gray
- light_gray
- yellow
- brown
- pink
- purple

Index